LIBRARY
University of Glasgow

ALL ITEMS ARE ISSUED SUBJECT TO RECALL

GUL 18-08

D1429415

POLIS AND REVOLUTION

During the turbulent last years of the fifth century BC, Athens twice suffered the overthrow of democracy and the subsequent establishment of oligarchic regimes. In an in-depth treatment of both political revolutions, Julia Shear examines how the Athenians responded to these events, at the level both of the individual and of the corporate group. Interdisciplinary in approach, this account brings epigraphical and archaeological evidence to bear on a discussion which until now has largely been based on texts. Dr Shear particularly focuses on the recreation of democracy and the city, both ritually and physically, in the aftermath of the coups and demonstrates that, whilst reconciliation after civil strife is difficult and contentious, it is also crucial for rebuilding a united society. Theories of remembering and forgetting are applied and offer a new way of understanding the dynamics in Athens at this time.

JULIA L. SHEAR is a Senior Associate Member at the American School of Classical Studies at Athens.

POLIS AND REVOLUTION

Responding to Oligarchy in Classical Athens

JULIA L. SHEAR

American School of Classical Studies at Athens

CAMBRIDGE
UNIVERSITY PRESS

CAMBRIDGE UNIVERSITY PRESS
Cambridge, New York, Melbourne, Madrid, Cape Town,
Singapore, São Paulo, Delhi, Tokyo, Mexico City

Cambridge University Press
The Edinburgh Building, Cambridge CB2 8RU, UK

Published in the United States of America by Cambridge University Press, New York

www.cambridge.org
Information on this title: www.cambridge.org/9780521760447

First published 2011

Printed in the United Kingdom at the University Press, Cambridge

A catalogue record for this publication is available from the British Library

Library of Congress Cataloguing in Publication data
Shear, Julia L., 1968–
Polis and revolution : responding to oligarchy in classical Athens / Julia L. Shear.
p.   cm.
Includes bibliographical references and index.
ISBN 978-0-521-76044-7 (hardback)
1. Athens (Greece) – Politics and government.   2. Athens (Greece) – History.   3. Democracy –
Greece – Athens – History – To 1500.   4. Social change – Greece – Athens – History – To 1500.
5. Political participation – Greece – Athens – History – To 1500.   I. Title.
JC73.S49   2011
938′.505 – dc22   2011001823

ISBN 978 0 521 76044 7 Hardback

For
Robin and Simon
and
Ian and Chloe

Contents

List of figures	*page* viii	
List of tables	x	
Preface	xi	
List of abbreviations	xiv	

1	Responding to oligarchy in Athens: an introduction	1
2	Revolution, oligarchy and the *patrios politeia*	19
3	Restoring Athens: democracy and the law	70
4	Reclaiming Athens: the *demos* and the city	112
5	Remembering and forgetting: rituals and the *demos*	135
6	The Thirty and the law	166
7	Reconciling the Athenians	188
8	Recreating democracy: documents and the law	227
9	The Agora and the democratic citizen	263
10	Forgetting or remembering: oligarchy, *stasis* and the *demos*	286
11	The strategies of democracy	313

References	323	
Index locorum	342	
General index	356	

vii

Figures

Cover *SEG* xxviii 45: honours for the Athenians returning from Phyle, fragment a (Agora ɪ 16). (Courtesy of the American School of Classical Studies at Athens: Agora Excavations.)

ɪ   Plan of Attica showing the places mentioned in the text. (Drawing: F. N. Ley.)   *page* 27
2   Restored plan of the Athenian Agora in *c.* 400 BC. (Courtesy of the American School of Classical Studies at Athens: Agora Excavations.)   28
3   Plan of the Peiraieus and the city of Athens in *c.* 405 BC. (Drawing: F. N. Ley.)   30
4   Plan of the city of Athens in *c.* 395 BC with some later structures. (Drawing: F. N. Ley.)   37
5   *IG* ɪ³ 104: the reinscription of the homicide law of Drakon (EM 6602). (Courtesy of the photographic archive of the Epigraphical Museum, Athens.)   77
6   Fragments of the sacrificial calendar and the trierarchic law (*IG* ɪ³ 236). (Courtesy of the American School of Classical Studies at Athens: Agora Excavations.)   82
7   State plan of the Stoa Basileios in the Agora. (Courtesy of the American School of Classical Studies at Athens: Agora Excavations.)   93
8   Roman copies of the Tyrannicides by Kritios and Nesiotes (Museo Archeologico, Naples G103–4). (Courtesy of the Deutsches Archäologisches Institute-Rom, Neg. D-DAI-Rom 1958.1789, photograph by Bartl.)   103
9   Restored plan of the Bouleuterion Complex in the Agora in *c.* 405 BC. (Courtesy of the American School of Classical Studies at Athens: Agora Excavations.)   116

10 Restored plan of the Athenian Akropolis. (Drawing: I.
    Gelbrich.)   124
11 Plan of the Erechtheion and the foundations of the
    late sixth-century Temple of Athena on the Akropolis.
    (Courtesy of the American School of Classical Studies
    at Athens: Archaeological Photographic Collection.)   125
12 Model of the Pnyx, period 1, from the northwest; built
    c. 500 BC. (Courtesy of the American School of
    Classical Studies at Athens: Agora Excavations.)   178
13 Model of the Pnyx, period 2, from the northwest;
    project started 404/3 BC. (Courtesy of the American
    School of Classical Studies at Athens: Agora
    Excavations.)   178
14 *SEG* XXVIII 45: honours for the Athenians who
    returned from Phyle. (Courtesy of the American
    School of Classical Studies at Athens: Agora
    Excavations.)   233
15 *SEG* XXVIII 46: the decree of Theozotides honouring
    the sons of the dead democrats. (Courtesy of R. S.
    Stroud.)   236
16 Restored section of the Stoa Basileios. (Courtesy of the
    American School of Classical Studies at Athens: Agora
    Excavations.)   245
17 Restored plan of the buildings for the courts in the
    northeast corner of the Agora in the fourth century
    BC. (Courtesy of R. F. Townsend.)   265
18 Restored plan of the Agora in *c.* 300 BC with the
    distribution of dikastic equipment. (Courtesy of the
    American School of Classical Studies at Athens: Agora
    Excavations.)   267
19 Restored plan of the Mint in the Agora. (Courtesy of
    the American School of Classical Studies at Athens:
    Agora Excavations.)   269

Tables

1   Thucydides' narrative of the Four Hundred   *page* 23
2   The Four Hundred according to the *Athenaion Politeia*   32
3   The 'Constitution for the future'   34
4   The 'Constitution for the present'   35
5   The 'Constitution of Drakon'   46
6   The preserved fragments of the Sacrificial Calendar
    (*SEG* LII 48)   80
7   The other preserved fragments of the laws   90
8   Dimensions of the slots in the south annexe and
    selected *stelai*   94
9   The distribution of Agora inscriptions before 393 BC   97
10 The reconciliation agreement of 403   192
11 Events in Boedromion   210

Preface

In years to come, the question of how society (re-)constructs itself as democratic after civil discord may come to be seen as a particular preoccupation of the early twenty-first century and this book very much reflects those contemporary concerns. It is not only a product of its time, but also of place: without the AHRB Anatomy of Cultural Revolution Project at the Faculty of Classics, University of Cambridge, this book would never have been written. I owe the deepest debt of gratitude to the members of this project: Robin Osborne, the director of the project, Simon Goldhill, the project's other senior member, Liz Irwin, my fellow post-doctoral researcher, and Ben Akrigg, Claire Taylor and Rob Tordoff, the project's three doctoral students. For four years while the project was underway, they all lived with and responded to my preoccupations with Athens, democracy and revolution as ideas in this book were tried out in the project's fortnightly seminars, in conversations and in drafts of conference papers. Robin and Simon, in particular, continued to engage with my project after I had left Cambridge. Without the engagement, help and support of the project's members, this volume would not exist. Unlike the Athenian *demos*, I cannot award them gold crowns to be announced in the theatre at the City Dionysia for their *eunoia* and *philotimia*, but, like Athenian benefactors, they are worthy of such honours for all their help and contributions. The project's fortnightly seminars drew a group of regular participants beyond the immediate team and their responses have also been invaluable in helping to shape my thinking.

In addition, I have incurred debts beyond Cambridge. Many of the ideas in this book were tried out on the honours students at the University of Glasgow who took my option Revolution and Democracy at Athens in 2007–8. Their questions and seminar discussions forced me to rethink various aspects and their second essays in particular helped to clarify where Sokrates and the trials after the Thirty fitted into this monograph. It is my pleasure now to thank them for their patience and their willingness to engage with my ideas. For their help and advice, thanks are also due to: Stephen Lambert, Polly Low, Margie Miles, Josh Ober, Anne Rogerson, Ian Ruffell, Michael Scott, T. Leslie Shear, Jr, Chloe Stewart, Ron Stroud, Stephen Todd, Steve Tracy and James Watson. For discussing unpublished material with me, I am indebted to: Kevin Clinton, Laura Gawlinski, Angelos Matthaiou, T. Leslie Shear, Jr and Peter Wilson. Some of the material in this book was presented, often in rather different form, at the annual meetings of the American Philological Association in 2004, 2005, 2007 and 2009; at the annual conferences of the Classical Association in 2004, 2006 and 2007; and at seminars at the universities of Cambridge, Warwick and Manchester. To all the participants at these various occasions, I extend my warmest thanks. I am also indebted to Susan Ashworth and Michael Given for their help and support during the very difficult period of September to November 2009. For their help with the illustrations, I would like to thank: John Camp, Michael Given, Annie Hooten, Daria Lanzuolo, Fred Ley, Nikos Manias, Craig Mauzy, Ron Stroud, Rhys Townsend and Natalia Vogeikoff-Brogan.

Several institutions have also made this book possible. For permission to study material in their care, I would like to thank Mrs Jan Jordan, the secretary of the Agora Excavations and the staff at the Stoa of Attalos; at the Kerameikos Excavations, Dr Jutta Stroszeck and her assistant Jan-Marc Henke; at the Epigraphical Museum, the emeritus director Dr Charalambos Kritzas and his assistant Dr Chara Karapa-Molisani, the current director Dr Maria Lagogianni and the staff at the museum. For her help in getting the necessary permissions, I am most grateful to Mrs Maria Pilali at the American School of Classical Studies. My four-year post-doctoral position at Cambridge was funded by the then Arts and Humanities Research Board. At Cambridge, the Faculty of Classics and King's College together provided the perfect place in which to begin this project and it is my great pleasure to thank the Faculty Board of Classics and the Provost and Fellows of King's College. Much of this book was written or rewritten in a carrel in the Davis Wing of the library of the American School of Classical Studies at Athens. For providing such a congenial setting, I would like to extend my warmest thanks to Professor Jack Davis, the current director, to Professor Steve Tracy, his predecessor, and to the staff of the School in Athens. Finally, at Cambridge University Press, Michael Sharp never ceased to believe that he would one day receive a manuscript and both he and his colleagues Elizabeth Hanlon and Laura Morris have graciously answered endless e-mails with queries. For their support and patience, I am most grateful. Tom O'Reilly, Linda Woodward and the rest of the production team skilfully turned an author's electronic files into a printed monograph and I would like to thank them for all their care and hard work. Thanks are also due to the two anonymous readers for the press whose comments and questions aided me in clarifying my own thoughts and ideas.

All of these individuals have in their own ways improved this book and the remaining imperfections are certainly no reflection on any of them. Without four of them, however, this book would never have been written and, for that reason, it is dedicated to them.

Abbreviations

Abbreviations of journal titles follow the scheme used in *L'Année philologique*. Abbreviations of the names and works of classical authors follow the *Oxford Classical Dictionary*, 3rd edition. The following abbreviations are also used.

Agora	*The Athenian Agora: Results of Excavations Conducted by the American School of Classical Studies at Athens.*
Agora XVI	Woodhead, A. G., *Agora* XVI: *Inscriptions: The Decrees.* Princeton, NJ, 1997.
Agora XIX	Lalonde, G. V., Langdon, M. K., and Walbank, M. B., *Agora* XIX: *Inscriptions: Horoi, Poletai Records, Leases of Public Lands.* Princeton, NJ, 1991.
Bekker	Bekker, I., ed., *Anecdota Graeca* I. Berlin, 1814.
Carey	Carey, C., ed., *Lysias: Orationes cum Fragmentis.* Oxford, 2007.
DK⁶	Diels, H., and Kranz, W., *Die Fragmente der Vorsokratiker.* 6th edn, Berlin, 1952.
FGrHist	Jacoby, F., *Die Fragmente der griechischen Historiker.* Berlin and Leiden, 1923–.
FHG	Müller, C., *Fragmenta Historicorum Graecorum.* Paris, 1841–70.
I.Eleusis	Clinton, K., *Eleusis: The Inscriptions on Stone: Documents of the Sanctuary of the Two Goddesses and Public Documents of the Deme.* Athens, 2005.
IG	*Inscriptiones Graecae.*
LSJ⁹	Liddell, H. G., Scott, R., rev. Jones, H. S., *A Greek–English Lexicon.* 9th edn, Oxford, 1940.
OCT	Oxford Classical Text.

PMG	Page, D. L., ed., *Poetae Melici Graeci: Alcmanis, Stesichori, Ibyci, Anacreontis, Simonidis, Corinnae, poetarum minorum reliquias, carmina popularia et convivialia quaeque adespota feruntur.* Oxford, 1962.
RO	Rhodes, P. J., and Osborne, R., *Greek Historical Inscriptions, 404–323 BC.* Oxford, 2003.
SEG	*Supplementum Epigraphicum Graecum.*
Thalheim	Thalheim, T., and Blass, F., eds., *Antiphontis Orationes et Fragmenta.* Stuttgart, 1966.
Theodoridis	Theodoridis, C., ed., *Photii Patriarchae Lexicon.* Berlin, 1982–.
Walbank, *Proxenies*	Walbank, M. B., *Athenian Proxenies of the Fifth Century BC.* Toronto, 1987.

Responding to oligarchy in Athens: an introduction

Just before the Great Dionysia of 409 BC, all the Athenians assembled by tribe and by deme swore an oath:

I shall kill both by word and by deed and by vote and by my own hand, if I can, anyone who overthrows the democracy at Athens, and if anyone holds office after the democracy has been overthrown in the future, and if anyone set himself up to be tyrant or if anyone helps to set up a tyrant. And if anyone else kills him, I shall consider him to be pure before both the gods and *daimones* (or spirits) because he killed an enemy of the Athenians, and, after selling all the property of the dead man, I shall give half to the killer and I shall not withhold anything. If anyone dies killing or attempting to kill such a man, I shall give benefits both to him and to his children just as to Harmodios and Aristogeiton and their descendants.[1]

In taking this oath, the Athenians were adhering to the decree moved by their fellow citizen Demophantos. About seven years later, another Athenian named Theozotides moved another decree which rewarded the sons of 'as many of the Athenian[s] as, [co]mi[ng] to the aid of the democracy, d[ie]d a [v]iolent death in the oligarchy . . . on ac[coun]t of the g[o]od deeds of t[h]eir fat[hers] towards [t]h[e *dem]os* (or people) of the Ath[en]ian[s and of their b]rav[e]r[y]'.[2] These boys were to receive the same support from the city as the sons of the men who died in war and their names were listed below this decree when it was inscribed on a *stele* or stone slab. As these two texts show, the Athenians in the last decade of the fifth century BC were concerned enough about both the safety of the democracy and also the threat of oligarchy and tyranny to take unusual and unprecedented measures and to reward their fellow citizens in distinctly new ways. Why were they so focused on democracy and so apprehensive that it might be overthrown?

---

[1] Andok. 1.96–8.   [2] *SEG* XXVIII 46.

For the Athenians, the last decade or so of the fifth century was a particularly turbulent and tumultuous time: the great war with Sparta suddenly lost, peace imposed, Spartan interventions, democracy overthrown by oligarchs twice, in 411 and, with civil violence, in 404/3, less than ten years apart. Never before had the democracy been in such peril. The city, however, did not fall apart under the dual threats of internal dissent and external aggression, as her enemies might well have expected. Instead, she continued fighting the Peloponnesians in the years after 411, while, in the aftermath of the defeat in 404, she was fighting the Spartans again by 394 and she was able to acquire a second league of allies again as early as 377. While the events of 404/3 showed that oligarchy (and perhaps tyranny) remained a potential problem for the city, after 403, the democratic *politeia* or constitution was stable and not seriously threatened until the Macedonian conquest in 322 after the death of Alexander.[3] The possibility of Spartan intervention to enforce the reconciliation made between factions in 403 and the subsequent changes to the city's constitution no doubt explain some of the reasons why Athens was able to regain power relatively quickly in the fourth century,[4] but these political developments do not tell the whole story. As I shall argue, how the Athenians chose to respond to the oligarchic revolutions in 411 and 404/3 and to rebuild their fractured society was also a critical factor in the city's recovery.

Having endured oligarchy and civil strife or *stasis* in both 411 and 404/3, the Athenians faced the same problem in 410 and in 403: how should they collectively and individually reconstitute the city? That such a response was necessary in both cases stemmed from the oligarchs' appropriation of the city's political traditions and practices, her *politeia* or constitution and even her very spaces for their own purposes. In short, not only did the democracy need to be re-established, but the city also needed to be made visibly democratic again. As I shall argue, the processes and methods which the *demos* used after 411 and 404/3 were very similar, but, after the Thirty, the Athenians did not simply continue the responses to the Four Hundred and Five Thousand. Instead, they adapted and changed various aspects to suit the circumstances after the Thirty. Understanding the Athenians' decisions and efforts, consequently, requires the parallel examination of their responses to both periods of oligarchy. These collective actions took place in a larger setting of time and space and they were not confined to a few moments or months after the *demos* regained power. As the Athenians

---

[3] Habicht 1997: 40, 44–7 with further references.
[4] Compare R. Osborne 2003: 266–7; Wolpert 2002b: 112; Todd 1985: 175–97; Phillips 2008: 147–9.

also demonstrated, democracy can successfully reconstitute itself after its very existence has been undermined, but the process is not accomplished easily or without dissent.

OLIGARCHY, DEMOCRACY, REVOLUTION AND REMEMBRANCE

To discuss the oligarchies of 411 and of 404/3 and the Athenians' responses to them in one study is to cut across one of the major divisions of the classical period: that the end of the Peloponnesian War in 404 should mark the end of the fifth century and the beginning of a new post-war era.[5] The consequences of this division have been profound: the oligarchies of the Four Hundred and the Five Thousand in 411 and probably early 410 are regularly separated from the oligarchy of the Thirty in 404/3. In terms of understanding how the Athenians responded to these oligarchies, a relatively recent scholarly focus, the traditional periodisation has meant that the Athenians' (re)actions have also been divided from each other.[6] Indeed, the effects of the division extend further because the responses to the events of 411 have not been considered.[7] All existing scholarship has focused on the ways in which the Athenians responded to the events in 404/3.

Of these studies on the responses to the Thirty, Nicole Loraux's essays and articles gathered together in 1997 to form *La cité divisée: l'oubli dans la mémoire d'Athènes* serves as an important starting point.[8] In a wide-ranging book, she addresses issues of remembering, forgetting, erasure and *stasis* in the democratic city. In terms of the Athenians, her focus is the reconciliation agreement made in 403 between the men of the city and the men of the Peiraieus, particularly its clause *me mnesikakein*, not to remember past wrongs, that is the misdeeds committed under the Thirty. For Loraux, this clause was intended to restore undisrupted continuity with the past, hence both the erasure and the construction of the past. The victory of the democrats was publicly remembered in circumscribed ways which erased the Thirty from existence and forgot that they were legitimate magistrates. Although Loraux places this particular clause of the

---

[5] See e.g. Lewis, Boardman, Davies and Ostwald 1992 and Lewis, Boardman, Hornblower and Ostwald 1994.

[6] For obvious reasons, Shear 2007a, which grew out of the project for this book, remains an exception.

[7] Again, for obvious reasons, Shear 2007b, which grew out of the project for this book, remains an exception.

[8] Her book has been translated into English as *The Divided City* and it will be cited in this edition (Loraux 2002).

reconciliation agreement in the more general context of remembering and forgetting in Greek culture in the period between the *Iliad* and *Odyssey* and the third-century reconciliation agreement of Nakone in Sicily, she is not interested in the relationship of the injunction *me mnesikakein* to the rest of the agreement or in this document's larger context of the Athenians' response to the Thirty. Her study's most significant contribution lies in its emphasis on the importance and consequences of remembering and forgetting and Loraux clearly brings out the ways in which these strategies inevitably work together.

Her influence is evident in Andrew Wolpert's book *Remembering Defeat: Civil War and Civic Memory in Ancient Athens* published in 2002. He focuses on how the Athenians 'confronted the troubling memories of defeat and civil war and how they reconciled themselves to an agreement that allowed past crimes to go unpunished'.[9] The arena for this investigation is 'civic discourse', by which Wolpert means speeches given in a public setting, such as the lawcourts, the *ekklesia* or assembly, or the commemoration of the war-dead, to a large mass of the Athenians in the period between 403 and about 377. This book is fundamentally a study of selected speeches written by Lysias and other speechwriters and given by individual men who were wealthy enough to commission them, but it does not focus on the ways in which these documents are part of a larger response to the Thirty.[10] Nor does it consider how a particular speech interacts with its specific public setting. Studying the legal speeches leads inevitably to the question of whether the Athenians obeyed the injunction not to remember past wrongs, but Wolpert does not concentrate on the legal dimensions of this issue. This focus on speeches, the individual and adherence to the reconciliation agreement also marks both Stephen Todd's doctoral thesis on Athenian internal politics between 403 and 395 and Thomas Loening's study of the reconciliation agreement.[11] These two projects particularly consider how the agreement was put into practice, especially in the courts, and Todd also stresses the important role played by the Spartan king Pausanias and the Athenians' fear of Spartan intervention in the years after 403.[12] Explaining the success of the agreement is the project as well of a pair of articles by James Quillin and Wolpert.[13] Collectively, this scholarship focuses on the contemporary literature and particularly on the speeches of the orators. As such, it concentrates on individual men and their particular

---

[9] Wolpert 2002a: xii.   [10] Compare also the similar focus of Wolpert 2002b: 117–24.
[11] Todd 1985; Loening 1987.   [12] See above note 4.
[13] Quillin 2002: 71–105; Wolpert 2002b: 109–24.

decisions which are not put in the larger context of Athens after the Thirty or the city's collective actions. That reconciliation is an on-going process which must be repeatedly constructed both individually and collectively is also not brought out by these studies.[14]

Since the revolutions of 411 and 404/3 were important political events, discussion of them appears regularly in studies of the political and social history of the period. In keeping with their different goals, these studies do not concern themselves with the Athenians' reactions to these significant events. In addition, political and military histories usually obey the traditional divisions between periods so that the two revolutions are separated from each other by the end of the Peloponnesian War.[15] For constitutional historians, the changes to the city's *politeia* in 403 often serve as a culmination, but their work is primarily concerned with the political system and they do not discuss events after 403.[16] With their focus on the political and the military, these studies are not interested in other types of history. In addition, they have a strong tendency to treat epigraphical evidence simply as texts on pages, rather than as monuments in their own right.[17]

The events surrounding the Four Hundred and the Thirty also make regular appearances in more specialised literature. Discussions of the reorganisation of the city's laws, for example, frequently refer to these oligarchs and the restoration of the democrats, but they do not look far beyond the collection and arrangement of the laws.[18] Either or both revolutions have also been invoked to explain archaeological remains. Rhys Townsend, for example, associates construction of the first permanent facilities for courts in the Agora with the events of 411 and 404/3 and the reorganisation of the laws, but he suggest no further connections.[19] Discussions of the reconstruction of the New Bouleuterion in the Agora make use of the evidence provided by Theramenes' trial by the Thirty, but, as with the buildings for the courts, the structure is not put into any larger context.[20] In the archaeological and architectural studies, there is also a very strong tendency to

---

[14] Despite Wolpert's comments, he does not demonstrate how these dynamics work; Wolpert 2002a: 138.

[15] See e.g. Kagan 1987; Strauss 1987; Krentz 1982; Lewis, Boardman, Davies and Ostwald 1992; Lewis, Boardman, Hornblower and Ostwald 1994.

[16] See e.g. Hignett 1952; Ostwald 1986.

[17] See e.g. Krentz 1982: 111–13 on *SEG* xxviii 45, 46 and RO 4; Kagan 1987: 254, 256–7 on *IG* i³ 102, 104, 105 and the decree of Demophantos (Andokides 1.96–8).

[18] E.g. Lambert 2002a: 354; Sickinger 1999b: 94–105; Todd 1993: 116–17, 120, 123–31; P. J. Rhodes 1991: 93–5, 99–100; Fingarette 1971: 332–5; Dow 1960: 291–2; Harrison 1955: 31.

[19] Townsend 1995: 44–5. As we shall see in chapter 9, the structures belong after 403; so also Shear 2007a: 103–4.

[20] Shear, Jr 1995: 178–80, 184–5; Roux 1976: 476–83.

discuss buildings and monuments individually without any reference to their surroundings so that they appear to float alone in undifferentiated space.[21]

As this brief survey makes clear, scholars have focused on the Athenians' responses to the events of 404/3 in contemporary literature and the legal sphere, but these discussions proceed as if the earlier responses to the oligarchies of 411 were irrelevant. Otherwise, these events are invoked in more general discussions of political, military and constitutional history or in more specialist studies. There is no consideration of the Athenians' overall responses to these oligarchies nor how they were instantiated in the city's material culture. Focusing only on the individual does not allow us to see the city's collective responses which created a culture requiring individual reactions. Inevitably, these public and collective actions shaped and affected the individual responses. That the Athenians need not have responded to the events of 411 and 404/3 is suggested by comparing the differing responses of Germany and Japan to the Second World War: in Germany, there has been significant discussion about the events which took place and the responsibility for them; in contrast, such dialogues have not taken place in Japan. The very different actions of these two countries have, in turn, affected their relationships with their neighbours so that Germany is much more integrated regionally than Japan is. In South Africa, the work of the Truth and Reconciliation Commission facilitated both individual and collective responses to apartheid and the damage which it caused; these efforts have been instrumental in rebuilding the country's civil society and reintegrating its formerly divided peoples. In contrast, in the area of former Yugoslavia, reconciliation and dialogues about past events have not taken place and tensions remain high between the different (ethnic) factions. These twentieth-century examples bring out the importance of responding both individually and collectively to traumatic events because the processes require both individuals and social groups to negotiate and to come to terms with the past.

MEMORY, MEMORIALISATION AND RITUAL: SOME APPROACHES

These processes of response and negotiation are fundamentally about the creation of collective and individual memories and they require both remembering and forgetting on the part of those involved. Memory is complex and works on different levels, as the extensive scholarship on

---

[21] See e.g. Camp and Kroll 2001: 127–62.

memory studies regularly brings out. Scholars frequently oppose individual memory with collective or social memory, even though individuals always remember as social beings within social contexts.[22] From our perspective, individual memory is easily identified: the ways in which one individual, for example the speaker of a speech, recalls past events. Collective or social memory, in contrast, is the memory of groups of individuals, who share their individual memories together so that 'a society's memory . . . might be regarded as an aggregate collection of its members' many, often competing, memories'.[23] Remembering is, therefore, a social activity and plays an important role in the functioning of groups.[24] This process also 'identifies the group, giving it a sense of its past and defining its aspirations for the future'.[25] Collective memory may be seen in the ways in which groups record and/or commemorate the past in public documents or monuments; for the Athenians, obvious examples include honorary decrees and monuments celebrating victory in battle. These memories, however, are not the final product, but a process and, as such, they are malleable and subject to (re)interpretation and (re)use.[26] Memory's fluidity can also lead to forgetting. The two processes are intimately linked so that each one can constitute the inverse of the other.[27] The possibility of forgetting also leads to specific injunctions to remember not to forget.[28] Consequently, we cannot discuss remembering without considering forgetting and these two processes constantly pose a choice: do individuals, do groups, choose to remember or to forget? And what aspects of the past will they choose to

---

[22] Individual vs collective/social memory: e.g. Fentress and Wickham 1992: ix–x; Olick and Robbins 1998: 111; Alcock 2002: 15; Young 1993: xi–xii; Geary 1994b: 10–12; Olick 1999b: 345; Cubitt 2007: 14. Individual in society: Cubitt 2007: 73–4, 118–25, 141; Olick 1999b: 346.

[23] Quotation: Young 1993: xi. Collective/social memory: Fentress and Wickham 1992: ix–x, 25; Young 1993: xi, 6; Cubitt 2007: 10–20; Olick 1999b: 333–48; cf. Olick and Robbins 1998: 111–12. Assmann's term 'cultural memory' seems too broad and inclusive to be especially useful; Assmann 1995; Assmann 2006: 24–30. For helpful introductions to collective or social memory, see Cubitt 2007; Fentress and Wickham 1992; Olick and Robbins 1998; Alcock 2002: 1–35; Nora 1989 with Wood 1994. Let the reader be warned: the topic is vast.

[24] Cubitt 2007: 118–21, 125–32, 166–7, 170; Olick 1999b: 342–3, 346; Sherman 1994: 186. The emphasis on the group goes back to Halbwachs; e.g. Halbwachs 1992: 38–40, 182–3; Olick 1999b: 334–5; Cubitt 2007: 158–65.

[25] Fentress and Wickham 1992: 25; see also Cubitt 2007: 132–40, 222–3 with further references.

[26] Memory as process: e.g. Olick and Robbins 1998: 122; Fentress and Wickham 1992: x; Cubitt 2007: 16, 18. Malleability: Young 1993: x, 2; Fentress and Wickham 1992: 29; Alcock 2002: 17; Cubitt 2007: 158–9, 202–3, 214.

[27] On forgetting, see e.g. Fentress and Wickham 1992: 39–40; Cubitt 2007: 52–5, 75–7, 223–4; Geary 1994b; Loraux 2002.

[28] As for example in Deuteronomy 25: 17–19: the people of Israel are told 'remember what Amalek [the Amalekites] did to you on the way as you came out of Egypt [Exodus 17: 8–15] . . . in the land which the Lord your God gives you for an inheritance to possess, you shall blot out the remembrance of Amalek from under heaven; you shall not forget'.

commit to memory?[29] Such decisions have important consequences as Patrick Geary's discussion of the reconstruction of the past in eleventh-century Europe makes clear: these processes completely shaped how we, as historians, have understood early medieval Europe.[30] As Geary also shows, there need be no clear divide between oral and literate when it comes to discussing memory and its construction, despite scholarly tendencies to impose such a division.[31] The kinds of memory processes which we are discussing, consequently, do not require a literate society. Nevertheless, writing is regularly understood by scholars as an important technology which enables and preserves memory.[32]

If texts provide one important vehicle for creating memory, public monuments provide another equally important venue. Their virtue lies in their very nature as commemorative structures set up in public spaces which are used by different groups in various ways. As such, they create shared public space in which different groups of people create a common past for themselves.[33] By themselves and in isolation, however, such structures remain simply masses of stone or metal devoid of meaning.[34] On their own, they also do not remember: 'by themselves memorials remain inert and amnesiac. . . For their memory, these memorials depend completely on the visitor. Only we can animate the stone figures and fill the empty spaces of the memorial, and only then can monuments be said to remember anything at all'.[35] Memory, accordingly, is created by the interaction between commemorative structures and viewers and those memories function both at the level of the individual and of the collective group. As inanimate objects, finished monuments normally ignore their own history, the processes by which they were brought into being, and so they are doubly amnesiac.[36] Texts on such structures usually do not indicate why they were created and the words merely record what is being commemorated. As we

---

[29] As Appadurai has shown, the past is a finite, not limitless, resource; Appadurai 1981.
[30] Geary 1994b. On the relationship(s) of history and memory, see Cubitt 2007: 26–65 with further references, and Le Goff 1992: 51–99. Cubitt stresses the inherent tensions between history and memory, while Le Goff sees memory as 'one of the bases of history'; Le Goff 1992: 212.
[31] On the divide, see Fentress and Wickham 1992: 44–6, 96–7; Geary 1994b: 12–15; and Cubitt 2007: 182–4, 188, all with further references.
[32] E.g. Cubitt 2007: 144–6, 182–4, 188–92; Le Goff 1992: 58–62, 65–75, 81–5, 90–7; Assmann 2006: 21, 41–3, 63–87, 97–100; Appadurai 1981; Fentress and Wickham 1992: 8–11; Olick 1999b: 344–5; Sivan 1999.
[33] Young 1993: 6–7; cf. Savage 1994: 130–1.   [34] Young 1993: 2.
[35] Young 1994: 38; cf. Young 1993: xiii, 97, 119, 156; Young 2000: 62. Note also: 'stories introduce a temporal dimension, making sites the markers of experiences of groups . . . not just markers of space'; Bruner 1984a: 5.
[36] Young 1993: 14; cf. Savage 1994: 140–1.

shall see, however, some monuments, notably inscribed Athenian decrees and laws, do not follow these rules and they do refer to the circumstances which brought them into being. Acknowledging their origin complicates both the ways in which these structures function to create memory and the ways in which viewers and readers interact with them.

Commemorative monuments also belong in larger spatial settings. In such a space, the structure 'becomes a point of reference amid other parts of the landscape, one node among others in a topographical matrix that orients the rememberer and creates meaning in both the land and our recollections'.[37] In this topography, commemorative structures are juxta-posed with each other so that they interact not only with their viewers, but also with each other. These multiple interactions add both depth and complexity to the memories created. There is also a layering effect as new monuments are added to the topography.[38] These different strata endow the structures with histories which, by their very nature, they would other-wise lack. The different layers may reinforce each other or they may create conflicts between the different earlier and later phases; these strategies either increase and deepen the memories created or they change them and so also the dynamics of the monument(s). If commemorative structures are places for remembering, they are also locations for forgetting and subject to the consequences of that process.

If monuments in and of themselves cannot remember and they must rely on interactions with viewers, then we must ask exactly how this memory process works at the level of the collective group. A monument may, like the Vietnam Veterans Memorial in Washington, DC, work primarily at the level of the individual. Individually, visitors touch the names on the black granite walls and leave their offerings which serve to tell their different stories.[39] As the repeated themes in these individual stories show, the structure is experienced by visitors in similar ways as a place of mourning, healing and connection with the individuals represented by the specific names;[40] they then leave with common memories experienced individually. Since, however, public monuments create shared public space, they must also be animated by and create memories for the collective group. In this

---

[37] Young 1993: 7; cf. Bruner 1984a: 4; Bruner and Gorfain 1984: 72; Leach 1984: 357–8; Savage 1994: 130–1; Sherman 2001: 220.
[38] For some examples, see Ma 2005; Lahiri 2003: 42–58; Hung 1991; Saunders 2003: 12; Young 1993: 104–12; cf. Savage 1994: 143; Rainbird 2003: 25–32.
[39] For visitors' dynamics, see Berdahl 1994: 88–111. For helpful introductions to the memorial, see Wagner-Pacifici and Schwartz 1991 with further references; Sturken 1991. Touching the names is not unique to this structure; for parallels after the First World War, see Winter 1995: 113.
[40] For some examples, see Berdahl 1994: 94–105.

fundamentally social interaction, the group must share or talk about its narratives because remembering is 'closely linked to communication'.[41] For such a process to be effective, there must be order and not the cacophony of many individuals speaking at once. That order is created through ritual, whether secular or sacred. At the same time, ritual makes remembering in common possible.[42] The repetition of the ritual implies continuity with the past and this relationship is made explicit when commemorative ceremonies re-enact a narrative of past events.[43] Consisting of an ordered series of speech acts, these rituals are also performative.[44] To carry out the ceremonies, accordingly, is to re-enact the past,[45] even if that re-enactment does not exactly replicate the original event. Furthermore, remembering together as a group creates a shared memory and, when this remembering is done as part of a ritual, it creates a memory both of the act of remembering and of the event being remembered.[46] In these ways, rituals create memories of the groups' past(s) which would otherwise not be available for the participants and, therefore, participation in these activities is extremely important.[47] These actions also present the group to itself and so create and disseminate its shared values.[48] Together with the commemoration and remembrance of important moments in the group's past, these shared values help to create an identity for the group which is both presented and reinforced by the rituals.[49] Since all members of the group share this process, the memory created is a 'national' one which is instantiated both in rituals and in commemorative monuments.[50] When this group is larger than a face-to-face society, these processes help to create an 'imagined community', such as the modern nation-state, which can only be perceived vicariously, rather than through personal experience, because of its size.[51]

---

[41] Cubitt 2007: 129 with 127, 179; cf. Fentress and Wickham 1992: ix–x; Young 1993: 6–7.
[42] Connerton 1989: 39–40; Cubitt 2007: 166–7, 181. Cubitt notes that ritual is not required for groups to remember their past; Cubitt 2007: 167.
[43] Connerton 1989: 45.   [44] Connerton 1989: 58–61.
[45] Connerton 1989: 61–71; Cubitt 2007: 181; Assmann 2006: 10–11.
[46] Young 1993: 6–7; cf. Cubitt 2007: 220–1; Olick 1999a: 382, 397.
[47] Participation: Cubitt 2007: 220. For further discussion of the role(s) of ritual in creating memory, see e.g. Cressy 1992; Young 1993: 263–81; Cressy 1994; Geary 1994a: 77–92; Hedrick, Jr 2000b: 89–91, 101, 106–7, 126–30, 220–41, and cf. 113–26; Sherman 2001: 261–308; Elsner 2003: 222–5; Olick 1999a; Cubitt 2007: 181, 219–21. For ancient Greece, see *Agora* XVI 114.19–24 (sacrifice as memorial) and *IG* II² 657.43–5 and 680 (games as memorial).
[48] Connerton 1989: 49–50; Cubitt 2007: 181.
[49] Compare Young 1993: 6–7; Connerton 1989: 70–1; Cubitt 2007: 222–5. For the link between national identity and memory, see the helpful papers in Gillis 1994 and also Olick and Robbins 1998: 124–6.
[50] Young 1993: 6, 280–1.
[51] For the 'imagined community', see B. Anderson 2006 and especially 5–7 for a definition of the term. For Anderson, imagined communities are the products of modern nationalism which is made

In turn, the 'national' memory provides unity for the group, irrespective of its size, and binds its members together.[52]

These commemorative rituals and monuments may reflect the long-standing traditions of the group, but they may also be expressly invented in order to perform their specific functions. In this way, they operate like other 'invented traditions', practices which promulgate particular values and behaviours through repetition.[53] Although the reiteration suggests that the invented traditions are directly connected with the past, the continuity is generally a fiction and the creation of such traditions is the response to novel situations and discontinuity.[54] They especially establish or represent the cohesion of social groups and they also create or legitimise authority.[55] In so doing, old traditions may be adapted for new purposes, but old material may also be used to create invented traditions which are new both in type and in purpose.[56] While the essays of the classic collection on invented tradition focus on the nineteenth and twentieth centuries, Geary's work on early eleventh-century Europe shows these same practices at work.[57] The invented tradition is not, therefore, a phenomenon of the industrialised world and we shall see it at work also in fifth-century BC Athens where the inventions will create legitimacy and continuity with the past. These processes require selected remembering and, therefore, forgetting is also a critical element in the invention of tradition.

Although commemorative rituals and monuments present themselves as the (inevitable) development of the past and the proper place for its remembrance, they frequently come into being only through extensive contestation over their form, appearance, language and even their very existence; these dynamics can make remembering recent events particularly problematic.[58] Contestation is particularly brought out by the process of creating commemorative structures and it is well documented for many twentieth-century memorial projects.[59] The competing views may be

possible by the demise of the medieval religious community and medieval dynastic realm; see especially 9–36. The concept is also applicable to the pre-medieval world. For its use in connection with classical Athens, see Ober 1989: 31–3 and Cohen 2000: 3–4, 104–29, both with further references.

52 For a modern example, see the rituals remembering World War I in Britain in the inter-war years; Bushaway 1992: 158–61; Laqueur 1994: 158.

53 Hobsbawm 1983: 1.   54 Hobsbawm 1983: 1–2.

55 Hobsbawm 1983: 9.   56 Hobsbawm 1983: 5–6.

57 For case studies of the invention of tradition, see the essays in Hobsbawm and Ranger 1983; Geary 1994b.

58 Cubitt 2007: 210.

59 See e.g. Young 1993: 81–90, 104–12, 287–96, 302–19, 323–35; Young 2000: 184–223; Wagner-Pacifici and Schwartz 1991: 385–96; Savage 1994: 132–5, 143–4; Sherman 2001: 215–60. Museum displays like the Enola Gay in the National Air and Space Museum in Washington, DC may be contested; Cubitt

based on differences about location, appearance, politics and even whether the structure should be built at all. In this respect, two monuments in Berlin are instructive. Although proposals were made for constructing a monument on the site of the former SS and Gestapo headquarters (the Gestapo-Gelände), which was bombed during the Second World War and then dynamited in 1949, strong objections to the winning design prevented its construction and the memorial project was left unresolved.[60] The Memorial for the Murdered Jews of Europe was only built after extensive argument and multiple designs.[61] Once a monument has been erected, however, this contestation is usually not apparent to its visitors; only archival work will make the earlier disagreements apparent. For the ancient world, these dynamics have important consequences because it is the monuments which are normally preserved, not the traces of contestation about their existence. As the modern parallels make clear, it would be wrong to equate the absence of evidence with an absence of disagreement about the memorial projects themselves. Nor does the physical existence of the structure guarantee that it was not controversial, as the Memorial for the Murdered Jews of Europe makes clear. The contestation connected with the creation of commemorative monuments also brings out the importance of context: both the historical context and the physical setting and relationships to other structures. Without attention to these different aspects, it is impossible to understand the memory politics involved and the ways in which collective memory is being created.

MONUMENTS, INSCRIPTIONS AND VIEWERS

Since monuments in and of themselves cannot remember and memory must be created through the interactions between viewers and the structures, these dynamics raise the issue of how visitors relate to them and particularly to texts which they may include. As we saw in the case of the Vietnam Veterans Memorial, reading the inscribed names is an important part of a visitor's experience and it is integral to remembering. For scholars working on commemorative structures of literate societies, reading is assumed and it is understood as a significant aspect of the

---

2007: 208–10. Rituals can also be subject to contestation, as, for example, the religious services for Guy Fawkes Day in England in the 1850s or the commemoration of the 8 May 1945 in the Federal Republic of Germany; Cressy 1992: 81–3; Olick 1999a. For contestation of the past more generally, see Cubitt 2007: 206–14, 222–31; Olick and Robbins 1998: 126–8; Appadurai 1981 (a case study).

[60] Young 1993: 81–90.

[61] Young 2000: 184–223. For subsequent developments, see Mügge 2008: 711–22.

dynamics.[62] Indeed, at Birkenau in Poland, inscriptions were considered so integral to the memorial in this concentration camp that they were removed after the dissolution of the Soviet Block for replacement with more suitable texts.[63] These researchers would very probably presume that ancient Athenian inscriptions were also read and so scholars of ancient Greece, and particularly epigraphists, have often understood this material.[64] More recently, this consensus has been called into question. In its most uncompromising formulation, '*stelai* . . . are symbolic memorials' and 'inscriptions may have been read by a few Athenians . . . but consultation of inscribed decrees – and apparently the laws, too – was not a deeply ingrained habit'.[65] As a result of these very different viewpoints, the scholarly dialogue has tended to become polarised and inscriptions are thought to have only one purpose.[66] These discussions regularly ignore the multiple functions of Athenian inscriptions and also the dynamics of writing on commemorative monuments.

For such structures to function, visitors must know what is being memorialised. If these Athenian inscriptions only had a commemorative function, then it would not have been necessary to inscribe whole documents, often at significant expense; the *stele* would simply have needed a short title: 'memorial of the alliance between the Athenians and the people of such-and-such city'. A rectangular block of blank stone set on end is, however, a poor monument because it provides little to remember and memory of events does not take place in the abstract. As the sculptor Nathan Rapoport once said about his Warsaw Ghetto Memorial, 'could I have made a stone with a hole in it and said, "Voilà! The heroism of the Jews"? No, I needed to show the heroism . . . I did not want to represent resistance in the abstract:

---

[62] E.g. Savage 1994: 131, 136–7; Laqueur 1994; Sherman 1994: 188–90, 204, 206–7; Wagner-Pacifici and Schwartz 1991: 400–1, 403, 412; Young 1993: 30, 34–5, 53–5, 64–7, 102–3, 121–3, 205–6, 257–8, 289, 295–6, 299–300; cf. Bushaway 1992: 139–52; Berdahl 1994: 98–9; Winter 1995: 95.

[63] Young 1993: 141–3, 208.

[64] See e.g. Meritt 1940: 89–91; D. Harris 1994: 215–16; R. Osborne 1999; Sickinger 1999a: 232; Sickinger 1999b: 64–5; P. J. Rhodes 2001a: 34–41; Liddel 2003: 34–41; Ma 2005: 141–83; Blanshard 2007; Gagarin 2008: 69–71, 176–80; cf. Rhodes and Osborne 2003: xiii–xiv; Hedrick, Jr 1994: 161–2.

[65] Thomas 1989: 52, 67. Compare 'Athenian inscriptions were intended to serve as symbols, more to be seen than to be read'; Hedrick, Jr 2000a: 127. Thomas' most recent discussion is less extreme; see Thomas 2009. For inscriptions as monuments, see Thomas 1989: 49–53; Thomas 1992: 84–8, 139–40; Hedrick, Jr 1994: 173; Steiner 1994: 64–73; Sickinger 1999a: 233–4; Sickinger 1999b: 65; P. J. Rhodes 2001b: 140–1; cf. D. Harris 1994: 216.

[66] Polarisation: see Stroud 1998: 46 note 95; Sickinger 1999b: 216, note 9; Hedrick, Jr 2000a: 133. Issues of literacy are closely bound up with these discussions, but they lie beyond the scope of this work. For a helpful recent discussion of literacy and writing in the particular context of Greek law, see Gagarin 2008: 66–92, 176–205. The evidence provided by Gagarin and Thomas together shows that reading would not actually have been foreign to many Athenians in the late fifth century; Gagarin 2008: 176–205; Thomas 2009.

it was not an abstract uprising'.[67] We could add here that, when modern monuments are abstract, they include inscriptions which are integral to remembrance, as, for example, on the Vietnam Veterans Memorial or the Pillar of Heroism at Yad Vashem in Israel.[68] So, too, the abstract and amnesiac form of this putative *stele* fails to memorialise this particular alliance. Furthermore, on the Akropolis, it would have been indistinguishable from many other similar *stelai*.[69] Inscribing the whole text of the alliance, in contrast, would create a unique monument and it would make clear what exactly was being commemorated. Even the addition of a document relief at the top of the block might not help to individualise this structure: a relief showing Athena and Hera shaking hands was used for both the decrees honouring the Samians in 403/2 and the inventory of the treasurers of Athena and the Other Gods in 399/8.[70] Without the inscriptions, it would be impossible to know that only one monument commemorated the relationships between Athens and Samos or that one document listed an inventory of sacred items. To understand these reliefs, the inscribed documents must be read.[71] In order for inscriptions to function as memorials, consequently, their texts must be known to viewers, a process which requires them to read the inscription, however well or however badly. Without any reading at all, they will not interact with the structures[72] and remembering will not take place. Monuments and texts are, therefore, not mutually exclusive and Athenian inscriptions must have served both functions at the same time.

RESPONDING TO OLIGARCHY AT ATHENS

These approaches to memory, memorialisation and ritual provide powerful analytical tools for understanding both the present and the past and they provide the basis for studying the Athenians' reactions to the oligarchies of 411 and 404/3 and their reconstruction of democracy. We shall consider their responses not just in one sphere such as literature or oratory, but across a range of areas, particularly inscribed documents, the buildings, monuments and spaces of the city and the city's public rituals, because an

---

[67] Nathan Rapoport as quoted by Young 1993: 168 and cf. 9, 155. For the Warsaw Ghetto Memorial, see Young 1993: 155–84.

[68] For the Pillar of Heroism, see Young 1993: 255–7, 259.

[69] For the Akropolis as the main place for erecting inscriptions, see Shear 2007a: 97–101; Liddel 2003.

[70] Samians: *IG* i³ 127 + RO 2 (= *IG* ii² 1); Blanshard 2007: 20 fig. 1.1; treasurers: *IG* ii² 1374; Blanshard 2007: 20 fig. 1.3.

[71] Blanshard 2007.

[72] Contra: Hedrick, Jr 1994: 174. I do not understand how citizens' 'active, social interaction' with inscriptions, to use Hedrick's phrase, can take place without reading the text.

interdisciplinary approach is necessary to understand these civic processes. These responses are both collective and public, the results of the Athenians' decisions as a group. As such, they had to be approved by the *demos* and the *boule*, the people in the assembly and the council, and they must represent at least a majority view, albeit one often only reached after debate, dissent and contention. Politics, consequently, will enter into our discussions, but governing Athens is not the primary focus of this study. Since we usually see only the results of these political actions, we should not forget the different opinions generated during the processes of approval. In some cases, individual dissent found its outlet in legal suits brought against specific measures such as Theozotides' and Thrasyboulos' proposals for honouring the men involved with the overthrow of the Thirty and the return of the *demos*.[73] Lawsuits brought against men for their actions, real or alleged, under the oligarchs, provided other occasions for contestation between individuals.[74] As the reactions of individual men, these speeches belong against the backdrop of the Athenians' collective responses in the public sphere and they show us some of the ways in which individual men negotiated their memories of oligarchy.

This contestation brings out for us the fractured nature of Athens in the aftermath of civil strife and differences over the appropriate form of rule for the city. Responding to oligarchy, consequently, also required reuniting the divided Athenians. In this riven society, agreement could not be assumed, particularly in the political sphere; instead, it needed to be deliberately created. In this difficult process, not all issues would be explicitly articulated because to do so was to open the possibility of disagreement which would lead to further disunity. Leaving contentious matters implicit, in contrast, removed the sources of contention and provided an area on which everyone could tacitly agree. These dynamics, however, did not preclude disagreement over other issues. In the Athenian democracy, difference was a fundamental part of a system in which debate and competition were critical aspects of both the assembly and the lawcourts.[75] Tacit agreement on the type of political system allowed disagreement on specific issues, but it did not spill out of control because of the implicit understanding that everyone would abide by the decision of the majority. Under these rules, there was also unity in division. In addition, differences and splits could be

---

[73] Theozotides: *SEG* xxviii 46 with Lys. fr. lxiv.128–150 (Carey); Thrasyboulos: Arist. *Ath. Pol.* 40.2; below chapters 7 and 8.
[74] Below chapters 2 and 7.
[75] Loraux 2002: 20–4, 98–104, 231–8; Loraux 1991: 39–44; Ober 1998: 39; Ober 1989: 76, 78–9; Yunis 1996: 11–12.

exploited by excluding specific individuals from the group so that they, not the divisions, became the focus; a new unity was, therefore, generated by exclusion.[76] As we shall see, the Athenians used these strategies to bring the warring factions back together and to begin to heal their divisions. These processes very much complemented the unities created through memorialisation and through rituals, particularly the swearing of oaths and the offering of sacrifices to the gods and these occasions became opportunities for displaying the city's new harmony.

Serious disputes and dissent among the Athenians began in 413 with the overwhelming defeat of the great expedition sent two years earlier to conquer Sicily: democracy, the city's established *politeia*, was now called into question as the only possible way of ruling the city. Out of the ensuing intense debate about the proper sort of constitution for Athens came the oligarchs in 411 who wished to overthrow the democracy and institute a different and, in their view, better *politeia*. As we shall see in detail in chapter 2, these men brandished the *patrios politeia*, the ancestral constitution, to legitimise their rule and they re-used the city's political past for their own ends. They also tried to lay claim to the city's spaces, which their actions made into contested areas. Although these strategies were begun by the Four Hundred, they were continued by the Five Thousand, a less extreme oligarchic regime which faced similar problems of legitimacy.

When the *demos* regained its full power, it faced two critical issues: how to make Athens democratic again and, in light of the oligarchs' appropriations of the city's political past, whether a history of the democratic city existed and could be identified. As we shall see, remaking Athens as the democratic city entailed displaying the rule of the *demos*, its processes and its control visibly in the city. In this way, the democrats laid claim to the city both through inscribed documents, which show the processes very clearly (chapter 3), and through construction projects in the Agora and on the Akropolis (chapter 4). In these spheres, these actions worked both at the level of the individual reader or viewer and at the level of the collective and they also allowed the *demos* to reclaim the city's past for its own use. The Athenians used rituals associated with the City Dionysia both to (re)create unity out of the fractures of oligarchy and to display the *demos* and its control (chapter 5). From the festival's dramatic competitions in 409, Sophokles' *Philoktetes*, one of the winning plays, shows how one

---

[76] The Athenian institution of ostracism, the practice in which the Athenians voted to send a man into exile for ten years, nicely illustrates these dynamics; on ostracism, see Forsdyke 2005: 146–77, especially 159.

man reacted to the city's collective response to the events in 411. These ceremonies at the City Dionysia also created memories of these occasions which served to unite the Athenians and to provide them with memories of specific significant moments in the response to oligarchy. By 405, the Athenians had remade Athens into the democratic city and they had recovered the past from the oligarchs, whom collective memory had publicly forgotten.

Forgetting the past, however, allows it to re-occur: in the aftermath of defeat in the Peloponnesian War, oligarchs once again gained control of the democratic *polis* or city. They responded to the democrats' earlier actions by starting to remake Athens as an oligarchic city with a suitable (new) constitution, as we shall see in chapter 6. Before this project could be completed, the driving forces lost out to the practical realities of retaining power at all costs. Nevertheless, when the *demos* returned from exile, they were again faced with the problem of recreating Athens as the democratic city and re-establishing the democracy. Not all of the strategies used after 411 had been successful: oligarchs had once again seized power. This time, they had not been overthrown without fighting between different groups of Athenians, the men of the Peiraieus on the side of the *demos* and the men of the city, who supported the oligarchs. Consequently, reconciling the different factions had to be the first step in responding to the Thirty, as we shall see in chapter 7. Involving an oath sworn by all the Athenians, this process created a memory of this crucial event and the inscribed text served as a locus for remembering the occasion, significant elements in the success of the reconciliation. Bringing the Athenians back together again, however, was not achieved by these actions alone. Instead, reconciliation was a process which had to be repeatedly performed by individual men. Their negotiations are now visible in the speeches generated by the trials in the years after 403; they show us both some of the strategies used and the difficulties of the process.

In response to the Thirty's actions, Athens also had to be made once again into the democratic city. As in the years after 411, decrees and the laws (chapter 8) and monuments in the Agora (chapter 9) were used to display the rule of the *demos* and its control of the city. These actions also allowed the democrats to complete the transformation of the Agora from multi-use space, which it had been before 410, to the space of the democratic citizen. Since forgetting the oligarchies of 411 had not been a successful strategy, the Athenians also had to ask how they were going to remember the Thirty and the consequent *stasis*. As we shall see in chapter 10, through rituals and monuments, they remembered the events of 404/3 selectively as external war, rather than *stasis*, which, together with the Thirty, was consigned to the gaps of memory. These rituals also served to re-unite the men of the city and the men of the Peiraieus and so to re-integrate the former supporters of the oligarchs into the Athenians *demos*. As in the years after 411, the creation of unity was once again an important (and difficult) part of responding to oligarchy. In the aftermath of the Thirty, however, the Athenians also implemented important new constitutional measures which created serious obstacles for anyone wishing to overthrow the democracy in the future.

By responding to oligarchy, the Athenians reconstituted themselves as a united *polis* and they reconstructed their political system. In the cityscape, the power and control of the *demos* was repeatedly displayed and Athens was visibly marked as democratic. So successful were these efforts that the city could once again turn her attention to the international stage. By 394, she was fighting Sparta again and had started to rebuild the fortification walls, which had been destroyed at the end of the Peloponnesian War as part of the peace terms.[77] In 394/3, an Athenian-led fleet soundly defeated the Spartans off the peninsula of Knidos and, in 377, the city set up a new league of allies to replace the one which she had lost by the end of the Peloponnesian War. No longer visibly divided, democratic Athens was once again an important force in the Greek world.

---

[77] The earliest evidence for rebuilding the walls dates to Skirophorion 395/4; *IG* ii² 1656. The project may have begun earlier at the start of the war with Sparta.

CHAPTER 2

Revolution, oligarchy and the patrios politeia

Civil strife or *stasis* was a common feature of many Greek cities in the fifth century BC and its divisiveness is particularly clear in Thucydides' narrative of the Kerkyrean *stasis*.[1] For Athenians in the 420s, however, civil strife was something which took place in other cities or in the past, but their own *polis* was certainly not disrupted by such events.[2] Not all of these Athenians were ardent democrats, but, at this time, political differences were confined to the *ekklesia* and the *boule* and then parodied in the Theatre of Dionysos in plays such as Aristophanes' *Knights*. Concurrently, there was also a lively debate over the ideal type of constitution. Now reflected in such sources as the 'constitutional debate' in Herodotos, the pseudo-Xenophontic *Athenaion Politeia*, Euripides' *Suppliants* and Thucydides, these discussions involved not only oligarchs of various stripes, but also democrats.[3] These debates, however, remained in the realm of theory, as the author of the *Athenaion Politeia* makes clear: he is concerned to tell his readers why democracy is bad, but he is also very clear that it works. He never suggests that it might be replaced with another system and, indeed, he tries to explain why such an attempt would be in vain. After the Sicilian disaster, this situation changed abruptly when *stasis* actually came to Athens: in 411, oligarchs seized power and the democracy was dissolved. Happily for the Athenians,

---

[1] Thuc. 3.69–85. On *stasis*, see Hansen and Heine Nielsen 2004: 124–9, 1361–2; Finley 2004: 166–7; Loraux 2002: 93–122; Loraux 1991; 44–50.

[2] As the list of Athenian *staseis* provided by Hansen and Heine Nielsen makes clear: they took place in the 630s, late seventh to early sixth century, 560s, 550s, 540s, 510, 508/7, 411, 404/3; Hansen and Heine Nielsen 2004: 1361; cf. Finley 2004: 181.

[3] Hdt. 3.80.1–84.1; [Xen.] *Ath. Pol.*; Eur. *Supp.* 399–466. For the date of [Xen.] *Ath. Pol.*, I follow the majority of scholars who place it in the 420s; see e.g. Forrest 1970; de Ste Croix 1972: 307–10; Mattingly 1997: 352; R. Osborne 2004: 4–10; Marr and Rhodes 2008: 3–6; for a date in the 440s, see Bowersock 1966: 33–8; for late dates, see Mattingly 1997 (414); Hornblower 2000: 363–76 (380s). On Thucydides' involvement with these issues, see Farrar 1998: 126–91; Ober 1998: 52–121. For democratic involvement in these constitutional debates, see helpfully Raaflaub 1990. For critics of democracy, see above all Ober 1998, but note that his real focus is on the period after 403; 14–51 discuss the 420s. On this decade, see also Yunis 1996: 36–58.

19

this state of affairs did not last long and it ended with minimal bloodshed: the decree of Demophantos shows that the full democracy was already back in power by the first prytany of 410/9.[4] Looking back at earlier events, democrats in 410 were faced with two questions: how did *stasis* come to Athens and how did the city now go on to rebuild democracy? For the Athenians, answering these two questions was a critical step in creating a future because otherwise the city had no hope either of recovering from internal strife or of continuing the war against the Spartans. These two questions also provide the structure for the first part of this book: like the Athenians, this chapter looks backward at the events surrounding 411 and the Four Hundred, while the following three chapters examine how the Athenians rebuilt democracy and remade the *polis* into the democratic city.

Our sources for the oligarchic revolutions of 411 are themselves constructed responses to the events and the two main accounts present us with radically different versions: Thucydides focuses on violence and the actions of a small group of fervent oligarchs, while the later Aristotelian *Athenaion Politeia* presents the events as a serious attempt at constitutional reform. These two sources have different leading figures and they focus on different areas of the city. In both cases, the individuals and places emphasised complement the image presented of these events. These two very different accounts of the events of 411 force us to consider some of the influences at work. Understanding the constitutional emphasis of the *Athenaion Politeia* requires us to locate and identify the documents cited in the text, particularly the 'constitution for the future' and the 'constitution for the present'.[5] As I shall argue, this material comes directly out of the fierce contemporary debates over the correct *politeia* for Athens and its relationship to the city's political past. Both the *patrios politeia* and the *patrioi nomoi* or ancestral laws were invoked as the proper models for the present and the issues were debated by oligarchs and democrats alike. These discussions made the city's past into an important focus of attention and the past was used to legitimise the oligarchs and their actions. Consequently, claiming the city's past became an issue which no regime after the Four Hundred could afford to ignore. In contrast, Thucydides' violent account shows a different set of influences. It reflects strategies used in the lawsuits brought against the oligarchs and their supporters after the fall of the Four Hundred. These tactics focused on violence, deceit and conspiracy, the actions of a small group of hard-core oligarchs who were

---

[4] Andok. 1.96–8 with *IG* I³ 375.1–3 for the date; see further the discussion below chapter 3.
[5] Arist. *Ath. Pol.* 30.1–32.1.

conveniently dead or exiled from Athens when these trials took place. The oligarchic supporters, in contrast, were portrayed as moderate men who certainly did not take part in such distasteful and extreme activities. These same strategies are visible in Thucydides' narrative and the influences of these trials help to explain both his particular focus and his lack of interest in the constitutional debates.

Scholars considering Athens at the time of the Four Hundred, however, have not particularly focused on these issues. Instead, they have concentrated on ascertaining which author provides a more accurate version of what actually happened and on how this account may be supplemented or augmented by other information at our disposal.[6] Scholars have also have discussed and disagreed over the extent to which the documents included in the narrative of the Aristotelian *Athenaion Politeia* represent actual documents passed by the assembly at Kolonos when the Athenians voted the oligarchs into power and dissolved the democracy.[7] In these discussions of the Four Hundred's rise to power, the *patrios politeia* has generally not been the focus of scholarly analyses and its absence from Thucydides' account has led scholars to question the importance of the whole debate.[8] When they have considered the *patrios politeia*, it has generally been from a different perspective. In one strand of scholarship, calls for a return to the *patrios politeia* are associated only with the moderate oligarchs and most particularly with Theramenes, the son of Hagnon, a general and sometime oligarch.[9] In contrast, Martin Ostwald has argued that individuals from various political backgrounds were appealing to the ancestral constitution at this time.[10] Building on his work, we shall see that these discussions and issues had important consequences and this debate over the conveniently

---

[6] See e.g. Kagan 1987: 106–210; Ostwald 1986: 337–411 and especially 368 note 122; Andrewes 1992: 471–81; Hignett 1952: 268–80, 356–78; Gomme, Andrewes and Dover 1981: 184–212, 240–56; P. J. Rhodes 1981: 362–9; P. J. Rhodes 1972b: 114–18; E. M. Harris 1990: 243–67; M. C. Taylor 2002b; Hornblower 2002: 176–80; P. J. Rhodes 2006: 160–5; cf. Hornblower 2008: 945–6.

[7] See e.g. P. J. Rhodes 1981: 365, 385–9 with discussion of earlier views; Gomme, Andrewes and Dover 1981: 242–6; Hignett 1952: 357–9, 367–78; Ostwald 1986: 367–87; R. Osborne 2003: 258–63; P. J. Rhodes 1972b: 117; Andrewes 1976: 20–1; E. M. Harris 1990; de Ste Croix 1956; Heftner 2001: 177–210; Kagan 1987: 159–60.

[8] R. Osborne 2003: 258. Constitutional debate barely figures in e.g. Kagan 1987: 106–57; Andrewes 1992: 471–9; Hornblower 2002: 172–81. It does not appear at all in M. C. Taylor 2002b.

[9] Especially Fuks 1953: 1–33, 107–10; Finley 2000: 35–9; Hignett 1952: 5–6, 273–4; cf. de Ste Croix 1956: 10; Bibauw 1965: 478–83; Cecchin 1969: 26–63; G. Anderson 2003: 47.

[10] Ostwald 1986: 242–3, 367–72, 377–8, 389–90, 406, 409–10; cf. also Lévy 1976: 191–7. Walters argues that the *patrios politeia* issue is a fourth-century construction created by Androtion's inability to understand fifth-century references to the *patrios politeia* and the *patrioi nomoi*; Walters 1976. As this chapter shows, our evidence does not support this interpretation; against Walters' interpretation, see Harding 1978; cf. Ostwald 1986: 367 note 119.

nebulous *patrios politeia* was not just empty theorising: both the Four Hundred and the Five Thousand in turn appropriated the city's political past to provide legitimacy for their regimes. In 410, these appropriations left the democrats with little choice: they, too, had to take over the city's past from the oligarchs as part of the process of remaking Athens into the democratic city.

(RE)CONSTRUCTING THE FOUR HUNDRED

Our difficulties in understanding exactly what took place to enable the Four Hundred to gain power and then to maintain it for four months stem from the problems of our sources. The vast majority of our information is coloured by later events, as well as the authors' prejudices, and contemporary evidence is limited to a small number of inscriptions.[11] Our two primary sources provide quite different accounts of what transpired. For Thucydides, the Four Hundred were a group of violent and unprincipled men who wanted power for their own ends. In his account, the self-serving oligarch Phrynichos is the critical figure; he functions very much as the leader of the coup and he eventually turns into a tyrant, complete with an appropriately bloody end. In contrast, the *Athenaion Politeia* presents a very different situation: the actions of the oligarchs represent a serious attempt to reform the democracy and the hero is the moderate oligarch Kleitophon; Phrynichos is not mentioned at all. The two accounts also focus on different areas of the city. Kolonos, the Agora and the Eetioneia in the Peiraieus all play important roles in Thucydides' story and these spaces have very different political charges. In contrast, the *Athenaion Politeia* does not focus on where the critical assembly at which the oligarchs gained power took place. Since the Bouleuterion is the only topographical site specifically mentioned, the importance of place is visible in this account only through omission.

Thucydides begins his story of the revolution on Samos where the Athenian *trierarchoi* (commanders of warships) and the most influential men (δυνατώτατοι) were eager to overthrow the democracy without the additional and independent stimulus of Alkibiades' actions intended to enable his return to Athens (table 1). Begun on the island, the revolution then spreads to the city. Once the preparatory groundwork has been done

---

[11] Period of the Four Hundred: *IG* ɪ³ 311.35–51; 335.30–2; 357.54–82; 373. Period of the Five Thousand: [Plut.] *X orat.* 833ᴇ–ꜰ = Krater. *FGrHist* 342 ꜰ5b; *IG* ɪ³ 312.52–68; 336.44–57; 374. Either the Four Hundred or the Five Thousand: *IG* ɪ³ 98. For all these texts, see the discussion below.

Table 1 *Thucydides' Narrative of the Four Hundred*

Event	References
Alkibiades advises Tissaphernes to wear down the two sides.	8.45.1–47.1
The Athenian soldiers on Samos perceive Alkibiades' influence with Tissaphernes.	8.47.2
Alkibiades sends word to the most influential men (δυνατωτάτους) to say the best men (βελτίστους) that he wished to return to Athens under an oligarchy.	8.47.2
The Athenian *trierarchoi* on Samos and the most influential men (δυνατώτατοι) independently decide to overthrow the democracy. The movement starts in the camp and, from there, spreads to the city.	8.47.2–48.1
A conference between the conspirators and Alkibiades.	8.48.1
They begin the conspiracy with promises of money from the king, if Alkibiades is restored and they are not ruled by the democracy (μὴ δημοκρατουμένων). The multitude (ὄχλος), though dissatisfied, keeps quiet.	8.48.2–3
Phrynichos' opposition, which is ignored. The conspirators prepare to send Peisandros and other envoys to Athens.	8.48.4–49
Phrynichos betrays Alkibiades to Astyochos, the Spartan commander, who immediately reports the information to Tissaphernes. Phrynichos then betrays the Athenians to Astyochos who reports it to Alkibiades.	8.50.1–51.3
Peisandros and the other envoys arrive in Athens and address the *demos*. They stress that, by recalling Alkibiades and by not having a democracy in the current form (μὴ τὸν αὐτὸν τρόπον δημοκρατουμένοις), they could have the Persian king as an ally and they could win the war.	8.53.1
The *demos* is initially displeased, but, persuaded by fear, it votes to send Peisandros and ten other men to conduct negotiations with Tissaphernes and Alkibiades.	8.53.1–54.2
Peisandros brings false accusations against the generals Phrynichos and Skironides; they are relieved of their commands and replaced by Diomedon and Leon.	8.54.3
Before his departure, Peisandros encourages the *hetaireiai* to work towards the overthrow of the *demos*.	8.54.4–5
The negotiations prove to be fruitless and the envoys return to Samos, where they continue plotting against the democracy, but without Alkibiades.	8.56.1–6, 63.3–4

(cont.)

Table 1 (*cont.*)

Event	References
Peisandros and half of the conspirators are sent to Athens, while the other half of the conspirators are sent to establish oligarchies in the allied cities.	8.64.1–65.1
Peisandros and his fellow conspirators arrive at Athens.	8.65.1
The previous actions of their associates: the secret death of the democrat Androkles; the open proposal that pay should be restricted to those fighting the war and no more than 5,000 should have a share in controlling affairs.	8.65.2–66.1
The agendas of the *demos* and democratically elected (ἀπὸ τοῦ κυάμου) *boule* are controlled by the conspirators.	8.66.1
The Athenians keep quiet through fear.	8.66.2–5
Upon arriving in Athens, Peisandros and his fellow conspirators call a meeting of the *demos* and propose the election of ten *sungrapheis autokratores* who will bring proposals for the best government on the appointed day.	8.67.1
The *ekklesia* meets at Kolonos.	8.67.2
The *sungrapheis* propose that: anyone who wished should be able to offer a proposal without penalty; the *graphe paranomon*, the prohibition against illegal proposals, should be suspended with heavy penalties for anyone who tried to use it.	8.67.2
The conspirators openly propose a motion establishing themselves in power (as the Four Hundred).	8.67.3
The ring-leaders: Peisandros, Antiphon the orator, Phrynichos ('most zealous' on behalf of the oligarchy) and Theramenes the son of Hagnon.	8.68.1–4
The proposals are passed without opposition and the *ekklesia* is dissolved.	8.69.1
The oligarchs evict the democratically elected *boule* and pay them off. They take over the Bouleuterion for their own centre of power.	8.69.1–70.1
Once in power, the Four Hundred kill a number of men and make peace overtures to King Agis at Dekeleia.	8.70.1–2
Agis brings his army up outside the walls of Athens, but without any success. More embassies are exchanged between the oligarchs and the Spartans.	8.71.1–3

Table 1   (*cont.*)

Event	References
A delegation of ten men is sent to the army on Samos to explain the situation.	8.72.1–2
The counter-revolution on Samos and the restoration of the democracy.	8.73.1–6
Chareas is sent to Athens to explain the situation.	8.74.1
Chareas' return and exaggerated report of the violence and bad situation in Athens.	8.74.3
Meetings of the army on Samos. They resolve to continue fighting the war.	8.75.1–77
The recall of Alkibiades to Samos.	8.81.1–82.2
Envoys from the Four Hundred to the army on Samos. Alkibiades tells them to depose the Four Hundred and re-establish the *boule* of 500.	8.86.1–7
Dissatisfaction starts in Athens. Among those critical are Theramenes, the son of Hagnon, and Aristokrates, the son of Skelias. There are demands for the appointment of the Five Thousand.	8.89.1–4
The opposition of men like Phrynichos, Aristarchos, Peisandros and Antiphon. They dispatch an embassy to Sparta and start construction on a fort at Eetioneia in the Peiraieus.	8.90.1–5
The return of the embassy and the assassination of Phrynichos.	8.91.1, 92.1–2
The Peloponnesian fleet sails towards Athens.	8.91.2, 92.3
The hoplites in the Peiraieus arrest the general Alexikles and the fort at Eetioneia is destroyed.	8.92.4–11
Meetings of the Four Hundred in the Bouleuterion and of the hoplites in the Peiraieus in the Theatre of Dionysos in Mounichia.	8.93.1–3
The arrival of the Peloponnesian fleet.	8.94.1–2
The Athenian fleet is manned and sent to Euboia. The defeat off Eretria.	8.95.1–7
News of the defeat reaches Athens.	8.96.1
A meeting of the *ekklesia* is called and it meets for the first time on the Pnyx.	8.97.1
The Four Hundred are deposed and power is transferred to the Five Thousand.	8.97.1–2

by the conspirators' associates, the arrival of the leading oligarch Peisandros from Samos leads quickly and directly to the fateful meeting of the *ekklesia* at Kolonos, the overthrow of the democracy, and the establishment of the Four Hundred.[12] In these early sections, Thucydides particularly focuses on two conspirators, Phrynichos and Peisandros, who are both with the army on Samos. Peisandros quickly emerges as one of the leading men of the conspiracy: he first appears among the conspirators' first delegation to Athens;[13] his actions there lay the groundwork for his second visit when he is instrumental in establishing the Four Hundred. On his first trip to Athens, he shows his true colours: he is already advocating a different form of democracy, which, he soothingly tells the *demos*, can be changed at a later date if it does not like it.[14] On this visit, he also shows his duplicity and deceit by falsely accusing Phrynichos of betraying Iasos and Amorges.[15] His commitment to the oligarchy is evident both in his charge against Phrynichos, whom he did not think was committed to the negotiations with Alkibiades, and in his encouragement to the members of the political clubs or *hetaireiai* to join together to overthrow the democracy.[16] These activities mark Peisandros out as instrumental in the conspirators' success and they also identify him as a solid oligarch. His leading role in the establishment of the Four Hundred comes as no surprise when Thucydides specifically mentions it.[17] He appears later among a list of the extreme oligarchic leaders and, when the Four Hundred is deposed, he seeks shelter with the Spartans at Dekeleia (fig. 1).[18]

If Peisandros is a typical oligarch, then the portrayal of Phrynichos is rather more elaborate. One of the generals on Samos, Phrynichos' first appearance in the rise of the Four Hundred is in opposition to the plans of the conspirators.[19] Although he rightly regards Alkibiades as an opportunist uncommitted to oligarchy, Phrynichos does not come off well in

---

[12] On Peisandros' career, see Ostwald 1986: 350–5.   [13] Thuc. 8.49.
[14] Thuc. 8.53.1, 3. Thucydides' account seems very compressed at this point. On the chronological problems, see Gomme, Andrewes and Dover 1981: 131, 184–93; Kagan 1987: 131 note 2; Ostwald 1986: 353 note 66; Sommerstein 1977: 113–16; Sommerstein 1990: 2–3; Henderson 1987: xxi–xxii, 132; Austin and Olson 2004: xxxviii–xxxix, xli–xliii; Avery 1999. The chronological problems are intimately connected with the issue of the dates of Aristophanes' *Lysistrata* (normally Lenaia 412/1) and *Thesmophoriazousai* (normally Dionysia 412/1); see Gomme, Andrewes and Dover 1981: 184–93; Sommerstein 1977; Sommerstein 1990: 1–3; Henderson 1987: xv–xxv; Sommerstein 1994: 1–4; Austin and Olson 2004: xxxiii–xliv; Avery 1999: 130–4.
[15] Thuc. 8.54.3.
[16] *Hetaireiai*: Thuc. 8.54.4. Thucydides says that these clubs existed to help members with lawsuits and elections; see also the helpful remarks of Gomme, Andrewes and Dover 1981: 128–31.
[17] Thuc. 8.68.1.   [18] Thuc. 8.90.2, 98.1.
[19] Thuc. 8.48.4–7. On Phrynichos' career, see Ostwald 1986: 348–50.

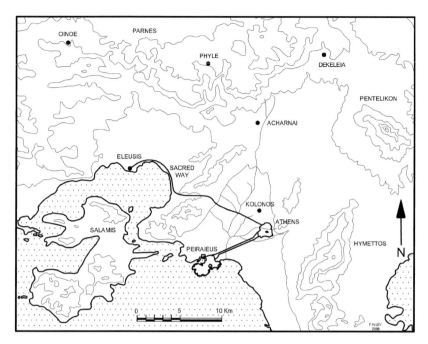

Figure 1   Plan of Attica showing the places mentioned in the text.

Thucydides' narrative. Instead of working against the nascent conspiracy, he betrays first Alkibiades and then the Athenians to the Spartan commander Astyochos.[20] At this point, only luck saves Phrynichos who will shortly be deprived of his command by the *demos* at Peisandros' instigation.[21] At this point, astute readers may wonder if Phrynichos' earlier refusal to fight off the city of Miletos was really as shrewd a move as Thucydides thought it was; perhaps Phrynichos was acting out of cowardice or, even worse, was already dealing with the enemy.[22] After such an introduction, Phrynichos' appearance among the main leaders of the Four Hundred should come as no surprise; now, however, he is described as 'most zealous' on behalf of the oligarchy, quite a change from his early position![23] Subsequently, he appears with Antiphon as one of the ambassadors to the Lakedaimonians

---

[20] Thuc. 8.50.1–51.3. Note that Phrynichos' first letter also contains a clear (σαφῶς) account of his other doings. On this passage, see also Hornblower 2008: 901–2.

[21] Thuc. 8.51.3.

[22] Refusal to give battle: Thuc. 8.27.1–6. For discussion of the military situation, see Kagan 1987: 64–8 with further references.

[23] Thuc. 8.68.3.

Figure 2   Restored plan of the Athenian Agora in *c.* 400 BC. The statues of the
Tyrannicides were located on the base between the racetrack and the Panathenaic Way.

so that he is included among the extreme oligarchs who want to make peace
with Sparta at any cost.[24] His return from the embassy presents us with a
final depiction: after arriving in Athens, he was assassinated in the crowded
Agora not far from the Bouleuterion by one of the *peripoloi*, the members
of the border patrol (fig. 2); while this man escaped, his Argive accomplice
was captured and tortured.[25] This episode is not merely the death of a
prominent oligarch because, through his description, Thucydides also suggests a parallel between Phrynichos and another Athenian assassinated by
two men near the Agora, Hipparchos, the brother of the tyrant Hippias,

[24] Thuc. 8.90.2.
[25] Thuc. 8.92.2. For the various versions of Phrynichos' assassination and their problems, see the
discussion below.

an event which had already been described in detail earlier in the work.[26] Although Thucydides places Hipparchos 'by the Leokoreion', the Tyrannicides' statues were located in the Agora where they connected Harmodios and Aristogeiton specifically with that space. Thucydides' description of Phrynichos' death, accordingly, casts him as a tyrant, the exact opposite of a democrat and a much worse state than being an oligarch.[27] Since Phrynichos was already depicted betraying the army to the Spartans, his violent end should come as no surprise to readers. His overall career emphasises his negative qualities and he very much stands as the ultimate example of the bad oligarch.

In addition to Peisandros and Phrynichos, Thucydides names a limited number of oligarchs: Antiphon, Aristarchos, Alexikles and Theramenes appear repeatedly.[28] Their actions divide them into two groups, Theramenes who appears as the moderate 'good' leader in the affair and the other whose actions identify them as extreme oligarchs. Two of Theramenes' supporters are named, Aristokrates and Hermon, and six other oligarchs are mentioned only once.[29] In contrast, groups of men are frequently unnamed: for example, Thucydides refers to certain men who go from Samos to Alkibiades, those men in the conspiracy or the conspirators, Peisandros and others/envoys, the *hetairoi* of Peisandros at Athens, some of the younger men, men sent by the Four Hundred to Agis and ten men sent by the Four Hundred to Samos.[30] This strategy focuses our attention on the individuals repeatedly named in the text; since they are the leaders of the extreme oligarchs, they are separated from the other, unspecified, oligarchs. Strikingly, all of these men except Theramenes were successfully prosecuted after the fall of the Four Hundred and their responsibility for the Four Hundred would already have become clear when Thucydides came to write this section. Thucydides' repeated references to these groups of nameless conspirators and oligarchs further bring out the uncertainty surrounding the Four Hundred's acquisition of power. As readers, we cannot always be sure who is on which side of the *stasis* and our uncertainty

---

[26] Thuc. 6.54.1–59.1.   [27] Phrynichos as tyrant: R. Osborne 2003: 258.

[28] Note especially Thuc. 8.68, 90.1, 98.

[29] Aristokrates: Thuc. 8.89.2, 92.2; Hermon: Thuc. 8.92.5. Other oligarchs: Dieitrephes: Thuc. 8.64.2; Charminos: Thuc. 8.73.3; Laispodias, Aristophon and Melesias: Thuc. 8.86.9; Thymochares: Thuc. 8.95.2. Contrast Xen. *Hell.* 2.3.46, where additional men are specifically described as directing the construction of the fort at the Eetioneia.

[30] Certain men: Thuc. 8.48.1; conspirators: Thuc. 8.49, 66.1, 69.2, 73.4; Peisandros and others: Thuc. 8.49, 53.1, 54.2, 54.5, 63.3, 64.1–2, 65.1, 67.1; Peisandros' *hetairoi*: Thuc. 8.65.2; some younger men: Thuc. 8.65.2–3; men sent to Agis: Thuc. 8.71.1; men sent to Samos: Thuc. 8.72.1, 77, 86.1, 89.1, 90.1. On this narrative strategy, see also Hornblower 2008: 945.

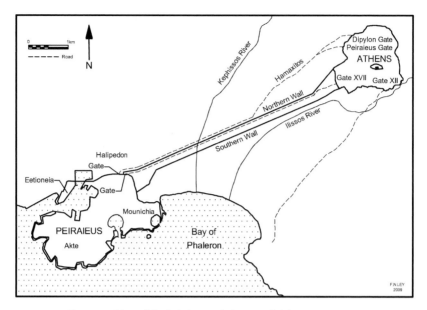

Figure 3   Plan of the Peiraieus and the city of Athens in *c.* 405 BC.

reinforces the description of the Athenians' confusion about the identity of the conspirators.[31] The Athenians' uncertainty about what was actually going on appears again in the description of the turmoil which erupted after the arrest of Alexikles and during the destruction of the oligarchs' fortress at the Eetioneia on the main harbour at Peiraieus, when it was unclear whether the Five Thousand actually existed or not (fig. 3).[32]

Phrynichos' bloody end fits in very well with the larger cycle of fear and violence in Thucydides' account. The oligarchs regularly use or threaten to use violence and they are depicted as a small group of individuals imposing their will on the Athenians.[33] The conspirators' first proposal to the Athenians, that they should recall Alkibiades and have a different form of democracy, is eventually passed by the *ekklesia* through fear.[34] Subsequently, shortly before Peisandros' return, when the conspirators are controlling the agendas of the *demos* and *boule*, the Athenians do not speak out against the growing conspiracy because they are afraid.[35] This fear was reinforced by the violence visited upon anyone who had the temerity to

---

[31] Thuc. 8.66.3–5.   [32] Thuc. 8.92.4–11.
[33] R. Osborne 2003: 258; E. M. Harris 1990: 267–8, 269. I am not persuaded by Taylor's efforts to downplay the importance of terror and deceit in Thucydides' narrative; M. C. Taylor 2002b.
[34] Thuc. 8.53.1–54.1.   [35] Thuc. 8.66.1–3.

speak out against the oligarchs; they had already resorted to violence shortly before Peisandros' return and put the democrat Androkles and others secretly to death.[36] When the Four Hundred evicted the democratically elected councillors from the Bouleuterion, they were accompanied by a band of young toughs; although no violence actually took place, its threat is clear.[37] The actual rule of the Four Hundred is described as *kata kratos* and they put some men to death.[38] Even more violence was later reported by Chaireas to the army on Samos; although Thucydides describes this report as false, it was believed by the soldiers.[39] The overall effect of his narrative is to emphasise the important role played by fear and violence in the Four Hundred's seizure of power. By focusing on these aspects of the situation, Thucydides also brings out the passivity of the *demos*, the way in which the Athenians continually acquiesced to the oligarchs' machinations.[40] Since the subsequent narrative focuses primarily on the military situation, both in Attica and in the eastern Aegean, and on the army in Samos, the details of the daily running of the city have been obscured. Consequently, confusion, fear and violence dominate the description of events surrounding the Four Hundred.

In contrast, the *Athenaion Politeia* presents a very different picture of these events (table 2). After the Sicilian disaster, the alliance between the Lakedaimonians and the Persians compels 'them' to overthrow the democracy and to set up the *politeia* of the Four Hundred.[41] At this point, we move directly to the proposals and documents which enable this political change. The initial decree was moved by Pythodoros of Anaphlystos and (part of) the text is quoted.[42] It was amplified by an important amendment which Kleitophon proposed. He specified that the *sungrapheis* or commissioners are to search for, or perhaps to investigate, (προσαναζητῆσαι) the *patrioi nomoi* which Kleisthenes had made when he was establishing the democracy so that, after also hearing these laws, they might advise the best course 'because the constitution of Kleisthenes was not democratic, but similar to that of Solon'.[43] In this version, the focus is firmly on the

[36] Thuc. 8.65.2, 66.2.   [37] Thuc. 8.69.
[38] Thuc. 8.70.1–2. On *kata kratos*, see Hornblower 2008: 963–4.   [39] Thuc. 8.74.3–75.1.
[40] The passivity of the *demos* in Thucydides' account is emphasised by M. C. Taylor 2002b.
[41] Arist. *Ath. Pol.* 29.1.
[42] Arist. *Ath. Pol.* 29.2. For Pythodoros, see P. J. Rhodes 1981: 370, 437; Ostwald 1986: 368–9.
[43] Arist. *Ath. Pol.* 29.3. On the meaning of προσαναζητῆσαι, see P. J. Rhodes 1981: 375–6 and Gomme, Andrewes and Dover 1981: 214–15, both with further references; Bibauw 1965: 469. For Kleitophon, see P. J. Rhodes 1981: 375. The amendment is generally thought to have ended with the words βουλεύσωνται τὸ ἄριστον and the last clause is understood as a comment on it; e.g. P. J. Rhodes 1981: 377; Gomme, Andrewes and Dover 1981: 215–16; Fuks 1953: 1–7; Ostwald 1986: 370; de Ste Croix 1956: 10; Bibauw 1965: 466–8; Andrewes 1976: 17; Walters 1976: 136–7.

Table 2   *The Four Hundred according to the* Athenaion Politeia

Event	References
The alliance between the Spartans and the Persian king compels 'them' to overthrow the democracy and set up the *politeia* of the Four Hundred.	29.1
Pythodoros of Anaphlystos makes the necessary proposal and the people acquiesce in order to get aid from the king.	29.1
Pythodoros proposes that: twenty *sungrapheis* be elected in addition to the ten *probouloi* to draft measures concerning the safety of the city; anyone else who wishes may also make proposals.	29.2
Kleitophon makes an amendment that: the *sungrapheis* search for, or perhaps investigate, (προσαναζητῆσαι) the *patrioi nomoi* which Kleisthenes made when he was establishing the democracy so that, after also hearing these laws, they might advise the best course 'because the constitution of Kleisthenes was not democratic but similar to that of Solon'.	29.3
The *sungrapheis* propose that: the *prutaneis* are required to put to vote all proposals concerning the safety of the city; the *graphe paranomon, eisangelia* or the process of denunciation and *proklesis* or the summons to a defendant are abolished with heavy penalties for anyone who tries to use them.	29.4
The *sungrapheis* then propose a *politeia*: the city's revenues are to be spent only on the war; for the duration of the war, pay for officeholders is abolished except for the nine *archons* and the *prutaneis*; for the duration of the war, the rest of the government is to be in the hands of those Athenians most able to serve the city with their persons and property and they are to be not less than 5,000 in number; their powers include the ability to make treaties; to enrol this Five Thousand, ten *katalogeis* over the age of forty are to be elected from each tribe.	29.5
These proposals are ratified and the Five Thousand chooses one hundred men to draw up a *politeia*.	30.1
Their work is presented.	30.1–32.1
The 'constitution for the future' (see table 3).	30.2–31.1
The 'constitution for the present' (see table 4).	31.1–3

Table 2 *(cont.)*

Event	References
Aristomachos puts the proposals to vote and they are approved by the multitude (*plethos*).	32.1
The *boule* in the archonship of Kallias is dissolved on 14 Thargelion before the end of its term and the Four Hundred come into office on 21 Thargelion. The oligarchy is set up in the archonship of Kallias.	32.1–2
The primary leaders are Peisandros, Antiphon and Theramenes.	32.2
The Five Thousand are only nominally chosen and the Four Hundred rule the city. They unsuccessfully send ambassadors to Sparta to make peace.	32.3
The Four Hundred remain in power for about four months.	33.1
The defeat off Eretria and the revolt of Euboia.	33.1
They dissolve the Four Hundred and transfer power to the Five Thousand; they also pass a proposal eliminating pay for office holding.	33.1
Aristokrates and Theramenes are primarily responsible for the dissolution of the Four Hundred.	32.2

constitutional process: the whole affair is presented as a very serious attempt to give the city a better constitution and it includes no less than three proposed *politeiai*: the *politeia* of the *sungrapheis*, the 'constitution for the future' (table 3) and the 'constitution for the present' (table 4).[44] Although we might regard this whole constitutional process as somewhat over zealous, the *Athenaion Politeia* portrays the events as a serious effort to rectify the excesses of the radical democrats.

Kleitophon's amendment with its specification that the *sungrapheis* investigate Kleisthenes' ancestral laws also signals that the new constitution will still be a form of democracy. This invocation of Kleisthenes further appeals to the earlier lawgiver as a source of legitimate authority for the type of government being proposed. Since he is specifically described as making *patrioi nomoi*, he cannot be understood as responsible for all that has been built on his foundations and he cannot be used to provide legitimacy to the supporters of the current regime. The power of the city's earlier political systems is also visible in the *sungrapheis*' proposal at Kolonos that pay

---

[44] Arist. *Ath. Pol.* 29.5, 30.2–31.3.

Table 3   *The 'Constitution for the future'*

	References[a]
Members of the *boule* are to be over thirty, hold office for one year and receive no pay.	30.2

From the *boule* are elected:
    the generals;
    the nine archons;
    the *hieromnemon*;
    the *taxiarchoi*;
    the *hipparchoi*;
    the *phularchoi*;
    the garrison commanders;
    ten treasurers of Athena and the Other Gods;
    twenty *hellenotamiai* in charge of both the league funds and the city's funds;
    ten *hieropoioi*;
    ten *epimeletai*.[b]
	30.2

All other offices are to be elected by lot and not from the *boule*.	30.2
Once elected, the *hellenotamiai* are to cease being members of the *boule*.	30.2
For the future, all men of the appropriate age are to be divided into four *boulai*, each of which will serve in rotation.[c]	30.3
The duties of the *boule* are outlined.	30.4
The *boule* is to meet every five days unless more meetings are necessary.	30.4
The order of business for the *boule* is specified.	30.5
Members absent from meetings are to be fined one *drachma* for each meeting missed.	30.6

[a]   All references are to Arist. *Ath. Pol.*
[b]   For this interpretation, see Rhodes 1981: 392; Gomme, Andrewes and Dover 1981: 219; R. Osborne 2003: 260; contra: E. M. Harris 1990: 249–51.
[c]   For this interpretation, see Rhodes 1981: 393; Gomme, Andrewes and Dover 1981: 222–3; R. Osborne 2003: 259–60. I am not persuaded by Harris' solution to the oddities of this passage; E. M. Harris 1990: 251–6.

for magistrates be restricted to the nine archons and the *prutaneis*.[45] In Athens, pay for office holding seems to have been introduced during the course of the fifth century and the earliest of these payments may have

---

[45] Arist. *Ath. Pol.* 29.5. *Prutaneis* are members of the (rotating) executive committee of the *boule*.

Table 4   *The 'Constitution for the present'*

	References[a]
The *boule* is to consist of 400 men *kata ta patria* with forty representing each tribe; the members are to be over thirty.	31.1
The duties of the *boule* include: the appointment of officials; establishing the form of the oath to be taken; taking actions about the laws, the *euthunai* and other matters.	31.1
They are to follow any laws which may be enacted concerning the *politeia* and they are not to change them or enact others.	31.2
The *boule* is to elect ten generals from the Five Thousand and also their secretary.	31.2
Also to be elected by the *boule* are: one *hipparchos*: ten *phularchoi*.	31.3
In the future, the *boule* is to elect these officials according to the procedures laid out above.	31.3
Only the members of the *boule* and the generals may hold office more than once.	31.3
At the appropriate point in the future, the one hundred men are to add the *boule* evenly among the four *boulai* of the 'constitution of the future'.	31.3

[a]   All references are to Arist. *Ath. Pol.*

been the stipends for jurymen which Perikles introduced in the middle of the century.[46] Here, the restriction serves to link the proposals to the city's past, to a time before such radically democratic measures were introduced. The offices function in a similar way because, of the nine archons, the archon, the *basileus* and the *polemarchos* certainly existed before the legislation of Solon and Drakon and the six *thesmothetai* also seem to have been in existence before Solon's day.[47] Retaining these offices connects the oligarchs with the city's political past, which, once invoked, gives legitimacy to their proposals. The presence of these different elements also signals that the *sungrapheis* are introducing a form of democracy. Strikingly, in the

[46] Arist. *Ath. Pol.* 27.3; P. J. Rhodes 1981: 338–40; Ostwald 1986: 183, 223–4; Hignett 1952: 219–20, 342–3; Jones 1986: 5. [Xen.] *Ath. Pol.* 1.3 specifically links the *demos* with offices for which there were stipends.
[47] Arist. *Ath. Pol.* 3.1–4, 8.1–2; Thuc. 1.126.8; P. J. Rhodes 1981: 99–100, 102–3.

whole account, the term oligarchy is only used once, towards the end when the various relevant dates are specified.[48] The effect is to emphasise the democratic aspects of the process and the constitutions presented, while the account particularly singles out Kleitophon as an important figure who makes the crucial amendment. As his proposal indicates, he is not a radical democrat and this version also suggests that he is the proper model for an Athenian citizen. This characterisation is unique in this narrative of Kolonos and it directs our attention to Kleitophon.[49] In contrast, Peisandros, Antiphon and Theramenes, who are explicitly identified as the main leaders, are not the focus of this text and they do not play critical roles here as they do in Thucydides' version.[50] The army on Samos and Alkibiades have been completely eliminated and their absence suggests that they are the kind of radical democrats whose mismanagement led to the need for constitutional change. The other missing figure is Phrynichos, who has no role at all in this narrative; violence is, consequently, not an aspect of this version and the leaders are all shown to be upright citizens rather than the isolated extremists of Thucydides' account.

In the Aristotelian *Athenaion Politeia*, the emphasis on the democratic process and the connections with Kleisthenes are further brought out by the one topographical feature mentioned in the text. In contrast to Thucydides' version, the critical meetings of the *demos* are not located in the city's topography and there is no indication that they did not take place, as usual, on the Pnyx (fig. 4). The only location mentioned is the Bouleuterion, but it is not described as being in the Agora (fig. 2).[51] The city's market square might be thought by some (fourth-century) readers to be closely connected with the *demos* and a more radical sort of democracy than is being championed here.[52] Focusing on the Bouleuterion rather than the Agora strengthens the connections between the Four Hundred, their *politeiai* and Kleisthenes because the council house had originally been constructed at the end of the sixth century to house the new Kleisthenic *boule* of 500 men.[53] In turn, these elements work together with the emphasis on Kleitophon to bring out both the moderate nature of the regime being implemented and its identity as a form of democracy. As readers, we are

---

[48] Arist. *Ath. Pol.* 32.1–2.
[49] The other named individuals are Melobios, Pythodoros and Aristomachos; Arist. *Ath. Pol.* 29.1–3, 32.1.
[50] Arist. *Ath. Pol.* 32.2.   [51] Arist. *Ath. Pol.* 32.3.
[52] Readers of the *Athenaion Politeia* will only have known the Agora after it became focused on the democratic citizen, as discussed in chapters 4 and 9 and Shear 2007a.
[53] Shear, Jr 1994: 231–6; Shear, Jr 1995: 157–71; Shear, Jr 1993: 418–27, 472–7.

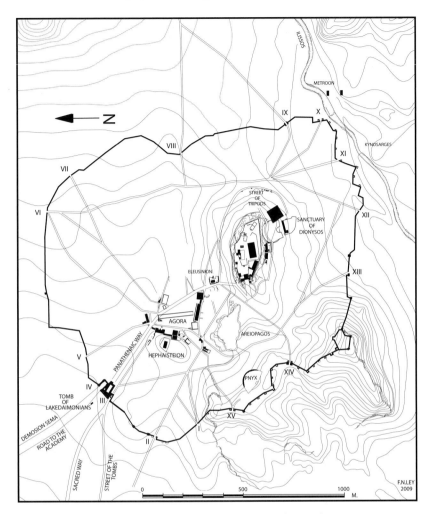

Figure 4   Plan of the city of Athens in *c.* 395 BC with some later structures.

not allowed to forget that what is described was an orderly constitutional process.

The politics of space in the *Athenaion Politeia* contrast sharply with the dynamics of Thucydides' account and its very strong emphasis on the different places involved in the coup. Most generally, Thucydides opposes Athens under the oligarchs with democratically controlled Samos,[54] the

---

[54] Most vividly at Thuc. 8.76.1.

location of the fleet, but space within Athens and Attica is also important. He makes a point of telling his readers that the critical assembly which voted the Four Hundred into power was convened at Kolonos and he adds 'there is a sanctuary of Poseidon about ten *stadioi* from the city' (fig. 1).[55] This sanctuary was sacred to Poseidon Hippios who was particularly connected with the *hippeis*, men whose devotion to the democracy might well be questioned.[56] In Aristophanes' *Knights*, the *hippeis* are described as the enemies of Kleon, *andres agathoi* and *kaloi k'agathoi* and as wearing their hair long; this constellation of terms indicates not only their position among the elite of Athenian society, but also their lack of political support for radical democrats like Kleon.[57] As individuals, they belong with the *trierarchoi* and most influential men (δυνατώτατοι) on Samos who initially wanted to overthrow the democracy and with the members of the *hetaireiai* whose aid Peisandros enlisted in Athens.[58] Kolonos, accordingly, is a place for elite Athenians. In Thucydides' narrative, this particular location outside of the city contrasts with the Pnyx, both the normal meeting place of the *ekklesia* and the proper home of the *demos*, as the *Knights* makes clear; the contrast emphasises that the *demos* is not meeting where it should. Instead, the *ekklesia* is being held where it does not belong and the unusual location alerts the reader to the extraordinary nature of the meeting which is about to take place. Under these circumstances, the dissolution of the democracy and the passivity of the *demos* should come as no surprise. Later in the narrative, the Four Hundred is overthrown at a meeting of the *ekklesia* which takes place 'then for the first time' on the Pnyx, a location which immediately indicates to the reader that the political situation is about to change from an oligarchy to a more democratic form. The rule of the Four Hundred is, consequently, bracketed by these two contrasting meetings and places. The locations suggest that there is something not quite right about the first meeting, while the Pnyx guarantees the legitimacy of the second.

If Kolonos is space for oligarchs and the Pnyx is the place of the *demos*, two other important locations, the Agora and the Peiraieus, are constructed as sites of contestation. After describing the meeting at Kolonos, Thucydides turns to the way in which the Four Hundred evicted the

---

[55] Thuc. 8.67.2.

[56] Poseidon and Kolonos: Paus. 1.30.4; Soph. *OC* 54–61, 887–9, 1156–9, 1491–5; cf. *IG* I³ 405; Poseidon and the *hippeis*: Ar. *Knights* 551–64; *Agora* XVI 270; on Poseidon, Kolonos and the *hippeis*, see Siewert 1979: 280–5; Ostwald 1986: 373; Spence 1993: 188–9.

[57] Ar. *Knights* 225–7, 580. On the wealth required for cavalry service, see Spence 1993: 272–86.

[58] Siewert 1979: 286; cf. Hignett 1952: 272.

democratically elected *boule* from the Bouleuterion, an episode not narrated in the *Athenaion Politeia*. Quite strikingly, the council house is not located in the city's topography and it is simply described on three occasions as the Bouleuterion.[59] Certainly, it is the home of the democratic *boule* of 500 and its members are described in the narrative as chosen by lot (ἀπὸ τοῦ κυάμου),[60] but the association with the democracy is not otherwise emphasised. Indeed, at this moment, the connection is contested because the Four Hundred are in the process of taking over the space for themselves and they will rule the city from this building. That the democratically elected *bouleutai* or councillors do not put up any fight should not blind us to the contest taking place. When the Bouleuterion next appears, however, it is in a completely different context: the assassination of Phrynichos which takes place in the crowded Agora when Phrynichos was not far from the Bouleuterion. As I have argued, Thucydides' description makes the oligarch into a tyrant and the assassins into tyrant slayers. The Agora is the home of the statues of Harmodios and Aristogeiton, which, with their cult, are distinctly democratic. Only at this moment, when power is beginning to slip from the hands of the Four Hundred, is the Bouleuterion connected with the marketplace and with democracy. That the act triggering this description is violent emphasises both the on-going contestation over this space and the important role of hostile force in this account.

The other point of dispute is the oligarchs' fort at the Eetioneia in the Peiraieus, a project started when the Four Hundred begin to realise that power is slipping from their hands (fig. 3).[61] Thucydides states that its purpose was to enable the oligarchs to admit the enemy whenever they wished, but it would also allow them to flee easily by sea, if they should lose power. Topographically, it forms a small piece of oligarchic territory in the Peiraieus, a location which would usually be closely associated with the *thetes* and the radical democracy; like the Bouleuterion in the Agora, it shows the oligarchs trying to extend their power into an area in which they do not belong. The fort's contested status is vividly depicted when the hoplites building the fort arrest the general Alexikles and a party is sent to rescue him.[62] With Theramenes' encouragement, the hoplites and 'many of the men from the Peiraieus' promptly demolished the structure while exhorting those in the crowd who want the Five Thousand to rule instead of the Four Hundred to help them; for Thucydides, the invocation of the

---

[59] Thuc. 8.69.1–70.1; cf. 8.92.6 and 8.93.1, references to the Bouleuterion again without any mention of the Agora.
[60] Thuc. 8.66.1, 69.4. [61] Thuc. 8.90.1–5. [62] Thuc. 8.92.4–9.

Five Thousand is actually a screen for the *demos* and so the democracy.[63] The oligarchs lose this contest for control of the Peiraieus because the fort is demolished. The inclusion of men from the Peiraieus among those destroying the structure emphasises that the winners are the democrats who are beginning to regain their power. At the same time, it looks ahead to the events of 403 when the democrats will regain control of Athens from their base in the Peiraieus. This episode in 411 is closely linked with the assassination of Phrynichos and the two events mark the turning point for the Four Hundred because they not only lose control of these disputed spaces, but they also start to lose their power. In the narrative, the contestations over the Agora and the Peiraieus signal the beginning of the end for the oligarchs and their final demise quickly follows.

What kind of regime the Four Hundred actually was depends very much on which source we believe. For Thucydides, the primary leaders were the extreme oligarchs who had no qualms about resorting to violence to gain power for their own ends. As Thucydides' continual references to their embassies to Sparta make clear, one of their goals was peace at almost any cost except their loss of power.[64] The only person who comes off reasonably well is Theramenes.[65] Thucydides' account is also a violent one which reaches a climax in the bloody death of Phrynichos the tyrant figure. He certainly demonises the oligarchs and it is not the version of anyone supporting an oligarchic regime of any kind. As such, it fits well with Cynthia Farrar's characterisation of Thucydides as a man supporting democracy, but not the radical democrats.[66] In contrast, the *Athenaion Politeia* presents the whole episode as an orderly and very serious constitutional process which aimed at reforming the radical democracy.[67] Through its focus on Kleitophon, it stresses that the solution to Athens' problems lies in moderate oligarchy, a stance which suggests the political orientation of its author.

These very different political stances make reconciling these two accounts an extremely difficult task, although scholars have not hesitated to do so. For anyone wishing to understand the events as largely a constitutional process, the excessive numbers of constitutions in the *Athenaion Politeia* remain a serious problem. Not only are there too many documents,

[63] Thuc. 8.92.10–11 and cf. 8.93.1.
[64] Thuc. 8.71.3, 86.9, 89.1–2, 92.2 and note especially the imperfect ἐπρεσβεύοντο in 8.71.3.
[65] On Theramenes, see Ostwald 1986: 364–6.
[66] Farrar 1998: 126–91. For Thucydides as a critic of democracy, see Ober 1998: 52–121 with a helpful summary of various scholarly views at 52 note 1; cf. Raaflaub 2006: 195–212.
[67] For this text as a critique of (fourth-century) democracy, see Ober 1998: 352–63.

but they are also incomplete and, as we shall see in the cases of the constitutions for the present and the future, they could not actually have functioned as instruments for ruling the city; they are unlikely to represent legislation actually passed at Kolonos.[68] Thucydides' account, however, also has its problems. In addition to its very particular political slant, the chronology of Peisandros' first visit to Athens seems very compressed and the number of *sungrapheis* accords ill with our other evidence.[69] To understand our two accounts of the Four Hundred better, we must consider their larger contexts, particularly the use of the *patrios politeia* and the political past and the trials of the oligarchs.

THE CONSTITUTIONS AND THE *PATRIOS POLITEIA*

The 'constitution for the future' and the 'constitution for the present' mark one of the significant differences between Thucydides' account and the version of the *Athenaion Politeia*. Their status and authenticity are extremely difficult issues; scholars have frequently argued that the 'constitution for the present' was, in fact, passed at Kolonos or shortly thereafter, while the 'constitution for the future' is generally interpreted as never having been put into practice, if it is not, in fact, a theoretical attempt at drawing up a constitution.[70] That these documents do not present constitutions which could actually have functioned suggests that they do not represent legislation passed at Kolonos.[71] Their poor formulation also makes it unlikely that they were intended to justify the regime of the Four Hundred or that they originated in Antiphon's defence speech.[72] Their most likely sources are pamphlets in circulation at this time. Even if these documents were

---

[68] R. Osborne 2003: 259.

[69] On the chronological problems of Peisandros' first visit, see above note 14. Thucydides' ten *sungrapheis autokratores* are usually rejected in favour of the twenty *sungrapheis* (plus the ten *probouloi*) of *Athenaion Politeia* 29.2; see Gomme, Andrewes and Dover 1981: 164–5; P. J. Rhodes 1981: 367, 372–3; Ostwald 1986: 359, 369–70; Kagan 1987: 145. On the number of *sungrapheis*, see also Androt. *FGrHist* 324 F43 and Philoch. *FGrHist* 328 F136, both cited by Harp. s.v. συγγραφεῖς; cf. also schol. Ar. *Lys.* 421a; *Suda* s.v. πρόβουλοι; Phot. *Lex.* s.v. καταλογεύς (Theodoridis); *Anecd. Bekk.* s.v. καταλογεύς, συγγραφεῖς (Bekker 190.24, 270.17, 301.13); *Etym. Magn.* s.v. συγγραφεῖς.

[70] P. J. Rhodes 1981: 365, 385–9; Gomme, Andrewes and Dover 1981: 242–6; Hignett 1952: 357–9, 367–78; P. J. Rhodes 1972b: 117; Andrewes 1976: 20–1; Kagan 1987: 159–60. 'Constitution for the present': Ostwald 1986: 379–85; P. J. Rhodes 1981: 365, 386–7; cf. de Ste Croix 1956: 14–15. 'Constitution for the future': de Ste Croix 1956: 14–20. That this constitution was actually implemented by the Five Thousand is unconvincingly argued in E. M. Harris 1990; de Ste Croix 1956.

[71] R. Osborne 2003: 259.

[72] R. Osborne 2003: 259. Justification: Gomme, Andrewes and Dover 1981: 244–6; Hignett 1952: 373. Connection with Antiphon, see Wade-Gery 1958: 141; contra: Andrewes 1976: 21–2; Gomme, Andrewes and Dover 1981: 248.

actually ratified at Kolonos, they could not have been created in the middle
of the (probably) tense meeting without advance preparation[73] and they
must belong to a larger context: the Athenians' debate over the *patrios
politeia* and the appropriate constitution for the city.

The reference to the *patrioi nomoi* in Kleitophon's amendment is usually cited to demonstrate the existence of such discussions.[74] This passage has led one group of scholars to conclude that the *patrios politeia*
and calls for a return to it should be associated only with the moderate
oligarchs.[75] In Thucydides' version of the events leading up to the meeting
at Kolonos (table 1), we hear of discussions between various conspirators
and conferences with Alkibiades, as well as Peisandros' encouragement of
the *hetaireiai*. On Samos, the conspirators openly called for the city not
to be ruled by a democracy (μὴ δημοκρατουμένων), while, during his
first visit to Athens, Peisandros specifically told the *demos* that, by recalling
Alkibiades and by not having a democracy in the current form (μὴ τὸν
αὐτὸν τρόπον δημοκρατουμένοις), they could have the Persian king as an
ally and they could win the war.[76] For the conspirators, overthrowing the
democracy required something to be put in its place and, for Thucydides'
descriptions to have any validity, they must presuppose an on-going and
perhaps contentious debate in various circles over the proper constitution
for the city. Peisandros' reference to another sort of democracy may also
suggest that, for some individuals, there was not a single type of democracy; the identification of multiple flavours of democracy is not likely
to have been done by oligarchs and particularly not by very committed
ones. Although the term *patrios politeia* does not appear in Thucydides'
account, such invocations, particularly when addressing the *demos*, would
have made calls for a different sort of constitution more palatable. Once
the city's *politeia* appeared on the agenda in the *ekklesia*, it would have been
discussed privately throughout Athens.[77]

Just such a context is presupposed by one of our independent pieces of
evidence for this debate, a fragment of a speech by the sophist Thrasymachos, which suggests that the arguments over the proper form of government for the city were widespread.[78] It was evidently written for delivery

---

[73] Ostwald 1986: 359; R. Osborne 2003: 260–1.
[74] Arist. *Ath. Pol.* 29.3. The style and language of this amendment suggests that this text derives from
a documentary source; P. J. Rhodes 1981: 375; Gomme, Andrewes and Dover 1981: 214; Andrewes
1976: 17; Ostwald 1986: 369–70.
[75] See above note 9.   [76] Thuc. 8.48.2, 53.1.
[77] For such discussions (in the fourth century), see the helpful comments of Vlassopoulos 2007: 40–6.
[78] Thrasymachos 85 B1 (DK⁶); for helpful discussions, see Fuks 1953: 102–5; Finley 2000: 36–8; Munn
2000: 135–6; Yunis 1997; Cecchin 1969: 12–25.

by a young Athenian at a time when the war was continuing and when the Athenians were in a state of enmity towards one another. Misfortune, says the speaker, has made the Athenians lose their heads and the orators and the others who are arguing with each other are actually saying the same thing rather than the opposite as they suppose. He asks his audience to consider the arguments of both sides (ἑκάτεροι) and continues 'the *patrios politeia* is causing an uproar (ταραχήν) among them, even though it is easy to understand and it is common to all citizens'. Now the Athenians must rely on accounts of their ancestors (τῶν παλαιοτέρων) and the advice of their elders. As a whole, the fragment indicates that there was an extensive and vociferous public debate over the proper sort of government for the city and that the participants were invoking the *patrios politeia*, presumably to justify their recommendations. Which side first used this expression is not clear from the preserved section of this speech, but it is easy to imagine oligarchs of various types invoking the *patrios politeia* as justification for changing the form of the democracy. The opening lines of the fragment would be consistent with an address to the *demos* itself.[79] The circumstances surrounding this extract would fit very well with the period immediately after Peisandros' arrival in Athens for his first visit and the speech has generally been dated to about this time.[80] Its particular value lies in its independence from both Thucydides and the constitutional tradition of the *Athenaion Politeia*.

In Aristophanes' *Lysistrata*, usually associated with the Lenaia of 412/1, the only alternative to democracy is tyranny, particularly the tyranny of Hippias.[81] His *Thesmophoriazousai*, normally associated with the Dionysia of 412/1, presents a more interesting situation.[82] The *arai* (curses) of the female herald at the beginning of the women's assembly curse anyone who conspires to harm the *demos* of women, who negotiates with Euripides or the Medes and who intends to become a tyrant or help to install a tyrant, as well as a host of morally unsavoury characters.[83] This passage seems politically harmless enough.[84] In the chorus' lyric *arai* which follow,

---

[79] Fuks 1953: 102; cf. more definitely Ostwald 1986: 367; Munn 2000: 136. For other possibilities, see Yunis 1997.

[80] E.g. Fuks 1953: 102–5; Cecchin 1969: 13–14; Finley 2000: 36–7; Ostwald 1986: 367; Munn 2000: 135–6; on the problems, see Yunis 1997: 64.

[81] Ar. *Lys.* 273–80, 616–35, 664–70, 1150–6. For the date of the play, see above note 14.

[82] For the date, see above note 14.

[83] Ar. *Thesm.* 335–51. Unsavoury characters: anyone who denounces a woman for passing off someone else's child as her own, the lover who deceives a woman with lies or does not give promised gifts and the old woman who gives a younger lover gifts.

[84] Compare Gomme, Andrewes and Dover 1981: 190; Austin and Olson 2004: xliii, 160, 163.

those who deceive the *demos*, break their oaths, seek to move the decrees and laws in the reverse direction, reveal secrets to the enemy, or invite in the Medes are cursed and described as wronging the city.[85] For us, the important section concerns the laws and decrees, ψηφίσματα καὶ νόμους ζητοῦσ' ἀντιμεθιστάναι, but the difficulty is to understand what exactly 'they seek to move the decrees and laws in the reverse direction' means. The form ἀντιμεθιστάναι is extremely unusual and it represents the only known occasion when this verb is used in the active; the word itself does not appear again until it is used by Aristotle in the passive.[86] In this passage, Antony Andrewes has suggested that it means 'move in reverse to normal' and Alan Sommerstein proposes 'put into reverse', but these two suggestions are not particularly helpful in elucidating what is going on here.[87] The word appears to be a specific invention for this context so that the term seems to be a parody of the verb μεθίστημι, which can be used in the active for political change, as it is, for example, by Thucydides.[88] That this word was politically loaded at this time is suggested by the title of Antiphon's defence speech, 'concerning the change in constitution' (περὶ τῆς μεταστάσεως), which he delivered when he was tried under the Five Thousand.[89] If Aristophanes is here parodying the catch words of some participants in the constitutional arguments, this passage would fit very well with the parodies in other clauses of these *arai* and it would also attest indirectly to the extent of the debates about the city's *politeia*: they were pervasive enough for Aristophanes to parody them.

This evidence that individuals from various parts of the political spectrum were discussing the city's ancestral constitution suggests that we should re-examine the passage in Thucydides' narrative which describes the reaction of the soldiers on Samos to the news that the Four Hundred had seized power. The soldiers immediately held an *ekklesia* and Thucydides summarises the arguments presented.[90] We are specifically told that the other party, i.e. the oligarchs, erred in abolishing the *patrioi nomoi*, while they, the democratic speakers, were saving them and would try to compel the oligarchs to do so.[91] Since both Alexander Fuks and Moses Finley believe that the *patrios politeia* was a slogan first used only by the

---

[85] Ar. *Thesm.* 352–71; on the textual difficulties of 365–6, see Austin and Olson 2004: 170–1.
[86] Gomme, Andrewes and Dover 1981: 191; Sommerstein 1977: 125.
[87] Gomme, Andrewes and Dover 1981: 191; Sommerstein 1977: 125.
[88] Thuc. 8.48.4; for other examples, see LSJ⁹ s.v. μεθίστημι ΑΙ.
[89] Gomme, Andrewes and Dover 1981: 176; see also the discussion below.
[90] Thuc. 8.76.2–77.   [91] Thuc. 8.76.6.

moderate oligarchs, they argue that, in this context, the *patrioi nomoi* are the traditional laws under which the Athenians had been living until the Four Hundred gained power and abolished them.[92] In view of our other evidence for the contemporary debates over the ancestral constitution, it seems more likely that this passage also represents yet another manifestation of this whole process. If this interpretation is correct, then Thucydides was not quite as immune to the whole issue as a hasty reading of his narrative might suggest.

So far, we have focused on speeches, proposals to the *demos* and allusions in comedy, all occasions of public performance, but such discussions also seem to have been carried on in more private settings which are now reflected in a political pamphlet incorporated into the *Athenaion Politeia*. This document, the 'constitution of Drakon', purports to be a *politeia* allegedly instituted by Drakon (table 5), but it is now generally recognised as a late fifth-century creation.[93] The restriction of citizenship to men capable of providing their own military equipment recalls the proposal made openly, perhaps in the *ekklesia*, by Peisandros' associates in Athens before his second return to Athens that no more than 5,000 should have a share in controlling affairs.[94] These 5,000 were also to be men especially able to use their property and persons on behalf of the city, and so they would have to have been of at least hoplite status. To be attractive to a large number of Athenians, such a proposal would have required justification of exactly the kind which the 'constitution of Drakon' could easily have provided. Its provision of fines for non-attendance of meetings suggests that pay for men holding office is not envisioned here.[95] Interestingly, Peisandros' associates are also said to have called for restricting pay to those fighting the war.[96] The absence of such pay, a fifth-century innovation, in this constitution shows the ways in which the past is being re-used in the present context. This document attributed to Drakon could also provide 'evidence' for anyone proposing the abolishment of such payments in contemporary Athens.

---

[92] Fuks 1953: 33–4; Finley 2000: 37–8. For the absence of the *patrios politeia* in Thucydides, see Hornblower 1987: 141–2; cf. Hornblower 2008: 980–1.

[93] Arist. *Ath. Pol.* 4.2–4; P. J. Rhodes 1981: 86–7, 115; Hignett 1952: 5–6, 7, 273; Ober 1998: 358; R. Osborne 2003: 259; G. Anderson 2003: 236 note 41. Since Fuks believes that the *patrios politeia* was championed only by the moderate oligarchs and the Drakonian constitution does not entirely match the 'constitution for the future' and the 'constitution for the present', he interprets it as a fourth-century document; Fuks 1953: 84–97. The document seems to belong better in the period of intense contestation over the proper *politeia* for the city in the late fifth century.

[94] Thuc. 8.65.3.   [95] Fuks 1953: 88–9.   [96] Thuc. 8.65.3.

Table 5   *The 'Constitution of Drakon'*

	References[a]
Citizenship is restricted to men providing their own arms.	4.2
Qualifications for office: nine archons and treasurers: an estate worth not less than ten *mnai*; lesser offices: from the men providing their own arms; generals and *hipparchoi*: an estate worth not less than 100 *mnai* and legitimate sons born in wedlock and over ten years old.	4.2
They are to accept security from the *prutaneis*, generals and *hipparchoi* of the previous year until their *euthunai*; four guarantors are to come from the same class as the generals and *hipparchoi*.	4.2
The *boule* is to have 401 citizens chosen by lot.	4.3
The *bouleutai* and the other magistrates are to be chosen by lot from among those over thirty years old.	4.3
No one is to hold the same office twice until all eligible men have held it once.	4.3
Fines for *bouleutai* not attending a meeting of the *boule* or the *ekklesia*: *pentakosiomedimnoi*: 3 *drachmai*; *hippeis*: 2 *drachmai*; *zeugitai*: 1 *drachma*.	4.3
The *boule* of the Areopagos is the guardian of the laws (*nomoi*).	4.4
A man treated unjustly may present an *eisangelia* to the *boule* of the Areiopagos with reference to the relevant law.	4.4

[a] All references are to Arist. *Ath. Pol.*

Two of its other provisions have similar connections with the city's political past. Until 462/1, the Areiopagos was the guardian of the laws and that role was evidently under discussion in the late fifth century because it appears again in 403/2 in the decree of Teisamenos.[97] The *boule* composed of 401 men recalls the Solonian *boule* of 400 citizens; the odd number of members is unusual for an Athenian council and it may have been chosen because the number 400 was firmly associated with

---

[97] Arist. *Ath. Pol.* 3.6, 8.4, 25.2; P. J. Rhodes 1981: 117, 315–17. Areiopagos and the decree of Teisamenos: Andok. 1.84.

the Solonian council which did not exist in Drakon's day.[98] Certainly, it would prevent evenly split votes on debates. The presence of the *prutaneis* is particularly striking because they belong with the *boule* of 500; they may, as Peter Rhodes has suggested, have been instituted by Ephialtes rather than Kleisthenes.[99] Their appearance here suggests that the author wished to associate them with a significantly earlier stratum of Athenian history. Attested in this appropriate 'historical' context, the *prutaneis* could then be retained by a regime claiming to return to the ancestral ways of running the city. In contrast, some of the other provisions, such as the complicated method for auditing the *prutaneis*, the generals and the *hipparchoi* (cavalry commanders), the particular property qualifications and the fines for not attending meetings, find no parallels in Athenian practices. They suggest that the author was as much theorising about the city's *politeia* as writing about its history. In the late fifth-century context, the document emphasises the importance of discovering the city's earlier constitutions. The parallels between some of its clauses and the proposals made by Peisandros' associates suggest that this constitution originated in oligarchic, rather than democratic, circles. Importantly, the document also shows that the discussions about the city's *politeia* could and did include elements associated with earlier phases of Athenian political history.

Similar strategies and a comparable mixture of history and theory are also evident in the 'constitution for the future' and the 'constitution for the present' in the *Athenaion Politeia*. Like the 'constitution of Drakon', the 'constitution for the future' (table 3) includes fines for *bouleutai* who do not attend meetings and it further specifies that the councillors are not to be paid. Doing away with pay for officeholders returned to earlier practices. Certain of the offices mentioned were also not new developments. Of the nine archons, the archon, the *basileus* and the *polemarchos* certainly existed before the legislation of Solon and Drakon and the six *thesmothetai* also seem to have been in existence before Solon's day.[100] That Solon regulated the appointment of the treasurers of Athena by lot indicates that these

---

[98] Solonian *boule*: Arist. *Ath. Pol.* 8.4 and cf. 21.3; Plut. *Sol.* 19.1–2; P. J. Rhodes 1981: 115, 153–4; P. J. Rhodes 1972a: 208–9. Hignett's and Mossé's arguments against the existence of the Solonian council of 400 are not convincing; Hignett 1952: 92–6; Mossé 2004: 257; against this position, see Cloché 1924. The number 401 also recalls the fourth-century *dikasteria* or courts, but this comparison need not indicate that the document belongs to the fourth century as argued by Fuks; P. J. Rhodes 1981: 115; Fuks 1953: 94–5.

[99] P. J. Rhodes 1972a: 17–19.

[100] Arist. *Ath. Pol.* 3.1–4, 8.1–2; Thuc. 1.126.8; P. J. Rhodes 1981: 99–100, 102–3.

officials, too, were active in the early sixth century.[101] Retaining these offices, accordingly, connected the present with the city's political past.

Some of the offices, particularly the *hellenotamiai*, or treasurers in charge of the tribute, did not have so antique a history, while other elements, particularly the fines for missing meetings of the *boule* and the complicated system of four rotating *boulai*, have no parallels at Athens. The closest parallels for the four *boulai* are the *boulai* in the cities of Boiotia and probably also the Boiotian federal council.[102] The combination of the proximity of the Boiotian *poleis* and the war with Sparta helps to explain why this model might be attractive to an oligarch theorising about the Athenian constitution at this time. Some of the provisions specified eventually came into use in Athens: by 410/9, there were twenty *hellenotamiai* and the boards of the treasurers of Athena and of the Other Gods were also amalgamated, perhaps in 406/5.[103] This 'constitution for the future', accordingly, is a *mélange* of items connected with the *patrios politeia*, the practical and impractical and the theoretical.[104] Nevertheless, it is the result of serious thought about constitutional issues and some research as well.[105] Juxtaposing it with the 'constitution of Drakon' brings out the similarities between the two *politeiai* and suggests that they are products of much the same circles and debates.

The 'constitution for the present' (table 4) should also belong to this same context. The 400 *bouleutai kata ta patria* are rather obviously derived from the Solonian *boule* of 400 and they are parallel to the 401 *bouleutai* of the 'constitution of Drakon'. In the 'constitution for the present', the Kleisthenic tribes are maintained so that connections are also established with this important figure; *ta patria* is evidently a rather broad term for this author, but the phrase also points to a context in the discussions about the ancestral constitution. The provisions for dividing the 400 *bouleutai* into the four *boulai* of the 'constitution for the future' link the two documents together and so they must come out of the same milieu. Much is left out of the 'constitution for the present' and its cursory nature suggests that it,

---

[101] Arist. *Ath. Pol.* 8.1, 47.1.

[102] *Hell. Oxy.* 16.2, 4; Thuc. 5.38.2–4; P. J. Rhodes 1981: 393; Gomme, Andrewes and Dover 1981: 222–3; Larsen 1955: 46–7, 50; R. Osborne 2003: 260–1; contra: E. M. Harris 1990: 252.

[103] *Hellenotamiai*: *IG* I³ 375. That, in 410/9, the *hellenotamiai* made payments previously made by the *kolakretai* must indicate that the two boards were amalgamated between 418/7, when the *kolakretai* are last attested, and 410/9; *IG* I³ 84.28; P. J. Rhodes 1981: 391–2; de Ste Croix 1956: 15; P. J. Rhodes 1972a: 98–102; Pritchett 1970: 111; E. M. Harris 1990: 257. Treasurers: Ferguson 1932b: 3–7, 104–9; de Ste Croix 1956: 19; W. E. Thompson 1970: 61–3; P. J. Rhodes 1981: 391; Gomme, Andrewes and Dover 1981: 220. The *kolakretai* made payments from state funds other than the tribute.

[104] On the impracticalities, see Gomme, Andrewes and Dover 1981: 243; Hignett 1952: 371–2.

[105] R. Osborne 2003: 260–1.

too, is a theoretical constitution rather than something which was actually approved and used.[106]

Our evidence for the 'constitution for the future' and the 'constitution for the present' suggests that these two documents are political pamphlets very similar to the 'constitution of Drakon', with which they share a number of themes. All three documents are the result of sustained consideration of the city's constitution and they show a particular interest in re-using the city's past. These elements serve to provide legitimacy to the projects and to suggest that they are not as great a departure from the current democracy as they might initially seem. These three constitutions come out of the debates about the *patrios politeia*, discussions which included individuals from all parts of the Athenian political system and not just the moderate oligarchs led by men like Kleitophon and Theramenes. In 412/1, (re)using the city's political past was very much part of theorising the Athenian constitution irrespective of one's political positioning. Since the 'constitution for the future' and the 'constitution for the present' are central to the *Athenaion Politeia*'s account of the Four Hundred, they also show how this version has been influenced by the *patrios politeia* debate. For an author concerned with the city's constitutional development, these documents would have been attractive because they were directly relevant to his overall project. As purported *politeiai* from important periods in Athenian political history, they would also have fit in with Aristotle's and his students' larger interests in gathering and producing the constitutional histories of different cities.[107] While there are traces of the discussions about the ancestral constitution in Thucydides' narrative, such debates did not drive events for him. These distinctions may perhaps indicate that the focus on the city's constitution was particularly strong in oligarchic circles.

USING THE PAST: THE FOUR HUNDRED AND
THE *PATRIOS POLITEIA*

Athenians who espoused a political regime other than the radical democracy current at the beginning of 412/1 did not cease considering the *patrios politeia* and the relationship between the city's past and the present when the oligarchic conspirators gained power in the *ekklesia* at Kolonos and the democracy was dissolved. Our literary evidence shows that both the Four

---

[106] On its incomplete nature, see Hignett 1952: 371–2; Gomme, Andrewes and Dover 1981: 243.
[107] On this context, see briefly P. J. Rhodes 1981: 1–2, 58–61. On the vexed question of the author's identity, see P. J. Rhodes 1981: 37–40, 58–63 (student) and Keaney 1992: 3–14 (Aristotle).

Hundred and the Five Thousand appealed to and re-used the Athenian political past while they were in power. Recycling and alluding to early parts of the city's history provided legitimacy for both regimes, while these decisions prevented their political opponents from employing the same strategies for their own ends. The epigraphical record provides further evidence for the use of these tactics by both the Four Hundred and the Five Thousand. Collectively, our material shows how these two regimes took over the past and made it into their own possession.

Pythodoros' decree and Kleitophon's amendment, as quoted in the *Athenaion Politeia*, make clear some of the ways in which the oligarchs appealed to the *patrios politeia* and the city's past. For Kleitophon, Kleisthenes clearly provided a potent name for conjuring. Further links to the past were created by the very number of men chosen as the primary governing group: the 400 oligarchs recall the 400 members of the Solonian *boule*; the number seems deliberately chosen to link the present with the Solonian past.[108] That these 400 oligarchs were intended to constitute the city's *boule* is suggested by the pseudo-Lysianic speech in defence of the oligarch Polystratos. On four different occasions, the speakers associate the Four Hundred specifically with the Bouleuterion and these references indicate that the oligarchs continued to use this space not only for the eight days when the defendant Polystratos was in Athens, but also for the entire time in which they were in power.[109] This independent evidence corroborates Thucydides' association of the oligarchs with the council house. Their use of the space further suggests that the oligarchs wished to be identified as the city's legitimate *boule*, although our sources avoid using this particular term.[110] Consequently, their number and their use of the Bouleuterion served to connect them with both Kleisthenes and Solon. Invoked in this fashion, these two men functioned as proper *exempla* for the new government of the city. When the oligarchs first seized power, these decisions would have indicated the legitimacy of the regime and its connections to the city's past. The decision to choose Mnasilochos as eponymous archon for the year beginning on 1 Hekatombaion 411 should also reflect this same strategy and would have made the links with the *patrios politeia* explicit.[111] Mnasilochos' name would be added to the list of previous holders of the

[108] Solonian *boule* of 400: above note 98. For this connection between the Four Hundred and the *patrios politeia*, cf. Ostwald 1986: 370–1; Hignett 1952: 273; Lévy 1976: 192–3; E. M. Harris 1990: 256.

[109] [Lys.] 20.1, 14 (twice), 16. Polystratos served as one of the *katalogeis* to enrol the Five Thousand, but he was sent to Eretria eight days after his office began; [Lys.] 20.13–14.

[110] Compare Hornblower 2009: 252.

[111] Arist. *Ath. Pol.* 33.1. His name and office are partially preserved in *IG* I³ 373.1–2.

office and henceforth, so the Four Hundred must have thought, the year would be known by his name.

This evidence should indicate that the desire to create connections with the ancestral constitution was widespread among the members of the Four Hundred because it represents decisions actually taken and put into practice. If these ideas had not been generally supported by the various oligarchs, then they could not actually have been instituted. It is very likely that they were supported by Peisandros and Antiphon whom both Thucydides and the *Athenaion Politeia* identify as among the leading oligarchs. Neither of them can be described as a moderate; subsequently they were both prosecuted under the Five Thousand and Antiphon was sentenced to death.[112] These ideas, however, were also supported by men, like Kleitophon, who were or later came to be moderates and/or associates of Theramenes. This evidence for the broad appeal of the ancestral constitution and the city's political past demonstrates that these issues were not being promulgated only by Theramenes and his associates. Instead, they received general support from the members of the Four Hundred; some men may have seen these measures as a purely pragmatic way of gaining and retaining power, but others may have believed that they really were returning to the *patrios politeia* and a time when the city had been well ruled and successful.

THE FIVE THOUSAND AND THE ANCESTRAL CONSTITUTION

Despite the Four Hundred's use of the past to provide both legitimacy and models for their regime, they were not able to retain their power for long, only four months according to the *Athenaion Politeia*.[113] As we saw, Thucydides locates the crucial meeting of the *ekklesia* on the Pnyx and notes that the assembly continued to be held there (fig. 4).[114] For the Five Thousand, the Pnyx was evidently a potent place and their use of this traditional meeting place of the *ekklesia* suggests that members of the Five Thousand wished to establish links with the city's past. Since the original form of the Pnyx seems to have been associated with the Kleisthenic democracy, the Five Thousand's use of it amounted to a reclaiming of this *politeia* for a more moderate regime which was also legitimised by

---

[112] On Peisandros and Antiphon, note also Thuc. 8.90.1; for their trials, see the discussion below.
[113] Arist. *Ath. Pol.* 33.1; P. J. Rhodes 1981: 410.
[114] Thuc. 8.97.1–2; on the reading πυκναὶ ἐκκλησίαι at 8.97.2, see the comments of Gomme, Andrewes and Dover 1981: 330.

this connection.[115] This particular layer of the city's past was probably also evoked by the *boule* which the epigraphical evidence discussed below shows existed at this time. It was presumably housed in the Bouleuterion and it may have consisted of 500 elected members (fig. 2).[116] In this building, such a council would certainly have reinforced the connections between Kleisthenes, the Five Thousand and the *patrios politeia*.

Other measures taken by the Five Thousand also forged links with the ancestral constitution. They maintained the traditional magistracies, albeit in at least some cases with different officeholders than those under the Four Hundred. They retained the office of eponymous archon, but the position was now held by Theopompos and Mnasilochos, the archon under the Four Hundred, was removed from the position.[117] As Aristotle's description makes clear, the year 411/0 was officially known as Theopompos' year and Mnasilochos' tenure was expunged from the official nomenclature of the city as if he had never held the position. Unlike Mnasilochos, Theopompos was identified as the legitimate archon whose name joined those of all his predecessors; his inclusion in this list emphasised the legitimacy of his tenure and created another link with the city's political past. Although the other traditional archons are not positively attested, it is likely that these offices continued to exist under the Five Thousand.

Although our evidence is limited, it shows the Five Thousand taking steps to create links with the city's political past. These measures also allowed them to reclaim the ancestral constitution, and especially Kleisthenes, from the now discredited Four Hundred; the oligarchic source of these strategies may have increased their attractiveness to men opposed to democracy. These decisions must have been widely supported because otherwise they could not have been enacted; re-using the past should not be connected only with a small group of individuals associated with one or two prominent men such as Theramenes. In addition, this process served to discredit the Four Hundred further because it showed that they were not a legitimate authority in the city even though their rule had actually

---

[115] Original form of Pnyx: Kourouniotes and Thompson 1932: 96–113; Stanton and Bicknell 1987: 73–6.

[116] The decree of Demophantos stresses that it was passed under the *boule* of 500 *chosen by lot*; Andok. 1.96. This designation may indicate, as Hignett and others have suggested, that this *boule* is to be distinguished both from the Four Hundred's council made up of its own members and another council of 500 instituted by the Five Thousand and composed of *bouleutai* elected rather than chosen by lot; Hignett 1952: 372; P. J. Rhodes 1972b: 117; P. J. Rhodes 1972a: 7; Ostwald 1986: 398–9; cf. de Ste Croix 1956: 22. This interpretation may explain Thucydides' and Aristotle's emphasis on the βουλὴ ἡ ἀπὸ τοῦ κυάμου in their discussion of the events of 411; see Thuc. 8.66.1, 69.4; Arist. *Ath. Pol.* 32.1.

[117] Arist. *Ath. Pol.* 33.1.

been sanctioned by the *demos* at Kolonos. Transferring the sanction of the past from the Four Hundred to the Five Thousand indicated that the new and more moderate regime was the legitimate one for Athens. In this situation, the Five Thousand had no choice except to reclaim the ancestral constitution and the city's past from the previous regime.

THE EPIGRAPHICAL EVIDENCE AND THE POLITICAL PAST

The meagre evidence provided by our literary sources for this process can be elaborated further with the help of the epigraphical record which confirms the manipulation and use of the city's past by both the Four Hundred and the Five Thousand. Our evidence includes both decrees and inventories and accounts of the treasurers of Athena, some of which can be closely dated to one of the two regimes, but at least one document has been associated with both groups and scholarly opinion is divided over its date; consequently, the epigraphical material for the whole period must be considered together. In addition to documenting the re-use of the city's past, the inscribed texts also bring out the continuity between the democracy, the Four Hundred and the Five Thousand, a situation which we might not have anticipated from our literary sources; similar continuity may well have existed in other spheres for which we now have no evidence.

Some of the inventories and accounts of the treasurers or *tamiai* of Athena can certainly be dated to the period of the Four Hundred in 411. They show little evidence for a sudden break with existing practices. In fact, the accounts of the Pronaos, the Hekatompedon and the Parthenon all indicate that the *tamiai* of Athena for 412/1 handed over their accounts as usual to their (oligarchic) successors and inscribed their accounts in the normal way under the accounts of the previous year.[118] It is likely, however, that their successors' term in office began early at the beginning of the archon year rather than at the Panathenaia on 28 Hekatombaion.[119] That the out-going treasurers were permitted to inscribe their accounts and to record the transition to their successors as usual suggests that the in-coming *tamiai* were to be seen as their legitimate successors. Since the treasurers of Athena existed already in Solon's day, these decisions allowed the Four Hundred to claim to be following the *patrios politeia* and they identified the oligarchic *tamiai* as legitimate additions to the lists of the goddess' servants. The treasurers' appearance in the 'constitution of Drakon' would

---

[118] *IG* I³ 311.35–51; 335.30–2; 357.54–82; Gomme, Andrewes and Dover 1981: 194.
[119] Ferguson 1932b: 145 note 1; Gomme, Andrewes and Dover 1981: 194.

also have allowed the Four Hundred to claim the authority not only of Solon, but also of Drakon, for themselves.

When the Four Hundred were replaced by the Five Thousand, their *tamiai* were allowed to inscribe their accounts for the Pronaos and the Hekatompedon as usual under the lists of their predecessors.[120] The *stele* with the accounts for the Parthenon seems not to have had sufficient room for the new entries.[121] As far as we can recover the prescripts for the accounts of the Pronaos and Hekatompedon, they appear to follow the model provided by the earlier version inscribed under the democracy except that the record for the Hekatompedon seems to have stated that the *tamiai* had received the treasures from their predecessors, a phrase not used in the accounts of 414/3, 413/2 and 412/1.[122] That the accounts of the treasurers of the Four Hundred were inscribed suggested to Andrewes that the *tamiai* did not flee to Dekeleia, but stayed in Athens and successfully passed their *euthunai* (examinations of conduct in office) under the Five Thousand.[123] If this assumption is correct, then these accounts would indirectly indicate that the new regime was making use of the system of *euthuna*. This explanation, however, does not entirely make clear why the Five Thousand allowed the accounts to be inscribed. These documents suggest the legitimacy of the out-going treasurers, that they were part of the legitimate sequence of *tamiai* of Athena. Such a message, we might think, was not in the interests of the Five Thousand, but inscribing the accounts showed that no misdeeds or peculations had taken place. It also allowed the new regime to demonstrate clearly its adherence to ancestral customs and to appropriate the city's political past for themselves. At the end of their tenure in office, the treasurers of the Five Thousand inscribed their accounts for the Pronaos and the Hekatompedon directly under the lists of their immediate (oligarchic) predecessors.[124] They were situated in the proper sequence of office and identified as the legitimate treasurers of the goddess. Since this decision must have been taken by the *demos*, now restored to its full powers, this choice also reflected on it: the democrats were shown abiding by the laws and customs of the city, an issue to which we shall return in greater detail in the next chapter.

---

[120] *IG* I³ 312.52–68; 336.44–57.   [121] W. E. Thompson 1966: 288–9.

[122] Compare *IG* I³ 336.44 with *IG* I³ 333.4; 334.18; 335.32.

[123] Gomme, Andrewes and Dover 1981: 195.

[124] *IG* I³ 313.72–86; 337.60–2. *IG* I³ 358, part of the list of treasures of the Parthenon, seems to belong either to the *tamiai* of the Four Hundred or of the Five Thousand, but, without the prescript, we cannot be certain which board it represents.

If the texts and history of the inventories of Athena's treasurers stress the connections among the various boards in office between late 412/1 and the beginning of 410/9, the accounts of the treasurers of the Four Hundred differ rather more strongly from the accounts of their (democratic) predecessors. Their extant document records payments made to the *hellenotamiai* on the 22 Hekatombaion.[125] After the heading specifying that the accounts are those of the archonship of Mnasilochos, the text begins immediately with the information about the board of *tamiai* and the board of *hellenotamiai* which received the money; it is followed by the authorisation of the *boule*, the date and the sums paid out. Unlike earlier accounts, the dating rubric does not include the name of the first secretary, the payment date is indicated by month and day rather than by prytany and day and the authorisation comes from the *boule* rather than the *demos*.[126] Dating by prytany and the first secretary has been abandoned, presumably because it was closely connected with the overthrown democracy. These accounts, however, were inscribed on the left side of a large *stele* bearing the accounts for the years 432/1 and 431/0 on the front and, on the back, for 414/3 and 413/2 (?).[127] This disposition placed the accounts of the Four Hundred firmly in the tradition of the earlier documents and identified them as products of the legitimate board of Athena's treasurers. As with the inventories, the legitimacy of the *tamiai* of the Four Hundred is emphasised by the placement of their accounts on the *stele*, while the new regime took over the past for its own purposes. Subsequently, another set of accounts was inscribed under that of the treasurers of the Four Hundred; this document seems to belong to the *tamiai* of the Five Thousand who thereby established their relationship to their predecessors and proclaimed themselves as their legitimate successors.[128] When the treasurers of 410/9 came to inscribe their accounts, however, they used a new *stele* as if to emphasise their distance from the boards of the previous year.[129]

This process of re-using the past and engaging with the *patrios politeia* was not limited to the inventories and accounts of the *tamiai* of Athena appointed by the Four Hundred and the Five Thousand and it is also visible in two decrees which belong to this overall period. As with the accounts of the treasurers, these two documents differ from decrees passed under the

---

[125] *IG* I³ 373.
[126] Gomme, Andrewes and Dover 1981: 194–5. For earlier accounts, cf. e.g. *IG* I³ 370 recording the accounts for the years 418/7 through 415/4.
[127] *IG* I³ 365, 366, 371, 372 with the comments of Lewis; cf. Meritt 1932: pl. 1 for the disposition of *IG* I³ 365, 371 and 373 on the stone.
[128] *IG* I³ 374 with the comments of Lewis. [129] *IG* I³ 375.

democracy, but a concern with the past is also evident. The first of the two documents is a decree honouring a certain merchant Pythophanes for his benefactions towards the city; his rewards consist of the inscription of a previous honorary decree and additional measures to provide security for his business.[130] As Russell Meiggs and David Lewis observe, the body of the decree in lines 8–28 is regular and the differences from previous practices are in the prescript, which is without parallel.[131] The fragmentary lines seem to record the names of the secretary and of the *epistates* or president of the *boule* followed by the phrase κ]αὶ μετ' αὐτõ π[– and probably four more names. Together with the *epistates*, we have a total of five men who seem to have presided over the *boule*; they may perhaps be the five *proedroi* or presiding officers whom Thucydides identifies as responsible for enrolling the Four Hundred, but we should also remember that the oligarchs elected *prutaneis* as soon as they took over the Bouleuterion.[132] Since the date of the inscription is unclear and it has been assigned to the periods both of the Four Hundred and of the Five Thousand, it is hard to know exactly what these men were doing.[133] The decree does show, however, that at least one benefactor was honoured with traditional language at this time and, as was customary, his decree inscribed on a *stele* and set up on the Akropolis. It also provides evidence for the existence of the secretary and *epistates* of the *boule*, as well as the *boule* itself.[134] The presence of the *epistates* is particularly interesting because the description of this office in the *Athenaion Politeia* makes it clear that it was an integral part of the democratic *boule*;[135] since the council was introduced by Kleisthenes, the position of *epistates* may also have been associated with him. Their appearance in this text suggests that the regime under which the decree was passed was interested in emphasising its connections with Kleisthenes and the city's political past and in co-opting them for itself. In addition, the prescript clearly indicated that the decree had not been passed under the full democracy.

[130] *IG* i³ 98.   [131] Meiggs and Lewis 1988: 249; Henry 1977: 14–15; de Ste Croix 1956: 18.

[132] *Proedroi*: Thuc. 8.67.3; *prutaneis*: Thuc. 8.70.1; Wilhelm 1922–4: 147; Meiggs and Lewis 1988: 249; Gomme, Andrewes and Dover 1981: 196; Walbank 1978: 389, 391; cf. de Ste Croix 1956: 17–19; against the possible association of these men with the *proedroi*, see P. J. Rhodes 1972a: 28–9; P. J. Rhodes 1981: 397–8; Develin 1989: 192.

[133] For the problems of the date and a summary of the various views, see Meiggs and Lewis 1988: 249 and the comments of Lewis in *IG* i³. Against the association of *IG* i³ 98 with this period, see Develin 1989: 191–2. He does not, however, account for the unusual form of the prescript.

[134] Secretary: *IG* i³ 98.3, 14, 28; *epistates*: *IG* i³ 98.4; *boule*: *IG* i³ 98.4, 14, 26.

[135] Arist. *Ath. Pol.* 44; cf. P. J. Rhodes 1972a: 23–4. For the usage in decrees, see the comments of P. J. Rhodes 1981: 534.

The second decree orders the arrest and trial for treason of the oligarchs Archeptolemos, Onomakles and Antiphon and is certainly dated to the regime of the Five Thousand.[136] As with the decree honouring Pythophanes, the prescript does not follow the form usually found in late fifth-century Athenian inscriptions: the date is given merely as the twenty-first day of the prytany.[137] The demotics of the secretary and the *epistates* are provided along with their names, but both men came from the tribe Antiochis, a situation which would not have been possible under the democracy.[138] If the decree originally gave the name of the archon, it is not included in our extant text. The body of the decree indicates that the accused were denounced by the generals, who, with up to ten members of the *boule*, are to produce them in court, and they are to play a role in the trial. The *thesmothetai* are to summon the accused on the following day. The document provides evidence for the activities of the generals and the *boule* as well as for the existence of the secretary of the *boule* and the *thesmothetai* and for the use of an *epistates*. These various officials connect the Five Thousand with the practices of the democracy and the city's political past; in this way, it would be identified as the upholder of the ancestral constitution. The somewhat unusual form of the prescript, however, would probably have made it clear that the decree was not passed by the full democracy.

When the decree was inscribed, these associations with the city's past would have been openly displayed in the city. The very process of publishing the document would also have created further links with the city's earlier practices. The verdict appended to the decree indicates that the documents are to be inscribed on a bronze *stele* and set up where the decrees concerning the dead Phrynichos were erected.[139] Bronze *stelai* were not the normal method of display for Athenian documents; if documents were inscribed, they were written up on stone *stelai*. Inscription on bronze had, however, been used before for the list of traitors headed by Hipparchos the son of Charmos and very probably also for the *stele* listing Peisistratos and his

---

[136] [Plut.] *X orat.* 833E–F = Krater. *FGrHist* 342 F5b; for the date, see [Plut.] *X orat.* 833D–E with Gomme, Andrewes and Dover 1981: 197.

[137] Gomme, Andrewes and Dover 1981: 197; P. J. Rhodes 1972a: 29 note 7; cf. de Ste Croix 1956: 16; for the standard form, cf. e.g. *IG* I³ 95.1–5; 97.1–5; 101.1–6; 102.1–6. There is no reference to the *demos* because the procedure was an *eisangelia* to the council; [Plut.] *X orat.* 833A, D; de Ste Croix 1956: 16–17; Hansen 1975: 27–8, 113–15; Ostwald 1986: 401. *Eisangelia* also seems to have been used against Peisandros; Jameson 1971: 557–9. The procedure of *eisangelia* is often thought to have been introduced by Solon; Hansen 1975: 15–19 with further references. Consequently, its use in these trials may represent another instance of the Five Thousand's re-use of the city's past.

[138] Gomme, Andrewes and Dover 1981: 197.   [139] [Plut.] *X orat.* 834B.

family.[140] These texts must have been inscribed after Hipparchos' ostracism in 488/7 and at the end of the sixth century respectively; as such, they were documents of the early democracy. Using this same medium for the documents concerning Antiphon, consequently, would have linked them to the practices of the Kleisthenic democracy. The earlier documents were certainly set up on the Akropolis and the sanctuary of Athena, the default location for inscribed documents in the fifth century, remains the most obvious setting for the inscriptions concerning Antiphon and Phrynichos. If this inference is correct, then the placement of the new *stelai* would have further emphasised the connections with the political past. This setting would also have constructed not just Phrynichos, but also Archeptolemos and Antiphon, as tyrants, as men on a par with the Peisistratidai.

Collectively, the epigraphical material provides evidence for the existence of a number of officials during the regimes of both the Four Hundred and the Five Thousand. The *tamiai* of Athena were active in both periods and the *hellenotamiai* received payment from them under the Four Hundred. The *boule* was active at both times and certainly had a secretary and an *epistates* under the Five Thousand; if the decree for Pythophanes was passed under the Four Hundred, then these two offices also existed at that time. For the period of the Five Thousand, both the generals and the *thesmothetai* are positively attested. On one level, the retention of existing offices and practices was a practical move which would have caused less disruption than the invention of a completely new system. Furthermore, keeping these elements of the existing system allowed the two regimes to position themselves in relation to the *patrios politeia* and to claim it for themselves. The *boule* of 400 was invented by Solon, the council of 500 by Kleisthenes; the archons, including probably the *thesmothetai*, existed before Solon's legislation and the senior archons existed before Drakon; the treasurers of the Athena were in office at the time of Solon. Retaining these positions maintained connections with the city's political past and provided venerable names, Drakon, Solon and Kleisthenes, with which to conjure. These associations suggested that the two regimes were going back to the good old days when these men had been active and before the radical democracy had been invented. They also indicated that the Four Hundred and the Five Thousand were legitimate successors of these earlier lawgivers and that they were not beyond the authority of the city's *politeia*.

---

[140] Traitors: Lykourg. *Leok.* 117–19. Peisistratidai: Thuc. 6.55.1–2; Gomme, Andrewes and Dover 1970: 324–5.

Keeping the offices allowed these two regimes to lay claim to the city's larger political past and to emphasise their relationship to it.

While the inscriptions fit very well with our other evidence for the ways in which the two regimes appropriated the ancestral constitution, they are set apart by the very fact of their publication on stone. Perusal of the corpus of Attic inscriptions shows that the inscribing of decrees did not begin any earlier than the last decade of the sixth century, while the earliest known accounts and inventories belong in the middle to third quarter of the fifth century.[141] Perhaps the inscribing of decrees was thought to have been an innovation of Kleisthenes, but the practice actually did not become common until the middle and second half of the fifth century, i.e. after the reforms of Ephialtes in *c.* 462; this chronology suggests that it was, in fact, a habit of the radical democracy which both the Four Hundred and the Five Thousand wished to destroy. Nevertheless, publication on stone was one of the city's political traditions as a brief visit to the Akropolis at the end of the fifth century would have made clear. By continuing this practice, these two oligarchic regimes were able to assert their control of this political past and to situate themselves in relationship to it as the city's legitimate political future. They could also put forward a visible claim to the sanctuary, now transformed by the projects of the democracy.

In addition, these inscriptions bring out the ways in which the debate over the ancestral constitution apparently developed. When the Four Hundred, and later the Five Thousand, gained power, it was not sufficient to adopt only those aspects of the *politeia* thought to have been promulgated by Drakon, Solon or Kleisthenes, nor could the *polis* survive in this fashion. The realities of the situation required that much more of the past be retained and it, in turn, provided legitimacy for the rulers. In this context, the phrase *patrios politeia* was wonderfully flexible because it could refer both very specifically to the ancestral constitution as well as more generally to the way of doing things in the past.[142] Its lack of specificity meant that it need not (immediately) cause alarm and it could be used by individuals from all parts of the political spectrum without necessarily committing themselves to specific future actions. Claiming this past also allowed the

---

[141] Decrees: *IG* I³ 1; 2; 5. Accounts: *IG* I³ 248 (Rhamnous; 450–440); 249 (*c.* 440); 253 (Ikaria; 450–425); 363 (Athena Polias and Nike; 441/0); 384 (Eleusis; *c.* 450; *I.Eleusis* 24: 450–430?); 402 (Delos; 434–432); building accounts: *IG* I³ 433 (*c.* 450); 436 (Parthenon; 447/6); 453 (gold and ivory Athena; 447/6 or 445/4); 461 (Parthenon doors; 438); 462 (Propylaia; 437/6). Inventories: *IG* I³ 292 (Pronaos); 317 (Hekatompedon); 343 (Parthenon; all 434). I give here the first or earliest examples only. *IG* I³ 435 has traditionally been associated with Pheidias' Bronze Athena and dated to *c.* 450, but the date and identification have now been called into question by Stroud; Stroud 2006: 26–32.

[142] On this point, see the comments of Finley 2000: 37–8; cf. Lévy 1976: 195.

regime in power to take it away from their opponents. For this reason, the Five Thousand had little choice except to continue the terms of the debate over the *patrios politeia* and to appropriate the past for themselves; to do otherwise would have given their opponents too many opportunities to undermine their regime.

THUCYDIDES AND THE TRIALS OF THE OLIGARCHS

Our evidence shows that the debate over the *patrios politeia* and the ways in which the city's political past could and should be used were very real and the process is evident both under the Four Hundred and the Five Thousand. As I have argued, the two constitutions of the *Athenaion Politeia* come directly out of this context and they also provide important evidence for it. Although Thucydides reflects this process in various places, his account does not belong in this setting and so we also need to ask about its background. His version, as we have already seen, focuses both on violence and deceit and on a small group of named oligarchs who are leaders of the extremists. They are clearly separated out from the ordinary and nameless oligarchs whose actions are described only collectively. Especial attention is reserved for Phrynichos, who, by his assassination in the Agora, becomes a tyrant. Thucydides' emphases are of particular interest because similar strategies can be seen in the trials of the oligarchs after the fall of the Four Hundred. As part of their defence, the accused sought to distance themselves from the hard-core oligarchs who were conveniently dead or exiled in Athens. Considering Thucydides' portrayal of Phrynichos from this perspective also suggests that the main traditions about his death probably originated in his posthumous trial.

These politically motivated trials began under the Five Thousand and continued until at least 405 when Aristophanes alluded to them in the *parabasis* of *Frogs*.[143] The earliest of these legal actions was the treason trial of the assassinated Phrynichos, to which we shall return below. Soon afterwards, as we know from Andron's decree and the accompanying verdict, Archeptolemos, Onomakles and Antiphon were charged with treason on the embassy sent by the Four Hundred to Sparta.[144] Since the verdict

---

[143] Ar. *Frogs* 687–702.

[144] Decree of Andron: above note 136; verdict: [Plut.] *X orat.* 834A–B = Krater. *FGrHist* 342 F5b. Fragments of Antiphon's defence speech are preserved: Antiph. frs. 1–6 (Thalheim); Gomme, Andrewes and Dover 1981: 198–9, 200; Gagarin 1997: 248–9; doubted by Hornblower 2008: 957. On the date of the trial, see Jameson 1971: 552 note 34; Hansen 1975: 114, 115 note 13; Ostwald 1986: 402 and note 226.

mentions only Archeptolemos and Antiphon, Onomakles must have escaped from Athens before the trial ended. Archeptolemos and Antiphon were found guilty of treason: they were killed, forbidden burial in any place ruled by the Athenians and, with their descendants, were made *atimos* (without citizen rights), while their property was confiscated. Peisandros also seems to have been brought to trial under the Five Thousand on a charge of *hubris* against Euktemon; Sophokles, apparently one of the prosecutors, is said to have requested the death penalty.[145] Present in Athens when the trial began, Peisandros got away to Dekeleia and so escaped being put to death (fig. 1); his property, however, was confiscated and at least part of it was later given to Apollodoros of Megara as a reward for killing Phrynichos.[146] Less prominent and well-known members of the Four Hundred also faced prosecution. Among them was Polystratos, a *katalogeus* known from the twentieth speech in the Lysianic corpus; he was brought to trial on unspecified charges under the Five Thousand and punished with a large fine.[147] Despite this trial, Polystratos was prosecuted again after the return of the democracy, the occasion of the composition of pseudo-Lysias 20.[148] The speech states that Polystratos was punished despite his relative insignificance, but many other men who spoke against the *demos* and remained in the Bouleuterion during the whole time of the Four Hundred were acquitted.[149] That 'many' men were acquitted suggests that the trials in question took place both under the Five Thousand and after the return of the full democracy.[150] Further evidence for large numbers of trials in this period may also be suggested by some Thucydidean manuscripts' use of the phrase ἐς ἀγῶνας in describing Antiphon's court case, but the text's corruption precludes certainty.[151]

Few details are preserved for the cases in and after 410/9. Lysias' twenty-fifth oration accuses Epigenes, Demophanes and Kleisthenes of enriching themselves by persuading the *demos* to condemn men to death without trial, by confiscating the property of many and by banishing and disenfranchising citizens.[152] The amnesty decree of Patrokleides, passed in the second half

---

[145] Arist. *Rh.* 1.14.3, 3.15.3, 3.18.6 with Jameson 1971: 541–64.
[146] Escaped: Thuc. 8.98.1; property: Lys. 7.4; Woodhead 1954: 145; Jameson 1971: 555–6, 557–8.
[147] [Lys.] 20.1, 13–14, 18, 22.
[148] Date: [Lys.] 20.17; de Ste Croix 1956: 11; Gomme, Andrewes and Dover 1981: 203; Todd 2000: 217. Issue at hand: note the prosecution's accusation that the Four Hundred were criminals; [Lys.] 20.16.
[149] [Lys.] 20.14–15.   [150] Jameson 1971: 553.
[151] Thuc. 8.68.2; Jameson 1971: 554–5, 566–8; Ostwald 1986: 404; Gomme, Andrewes and Dover 1981: 174–6; Hornblower 2008: 956–8.
[152] Lys. 25.25–6; Ostwald 1986: 421.

of 406/5, excludes from its provisions those who, having been tried by various courts, were condemned to death as tyrants.[153] The references in the preceding clause of the document to men registered as members of the Four Hundred and to records of deeds done under the oligarchy may also refer to the results of other court cases.[154] Despite all this general evidence for activity in the courts against members of the Four Hundred, we are not well informed about the trials of specific men. Aristarchos, a defender of Phrynichos, was certainly tried at some time before the battle of Arginousai in 406. At the time of the trial of the Arginousai generals, he was described as having betrayed Oinoe to the Thebans (fig. 1) and as having dissolved the democracy, but we do not know if these charges were made at his trial.[155] Aristarchos was certainly found guilty, killed and refused burial in the country.[156] Lykourgos describes Alexikles, who also defended Phrynichos, as suffering the same punishment and he, too, was probably tried for his role in the earlier trial.[157]

As this brief summary brings out, prosecuting the Four Hundred was not easy and we know of no certain cases in which the charge was actually membership in the oligarchy. The trial of Archeptolemos, Onomakles and Antiphon clearly brings out the difficulties involved. Although the real issue in this case was the establishment of the oligarchy and Antiphon's speech circulated under the title 'concerning the change in constitution' (περὶ τῆς μεταστάσεως), the men in question could not be so charged because both Andron, who proposed the decree, and three of the prosecutors, Theramenes, Apolexis and Thymochares, had also been members of the Four Hundred, as had other members of the Five Thousand;[158] for them, attack was evidently the best form of defence. Prosecuting any member of the Four Hundred, accordingly, required a charge other than membership in the oligarchy, even though such participation was the real reason for the trial. Such men could also expect severe punishments, including, for the most heavily implicated, death, but there were also lesser penalties, such as the fine imposed on Polystratos. These trials were not just about ridding the city of hated oligarchs: by bringing these charges, the Athenians stressed the lack of legitimate sanction of the Four Hundred and Five Thousand; if they had been legitimate regimes, then their members would not subsequently have been brought to trial.

---

[153] Andok. 1.78.   [154] Andok. 1.78 and cf. 1.75.
[155] Xen. *Hell.* 1.7.28; Jameson 1971: 552–3. For his betrayal of Oinoe, see Thuc. 8.98.1–4.
[156] Lykourg. *Leok.* 115.
[157] Jameson 1971: 552–3; more cautiously Gomme, Andrewes and Dover 1981: 340.
[158] Jameson 1971: 551–2; Gomme, Andrewes and Dover 1981: 176.

The Lysianic speech for Polystratos shows some of the strategies by which these oligarchs might defend themselves.[159] The extant text begins with the statement that the jury should not be angry at the name of the Four Hundred, but at the actions of *some* of its members; these men plotted against the *demos*, while the rest intended no harm either to the city or to anyone of the *demos*. Polystratos was, of course, in this later group.[160] The oligarchs are divided into two groups, the bad men who allegedly did all the evil, and the good men who were well disposed to the *demos*. By implication, this second group is not responsible for the actions of the bad oligarchs and should not be blamed for their deeds. A few sections later, the speaker picks up on this thought and stresses that the guilty men are those few who held offices not for the greatest good of the city and that the city was betrayed by the dishonest office-holders.[161] Polystratos, however, was loyal to the *demos* and this city and this characterisation is repeated on six more occasions.[162] In addition, Polystratos is described as having done no wrong to the *demos* and as being *demotikos*.[163] The true oligarchs' behaviour is contrasted with that of Polystratos and their violence is stressed. They put to death or exiled those who spoke against them so that fear deterred the opposition and most men gave up entirely.[164] They even punished Polystratos himself when he was unwilling to swear the oath and act as *katalogeus* for them.[165] This strategy for defending Polystratos could only succeed if the speakers could draw a sharp distinction between his actions and those of the 'true' oligarchs and it requires them to emphasise the violence and deceit of the main members of the Four Hundred. In contrast, the prosecution's tactic was to maintain that all members of the Four Hundred were equally responsible and to accuse them of being criminals.[166]

Dividing the Four Hundred into guilty hard-core leaders and less important moderate followers was a strategy deployed in several slightly later speeches. In his twelfth oration, Lysias accuses Theramenes both of being very responsible for the Four Hundred and of having done great evils, rather than great good, for the city.[167] In describing Eratosthenes, Lysias emphasises that he set up an oligarchy in his camp at the time of the Four

---

[159] Although the extant text seems to preserve parts of two speeches, sections 1–10 and sections 11–36, these tactics are evident in both parts. On the problems of the text, see Gomme, Andrewes and Dover 1981: 201; Todd 2000: 217, 221; cf. Todd 2007: 2 note 7.

[160] [Lys.] 20.1.   [161] [Lys.] 20.5.

[162] [Lys.] 20.6, 7, 8, 9, 13, 16 and it is implied in section 10.   [163] [Lys.] 20.19, 22.

[164] [Lys.] 20.8–9. Reiske attractively suggested that the manuscripts' τὸ δέος καὶ ὁ φόβος should be amended to τὸ δέος καὶ ὁ φόνος, but this suggestion does not seem to have found favour with other editors; see the apparatus criticus of Carey's OCT edition of Lysias and Todd 2000: 220.

[165] [Lys.] 20.14.   [166] Compare [Lys.] 20.16.   [167] Lys. 12.64–5; cf. 78.

Hundred, hardly the actions of a moderate man, and later he links him closely with Theramenes.[168] In his speech against Hippotherses, his opponent is described not merely as being an oligarch in 411, but the sort of man who then went into exile at Dekeleia and joined the Spartans in attacking his fatherland.[169] He is not a moderate oligarch. The speaker of Lysias 25 distinguishes between Phrynichos, Peisandros and the demagogues with them and the sort of members of the Four Hundred who, in 403, returned from exile with the *demos*.[170] Later in the speech, he stresses that he himself was never a member of the Four Hundred (nor, for that matter, of the Thirty).[171] In this way, he creates a scale going from hard-core oligarchs to moderate oligarchs to non-oligarchs. The speaker of Lysias 30 states that Nikomachos accused him before the *boule* of being a member of the Four Hundred, a claim made with slanderous intent, but, in fact, he was not even a member of the Five Thousand.[172] His evident indignation and his efforts to disassociate himself from all the oligarchs of 411 suggest that Nikomachos tried to paint him as an extremely oligarchic individual. The tactics used in these speeches presuppose a strong division between hard-core oligarchs and moderate men who argue that they were always really on the side of the *demos*. Violence on the part of these truly anti-democratic men is at least implied, if it is not indicated more openly.

These tactics were apparently employed not only by relatively unimportant oligarchs, but also by leading members. Antiphon seems to have made the argument that there were good and bad oligarchs and, of course, he was a good one; it was the other oligarchs who were part of the hard core and turned a reasonable reform into an undeniable oligarchy.[173] In the papyrus fragments of his speech, there is a partially preserved reference to Phrynichos and apparently Peisandros; it is likely that Antiphon tried to shift the blame for what actually transpired onto them.[174] In order for this tactic to work, all violence and deceit must have been attributed to everyone but Antiphon. Since Phrynichos was dead and his trial concluded, he would have made a particularly attractive scapegoat for Antiphon, as he certainly did for Aristophanes.[175] Another possible defence for Antiphon or other prominent members of the Four Hundred would have been to stress the legality of the oligarchs' actions and the role of the *demos* in their rise to

---

[168] Lys. 12.42, 62–3.   [169] Lys. fr. LXX.170 lines 182–92 (Carey).   [170] Lys. 25.9.
[171] Lys. 25.14. This speaker does have the problem that he remained in Athens under the Thirty, as we shall see in chapter 7, hence his efforts to position himself appropriately in the political sphere.
[172] Lys. 30.7–8.
[173] Gomme, Andrewes and Dover 1981: 199.
[174] Antiph. fr. 1c, col. 6 lines 17–18 (Thalheim); Gomme, Andrewes and Dover 1981: 198–9.
[175] Ar. *Frogs* 689–91. Here, all blame is placed on Phrynichos and no one else is mentioned.

power.[176] In such a situation, stressing that things were done according to the dictates of the *patrios politeia* also would not have been out of place. For Antiphon, emphasising the legality of what was done need not conflict with the argument that the whole affair began as a reasonable reform which was then co-opted by the extreme oligarchs.[177]

One manoeuvre for men facing allegations of belonging to the Four Hundred, therefore, was to divide the oligarchs into good and bad factions, a tactic which limited the evil deeds to a small group of extreme individuals and absolved everyone else, including themselves, of guilt.[178] For us, this explanatory strategy should be familiar because we have seen Thucydides employing the same approach in his narrative of the Four Hundred. Few men are specifically and repeatedly named; with the exception of Theramenes, they are the leaders of the extreme oligarchs and they do not hesitate to use violence to gain their ends. That the fear induced by this violence deterred opposition is also stressed both by Thucydides and by the author of the speech for Polystratos.[179] Thucydides' narrative, consequently, has been significantly influenced by the court speeches against the oligarchs and their tactics, which were probably widely used, provided him with an important interpretative framework for his narrative.[180] These approaches would also fit with Thucydides' stance as a supporter, rather than a critic, of democracy.

These strategies further allowed Thucydides to emphasise the violence of the events under the Four Hundred. In this way, he links his account of *stasis* at Athens back to the civil strife at Kerkyra where violence is an important part of events.[181] Through this approach, Thucydides is able to present a strong critique of oligarchy and its excesses: oligarchy is shown not to be a positive or desirable form of *politeia* in any way.[182] Adopting a narrative focused on orderly constitution-making, in contrast, would

---

[176] P. J. Rhodes 1981: 367.

[177] Gomme, Andrewes and Dover 1981: 247–8; Andrewes 1976: 19.

[178] This strategy may explain why, as de Ste Croix notes, Antiphon seems persistently to contrast the Four Hundred with 'the democracy'; de Ste Croix 1956: 12. Of course, the Five Thousand may also have presented themselves as 'the democracy' in order to distance themselves from the Four Hundred and to stress their relationship to the *patrios politeia*. The focus on the extreme leaders may also explain why later orators tended to elide any distinction between the *demos* under the democracy and the Athenians under the Five Thousand, a trend noted in Ferguson 1932a: 364 note 1 and de Ste Croix 1956: 11.

[179] Compare Thuc. 8.66.2 and [Lys.] 20.8–9.

[180] Since Thucydides was not in Athens at this time, he presumably learned these strategies from written versions of the speeches, just as he knew Antiphon's oration in its written form; Thuc. 8.68.2. For his exile from Athens, see Thuc. 5.26.5; Hornblower 2008: 50–3, 958.

[181] E.g. Thuc. 3.70.6, 72.3–74.2, 81.2–5.   [182] Compare Raaflaub 2006: 213–14, 221.

not have shown the events in Athens conforming to his existing paradigm for civil strife and it would not have enabled him to show the problems of the rule of a small group of men. The speeches' emphasis on a few principal oligarchs also fits with what seems to be the increased importance of individuals in the second half of Thucydides' overall narrative.[183] This focus in turn brings out the destructive personal competitions between specific men which lead not only to the defeat in Sicily, but also to *stasis* and the eventual defeat of the city, as the historian makes clear already in his 'obituary' of Perikles.[184] That the strategies of these court speeches correspond to the existing dynamics of his text would have increased their attractiveness to Thucydides, while his use of them constitutes his own response to the events of 411.

The reflections of these forensic sources in Thucydides' narrative further suggest that his image of Phrynichos the tyrant may belong to this tradition. Thucydides is not our only source for the death of Phrynichos: it is mentioned by both Lysias and Lykourgos and the decree honouring one of the assassins is preserved.[185] In contrast to Thucydides, Lysias and Lykourgos identify the assassins as Thrasyboulos of Kalydon, who is also honoured in the decree, and Apollodoros of Megara. Lysias states that Phrynichos was killed while he was out walking and that the assassins disappeared when an outcry arose, while Lykourgos locates the deed at the fountain in the osier beds at night and reports that the assassins were caught and put in prison. In these versions, Phrynichos does not appear as a terrible tyrant, although perhaps hanging around a fountain at night does not suggest a perfectly upright character. Since Thucydides elsewhere drew on the material generated by the trials of the oligarchs, his depiction of Phrynichos' death may also be derived from the prosecution speech at the trial, an occasion when the equation with a tyrant would have been very appropriate. This image would subsequently have been repeated when the bronze *stele* with the verdict was set up on the Akropolis in close proximity to the *stelai* for traitors and the Peisistratidai. In contrast, the tradition reflected by Lysias and Lykourgos would then originate in the statements of Phrynichos' defenders.

These two characterisations differ strongly from the information in the honorary decree for Thrasyboulos, which was passed in the eighth prytany

---

[183] Hornblower 1987: 146–50, 188; Westlake 1968: 13–15, 308–19; Gribble 2006: 443, 458.
[184] Thuc. 2.65.7, 11–13; Gribble 1999: 169–75.
[185] Lys. 13.70–3; Lykourg. *Leok.* 112; *IG* I³ 102 = M. J. Osborne 1981–82: D2. On the evidence of Plut. *Alk.* 25.14, see the comments of Gomme, Andrewes and Dover 1981: 309.

of 410/9 and belongs to the period of the full democracy.[186] In this document, the deed for which Thrasyboulos is honoured is never mentioned, but its two amendments indicate that it was highly contested. The first amendment provides honours for an additional group of men, while the second instructs the *boule* to investigate the bribery which allegedly accompanied the passing of Apollodoros' honours; bribery is also mentioned by Lysias.[187] What seems to be at issue here is responsibility for assassinating Phrynichos and our extant decree represents the middle of the process after honours had been awarded to Apollodoros.[188] The importance of the deed itself, however, does not seem to be the problem. References to tyrants, tyrant slaying and Harmodios and Aristogeiton are, perhaps strangely, absent from the inscription, which carefully avoids describing the event. The importance of the deed has apparently already been acknowledged, as it would have been by the guilty verdict of Phrynichos' trial. The focus on the participants, rather than the event, suggests that our various traditions about his death do not reflect the wrangling between Apollodoros, Thrasyboulos and others; instead, they should be linked to the earlier stage of his trial. Thucydides' Phrynichos the tyrant belongs very much to the same tradition as the emphasis on violence and a small group of extremist leaders.

THE INVENTION OF TRADITION

Our two different accounts of the Four Hundred, accordingly, are associated with significantly different traditions. Like the two constitutions which it includes, the version in the *Athenaion Politeia* comes out of the extensive debate over the *patrios politeia* and the city's past, while the emphasis on constitutional issues also fits closely with the larger purposes of the project. The crucial figure is the moderate oligarch Kleitophon who moves the amendment instructing the *sungrapheis* to look at Kleisthenes' *politeia* and the orderly process is about creating a suitable moderate constitution for the city. In contrast, Thucydides' violent account with its demonisation of Phrynichos as tyrant has been strongly influenced by the strategies used in the trials of the oligarchs under the Five Thousand and the full democracy. Since Thucydides certainly knew Antiphon's defence speech,

---

[186] *IG* I³ 102; see also the discussion below chapter 5. The date of the inscription is provided by comparison with *IG* I³ 375.27.

[187] First amendment: *IG* I³ 102.25–38. Second amendment: *IG* I³ 102.38–47. Bribery: Lys. 13.72.

[188] Apollodoros' claim was evidently upheld because he eventually sold the land awarded to him by the *demos*; Lys. 7.4.

his use of material from other trials is not surprising; in written form, these orations will have provided him with information which his exile would have prevented him from hearing in person.[189] He also alludes to the constitutional debate and the city's political past, but, for him, these issues, which Aristotle stresses, did not sufficiently explain how and why the Four Hundred first gained power and then subsequently lost it.[190] By removing most traces of the *patrios politeia* debate from his narrative, Thucydides also reduced the number of causes for the oligarchic revolution and sharpened his focus on the actions of the oligarchs. These decisions further absolved the majority of the Athenians from any responsibility for their role in the revolution. By responding to the events in this way, Thucydides was able to emphasise that oligarchy was not, in his view, a workable solution to the radical democracy which it replaced and to demonstrate that *stasis* in Athens was no different from civil strife in other cities.

The small role which Thucydides accords to the discussions over the city's political past, however, should not blind us to the very real existence of such a debate. Initially carried on by Athenians of all political persuasions, the *patrios politeia* proved to be a wonderfully vague concept which could easily embrace innovations attributed to Kleisthenes, as well as to Solon and Drakon. That the ancestral constitution was not merely a specious excuse used by the oligarchs in their quest for power is made clear by their actions after they gained control of the city: they continued to use the city's political past as a way of providing legitimacy for their regime. Conjuring up the past allowed the Four Hundred to portray their regime as a return to earlier forms of the city's *politeia* and to co-opt that past for their own use. Any innovation which they wished to make could be provided with legitimacy and any men seeking to overthrow them were deprived on the sanction of the past. For the Five Thousand, the constitutional debates were also critical because their power could not have been established so quickly without them.[191] Like their oligarchic predecessors, the Five Thousand used the past to give legitimacy to their regime. In 410, these actions raised a crucial question: was there still a past for the democratic city?

In contrast to his treatment of the *patrios politeia*, Thucydides accords a much larger role to the space of Athens. Some areas, like the Peiraieus and the Agora, are contested ones which the oligarchs try to recover from the democrats. Their failure to control these two spaces signals the imminent

---

[189] Above note 180.
[190] Note also Harris' emphasis on Thucydides' lack of interest in ideology; E. M. Harris 1990: 271–2; Hornblower 1987: 141–3, 159.
[191] R. Osborne 2003: 258–9.

fall of their regime. Thucydides was not the only Athenian interested in the politics of space. Erecting inscriptions on the Akropolis allowed the oligarchs to make a claim on Athena's sanctuary through their inventories, accounts and decrees and to suggest that this place was not just the territory of the democrats who had overseen its transfiguration. Setting up the bronze *stelai* concerning Phrynichos, Archeptolemos, Onomakles and Antiphon on the Akropolis certainly aided this process, but it also brought the documents into contact with the bronze *stelai* for traitors and the Peisistratidai, a juxtaposition which constructed the oligarchs themselves as traitors and tyrants of Athens. Controlling space and the images set up in it was an important way of legitimising a regime. Political domination, consequently, was literally played out on and through Athenian topography. In 410, the democrats needed to reclaim Athens for their own and to ask: how can the city be made democratic again?

As we shall see in the following chapters, the democrats thoroughly reclaimed the Athenian political past and they remade Athens as the democratic city. Their actions completely eclipsed anything which either the Four Hundred or the Five Thousand had managed to do and the result was a radically different Athens. The politics of this process bear a striking similarity to the concerns of Thucydides' narrative of the Four Hundred. Like his decision to portray Phrynichos as a tyrant, using the strategies of the trials of the oligarchs and focusing on the importance of place are not the actions of a committed oligarch. Instead, they fit with Farrar's portrait of Thucydides as a democrat: his treatment of the extreme leaders of the Four Hundred serves as the counter-example to his focus on Perikles' leadership and his emphasis on the importance of the unified political community finds a strong parallel in the actions of the democrats in and after 410.[192] For both the historian and the Athenians, understanding and responding to the events of 411 were of critical importance, if there was to be a future. Having that future required the Athenians to create a sustained response to the oligarchic revolutions, a response to which we must now turn.

---

[192] Perikles as political leader: Farrar 1998: 158–77, 186. Unified political community: Farrar 1998: 130, 153–87.

CHAPTER 3

Restoring Athens: democracy and the law

In the previous chapter, we looked back with the Athenians on the events of 411 and we considered how Thucydides and the Aristotelian *Athenaion Politeia*, our two main sources, portray the Four Hundred and their rise to power. Discussing the larger contexts to which these two works belong brought out two particularly important issues: the ways in which first the Four Hundred and then the Five Thousand used and appropriated the city's political past and the *patrios politeia* for themselves and the importance of the city's space, especially the Akropolis and the Agora, areas to which the oligarchs attempted to lay claim. In 410, the Athenians had not only to look back at what had happened, but also to look ahead to the future, to what they would create. The over-riding question at that moment was: how do we, the democratic Athenians, respond to oligarchy? Indeed, the Athenians had to ask whether oligarchy would be remembered at all or whether it would be thoroughly effaced and forgotten. As part of this process of responding to the events of 411, the Athenians needed to face two other important issues: how could the city be made (visibly) democratic again and, in light of the Four Hundred's and Five Thousand's actions, was there even a past for the democratic city?

How the Athenians undertook this process is the subject of the next three chapters as we look at the spheres of democracy and law (this chapter), of building and topography (chapter 4) and of ritual (chapter 5). Our discussion begins with democracy and law not only because democracy is the most critical issue in the city's response, but also because these two related topics with their associated documents most clearly show the Athenians' various strategies at work. This evidence further elucidates the changes in Athenian topography and the ways in which these developments formed part of this process (chapter 4). Understanding the documents preserving the rituals and the spaces in which they occurred allows us to see how rites were used to respond to oligarchy (chapter 5). To anticipate some overall conclusions, we shall see that the Athenians did, indeed, find ways to remake the democratic city and to recover her past for the *demos*. They also effaced the oligarchs' presence in the city's memorial spaces. Creating this response caused significant changes to the city's topography. Most importantly, these actions shifted the topographical focus from the Akropolis to the Agora and they began the process of making the Agora into space for the democratic citizen, rather than the multi-use space which it had previously been. The places in which decrees and other public documents were set also changed because, for the first time, inscriptions began to be set up in the Agora, rather than in sanctuary spaces and most especially the Akropolis, as they had been before 410.[1]

In 410, the Athenians' focus was on making the city democratic. Whether the city should be democratic seems not even to have been asked; certainly there are no traces of any public debate over the appropriateness of the rule of the *demos* nor were significant changes made to the system. Instead, the emphasis was on the instantiation of that rule. As I shall argue, erecting particular *stelai*, namely those bearing Demophantos' decree and the oath quoted at the beginning of chapter 1 and the newly gathered and reorganised laws, showed that the democracy was functioning properly. These documents also allowed the *demos* to write its control of the city firmly on the topography and particularly on the Agora. The laws further enabled the Athenians to begin the process of reclaiming the city's past for the *demos* and of making that past democratic. As with the Four Hundred and the Five Thousand, the past was once again used to legitimise the current political system, in this case, the rule of the *demos*. Since these documents are closely dated, they also confirm that the Athenians began responding to oligarchy at the beginning of 410/9 as soon as the full democracy was back in power. For the *demos*, creating these responses was no small matter.

Nevertheless, the scholarship on these documents has not focused on these issues and neither the decree of Demophantos nor the extant fragments of the laws have been associated with the Athenians' response to the oligarchs. Instead, scholars have concentrated on other matters. The decree of Demophantos is regularly cited in discussions of the politics of late fifth-century Athens, in part because it provides our first evidence that the full democracy was back in power.[2] In such contexts, the decree is

---

[1] I have briefly discussed these issues in Shear 2007a: 91–101. The multiple uses of the Agora included activities connected with democracy, but also many other things. The multi-purpose form of the fifth-century stoas emphasised the different ways in which the space could be used.
[2] See e.g. Plescia 1970: 78; Ostwald 1986: 414, 418; Munn 2000: 159–60; Ober 2003: 223; Raaflaub 2003: 70; cf. Ostwald 1955: 112–14. For obvious reasons, Shear 2007b is an exception to this trend and discusses the construction of Athenian identity in the decree.

understood pragmatically as 'intended to ensure that the democracy was not overthrown again' and it has also been examined in the context of the development of the Athenian legal system.[3] Since the Athenians undertook a major reorganisation of their lawcode after 411, the laws have naturally featured in that discussion; scholars have concentrated extensively on the political and practical aspects of the process and on the need to establish with certainty what the laws actually were.[4] The laws have also recently been considered in the context of writing law and writing more generally.[5] Discussion has further focused on the extant inscribed remains of the laws: Drakon's law on homicide, laws concerning the *boule*, the trierarchic law, another fragmentary law and the sacrificial calendar fragments.[6] Since Sterling Dow's seminal work on the trierarchic law and the calendar fragments, scholars have been content to repeat his observations, sometimes without autopsy, and without consideration of the new interpretations required by the discovery of the Stoa Basileios in 1970.[7] In fact, re-examining the extant inscriptions in light of the stoa's preserved remains requires serious rethinking about the inscribed laws' setting and display. Consideration of minute details dear to epigraphical and archaeological hearts shows that the laws' history as monument is considerably more complicated and more important than has been previously recognised. Inscribed on huge marble *stelai*, the laws were displayed prominently in purpose-built annexes of the Stoa Basileios, as well as in front of the building. In the northwest corner of the Agora, they emphasised democracy's control of the area and they served as physical reminders of its proper functioning.

DATES, LAWS AND BEGINNING A RESPONSE

The documents and the processes which generated them can be dated with some precision and this material testifies to the speed with which the Athenians began responding to oligarchy. Our earliest evidence is provided by the decree of Demophantos which specifies what Athenians should do if the democracy were overthrown in the future and is quoted, perhaps in

---

[3] Overthrow of democracy: MacDowell 1962: 135. Legal system: Ostwald 1955; Carawan 1993: 312–19.
[4] See e.g. P. J. Rhodes 1991; Robertson 1990; Dow 1953–7; Dow 1960; Sickinger 1999b: 93–113; Todd 1996; Ostwald 1986: 409–11.
[5] Gagarin 2008: 183–8; Pébarthe 2006: 129–46.
[6] *IG* i³ 104, 105, 236 (= *SEG* LII 48 fr. 3B), 237. For the texts of the calendar, see Lambert 2002a = *SEG* LII 48. The fragments are cited by his numeration system.
[7] Dow 1961 and Lambert 2002a are critical for the fragments; see also e.g. Dow 1941; Fingarette 1971; Clinton 1982. Without autopsy or the archaeological evidence: e.g. P. J. Rhodes 1991; Robertson 1990. For Drakon's law on homicide, see importantly Stroud 1968.

its entirety, by Andokides in his speech on the Mysteries.[8] The prescript indicates that the document was passed by the *boule* and the *demos* when the tribe Aiantis was in prytany, when Kleigenes was first secretary and when Boethos was *epistates*. Comparison with the accounts of the loans of Athena Polias and Nike from 410/9, the archonship of Glaukippos, indicates that Kleigenes of Halai was first secretary and that Aiantis held the first prytany.[9] Demophantos' decree, therefore, belongs to the first prytany of this year, i.e. to the beginning of the Athenian official year.[10] In order for these various officials to have been democratically elected, the democrats must have come back to power before the end of the previous archon year. Like the decree of Demophantos, the reinscribed version of Drakon's law on homicide is also firmly dated by prescript, in this case of the authorising decree.[11] It shows that the reinscription was authorised by the *boule* and the *demos* when Diognetos of Phrearrhioi was secretary and when Diokles was archon, hence in 409/8; although the tribe in prytany is specified as Akamantis, we do not have enough information to know when in the official year the document was passed. We should also note the decree's specification that the *anagrapheis* or 'recorders' of the laws (οἱ ἀναγραφēς τōν νόμον) are to publish Drakon's law on homicide on a stone, i.e. marble, *stele*.[12] No further details are given about this board and its identity is evidently intended to be known by the readers of the document.

Further evidence for dating the reorganisation of the laws and for the *anagrapheis* of the laws is provided by Lysias 30, a speech written against a certain Nikomachos, one of the participants in the project. In the opening paragraphs, the speaker states that Nikomachos was an *anagrapheus* of the laws (ἀναγραφεὺς τῶν νόμων), the same term used in the authorising decree of Drakon's law; despite later references to him as a *hupogrammateus* (undersecretary), his correct title seems to have been *anagrapheus* of the laws and he must have been one member of a board of ten.[13] He was instructed 'to write up' (ἀναγράψαι) the laws of Solon during a four-month term, but the process actually took six years.[14] He did not give

<hr />

[8] Andok. 1.96–8.   [9] *IG* i³ 375.1–3.
[10] On the absence of Glaukippos' name from the preamble, see Shear 2007b: 252 note 13.
[11] *IG* i³ 104.1–9; the prescript occupies lines 1–4.   [12] *IG* i³ 104.4–6, 7.
[13] Two boards of *anagrapheis* the same: Robertson 1990: 52–3; P. J. Rhodes 1991: 88–9; Stroud 1968: 20; Ostwald 1986: 416–17; Clinton 1982: 30; Dow 1953–7: 7–8; cf. Dow 1960: 279; uncertainty: Todd 1996: 106. Correct title: Lys. 30.2 and cf. 4, 17, etc.; Todd 1996: 104; Robertson 1990: 52 with note 26; Dow 1960: 271; Stroud 1968: 20; Ostwald 1986: 416, 511–12; Harrison 1955: 29–30; contra: Hansen 1990: 68–9; Munn 2000: 207, 221, 274–7. *Hupogrammateus*: Lys. 30.27, 28, 29. In the title of the speech, he is called a *grammateus* or secretary.
[14] Lys. 30.2.

up his office and undergo his *euthuna* until the city 'was reduced to the greatest disasters' (τὰς μεγίστας συμφοράς), Lysias' standard euphemism for the events at the end of the war: the great defeat at Aigospotamoi in the summer of 405, the siege of the city during the winter of 405/4 and the surrender to the Spartans in the spring of 404.[15] This evidence suggests that Nikomachos was appointed soon after the democrats regained power in 410 and continued to hold office until sometime in the year 405/4.[16] Later in the speech, Lysias implies that Nikomachos was still in office at the time of the democratic politician Kleophon's trial in the winter of 405/4.[17] If this inference is correct, and we have no independent evidence to support it, then the *anagrapheis* were still at work during this winter. That Nikomachos did, indeed, undergo an *euthuna* should indicate that he laid down his office while the city was still democratic and before the Thirty gained power.[18] Since the decree of Demophantos shows that the *demos* was already beginning to respond publicly to the oligarchs at the beginning of 410/9, it is very likely that Nikomachos was appointed earlier rather than later in this year; his term may have finished at the end of 405/4. We shall consider his subsequent term of office, which lasted for four years and must belong after the return of the democrats in Boedromion of 403, in greater detail in connection with the democratic responses to the Thirty.[19]

For the *demos'* reactions to the oligarchs of 411, our collective evidence shows that the process began as early as the first prytany of 410/9 and continued into 405/4. Since two of the relevant documents were approved by the *boule* and the *demos*, they must have been widely supported by the Athenians from all parts of the political spectrum. For us, they emphasise that this programme of responses could not have occurred without the authorisation of the *boule* and the *demos*. Of course, we should not imagine that the relevant decrees were passed unanimously or without

---

[15] Lys. 30.3. On the expression, see Todd 1996: 102–3; Todd 2007: 468.

[16] Todd 1996: 103, 109; P. J. Rhodes 1991: 88–9; Robertson 1990: 53 note 29; cf. Dow 1960: 271; contra: Ostwald 1986: 407–10, 416.

[17] Lys. 30.10–14.

[18] MacDowell 1962: 197; Todd 1996: 109; Clinton 1982: 28, 30. Lysias' text does not support Rhodes' belief that Nikomachos never underwent an *euthuna* after his first term in office; P. J. Rhodes 1991: 89.

[19] Lys. 30.4; Todd 1996: 103. Nikomachos cannot have been appointed by the Thirty because, as Todd notes, Lysias would certainly have used this detail against him. The speaker admits that Nikomachos was in exile under the Thirty, although they are not specifically mentioned; Nikomachos' second term must belong to a time when he was in Athens; Lys. 30.15–16. For further discussion, see below chapter 8.

discussion, which may well have been heated, as comparison with modern memorial projects and responses to past events indicates.[20]

THE DOCUMENTS AND THEIR CONTENTS

For us, the importance of the decree of Demophantos and the fragments of the laws lies not only in their existence and the process which they indirectly record, but also in the concerns and specifications of their texts which show us some of the dynamics of making Athens and her past democratic again. Democracy is very explicitly the concern of Demophantos' decree and its accompanying oath.[21] After the details of the prescript, the text specifies that anyone who overthrows the democracy or holds office after the democracy has been overthrown is to be a public enemy (*polemios*) of the Athenians and may be killed with impunity.[22] His property is to be confiscated with a tenth given to the goddess and his killer and any accomplices are to be pure and free from pollution (εὐαγής). The Athenians, organised by tribe and by deme, are to swear to kill such a man and the oath is provided in the text of the decree. The oath adds further details: the individuals proscribed include not only the man overthrowing the democracy or holding office after it has been overthrown, but also the man setting himself up as a tyrant or helping to set up a tyrant. If anyone dies while trying to kill such a man, both he and his sons will receive the Tyrannicides' benefits.[23] The document concludes by repeating the specifications for swearing (all the Athenians before the Dionysia) and adds that the Athenians are to pray for many good things for the man keeping his oath and destruction for anyone breaking it and for his *genos*. Both the text and tone of this decree are strikingly uncompromising and it sets up a stern model for the Athenians: they are all now to become the slayers of tyrants.

The dossier of the laws is far more heterogeneous and the extant inscriptions concern a variety of subjects, many more complex than Demophantos' decree. The best preserved of this group is the *stele* bearing the republication of Drakon's law on homicide.[24] After the dating preamble of the

---

[20] Above chapter 1.   [21] Above note 8.

[22] On killing with impunity, see Velissaropoulos-Karakostas 1991 and Carawan 1991.

[23] Harmodios and Aristogeiton received bronze statues in the Agora and a cult; on the cult, see M. W. Taylor 1991: 5–9; Parker 1996: 123, 136–7. Their descendants received *sitesis, proedria* and *ateleia*; Isai. 5.47; Dem. 20.18, 127–30; *IG* I³ 131.1–9; Shear 2007b: 152, 252–3 notes 23–4 with further references.

[24] *IG* I³ 104. I remain unconvinced by Gallia's attempts to separate this document from the project of republishing the laws of Athens; Gallia 2004: 455–6, 459–60.

decree authorising the publication of the following document, the text specifies that the *anagrapheis* of the laws (οἱ ἀναγραφῆς τῶν νόμον) are to publish Drakon's law on homicide on a stone, i.e. marble, *stele* after they have received it from the *basileus*, with the secretary of the *boule*, and they are to set it up in front of the Stoa Basileios; payment for the project is also specified.[25] The next line reads 'first *axon*' and the text of Drakon's law, as it was inscribed, begins in the following line.[26] Inscribed in slightly larger and more widely spaced letters, this line serves as a heading, as well as providing the specific source of the following text (fig. 5).[27] Indented some twelve letter spaces, the text proper begins in the next line with the words 'even if' or possibly 'and if' (καὶ ἐάμ) and Drakon's law on involuntary homicide follows. Whether this phrase marks the original beginning of the law is a notorious problem on which there is no scholarly consensus, but, for our purposes, this issue is not particularly important.[28] More significant is the text at line 56, a second heading with the words 'second *axon*', [δεύτ]ερος [ἄχσον]; although fragmentary, enough is preserved to indicate that this heading was treated exactly like the heading in line 10.[29] In line 57, the text of the law, probably indented as it was in line 11, continued.[30] Shortly thereafter, the extremely fragmentary text breaks off, but the extant bottom was created when the *stele* was cut down for secondary reuse.[31] Originally, the text will have continued and the free-standing *stele* was presumably set into the socket of its stone base, the regular means of setting up an Attic inscription. Significant amounts of the text are now lost, but it is not clear what it covered.

A second similar *stele* bears texts of laws pertaining to the powers of the *boule*, but the very fragmentary remains preserve no traces of any decree authorising the publication of the documents.[32] Part of the text concerns the oath of the *bouleutai* and it is followed by a text introduced with the

[25] *IG* I³ 104.1–9.   [26] *IG* I³ 104.10–11.

[27] The letters are about 0.002 m. higher than those of the rest of the text and the eleven letters are spread out over twelve letter spaces; Stroud 1968: 4, 9, fig. 1.

[28] For καὶ ἐάμ as the beginning, see e.g. Stroud 1968: 34–40, 60–4; Gagarin 1981: 65–110 and Sickinger 1999b: 16–23, all with discussion of opposing views; Carawan 1998: 34–8, 80; cf. Humphreys 1991: 20; against this phrase as the beginning, see e.g. P. J. Rhodes 1991: 91; Robertson 1990: 55; Wallace 1985: 16–18; Sealey 1983: 290–4; Figueira 1993: 291–5. The architecture and language of the inscription as marshalled by Stroud and Gagarin indicate to me that the whole text of the first *axon* was inscribed and, therefore, the first words of line 11 represent the beginning of the law.

[29] *IG* I³ 104.56–7; Stroud 1968: 16–18, fig. 1.

[30] Line 57 indented: cf. Lewis' text in *IG* I³; Stroud 1968: 6, 18.   [31] Stroud 1968: 4, pl. 3.

[32] *IG* I³ 105. Similar appearance to Drakon's law: e.g. Lewis in *IG* I³; Lewis 1967: 132; Ostwald 1986: 31–2; Wade-Gery 1932–3: 113; Ferguson 1936: 148 note 19; Natalicchio 1990: 66; Robertson 1990: 58; Gagarin 2008: 94 note 4.

Figure 5   *IG* ɪ³ 104: the reinscription of the homicide law of Drakon (EM 6602).

phrase 'the following was decreed by the *d[emos* of the A]the[ni]ans in the Lykeion'.[33] The provisions of this decree are not entirely clear, but it concerns actions which cannot be taken without the approval of 'the full

---

[33] Oath: *IG* ɪ³ 105.23–34; decree: *IG* ɪ³ 105.34 ff.   It is not quite clear to me where the decree ends and whether the financial matters of lines 44–51 are part of it.

demos of the Athenians' (ὁ δῆμος ὁ Ἀθηναίων πληθύων); they certainly include making war and peace, imposing the death penalty and levying a fine on an Athenian.[34] At line 43, the text is broken by three interpuncts which may indicate that the original text was illegible at this point.[35] There are repeated references to the *demos* of the Athenians and especially to the archaic phrase 'the full *demos* of the Athenians'; also mentioned are the *boule*, the Bouleuterion, the *ekklesia* and the *prutaneis*.[36] Context shows that two additional references to the 500 pertain to the council of 500.[37] If lines 7–10 have been correctly restored on the basis of a passage in Demosthenes' speech against Timokrates, they prohibited the imposition of a fine on any Athenian offering three sureties unless he betrays the city, overthrows the *demos*, or defaults on taxes or on sureties. We are evidently dealing with documents of various periods which have been brought together and inscribed to form our extant text.[38]

Two fragments recording laws of the city should be associated with these documents. Represented by part of the right side of an opisthographic (i.e. inscribed on both sides) *stele*, the first preserves the fragmentary text of a naval law concerning hanging and wooden equipment of *triereis* (warships) and the obligations of out-going *trierarchoi* to their successors; a *dikasterion* is also specifically mentioned.[39] On its reverse, the stone preserves part of a sacrificial calendar inscribed in Ionic letters, a document which has generally been associated with the second term of Nikomachos and his colleagues.[40] Since the text on the naval law was inscribed using Attic letters, it has been universally associated with the *anagrapheis*' first term of office between 410/9 and 405/4 and before the Ionic alphabet was officially introduced in the archonship of Eukleides in 403/2.[41] The second fragment preserves part of the left side of a *stele* and the lacunose text mentions various payments, including rents, and several kinds of farm products including

---

[34] *IG* i³ 105.34–5, 36, 40–1; P. J. Rhodes 1972a: 183–4, 196–7. For helpful discussion of the 'full *demos* of the Athenians', see P. J. Rhodes 1972a: 197–8.

[35] Lewis 1967: 132; Robertson 1990: 57 with note 43; Sickinger 1999b: 214 note 96.

[36] *Demos*: *IG* i³ 105.17, 18, 34 and 9 (restored on the basis of Dem. 24.144); full *demos*: *IG* i³ 105.25, 35, 36, 37, 40–1; 42, 43, 45–6; *boule*: *IG* i³ 105.27, 33, 40, 47, 52, 56–7; Bouleuterion: *IG* i³ 105.33; *ekklesia*: *IG* i³ 105.27, 53, 54; *prutaneis*: *IG* i³ 105.49, 59.

[37] *IG* i³ 105.30, 45.   [38] Compare P. J. Rhodes 1972a: 198; Ryan 1994: 121; Ostwald 1986: 31–2.

[39] *IG* i³ 236 = *SEG* lii 48 fr. 3B.

[40] *SEG* lii 48 fr. 3A. For the association of the Ionic sacrificial calendar with the second term of the *anagrapheis*, see Lambert 2002a: 355; P. J. Rhodes 1991: 93–5; MacDowell 1962: 198–9; Sickinger 1999b: 103; Dow 1960: 278–9; Dow 1953–7: 8; and the further discussion below chapter 8.

[41] Lambert 2002a: 355; P. J. Rhodes 1991: 89–90; Robertson 1990: 56–8; Sickinger 1999b: 103; J. H. Oliver 1935: 7–9, 15; Dow 1960: 278; Dow 1953–7: 8. Introduction of the Ionic alphabet: Theopomp. *FGrHist* 115 f155, cf. f154; Douris *FGrHist* 76 f66; D'Angour 1999.

grape must and honey.[42] Also extant are references to types of settlements overseas (ἀποικίαις καὶ κλεροχία[ις]), to the second prytany, to the *boule* and the sovereign or principal *ekklesia*; it is perhaps part of a law about taxes.[43] Lewis identified the mason who inscribed this *stele* as the same man who produced the earlier side of one fragment of the sacrificial calendar; this observation, together with the content and appearance, suggested to him that this inscription was part of the work produced by the *anagrapheis* during their first term.[44]

The project of reorganising the laws is represented by a further group of fragments which record parts of a sacrificial calendar in Attic script (table 6: frs. 1, 4, 5, 8–13; fig. 6).[45] Like the *stele* with the trierarchic law, five of these stones are opisthographic and preserve a sacrificial calendar inscribed in Ionic on their second side (table 6: frs. 1, 5, 8, 9, 12; fig. 6).[46] The similarities with the trierarchic law confirm the association of the fragments with the reorganisation of the laws. The texts preserve a series of entries with the relevant information: the name of the deity or hero, the animal to be sacrificed, any extras and any payment to the officials involved. The names of the festivals are not listed, but, in one case, the date on which the offerings are to be made is specified. When it was originally inscribed, the entire text would have laid out with great clarity exactly what the Athenians were to sacrifice to which deity or hero on what occasion. Collectively, the epigraphical evidence suggests that the project of reorganising the laws included both secular documents like Drakon's law, the laws about the *boule*, the trierarchic law and the text about taxes and sacred laws now represented by the calendar fragments. On any reckoning, we must have only a very small fraction of the material involved.

THE *ANAGRAPHEIS* AND THE LAW

Further information about the project is provided by Lysias' speech against Nikomachos. As we saw earlier, Nikomachos was one member of the board of *anagrapheis* who were to write up the laws of Solon. Lysias accuses Nikomachos of having made himself into a *nomothetes* (lawgiver) and having inscribed some laws while erasing others, a nefarious activity done

[42] *IG* i³ 237.   [43] So P. J. Rhodes 1991: 90 and, with more confidence, Robertson 1990: 57.
[44] Lewis on *IG* i³ 237, 237*bis* (= *SEG* LII 48 fr. 13B).
[45] For the texts, see Lambert 2002a: 365–7, 394–5 = *SEG* LII 48. One fragment assigned by Dow (his fr. K = *IG* i³ 240K) has been disassociated from the group by Lambert who identifies it most probably as part of *IG* i³ 1185; Lambert 2002b; Dow 1961: 68–9; Dow 1941: 34, fragment D.
[46] Fragment 4 is also opisthographic, but the preserved section was not inscribed.

Table 6 *The preserved fragments of the Sacrificial Calendar* (SEG LII 48)

Lambert fr. number[a]	Dow fr. letter[b]	Location Found	Faces preserved	Thickness	Group	Surface treatment	Text inscribed	Anathyrosis (side A up)	Top
Fr. 1	Fr. A	Akropolis S. slope (EM 8001 only)	A, B	0.119 m.	A	A: smoothed, polished / B: smoothed, polished	A: stoich / B: stoich	left, 1 band	
Fr. 2	Fr. E	Agora: S. side (M 16)[c]	A	0.144 m. (as preserved)	A	A: *in erasure*, worn; no traces of claw-toothed chisel*	A: stoich	right, 1 band	part of cutting for clamp
Fr. 3	Fr. C	Agora: SW corner, over drain (I 12)	A, B	0.119–0.120 m.	A	A: *in erasure*, smoothed, polished / B: worn; no traces of claw-toothed chisel*	A: stoich / B: stoich (= *IG* I³ 236)	left, 2 bands	cutting for clamp
Fr. 4[d]		Agora: NW corner, section BΓ	A, B	0.1195 m.	A	A: smoothed, polished / B: smoothed, polished	A: not inscribed / B: stoich		
Fr. 5[e]		Agora: NW corner (I 4)	A, B	0.115 m.	A	A: worn* / B: smoothed, polished	A: non stoich / B: stoich	right, 2 bands	
Fr. 6	Fr. B	Akropolis NW slope	A	not pres.	A	A: worn	A: stoich		
Fr. 7	Fr. D	Agora	A	not pres.	A	(now lost)	A: stoich		

								right, 1 band
Fr. 8	Fr. G	Agora: SW corner (H 12–13)	A, B	0.095 m.	B	A: worn* B: worn	A: non stoich B: numerals only	
Fr. 9	Fr. J	Agora: SW corner (I 12, I 11, H–I 11)	A, B	0.092–0.093 m.	B	A: smoothed, polished B: claw-toothed chisel	A: non stoich B: non stoich	
Fr. 10	Fr. H	Agora: SW corner (H 12)	B	not pres.	B	B: smoothed, polished	B: non stoich	
Fr. 11	Fr. I	Agora: SW corner (I 11)	B	not pres.	B	B: smoothed**	B: non stoich	
Fr. 12	Fr. F	not known	A, B	not known	A or B	(now lost)	not known	
Fr. 13		Agora: NW corner (E 3)	B	not pres.	A?	(now lost)	B: stoich?	

Notes: Side A = the later side inscribed in Ionic letters and dated to 403–399 BC

Side B = the earlier side inscribed in Attic letters and dated to 410–404 BC

    * preserved surface consistent with smoothing and polishing

   ** preserved surface consistent with polishing

^a Lambert 2002a = *SEG* LII 48.

^b Dow 1961.

^c The Agora grid co-ordinate was accidentally given as M 1 by Lambert 2002a: 358.

^d Partially published: Clinton 1994: 18–21.

^e Published: Gawlinski 2007.

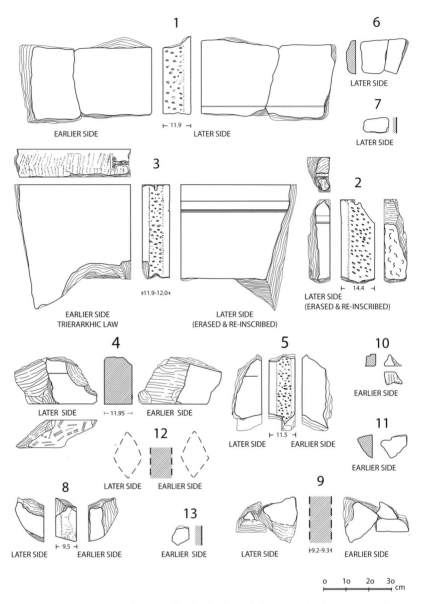

Figure 6   Fragments of the sacrificial calendar and the trierarchic law (*IG* I³ 236).

while he received daily payment; as Todd notes, while this phrase implies that Nikomachos was accepting bribes in return for changing the laws, it may mean only that he was paid on a daily basis for his maintenance and/or his work.[47] The laws, says Lysias, were being dispensed from Nikomachos' hands and parties in lawsuits brought into court contradictory laws which they had received from him.[48] Nikomachos is alleged to have produced a law on request at the time of Kleophon's trial in the winter of 405/4.[49] Lysias also states that, when the archons imposed fines and brought matters into court, Nikomachos refused to hand over the laws, and, we must understand, impeded their work.[50] Later in the speech, Nikomachos is described generally and without reference to a specific term of office as an *anagrapheus* of both secular and sacred matters (καὶ τῶν ὁσίων καὶ τῶν ἱερῶν).[51] These various statements indicate that the *anagrapheis'* project took a long time, hence the six years in which they were active. That they produced contradictory laws suggests that the laws of Solon were not gathered together in one place, but scattered about the city; part of their mandate must have been to collect this material. The charge that Nikomachos erased some laws and added others should indicate that not all the material which the *anagrapheis* amassed was included; laws which had been rendered obsolete by subsequent legislation did not need to be included and others may have needed to be amended in light of later documents. If this inference is correct, it is easy to see how a hostile speaker could describe this process as inscribing some laws and erasing others. The prescription that the board 'write up' (ἀναγράψαι) the laws of Solon naturally suggests that they published their work in a form which could be consulted by whoever wished to do so.[52]

The epigraphical evidence fits with the information in Lysias' speech. It is compatible with the statement that the *anagrapheis* were involved with writing up both sacred and profane legislation. The inscriptions also contain information which cannot have been drafted by Solon himself: the naval law is recent enough to include references to *trierarchoi* and a *dikasterion*.[53] The

---

[47] Lys. 30.2; Todd 1996: 109.   [48] Lys. 30.3.   [49] Lys. 30.10–13.
[50] Lys. 30.3. On the interpretation of this passage, see Todd 1996: 109 with note 16 and Robertson 1990: 54 note 36.
[51] Lys. 30.25. Compare at the end of this section, οὗτοι δ᾽ ἐπὶ τῇ τῶν νόμων ἀναγραφῇ [καὶ τῶν ἱερῶν] δῶρα λαμβάνοντες, 'they (Nikomachos and his colleagues) took bribes for the writing up of the laws [and the sacrifices]'. In light of the earlier passage, it is not clear that Franken was correct to delete the words καὶ τῶν ἱερῶν; Hansen 1990: 69–70. On the terms ὅσια and ἱερά, see the helpful comments of Connor 1988.
[52] Todd 1996: 108; P. J. Rhodes 1991: 91–3; contra: Robertson 1990: 53–5, 58.
[53] P. J. Rhodes 1991: 90.

laws about the *boule* seem to incorporate documents from different periods, hence the references to both the *demos* and the full *demos*.[54] Furthermore, the law on homicide is explicitly identified as Drakon's and not as Solon's. The epigraphical remains suggest, accordingly, that, at this moment, the phrase 'laws of Solon' meant, not the legislation passed by the man himself, but the laws currently in force in the city, a usage attested in the fourth century.[55] That the *anagrapheis* were involved with collecting and organising the legislation in use at the time would also explain how Nikomachos could provide contradictory laws to both sides of a lawsuit or produce a law on request for Kleophon's trial and how he was able to impede the archons' abilities to impose fines and bring matters to court. Similarly, the need to remove contradictions between legislation passed at different times would explain Lysias' charge that Nikomachos had erased some laws and inserted others. This project was evidently a very complicated and ambitious undertaking, hence the six years which it took. It also seems to have evolved and changed as it progressed. Such a situation would explain why Drakon's law has its own authorising decree and it certainly explains why the inscribed fragments differ in appearance, an issue to which we shall return shortly.

Given the current state of our evidence, it is impossible to determine how much of the material produced by the *anagrapheis* was actually inscribed on stone.[56] Before any document was inscribed, a copy on perishable materials had to be prepared and the mason worked from such a copy. As James Sickinger has shown, this version, written on either papyrus or a wooden tablet, was an official copy and such documents were preserved at least as early as the 460s.[57] These documents, he stresses, were saved by the relevant officials and they constituted an official record regardless of whether the texts were inscribed on stone. In 410/9, such documents were kept in various collections located in the same place as the official under whose direction they were produced. The laws, accordingly, were scattered in different places around the city and one of the tasks of the *anagrapheis*

---

[54] Compare Ryan 1994: 121; Hignett 1952: 153–4. That line 43 seems to have been copied from a damaged original text does not require the entire inscription to have been taken from the same source despite Lewis' comments; Lewis 1967: 132.

[55] P. J. Rhodes 1991: 89–93; Robertson 1990: 54–5; Sickinger 1999b: 98, 227 note 20; cf. Hansen 1990: 65–8; Ostwald 1986: 416–17; contra: Clinton 1982: 29–30, 37; J. H. Oliver 1935: 7.

[56] For various views on how much was published, see e.g. Sickinger 1999b: 102–4; P. J. Rhodes 1991: 90–1, 100; Fingarette 1971: 333–5; Ferguson 1936: 146–7; Robertson 1990: 56–60; Clinton 1982: 30–3, 37; Hansen 1991: 162–3.

[57] Sickinger 1999b: 62–92. Some documents seem to have been saved already in the sixth century; Sickinger 1999b: 35–61.

must have been to collect them together.[58] Their work also resulted in a single collection of the city's legislation in one place, hence the creation at this time of the city's first central archive.[59] Once these documents were collected together and organised, they were available for consultation by individuals. Inscribing the laws on *stelai* was not primarily about access, but about issues related to their place of erection, the recreation of the democratic city and (re)appropriation of the city's past for the *demos*.

STELAI AND THE PRESENTATION OF THE LAWS

Our discussion so far has focused on the dates and the contents of Demophantos' decree and the documents collected by the *anagrapheis*, the aspects most of interest to modern scholars. In late fifth-century Athens, however, these texts had a physical presence in the city both as visible monuments and as documents erected in a particular location. If we are to understand the ways in which these inscriptions fitted into their settings and the ways in which the *demos* used them to remake the democratic city and reclaim the past, then we must understand how they would have appeared physically. In the case of the sacrificial calendar, the evidence for its appearance provides important clues for both the appearance of the inscriptions as individual free-standing *stelai* and their setting. Neglecting these details has led scholars to misunderstand in important ways the setting of these documents.

Several of these documents were clearly free-standing *stelai* of the type which we usually associate with Attic inscriptions. Demophantos' decree is described by Andokides, Demosthenes and Lykourgos as a *stele*;[60] since the text was not especially long, we may imagine that it was not inscribed on both sides. The preserved remains of Drakon's law show that it, too, was inscribed on one side of a marble *stele*, while the back is roughly worked except for the fine decorative band along the edges of the block (fig. 5).[61] Now cut down, it must originally have been at least 1.70 m. tall and its height might have been as much as *c.* 2.30 m.[62] The laws about the *boule*

---

[58] Sickinger 1999b: 95–9. On the scattered nature of the city's laws and decrees, see also Ostwald 1986: 410 and Todd 1996: 123–4; cf. Boegehold 1972: 29 with further references. On the basis of the Thirty's destruction of the laws of Archestratos and Ephialtes (and similar examples), Todd believes that only inscribed documents were official; Arist. *Ath. Pol.* 35.2. That whole classes of Athenian documents are absent from the epigraphical record but are otherwise indirectly attested should be food for thought; see further Sickinger 1999b: 4–5, 66–74, 79–80, 91–2; cf. R. Osborne 1999: 342.

[59] Sickinger 1999b: 102–13. For further discussion of the contents of this archive, see Sickinger 1999b: 114–38.

[60] Andok. 1.95–6; Dem. 20.159; Lykourg. *Leok.* 124, 126.   [61] Stroud 1968: 3, pl. 2.

[62] Stroud 1968: 58–9.

were also inscribed on a *stele* of similar width. Since, in its later life, this inscription was re-used for a threshold and its reverse side is heavily worn by foot traffic, we do not know if it was opisthographic or not. Like Drakon's law, it was also 0.725 m. wide, but it was not quite as thick, 0.113 m. rather than 0.135 m.; now broken at both the top and bottom, the *stele* about the *boule* may also have been similar in height to Drakon's law. Originally, the inscribed surface was carefully smoothed. The fragment with the text about taxes preserves the left edge of a *stele*, but no other part; consequently, we do not know if this stone was opisthographic or not. It will, however, have been free-standing and its surface was carefully smoothed. As this evidence indicates, these extant documents represent four different *stelai*, at least two of which were substantial monuments.

The appearance of the naval law and the calendar fragments requires rather more discussion because the preserved remains indicate that the scholarly *opinio communis*, that they formed three 'walls' or '*stele*-series', is incorrect for the period 410/9–405/4.[63] Instead, our evidence shows that these texts were inscribed on free-standing *stelai*, as we would normally expect an Athenian inscription to be, and it was only between 403 and 399 that the *stelai* were joined together. In discussing contents of the trierarchic law, we saw that the inscription was opisthographic with the law in Attic letters on one side and a sacrificial calendar in Ionic letters on the other (table 6: fr. 3). This Ionic calendar is represented by eight other fragments (table 6: frs. 1, 2, 5–9, 12); of them, five stones bear on the reverse the calendar in Attic script, the text of which we discussed earlier (table 6: frs. 1, 5, 8, 9, 12; fig. 6). The Attic calendar allows these fragments to be associated with four others preserving only this document (table 6: frs. 4, 10, 11, 13; fig. 6); of these stones, only fragment 4 preserves its back, a beautifully smoothed and polished surface which was never inscribed, while the backs of the other three are broken away. Fragment 3 preserves further important evidence because the later Ionic calendar was cut in an erasure which runs from the bottom of the decorative fascia or horizontal band to the bottom of the stone (fig. 6).[64] Since the trierarchic law begins right at the top of the other side of the fragment, there is no space for a decorative fascia and, consequently, as Dow observed, the face now bearing the later calendar must always have been the principal face of this block, regardless of what text was inscribed on it, hence Lambert's designation of

---

[63] See e.g. Lambert 2002a: 355–6 with note 17; Robertson 1990: 56–7; P. J. Rhodes 1991: 89–90, 93–5; Sickinger 1999b: 103; Clinton 1982: 32–3, 35; Dow 1961: 69–73; cf. Dow 1960: 277–9; contra: Kuhn 1985: 216.

[64] Dow 1961: 63–4; Lambert 2002a: 355, 361.

the Ionic side as face A and the Attic side as face B.[65] This fascia is also extant on fragment 2, which preserves only the later side A (fig. 6). The text of fragment 2 was certainly cut in an erasure, a fact which indicates that both faces were originally inscribed because, otherwise, the later text could have been cut on the uninscribed back. Originally, then, fragments 2 and 3 were opisthographic, but the text on side A was erased in order that the later calendar could be inscribed.[66]

Five fragments preserve parts of the sides of their *stelai* and they provide further important information about their original appearance. Both fragments 1 and 3 preserve their blocks' left sides with side A (Ionic) uppermost, while fragments 2, 5 and 8 both preserve the right sides of their *stelai* with side A (Ionic) uppermost (table 6; fig. 6). In and of itself, the preservation of the sides of the stone blocks is not unusual; what is unusual is the clear anathyrosis preserved on these five sides.[67] This treatment indicates that, at some stage in their history, these *stelai* were set next to other blocks; the top surface of fragment 3 preserves a cutting for the T-clamp attaching it to its neighbour, while the top surface of fragment 2 preserves part of a similar clamp (fig. 6). Surprisingly, on fragments 1 and 8, the anathyrosis exists only on the edge adjacent to side A (Ionic) and there are no traces of anathyrosis on the other edge adjacent to side B (fig. 6).[68] On fragment 3, there is anathyrosis on both edges, but, as Dow noted, the contact band adjacent to the earlier side projects 0.002 m. less than the band next to the later side (fig. 6).[69] Consequently, the anathyrosis only functions properly with the later side and the clamp cutting also functions with this side. Fragment 5 preserves anathyrosis adjacent to both faces, but the band next to face A is considerably wider than its mate, a situation which indicates that the anathyrosis was designed to function with the later side (fig. 6).[70] Since fragment 2 only preserves face A and the back is broken away, we do not know if it originally had anathyrosis adjacent to the now destroyed face B (Attic) (fig. 6). Collectively, this evidence indicates that the anathyrosis

---

[65] Dow 1961: 71–2; J. H. Oliver 1935: 14, no. 1.

[66] Dow thought that side A of fragment 1 had also been erased, but Lambert does not so describe it; Dow 1961: 60, 71; Lambert 2002a: 361. At autopsy, it was impossible to determine if the text on this side was in an erasure.

[67] Anathyrosis is the treatment of a block's vertical joint surface. Finely worked bands are left along the edges of the side and the centre is worked down so that it does not contact the next block.

[68] Compare Dow 1961: 60–1, 68, 72–3. Lambert describes the anathyrosis of fr. 1 as 'towards the front and (damaged) towards the back'; Lambert 2002a: 361. At autopsy, I saw no traces of anathyrosis on the edge with the earlier side.

[69] Dow 1961: 64.

[70] Width of band adjacent to face A: 0.036 m.; width of band adjacent to face B: 0.020 m.; Gawlinski 2007: 38 fig. 1.

only belongs with side A. When these *stelai* were first erected at some time between 410/9 and 405/4 BC, they were free standing and were not clamped together, a development belonging to their second phase between 403 and 399 BC as we shall see in greater detail when we discuss the Athenians' response to the Thirty.[71]

That these *stelai* were not linked together in their first phase is further suggested by the disposition of the texts and the varied treatments on the surface on side B (Attic) of these stones. On the early side B, the Attic calendar in no case certainly runs across the joint on to a putative adjoining block as the Ionic text regularly does on later side A.[72] The different ways in which the surfaces of the earlier Attic side have been treated reinforce this observation (table 6). On fragment 9, the well-preserved surface of side B was certainly finished with a claw-toothed chisel because its face contains abundant traces of this tool.[73] In contrast, side B of fragments 1, 4, 5 and 10 were both smoothed and then polished. On fragment 11, the surface of side B was carefully smoothed and the remains are consistent with polishing, but the surface need not have been treated this way. The surfaces of side B on fragments 3 and 8 are worn; fragment 3 preserves no traces of a claw-toothed chisel on this side and the surface is consistent with smoothing and polishing. Since fragments 12 and 13 are now lost, we do not know how the surface of side B was treated. This variety of surface treatments reinforces the arguments that the *stelai* now represented by these inscriptions were originally free standing.

This physical information also permits an estimate of the minimum number of *stelai* represented by these inscriptions. On fragments 1, 2, 3 and 8, the anathyrosis is slightly different on each stone and each one seems to have been worked by a different mason.[74] The anathyrosis on fragment 5 also differs from that on the other four inscriptions. Accordingly, they should represent five different *stelai*. The surface of side B on fragment 4 is notable for its excellent preservation and its high-quality polish which are now not matched by any other piece; possibly it could go with fragment 1 because they both have the same thickness, text inscribed stoichedon,[75] and the same basic surface treatment (table 6: frs. 1, 4), but the different quality of their surfaces suggests that they had a different history and represent two

---

[71] See the discussion below chapter 8.

[72] The only exception may be fr. 1B.14; Lambert 2002a: 361–2, 386, 388.

[73] Dow 1961: 68. These chisel marks are clearly visible in Dow's photograph; Dow 1941: 33, no. 2.

[74] Dow 1961: 73.

[75] When a text is inscribed stoichedon, the letters are aligned both vertically and horizontally, as if centred in the middle of the squares of a grid. When a text is described as non stoichedon, the letters are only aligned horizontally in lines, but not vertically.

different slabs. As the only piece with claw-toothed chisel marks on the surface of side B, fragment 9 must represent its own *stele* to which no other fragments can belong.[76] On fragments 10 and 11, the Attic text on side B was inscribed non stoichedon and, for this reason, these two pieces cannot be associated with fragments 1, 3, 4 and 5 (table 6); they should represent yet another individual *stele*. Collectively, these fragments should represent a minimum of eight different *stelai*. If it is significant that the surfaces of fragments 10 and 11 are now slightly different (smoothed and polished vs. smoothed; table 6: frs. 10, 11), then we would have parts of at least nine different inscribed blocks preserved. Focusing on the detailed differences between the fragments obscures their overall similarity in their appearance and their character as an identifiable group would have been reinforced by their content. Very probably, they were set up in close proximity to each other. Like both the republication of Drakon's law, the documents about the *boule* and other *stelai* in the city, they were presumably set into sockets cut into the bases on which they stood.[77] As comparison of tables 6 and 7 indicates, the fragments with the sacred calendar are physically quite comparable with the other inscribed fragments of the laws with an important exception: as the erasures on the Ionic sides (A) of fragments 2 and 3 indicate, these particular *stelai* were opisthographic unlike, it appears, the other preserved inscriptions from this project.

DISPLAYING THE LAW IN THE CITY

These physical details are also important because they can help us to locate the laws in the cityscape of Athens and they complement our other evidence for their setting. As we shall see, these documents were erected in an unprecedented location, the Agora, and they stood in an equally novel setting. Demophantos' decree is described by Andokides as the law 'which is on the *stele* in front of the Bouleuterion' and this location is confirmed by Lykourgos in 330 BC (fig. 2).[78] In 410/9, this inscription was set up somewhere in front of the (Old) Bouleuterion; it may have stood

---

[76] For this reason, fragments 9, 10 and 11 cannot be part of the same slab as suggested by Dow; Dow 1961: 73.

[77] Dow identified the extant bottom of fr. 10 as original; Dow 1961: 68–9. Fr. 4 also preserves an identical treatment, but these remains are incompatible with free-standing *stelai*. As we shall see in chapter 8, these bottom surfaces belong to the inscriptions' second phase.

[78] Andok. 1.95: ὃς ἐν τῇ στήλῃ ἔμπροσθέν ἐστι τοῦ βουλευτηρίου. Lykourgos described the *stele* twice: once as the *stele* ἐν τῷ βουλευτηρίῳ and once as the *stele* which they set up εἰς τὸ βουλευτήριον; Lykourg. *Leok.* 124, 126. In both cases, comparison with Andokides' statement indicates that the inscription should be 'at' rather than 'in' the building.

Table 7 *The other preserved fragments of the laws*

Text number	Description of text	Location found	Faces preserved	Thickness	Original width	Front surface treatment	Text inscribed	Back
IG i³ 104	Drakon's law	under Metropolitan Church	front, back	0.135 m.	0.725 m.	worn	stoich	roughly worked with smooth band
IG i³ 105	documents pertaining to the *boule*	Akropolis	front, back	0.113 m.	0.725 m.	smoothed	stoich	re-used as a threshold when partially cut down; now very worn from foot traffic
IG i³ 236 (= *SEG* LII 48 fr. 3B)	trierarchic law	Agora: SW corner, over drain (I 12)	front (= B), back (= A)	0.119–0.120 m.	estimated *c.* 1.095 m.	worn; no traces of claw-toothed chisel*	stoich	opisthographic: inscribed in Ionic letters with the sacrificial calendar (= *SEG* LII 48 fr. 3A); in erasure, smoothed and polished
IG i³ 237	concerns taxes (?)	Akropolis: near Erechtheion	front	not pres.	not pres.	smoothed	stoich	back is broken away

Note: * preserved surface consistent with smoothing and polishing

next to the building's entrance, but the remains' poor state of preservation precludes certainty. The placement of Drakon's law is prescribed in the authorising decree which specifies that it is to be erected in front of the Stoa Basileios, the home of the *basileus* from whom the *anagrapheis* received the text (fig. 2).[79] In contrast, none of the other fragments of the laws contain publication clauses and their original setting must be otherwise identified. For our purposes, the places in which they were found are not particularly helpful because they appeared in various locations around the ancient city and they were all discovered in secondary contexts (tables 6 and 7). Even the sizable fragment of Drakon's law travelled from the Agora to the area of the modern Metropolitan Church of Athens, a distance of about half a mile.[80]

More helpful is a decree moved by Teisamenos in 403/2 and quoted by Andokides, a document which we shall consider in more detail when we come to the period after the fall of the Thirty.[81] The text specifies that the Athenians are to use the laws of Drakon and Solon and any additional laws which are needed are to be written up by the *nomothetai* or lawgivers appointed by the *boule*. Initially, the new laws are to be written up on *sanides* or wooden boards and erected in front of the Eponymous Heroes, but, 'when the laws have been passed, let the *boule* of the Areiopagos take charge of the laws so that the magistrates may use the laws which are in force. The laws which are being ratified are to be written up on the wall, where they were written up before, for anyone who wishes to inspect'.[82] These two sentences mark the culmination of the extant decree, which establishes the approval process for new laws, and they must concern the final publication of the approved laws.[83] In introducing this decree, Andokides states that the Athenians 'decreed that all the laws be examined and then that those laws which had been examined and approved be written up in the stoa'.[84] Immediately after the decree, he continues 'so, gentlemen, the laws were examined in accordance with this decree and the ones ratified were written up in the stoa'.[85] If Andokides had invented 'the stoa', then his audience would have recognised the fabrication; this detail, consequently, is unlikely to have been his invention. Together, the speech and the decree indicate that, in 403/2, the newly ratified laws were set up in a stoa and they were

[79] *IG* i³ 104.5–8. [80] Stroud 1968: 2.
[81] Andok. 1.83–4; see further below chapter 8. [82] Andok. 1.84.
[83] Compare Sickinger's summary; Sickinger 1999b: 99–100; contra: Robertson 1990: 46–9.
[84] Andok. 1.82. I remain unconvinced by Carawan's attempt to divorce the text of Teisamenos' decree from the surrounding text of Andokides' speech; Carawan 2002.
[85] Andok. 1.85.

written up on the wall where they had been written up before, a rather opaque phrase in the context of this decree.[86]

The location of the draft laws in front of the Eponymous Heroes in the Agora suggests that 'the stoa' should be located in the marketplace, where Drakon's law had already been set up in front of the Stoa Basileios. By the last decade of the century, the market square boasted a total of four stoai: the Stoa Poikile, the Stoa Basileios, the Stoa of Zeus Eleutherios and South Stoa I (fig. 2). Of these four structures, only the Stoa Basileios has the necessary bases for *stelai* and it must be 'the stoa' which Andokides mentions.[87] These bases were installed in the last decade of the century, when this small stoa was augmented by the addition of two annexes at its northeast and southeast corners (fig. 7).[88] For our purposes, the south annexe is most helpful. As is normal in Greek architecture, the columns stood on a continuous stylobate, but unusually the intercolumniations were filled with slots for great *stelai*; the two slots on the north side and the slot between the south anta of the stoa and its first column are now preserved.[89] Since a threshold between first and second columns of the stoa provided access to the annexe, we can be certain that all of the intercolumniations of the annexe were blocked by *stelai*. As the dimensions of the slots indicate, these slabs were extremely large, particularly in their width, and, as architectural elements, they must have been equally tall (table 8). That the annexe was provided with a door indicates that the *stelai* were both tall and opisthographic because otherwise this entrance would have been unnecessary. The slightly earlier north annexe was also fitted with a base for *stelai* placed edge to edge and dowelled into the slot of a single base (fig. 7); the intended dimensions of the *stelai* have been estimated as *c.* 0.72 m. wide and *c.* 0.19 m. thick.[90] Since the details about the original phase of this wing are now obscured by later alterations and rebuildings, it provides us with less information than the south annexe.

None of our preserved fragments can originally have stood in the base of the north annexe because none of these *stelai* were erected edge to edge

---

[86] To the best of my knowledge, no one, not even Robertson, has denied that the laws were erected in a stoa, although Fingarette only places them here in the period after 403; see Robertson 1990: 58–60; Fingarette 1971: 334–5. The *opinio communis* places them in the Stoa Basileios; e.g. P. J. Rhodes 1991: 90–1; Lambert 2002a: 356; Clinton 1982: 32–3; Dow 1960: 277; J. H. Oliver 1935: 8–9; Ostwald 1986: 513 with note 60, 519; Ferguson 1936: 146–7; cf. Sickinger 1999b: 103.

[87] Contra: Robertson 1990: 59–60, 64–5.

[88] Shear, Jr 1971: 250–2, 254–5; Shear, Jr 1975: 366–8; see also the further discussion below chapter 4.

[89] Shear, Jr 1971: 251–2.

[90] Shear, Jr 1971: 251. This base is now preserved on the south side of the north annexe, but it is re-used in its present location after being recut and reduced in length. It may always have been located in this intercolumniation, but we cannot be sure. Dimensions of *stelai*: Shear, Jr 1971: 251 note 18.

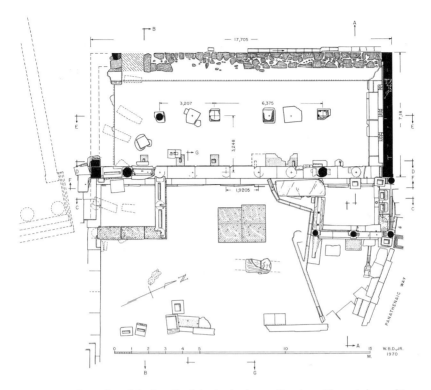

Figure 7   State plan of the Stoa Basileios in the Agora. Onesippos' herm is located in front of the first exterior column from the north, while the *lithos* is in front of the second and third exterior columns from the north.

as that base requires.[91] In the south annexe, only three of the seven original slots are preserved. The extant cuttings are not precisely cut: in the case of the western slot on the north side, the width varies 0.015 m. from end to end (table 8). The slots themselves are treated like *stelai* bases: they have not been cut with the care of architectural blocks and the inscriptions inserted into them were secured with lead. If we allow a minimum of 0.005 m. on all four sides for the lead, then fragment 2 of the sacrificial calendar can only fit in the eastern slot on the north side of the annexe (table 8).[92] Although the width of the trierarchic law (fr. 3) would allow this *stele* to fit in any of the

---

[91] Compare Kuhn 1985: 213.

[92] 0.005 m. is the minimum amount of lead used to secure the grave *stele* of Pythagoras of Selymbria (*IG* i³ 1154; *c.* 460–450) in its base in the Kerameikos. On the *stele* for the Kerkyrean envoys Thersandros and Simylos (*IG* ii² 5224), as much as 0.031 m. has been used.

Table 8   *Dimensions of the slots in the south annexe and selected* stelai

Slot	Length	Width	Maximum thickness of inscription
S. Annexe: west side, slot	0.949 m.	s. end: 0.145 m. n. end: 0.140 m.	0.138 m.
S. Annexe: north side, west slot	0.962 m.	w. end: 0.138 m. e. end: 0.153 m.	0.136 m.
S. Annexe: north side, east slot	1.042 m.	w. end: 0.187 m. e. end: 0.181 m.	0.179 m.

Inscription number	Description	Height	Width	Thickness
SEG lii 48 fr. 2	sacrificial calendar fr. 2	not pres.	not pres.	0.144 m. (as preserved)
IG i³ 236	trierarchic law and sacrificial calendar fr. 3	not pres.	est. *c.* 1.095 m.	0.119–0.120 m.
IG i³ 104	Drakon's law	0.96 m. (as preserved); min. est. *c.* 1.70 m.	0.725 m.	0.135 m.
IG i³ 105	documents pertaining to the *boule*	0.85 m. (as preserved)	0.725 m.	0.113 m.
IG i³ 84	decree concerning *hieron* of Kodros, Neleus and Basile	1.49 m. (including relief)	0.60 m.	0.19 m.
IG i³ 102	decree for Thrasyboulos of Kalydon	1.15 m.	not pres.	0.16 m.
IG i³ 127 + Rhodes and Osborne 2 (= *IG* ii² 1)	decrees for the Samians	*c.* 1.640 m. (as preserved including relief)	0.515 m. (just below relief)	0.120 m.
SEG xxviii 46	decree of Theozotides	1.53 m.	0.645–0.67 m.	0.135 m.

extant slots, the estimated minimum length of the block, 1.0914 m., is too long for these slots (table 8). It would, however, easily fit in either of the two intercolumniations on the east side or in the western intercolumniation on the south side.[93] As this exercise shows, the two opisthographic fragments 2 and 3 have dimensions suitable for the slots in the south annexe, where we should restore them standing with side B facing into the building. This annexe is also the most likely place for the erection of the small fragment apparently pertaining to taxes (*IG* I³ 237). Although it was found on the Akropolis, it is a small piece which could easily have been taken up the hill for building material.[94] Since it otherwise seems to fit with the rest of the laws, it is more likely that it was erected with them in the Agora, rather than on the Akropolis, where it would have been separated from the other laws and lost among all the other different sorts of inscriptions.

These three fragments (*IG* I³ 237 and fragments 2 and 3 of the calendar) most probably belong in the south annexe of the Stoa Basileios, where they would have stood with the other *stelai* inscribed with the city's laws. The north annexe will have held similar *stelai* also inscribed with the laws. This reconstruction further explains Teisamenos' specification that the laws 'are to be written up on the wall where they were written up before': the term 'wall' describes the screen construction created by the inscriptions and the columns in the two annexes. In 403/2, the phrase 'where they were written up before' refers to the laws inscribed by the *anagrapheis* during their first term of office[95] on the *stelai* in the intercolumniations of the stoa's two wings. The other fragments of the sacrificial calendar, however, do not belong in these annexes because they were evidently not opisthographic. Instead, these *stelai*, at least six in number, were very probably erected in the area in front of the Stoa Basileios,[96] just as Drakon's law was. The location of the inscription with the documents about the *boule* is not

---

[93] Since the text is inscribed stoichedon with *c.* 107 letters per line and the width of the stoichos is 0.0102 m., the minimum original width of the *stele* is 1.0914 m.

[94] Compare the slightly larger *IG* II² 2720, a security *horos* found on the Akropolis where it almost certainly was not originally erected; Lambert 1996: 77 note 3.

[95] So also J. H. Oliver 1935: 8; cf. Fingarette 1971: 334; see further below chapter 8.

[96] Contra: Robertson 1990: 58–60; Kuhn 1985: 215–16. Of the thirteen fragments of the calendar, ten (frs. 2–5, 7–11, 13) were found in the Agora (table 6), but only fragments 3, 4 and 5 are inscriptions of some size. Fr. 3 was found re-used to cover a section of the fork of the Great Drain in the southwest corner of square (I 12), while frs. 4 and 5 were both discovered in the northwest corner of the Agora in section BΓ (table 6). The small fr. 13 was also found in the northwest corner of the marketplace (E 3). The remaining Agora fragments are all small and their findspots not necessarily significant. Contrary to Robertson, there is no reason to locate them in South Stoa I, the floor of which does not contain the necessary beddings for *stelai*; cf. P. J. Rhodes 1991: 91 note 22. For the places of discovery of the Agora fragments, see Lambert 2002a: 358–60, but note that the Agora grid co-ordinate for fr. 2 was accidentally given as M 1 rather than M 16; for the other fragments, see J. H. Oliver 1935: 6.

specified by the extant text. The fragments were found broken up on the Akropolis, but this location would separate the *stele* from the other laws with which it otherwise fits very well. Set up in Athena's sanctuary, it would not have stood out from the many other *stelai* erected there and it would not easily have been associated with the rest of the laws in the Agora. In this location, it would also have been divorced from the council with which it was specifically concerned. For these reasons, the marketplace remains a much more likely setting for this document than the Akropolis. Here, the document can be brought into proximity with the *boule* and this association suggests that the area in front of the Bouleuterion is the most likely location for its erection.[97] If this suggestion is correct, then the *stele* may well have begun with an authorising decree similar to the one preceding Drakon's law. By 405/4, accordingly, the space of the Agora had received a whole series of new inscriptions clustered in and around the Stoa Basileios, as well as two *stelai* erected in front of the (Old) Bouleuterion (fig. 2). For the first time, single copies of inscriptions had been erected in the Agora (table 9).[98]

DEMOCRACY, THE LAW AND THE CITY

Inscribing the texts of Demophantos' decree and of the laws and setting them up in the Agora served to focus attention on this particular area of the city. It also displayed graphically the importance of democracy to the Athenians and marked out the rule of the *demos* as the proper *politeia* for the city. These actions served to recover the city's past for the *demos* and to show that the democratic city did, indeed, have a history which was neither oligarchic nor tyrannical. Collectively, these actions played an important role in remaking the city as the democratic city. They allowed the *demos* to begin to recover a part of the city which Thucydides portrays as a site of contestation between oligarchs and democrats. That process involved not only the inscribed texts, but also various new structures which we shall discuss in greater detail in the following chapter.

The emphasis on democracy appears immediately in the decree of Demophantos because this document establishes the proper behaviour for Athenians if the rule of the *demos* were to be overthrown in the future. *Demokratia* is the third word of the decree proper and it appears three more times in

---

[97] So also Robertson 1990: 58–9. Lewis without argument located the *stele* on the Akropolis; Lewis 1967: 132. It seems unlikely that this text was erected both on the Akropolis and in the Agora because none of the other related documents existed as copies and multiple copies are rare at Athens; on copies, see Liddel 2003: 85 table 1; Pébarthe 2006: 256–7.

[98] See further Shear 2007a: 97–101; Liddel 2003.

Table 9   *The distribution of Agora inscriptions before 393* BC

	In front of Bouleuterion	In front of and in Stoa Basileios	In front of Stoa of Zeus
before 430	*IG* ɪ³ 27 (+ copy on Akropolis) (*c.* 450/49)		
430–411	*IG* ɪ³ 71 (+ copy on Akropolis) (425/4)		
410–404	Demophantos' decree (Andok. 1.96–8) (410/9) probably the documents about the *boule* (*IG* ɪ³ 105) (*c.* 409)	Drakon's law (*IG* ɪ³ 104) (409/8) Laws (completed by 404)	
403–395	Honours for Athenians from Phyle (*SEG* xxvɪɪɪ 45) (403/2?) probably documents for sale of property of Thirty (*SEG* xxxɪɪ 161) (402/1)	Laws (403–399) probably Theozotides' decree (*SEG* xxvɪɪɪ 46) (403/2?)	
394/3			Honours for Konon (Dem. 20.69–70) (394/3) Honours for Euagoras (RO 11) (394/3)

the text which follows. The *demos* of the Athenians is also mentioned as are the tribes and demes, the hallmarks of the system introduced by Kleisthenes. Since the decree was approved after the full democracy returned to power, the prescript follows the normal form for a decree of the *boule* and *demos*. It also contains the added specification that the starting date for the document is the '*boule* of 500 elected by lot (τῷ κυάμῳ) for which Kleigenes is first secretary'. This detail focuses our attention on the democratically elected council and it ensures that there is no confusion about this document: it is a product of the *demos* about democracy.

The extant text of the regulations concerning the *boule* (*IG* ɪ³ 105) also focuses on the *demos* with a series of clauses which prevent the *boule* from acting without the 'full *demos* of the Athenians'. This particular section is concerned with restricting the powers of the council and it recognises the people's sovereign power for such acts as making war and peace, imposing the death penalty and levying fines on Athenians.[99] As presented here, the *boule* is very much the servant of the (full) *demos*, without which it often may not act. This text establishes the supremacy of the people and its emphasis serves to focus attention specifically on democracy and what the rule of the *demos* actually entails. This focus is reinforced by the inclusion of at least one document explicitly decreed by the Athenian people;[100] if, as seems likely, the inscription originally included a series of such documents, the repeated notation that they were decrees of the *demos* would have reinforced this emphasis on the importance of democracy, the rule of the people.

If this inscription was originally introduced by a decree authorising its publication, as Drakon's law was, then this document would further have emphasised the importance of democracy to the Athenians. These dynamics are clearly visible in Drakon's law. The authorising decree states specifically that the *stele* exists because it was approved by the *boule* and the *demos*, that is by the Athenians exercising their democratic power to decide what was best for the city. The emphasis on the democracy continues in the rest of the prescript which follows the usual formula with the tribe in prytany, the secretary, the *epistates* and the name of the man who made the motion. All these items are regular features of decrees passed by the democracy and so they also appear in Demophantos' decree. In both cases, this form emphasises that the document is the product of the *demos* and it maintains the focus on democracy. The prescripts also perform a further important function: they show that the rule of the *demos* was functioning as it should because all the officials have been selected according to proper (democratic) procedures, a situation emphasised in Demophantos' decree by the specification that the *boule* was elected by lot.

These documents do more than just focus on democracy. They also show that the rule of the people is the only proper form of *politeia* for the city. This process is particularly clear in Demophantos' decree because it proscribes both overthrowing the democracy and holding office after it has been overthrown.[101] If no office may be held after the rule of the *demos* has been dissolved, then the city cannot have any other type of *politeia*. In the more concrete terms of the oath, this situation is further elucidated by additional specifications: setting oneself up as a tyrant or helping to set up a tyrant are also proscribed. These clauses obviously apply to the Four Hundred and the situation in 411, but they are also more general: while one

---

[99] *IG* I³ 105.34–5, 36, 40–1. Restriction of *boule*'s powers: P. J. Rhodes 1972a: 183–4.
[100] *IG* I³ 105.34.   [101] See further Shear 2007b: 150–1.

man will set up a tyranny, a man holding office after the overthrow of the democracy is a member of an oligarchy which is using democratic offices to legitimate itself. Neither tyranny nor oligarchy are possible options for the city's *politeia*. In the document concerning the *boule*, both the council and the assembly are specifically mentioned and the clauses requiring the approval of the 'full *demos*' for the actions of the *bouleutai* require the two parts of the system to work together. In the immediate aftermath of 411, such co-operation contrasts with the situation under the Four Hundred which constituted itself as the city's *boule* and did not consult a larger body of the Athenians, much less anything which might be described as the (full) *demos*. In the inscription, the clauses set up a contrast between the democratic system which it authorises and all other possible *politeiai*, which, in the preserved text at least, are not even possibilities. In the other extant sections of the laws, references to the city's officials, the *boule* and the *ekklesia* reinforce this idea that democracy is the only possible form of government for the Athenians.[102] Collectively, the inscribed laws indicate the statutes now in force in the city. Since they make the current system, the democracy, possible, they also suggest that oligarchy and tyranny are not viable alternative forms for Athens' *politeia*. In the context of the years after 411, the image which these documents present as a group is emphatic: the city can only be ruled by the *demos* and experimentation with other forms is not an alternative which may be countenanced.

These inscribed documents have a further important role to play in remaking the democratic city because they actively display that democracy in a permanent and monumental form, namely the inscribed marble *stele*. In this inscribed form, the documents also serve as permanent witnesses and memorials of the democratic process, activities which would otherwise not be visible except when the *ekklesia* and the *boule* were meeting on the Pnyx and in the Bouleuterion respectively. The opening prescripts of Demophantos' decree and the decree authorising the republication of Drakon's law show some of the ways in which this process works. They make it clear that these documents exist because the actions of the *boule*, the *demos* and the officials of the democratic city created them. In the case of Drakon's law, other officials, the *basileus*, the *poletai* and the *hellenotamiai*, needed to act so that this document as it was inscribed could be brought into existence and made visible in the city. The *stelai* are the visible effects of these activities and they put the process itself on display in this monumental form. With Drakon's law, in case the inattentive reader failed to focus

---

[102] Officials: *IG* i³ 104.5–9; 236.5–6, 9; *boule*: *IG* i³ 104.7; 236.38, 41; 237.13; *ekklesia*: *IG* i³ 237.13.

on this display, the names of the secretary of the *boule*, Diognetos of Phrearrhioi, and the archon, Diokles, were written in larger letters above the first full line of text (fig. 5).[103] Since the secretary is mentioned in the prescript, as we would expect, the first two lines are as much about display as they are about dating and authorising the document. If the inscription delineating the powers of the *boule* had a similar authorising decree, then it will also have displayed the democracy which made the document possible.

This idea of putting the actions of the *demos* on show certainly appears in the extant portions of this text. It contains at least two embedded documents: the decree of the *demos* which starts in line 34 and the bouleutic oath. Whatever their original history, in this context, they are presented as the products of the democracy. As such, they also show that it is functioning properly because the *demos* is able to create such documents and make them available for their publication on this *stele*. The sacrificial calendar testifies to the activities of the *demos* in a further way because it shows not only what the people have done so far, namely authorise the inscription of the calendar, but also what they will do, sacrifice to the city's gods and heroes as specified in this document. In some cases, these actions will require the participation of selected officials, but, in others, it will require the presence of the whole *demos*, which will act collectively and display itself in the process.[104]

The overall process of collecting and inscribing the city's laws should be understood as a further way of displaying the democracy in action, as it were, despite the overtly partisan complaints of the speaker of Lysias 30.[105] Without the appropriate legislation by the *demos* and the *boule*, the project could never have been begun.[106] Once it had started, the activities of the *anagrapheis* would have been visible to people in the city and they would have reminded them of the importance of democracy. When the results were ready for inspection, either in the archive or inscribed on *stelai*, they would have showed off the actions of the democracy yet again. The decision to inscribe at least some of this material on stone meant that the democracy was, in a sense, continually and permanently functioning. Both the laws and the system which generated them had a permanence now made visible in the city. Once these various texts had been erected in the city, reading them repeated the very process which brought them into being because the reader said out loud 'it was decreed by the *boule* and the

---

[103] *IG* I³ 104.1–2. The letters in these two lines are 0.020–0.028 m. high, while the letters in the other lines, with the exception of lines 10 and 56, are 0.010 m. high; Stroud 1968: 4, fig. 1, pl. 1.

[104] Officials: e.g. *SEG* LII 48 fr. 1B.14; 9B col. 2.8; *demos*: e.g. *SEG* LII 48 fr. 9B col. 2.7.

[105] See e.g. Lys. 30.5–6, 9–14, 17, 30, 35.   [106] Compare Lys. 30.17; Andok. 1.83–4.

demos . . . so-and-so made the motion'. In the case of Demophantos' decree and the documents about the *boule*, the reader repeated the oath included in the text and so reperformed the action.[107] Of course, this reperformance was not exact because the sacrificial victims necessary for swearing an oath would not have been present;[108] in the case of the inscription about the *boule*, the reader need not have been a *bouleutes*, while, with Demophantos' decree, he would not have been arrayed with his tribe and his deme. Even in this imperfect fashion, reading these documents brought them to life and exhibited yet again processes of democracy, the actions which had originally created these texts.

The location in which these inscriptions were erected also participated in this display of the rule of the *demos*. How this dynamic functioned is evident from the *stele* with Drakon's law. As the authorising decree shows, the inscription was to be erected in front of the Stoa Basileios, the specific location approved by the *demos* and the *boule*.[109] Erecting the inscription in front of the stoa reflects the decision of the Athenian people and council and its presence reflects the whole democratic process which culminated in the placement of the *stele* in the Agora. The other inscriptions with the laws and Demophantos' decree will have interacted with their settings in the same way as Drakon's law and they, too, were displayed as the products of decisions made by the *demos* and *boule*.

Within the context of the Agora, however, these documents were not erected haphazardly. Instead, as we have already noticed, they are clustered in two areas: in front of the Bouleuterion and in front of and in the Stoa Basileios (table 9; fig. 2). Erected here, the *stelai* focus attention on these two monuments and the areas surrounding them. In the case of the Bouleuterion, the documents serve as exempla for democratically elected *bouleutai*, as indications of how they should act. Demophantos' decree shows the councillors how they should behave if the democracy were to be overthrown in the future: out of office with the change of the regime, they are to imitate Harmodios and Aristogeiton and kill or attempt to kill the men who overthrew the rule of the *demos*. That this decree was understood as a model for the actions of the *bouleutai* is brought out by Lykourgos' description of it in precisely these terms: 'these words, gentlemen, they inscribed on the *stele* and set it up at the Bouleuterion to remind those meeting each day and deliberating over the business of the

---

[107] For Demophantos' decree and these dynamics, see Shear 2007b: 159.
[108] For the rituals of oath-taking, see Cole 1996: 230–3 with further references; for the taking of Demophantos' oath, see Shear 2007b: 153–8 and below chapter 5.
[109] *IG* I³ 104.7–8.

fatherland how they should treat such men'.[110] The decree, consequently, invites the councillors to be active on behalf of the city: they should not imitate the councillors who, in Thucydides' version, meekly took their pay and departed when ordered to do so by the Four Hundred. If, as I suggested, the *stele* with the documents about the *boule* also stood in front of the Bouleuterion, then it will have worked together with Demophantos' decree. On a regular basis, the members of the council will have walked by the inscription with the oath which they had sworn when they took office. The list of actions not to be undertaken without the approval of the 'full *demos*' delineated the power of the *bouleutai* and it provided them with a further, albeit negative, exemplum for their behaviour. Hedged around in these ways, the council was prevented from acting independently of the *demos* and without its consent. The document emphasises the interconnection between the *demos* and the *boule*, a relationship ignored by the Four Hundred in their efforts to act as the city's council, while it prevents the *bouleutai* from becoming a second Four Hundred, a second oligarchic council. In this setting in front of the Bouleuterion, the two documents worked together to provide the democratically elected councillors with a very specific image of the behaviour appropriate to their office, a position emphatically mentioned in the prescript of Demophantos' decree.

The interaction between the topography and the decree of Demophantos is not limited to these dynamics on the terrace in front of the Bouleuterion. Demophantos' oath with its reference to Harmodios and Aristogeiton also serves to connect the text to the statues of the Tyrannicides in the middle of the Agora between the racetrack and the Panathenaic Way (fig. 2).[111] This setting reinforced the oath's stipulation that the Athenians follow the model of Harmodios and Aristogeiton and become the slayers of tyrants because the sculpted figures themselves served as models for the proper behaviour for Athenians (fig. 8).[112] With the possible exception of a statue dedicated by Leagros to the Twelve Gods, the Tyrannicides were the only sculpted human figures in the Agora at this time: their connections with the inscribed oath would, therefore, have been extremely clear.[113] Depending on

[110] Lykourg. *Leok.* 126.
[111] Location of statues: Paus. 1.8.4–6; Arr. *Anab.* 3.16.8 with Vanderpool 1974: 308–9; Val. Max. 2.10.ext. 1; Thompson and Wycherley 1972: 157–8.
[112] For the statues as models, see Ar. *Lys.* 630–5; Hdt. 6.109.3; see also M. W. Taylor 1991: 19; Castriota 1998: 205; Shapiro 1998: 130; Hölscher 1998: 160.
[113] Statues of figures of cult showed Zeus Soter and the Eponymous Heroes. Demosthenes specifies that Konon was the first person after Harmodios and Aristogeiton to receive a bronze statue and his figure was accompanied by that of Euagoras, the king of Cypriot Salamis; Dem. 20.70; Isok. 9.57; Shear 2007b: 96, 107–9; below chapter 9. Leagros' dedication: *IG* i³ 951; Gadbery 1992: 472–4.

Figure 8   Roman copies of the Tyrannicides by Kritios and Nesiotes (Museo Archeologico, Naples G103–4). The bronze originals were erected in the Athenian Agora in 477/6 BC.

where exactly the *stele* was located on the Bouleuterion terrace, viewers may actually have been able to look directly from the text to the figures of the Tyrannicides in the centre of the marketplace. The group's composition was overtly anti-tyrannical: Hipparchos, whom Harmodios and Aristogeiton were about to slay, was not shown so that the viewer standing immediately in front of the monument took his place and became the tyrant (fig. 8).[114] This connection made all opponents of democracy into tyrants, the true opponent of the *demos*, and it should have reinforced the injunctions of Demophantos' decree. This setting constructs the ideal reader of the decree equally as the ideal viewer of the sculpture group and it aligns the messages which the two monuments promulgate. Since the killing of Hipparchos was considered the foundational moment for the democracy, this design also helps to identify the space of the Agora as an area now being orientated specifically towards citizens of the city.

If Demophantos' decree and the inscription about the *boule* focus particularly on the Bouleuterion and the councillors, Drakon's law, the other secular laws and the sacrificial calendar focus on the Stoa Basileios, the *basileus* and the other archons (fig. 2). The stoa provided a particularly appropriate setting for Drakon's law because the *anagrapheis* had received the text of the law from the *basileus* who was located in this building.[115] Since the *basileus* presided over all homicide trials, Drakon's law fell very much into his sphere, hence his possession of the text used for the inscription.[116] Erecting the *stele* in front of his building replicated in a permanent form his relationship with the text now written on the marble *stele*. Instead of being kept in his archive inside the stoa, Drakon's law was now set up in front of it and it was inscribed in a familiar, modern form on a modern marble *stele*; now, it was available for anyone who wished to consult it. Drakon's law had a further connection with this building because the structure seems to have been particularly associated with the city's laws: since at least the reforms of Ephialtes in 461, it had housed the *kurbeis*, triangular bronze pillars, with Solon's laws; they may even, as T. Leslie Shear, Jr suggests, have been transferred there when the building was originally built for the *basileus* at the end of the sixth century.[117] Created in the early sixth century, the *kurbeis* in 410/9 will have been old and unfamiliar documents inscribed in antique letters; reading them cannot have been easy. Located in the stoa, they were under the control of the *basileus*, but they were not necessarily very easy to consult. After 410/9, in contrast, both Drakon's law on homicide and the other reinscribed laws were made easily available in

---

[114] For the group's anti-tyrannical nature, see e.g. Boardman 1985: 25; Stewart 1996: 73; Ajootian 1998: 1, 9; Steiner 2001: 221.

[115] *IG* I³ 104.5–7.   [116] Arist. *Ath. Pol.* 57.2–4; cf. Sickinger 1999b: 17.

[117] Stroud 1979: 41–4; Shear, Jr 1994: 240–1. For the ancient testimonia, see Stroud 1979: 3–40. Those unconvinced by Stroud's arguments include P. J. Rhodes 1981: 131–4, P. J. Rhodes 1991: 91 with note 23 and Sealey 1987: 140–5. Neither Rhodes nor Sealey engages with the archaeological material described by Stroud and Shear.

a well-known, modern medium, which, in the area of the Stoa Basileios, maintained the traditional connection between the laws and the *basileus*. Just as the homicide law reflected one of the *basileus'* duties, presiding over homicide trials, in the same way, the sacrificial calendar reflected his role as the magistrate presiding at impiety trials and responsible for the ancestral sacrifices.[118] In both cases, the inscribed *stelai* made his roles and spheres of activity visible in concrete form in front of the building in which he was located. These connections between archon, office and documents further suggest why Drakon's laws and the calendar were inscribed on separate *stelai* and treated differently from the other laws: they belonged to the sphere of the king. Separated out from the rest of the laws, they proclaimed both the stoa and the court in front of it as his particular space.[119] At the same time, these documents reminded the *basileus* of his duties in much the same way that the inscription about the *boule* reminded the *bouleutai* of theirs.

Erecting this monumental display of the laws in and around the Stoa Basileios had further consequences for uses of this space because the building was also the location of the *lithos*, the stone upon which the nine archons stood to take their oath to uphold the laws of the city and not to accept bribes.[120] Since the *lithos* stood on the step of the stoa with its north end projecting into the north annexe, the annexes with their *stelai* and inscribed texts surrounded anyone standing on the oath stone (fig. 7).[121] When the archons took their oath to uphold the city's laws, they would quite literally have been surrounded by the relevant legislation. Becoming an archon of the democratic city now had to take place in the physical presence of the laws. Just as the magistrates entered into a relationship with the gods through their oaths, they could also be seen in this setting to enter into a comparable one with the laws themselves.[122] Activities necessary to the running of the democratic city, accordingly, took place in the actual presence of the laws.

Collectively, these inscriptions helped to redefine and reform the space of the Agora. They functioned as memorials in their own right which

---

[118] Arist. *Ath. Pol.* 57.1–2. He also oversaw suits concerning disputed claims to priesthoods and adjudicated in disputes between both *gene* and priests over privileges and perquisites.

[119] For the court, see Shear, Jr 1971: 252; Shear, Jr 1975: 366–8.

[120] Arist. *Ath. Pol.* 7.1, 55.5; Poll. *Onom.* 8.86; Plut. *Sol.* 25.3; cf. Harp., Phot. *Lex.* and *Suda* s.v. λίθος. The arbitrators (*diaitetai*) also took oaths on the *lithos*, but the *diaitetai* served for the first time only in 399/8 and belong to the period after the Thirty; MacDowell 1971b and especially 270–1.

[121] Location of *lithos*: Shear, Jr 1971: 259–60; Shear, Jr 1994: 242–5.

[122] For oaths creating bonds between humans and gods, see Rudhardt 1958: 209–10; Cole 1996: 230.

celebrated the democratic processes and made them perpetually visible. As commemorative monuments, these inscriptions are unusual because they explicitly tell us through their texts how they came into being, a process which such structures usually ignore.[123] In this case, however, the texts are crucial because they allow these *stelai* to commemorate and to display the actions of the *demos* and also to create a series of interconnections between different structures in the topography of the Agora. As the products of Athenian citizens, of the men who governed the city, the inscriptions focused attention on their activities. Through their function as memorials, the *stelai* brought the activities of the Pnyx and the Bouleuterion itself into the multi-use space of the Agora and they wrote the presence of the democratic process visibly onto the fabric of the marketplace. They interacted with the activities of the *demos*, particularly the actions of the *boule* and the *basileus*, and they served as reminders of the proper activity for (democratic) Athenians. As physical markers of the rule of the *demos*, the inscriptions also help to recover this particular area, which Thucydides portrays as contested space, for the *demos* and to mark it as democratic, not oligarchic, territory. Consequently, these documents mark the beginning of the Agora's transformation into a place focused on the citizen rather than on everyone who made use of it, a process which we shall examine further in the next chapter and in discussing the response to the Thirty.[124]

RECOVERING THE PAST FOR THE *DEMOS*

Erected in the Agora in the years after 411, these inscriptions helped to define this particular space in new ways and to begin the process of making it overtly democratic. They also allowed the *demos* to begin the process of (re-)identifying the democratic city's past, a task made particularly urgent by the ways in which both the Four Hundred and the Five Thousand had manipulated the past for their own ends. In this process, the democrats focused particularly on three figures, Drakon, Solon and Kleisthenes, as well as more generally on the *patrios politeia*. As part of this project, the collection and reinscription of the city's laws had a particularly important role to play because of the multiple pasts represented in them. Drakon's law shows how some of these dynamics work. The authorising decree specifies that the document to be inscribed is Drakon's law on homicide and its publication was authorised by the *boule* and the *demos*. This document, accordingly, was important enough to these two bodies of the Athenians

[123] Young 1993: 14.   [124] See also the discussion of Shear 2007a.

that they republished it. By doing so in this particular form, they laid claim to Drakon as part of their past, a proto-democrat, as it were, who had produced a law still valid under the rule of the *demos*. Similar dynamics are also at work with the republication of Solon's laws: these documents connected the *demos* with this seminal archaic figure who legislated how the city ought to be governed and they identified the democrats as his proper successors. For these connections to function, it is immaterial whether Solon actually made all the laws in question or whether Athenians in the late fifth century merely attributed them all to him; the perception of the *demos* rather than historical accuracy was the critical factor in this process. Since the Four Hundred apparently constituted themselves as the city's *boule* on the model of the Solonian *boule* of 400, it was especially important for the *demos* to reclaim Solon from the oligarchs and to show that his legislation in no way could be thought to authorise an oligarchic *politeia*.

The process of recovering Kleisthenes is visible in these documents in rather more detail. In Demophantos' decree, the Athenians are to swear the oath arrayed 'by tribe and by deme', i.e. in the democratic divisions as instituted by Kleisthenes. Since the document identifies democracy as the only possible *politeia* for the city, the democratic nature of the tribes and demes is further brought out by the text itself. The prescript's focus on the *boule* of 500 elected by lot stresses that it also is properly part of the system of rule by the *demos*, the system legitimised by this document. Since Kleisthenes established this council, as well as the tribes and demes, he also is reclaimed by these references to important parts of the system which he instituted.

A similar process is at work in the documents about the *boule*. The text contains two clear references to the *boule* of 500, one of which is associated with the Bouleuterion;[125] the council and its meeting place are shown here to belong together and their institution belongs to the end of the sixth century BC. On two occasions, the *boule* and the *ekklesia* are linked together, an association which again is one of the characteristic features of the Kleisthenic system.[126] Including the bouleutic oath in the inscription also helps to keep the focus on Kleisthenes because the oath, which we know to have been instituted in 501, logically belongs with the process of setting up the new council.[127] The overall effect in this inscription is to identify Kleisthenes as the person who created this part of the democracy.

---

[125] *IG* I³ 105.30 (Bouleuterion), 45.   [126] *IG* I³ 105.27, 44–5.
[127] Arist. *Ath. Pol.* 22.2 with P. J. Rhodes 1981: 262–4.

Linking him together with his council also allows him to be reclaimed as a democrat and the founder of the current *politeia*. Every *bouleutes* must swear this oath as part of his entry into office and, consequently, the inscription also reclaims the *boule* of 500 for the democracy. Since the Four Hundred had attempted to set themselves up as the city's council, the link between the rule of the *demos*, the *boule* and Kleisthenes needed to be clearly re-established. Once these documents were inscribed and erected, the association between the council and the Bouleuterion will have been reinforced by the topography. The focus on this area and the erection of *stelai* here will further have helped to reclaim Kleisthenes because, as we shall see in further detail in the next chapter, the structure was originally built at the end of the sixth century as part of the process of laying out the new Agora for the new democracy.[128]

In addition to laying claim to these three iconic figures, the *demos* also reappropriated the past more generally. This process appears perhaps most clearly in the documents concerning the *boule*. Collecting documents belonging to different times in the city's past together and inscribing them in one inscription indicated not only that the texts themselves were relevant to the *demos*, but also that the different time periods which they represented were important. These chronological differences will have been particularly brought out by such archaic terms as the 'full *demos*' which were no longer in regular use in the late fifth century and the opening formula for the decree of the *demos* meeting in the Lykeion. Including these texts suggested that the *demos* had been ruling the city when the original documents were passed. A similar process will also have occurred with the inscribed laws in the Stoa Basileios. The different texts collected by this project may well have belonged to more periods than the material concerning the *boule* and so the laws potentially allowed other pasts to be reclaimed. As documents approved by earlier generations of Athenians, they also showed that the democracy had a history of past actions, that it was, in fact, *patrios*. Collectively, they represented the *patrios politeia* so that their publication and display demonstrated that the ancestral constitution was, in fact, the democracy. In this way, the *demos* also very clearly laid out their claim to this constitution and showed that it was not the possession of the oligarchs.

Focusing on the *basileus* and the Stoa Basileios through the display of the laws also demonstrated that the king was a part of the democratic system; by extension, the *demos* was also able to reclaim the archons and other officials of the city for the democracy. Any references to them in the

---

[128] Shear, Jr 1994: 231–6; Shear, Jr 1995: 157–71; Shear, Jr 1993: 418–27, 472–7.

inscribed documents, such as the preamble of Drakon's law, will also have reinforced this connection. Since the oligarchs had made a concentrated effort to show that the city's officials actually belonged to their past rather than to that of the *demos*, these moves were of considerable importance. The *demos* was not obliged to invent a new way of ruling the city and it made the claim that these officials were actually part of the democratic past. These actions also indicated that the democratic city's history went further back in time than the days of Solon and Drakon. The sacrificial calendar must have complemented this process because the rituals listed here will have included the ancestral sacrifices for which the *basileus* was responsible. Almost certainly the text included archaic terms which, by this time, were only used in specific ritual contexts. They will have reinforced the impression that the origins of the democracy went back to the city's deep past.

The laws and the other inscriptions, accordingly, allowed the *demos* to begin to forge a new relationship with the past and to identify it as relevant to the democratic city. As part of this process, the iconic figures of Drakon, Solon and Kleisthenes were shown to have been democrats and not the authors of an oligarchic or limited system as the Four Hundred and the Five Thousand had presented them. Since at least some of their legislation was now prominently displayed, its popular nature could easily be verified by anyone who wished to do so. The *demos* also reclaimed the *patrios politeia* from the oligarchs and showed that democracy was historically the proper form of constitution for the city. By using inscriptions as part of this process, the democrats were able to begin to write their new past on the very topography of the city. Choosing to erect them in the Agora, an area without oligarchic inscriptions, allowed the focus to remain resolutely on the rule of the *demos* and it de-emphasised the recent oligarchic past.

CONSEQUENCES

As we have seen in this chapter, the process of creating a collective, public response to the oligarchic revolution began already in the first prytany of 410/9. Through inscriptions erected for the first time in the Agora, the *demos* was able to display its power and the importance of its rule to the city. By focusing on the type of *politeia* and its constituent parts, particularly the *boule*, these texts directed attention from individual to institutional power, a strategy which contrasted with the oligarchs' much greater focus on the personal and their disregard for the city's institutions. Indeed, these documents constructed democracy not only as the proper *politeia* for

Athens, but also as the only possible one. Inscribed on marble *stelai*, these texts put this rule of the *demos* physically on display in monumental form in the Agora, where the documents were juxtaposed with the Bouleuterion, the home of the council of 500, and the Stoa Basileios, the home of the *basileus*. In the years immediately after 411, the physical form of these inscribed texts may have been particularly reassuring to Athenians and it may have suggested to them that this democracy was stable and would not be overthrown as easily as it had been by the oligarchs. These documents also allowed the *demos* to begin to reclaim the city's earlier history and to show that there was a democratic past for Athens. In so doing, the democrats put special emphasis not only on the *patrios politeia*, but also on the important figures of Drakon, Solon and Kleisthenes, all of whom had been co-opted by the oligarchs for their own purposes. By its actions, the *demos* was now able to redeem them for itself.

Using decrees, the laws and the Agora to respond to oligarchy and to display democracy, however, had further consequences for the Athenians because they also created a new image of what it meant to be Athenian. Demophantos' decree played a large role in this process and it set out a very uncompromising image.[129] The text identifies the good Athenian as a male citizen who kills tyrants and oligarchs and so upholds the rule of the *demos*. The bad Athenian is also identified: the citizen who is or aspires to be an oligarch or tyrant. Since this person is described in the text as a *polemios*, an external enemy of the city, all threats to Athens and her democracy are construed as external and so all appropriate measures are also authorised in the decree. This image was reinforced by the juxtaposition of Demophantos' document and the statues of Harmodios and Aristogeiton: the ideal reader and the ideal viewer were the same man, the democratic Athenian, who, if necessary, would imitate the Tyrannicides to maintain the rule of the *demos*. The juxtaposition with the inscribed laws further suggests that this democratic Athenian is also the ideal reader of the laws and the sacrificial calendar. In this overall setting, then, the ideal Athenian is also constructed as following the rule of law, which entails making the appropriate offerings to the city's gods and heroes on the appropriate occasion. These divine powers have, in turn, a reciprocal obligation to protect and defend the city.[130]

In this context, it is activities which identify the good (and the bad) Athenian, but they are located either in the present or the future. The

---

[129] For more detailed discussion, see Shear 2007b: 151–2.
[130] For the reciprocal relationships created by sacrifice, see Parker 1998.

past is relevant in as much as it is a democratic past which provides the foundation for the present. Individual Athenians are not named unless they hold office or move decrees. While these strategies stress the unified nature of these Athenian democrats, they also serve to obscure the events that led to this response to oligarchy. On the basis of these documents erected in the Agora, we would not know that two different oligarchic regimes had controlled the city during 411 and 410; in this space, it is as if they had never been. Similarly, the actions which led to the removal of the oligarchs are also not mentioned, much less celebrated, although there was not necessarily very much to commemorate; nevertheless, their absence in this space represents a deliberate decision by the *demos*.[131] This effacement of the oligarchs in the Agora further suggests that the city had always been ruled by the *demos*, the political system here identified as the proper *politeia* for the city.

The decision of the *demos* to erect these documents in the Agora had further consequences. As we have seen, the inscriptions interact both with each other and with their setting in the market square and the interrelationships created are integral to the response to oligarchy. Since they represent a new departure in the way in which this particular space was used, they also serve to focus attention on the Agora. This dynamic is particularly clear in Demophantos' decree with its specific reference to Harmodios and Aristogeiton, memorialised in bronze not very far away. If, as I have argued, the documents concerning the *boule* were, indeed, erected on a *stele* at the Bouleuterion, they, too, will have emphasised the relationship between the council and that particular location. Meanwhile, the laws and the sacrificial calendar drew attention to the *basileus* and the Stoa Basileios. These interrelationships bring out both the power which specific places in the city held for the *demos* and the importance of using that power as part of the response to oligarchy. As we shall see in the following chapter, both the Agora and the Akropolis were spaces which needed to be reclaimed for the democratic city, an entity made up not only of documents, actions and institutions, but also of topography and monuments.

---

[131] This strategy also avoids the complication that there were two different regimes, the Four Hundred and the Five Thousand, and it makes room for men like Theramenes and Polystratos to be(come) good democrats.

CHAPTER 4

Reclaiming Athens: the demos and the city

In the years after 411, the Athenian *demos* made a concentrated effort to reclaim the city through the city's laws and her very democratic practices, as we saw in the previous chapter. The documents also allowed the *demos* to recover the past for themselves, the same past which the Four Hundred and the Five Thousand had invoked to legitimise their own regimes. Now the actions of the democrats showed that this past, with its iconic figures of Drakon, Solon and Kleisthenes, was, in fact, their own. Consequently, the rule of the *demos* had a historical lineage: it was, indeed, *patrios*. Reclaiming the city and identifying her as democratic, however, was not a process limited to the laws and the display of the rule of the *demos*. As we saw in chapter 2, the oligarchs made use for their own purposes not only of the city's documents, but also of her spaces. Thucydides portrays the Agora as a hotly contested space which both sides were endeavouring in 411 to control for their own ends. His narrative also makes clear that the Four Hundred were using the Bouleuterion as the seat of their own power and they were intent on establishing themselves as the city's *boule* which, in their eyes, would be legitimately constituted.[1] This version of events also brings out the power of place, in this case the power of the Agora, a place worth fighting over for both oligarchs and democrats. Space and its control, accordingly, mattered to the different sides in Thucydides' narrative and not only to them. In the narrative of the *Athenaion Politeia*, the Bouleuterion again appears as the seat of the oligarchs' actual power, while the ways in which the oligarchs used inscriptions on the Akropolis also allowed them to lay claim to that sanctuary, the most important in the city and the symbolic centre of Athens.[2]

In the years after the oligarchies, consequently, the *demos* needed not only to show that the city was once again democratic, but it also needed

---

[1] Thuc. 8.69.1–70.1; above chapter 2.

[2] Arist. *Ath. Pol.* 32.3; above chapter 2. For further discussion of the Akropolis as symbolic centre, see Loraux 1993: 37–71.

to reclaim the spaces of the Agora and the Akropolis from the oligarchs for its own purposes. As we shall see, the inscriptions with the laws and the oath and decree of Demophantos played an important role in this process not only through their texts, but as monuments in their own right. Reclaiming the space of the Agora further involved new construction projects which complemented the messages presented by the texts of the inscriptions. These structures, the annexes on the Stoa Basileios and a new council house, were explicitly spaces necessary for the democratic rule of the city. Construction was not limited to the marketplace because the *demos* also resumed work on a new temple for Athena Polias, now known as the Erechtheion, on the Akropolis. Halted some years previously, possibly as a result of the Sicilian disaster, this project allowed the *demos* to project its claim over the space of the Akropolis, as well as in the Agora. The *demos*, however, was intent on more than physically writing its control of Athens upon the city's topography. As we shall see, these building activities allowed the *demos* to display the democracy itself and its processes and to reclaim the city's past which was now made manifestly visible through the new construction. The Athenians' identity as democrats was also emphasised and the oligarchs were effaced from the physical spaces of the city. In the contest for controlling the cityscape, a process left incomplete in Thucydides' narrative, the democrats had won resoundingly: now the city of the *demos* visibly complemented the messages presented by the new inscriptions in the Agora.

RECLAIMING THE AGORA: THE MONUMENTS

As we saw briefly in the preceding chapter, inscriptions first began to be erected in the Agora in the years immediately after 411, the first time when single copies of inscriptions were set up in the marketplace.[3] These documents, however, were not erected randomly within the overall space; instead, they were gathered in two distinct areas: in front of and in the Stoa Basileios and in front of the (Old) Bouleuterion (table 9), locations which complemented the texts of the documents (fig. 2). Sited in close connection to these two structures, the *stelai* also served to draw attention specifically to them and to their setting. This focus was reinforced by the activities now taking place around these buildings because both of them were the sites of new construction.

---

[3] See also Shear 2007a: 97–101.

The first of these structures, the Stoa Basileios in the northwest corner of the Agora, became between 410 and 404 the location for presenting the great marble *stelai* inscribed with the city's laws. The small and venerable stoa was evidently considered insufficient to accommodate this new display as it was currently configured. Two small annexes were added to its northeast and southeast corners and the building changed from being a purely ordinary stoa into a more elaborate structure along the lines of the neighbouring Stoa of Zeus with its two wings (fig. 7). The construction seems to have taken place in two phases which help to explain the different building techniques used for the two annexes. Of these two wings, the northern one seemed to the excavators to be slightly earlier (fig. 7).[4] Subsequently heavily rebuilt, probably on more than one occasion, the north annexe no longer preserves its original appearance.[5] At that time, it seems to have been a simple structure: three unfluted columns along the east front and one next to the anta of the original stoa and an earth floor.[6] In contrast to normal Greek architectural practice, there were no stylobate blocks between the columns in this original phase and the columns stood on isolated square blocks.[7] The space between them, however, was not left open, but it was filled with bases designed to support a series of *stelai* placed edge to edge; one of these bases, now recut and re-used, was found by the excavators in place on the south side of the annexe.[8] That there was no proper stylobate further suggests that the intercolumniations of this wing were not intended for regular traffic which would have worn away the floor at precisely these points. Once the bases and their *stelai* were in place, the oddities of construction, which are so striking in the preserved remains, would probably not have been visible.

In contrast, the south wing was built in a more orthodox fashion (fig. 7). On its front side, three columns stood on a standard continuous stone stylobate, while another column stood in the middle of the stylobates of the north and south sides.[9] As we saw in the preceding chapter, the stylobates between these columns contained cut slots for the insertion of *stelai* and the whole annexe was entered through a door now marked by a threshold.[10] The structure was clearly intended for the display of great *stelai* which we have identified as the *stelai* carrying the newly inscribed laws. As part of the process of building the south annexe, the old stoa was given a new clay floor and the platform surrounding the north, west and south sides of the building's interior was removed to make way for a bench, the

---

[4] Shear, Jr 1971: 252.   [5] Shear, Jr 1971: 250–1.   [6] Shear, Jr 1971: 250, 252.
[7] Shear, Jr 1971: 251.   [8] Shear, Jr 1971: 251.   [9] Shear, Jr 1971: 251.   [10] Shear, Jr 1971: 251.

supports of which are still preserved at the north end of the structure.[11] At the same time, the floor of the north annexe was raised to the same level as the floors of the rest of the building. The uniform level of the floors would have helped to unify the structure and it would perhaps have obscured the different construction techniques used for the two annexes. If both wings had unfluted Doric columns, then this repetition would also have made the resulting structure more visually coherent.[12]

On the basis of the archaeological evidence, we can restore the appearance of the Stoa Basileios at the end of this construction project with some certainty, but the material remains do not explain the chronological sequence observed by the excavators. The connections between the inscribed laws, the building and the *anagrapheis*, as discussed in the previous chapter, suggest an explanation. We saw that the project of collecting, organising and inscribing the laws seems to have developed over time and it is likely that neither the scope nor the complexity of the project were apparent when it first started. If construction at the Stoa Basileios began with the north annexe and then continued to the south annexe, the sequence observed by the excavators would be explained. It is very possible that originally one annexe was considered sufficient for the display of the laws, but, as more material was collected and the scope of the project increased, the need for more display space may have become clear. The construction of the north wing suggests an effort to execute the project with as little expense as possible. If its appearance was not considered satisfactory when it was completed, then the use of the more usual techniques observed in the south wing could be simply explained. The chronological differences between the two wings, however, very probably represent a very short period of time, perhaps only a matter of months. That the whole structure was given a uniform clay floor at the end of the project indicates that the rebuilt Stoa Basileios was intended to be understood as a uniform whole; its new overall appearance need not have been as ramshackled as the archaeological remains might now suggest.

---

[11] Shear, Jr 1971: 244–8. That this bench ran around all three sides of the building is suggested by the stylobate block between the south anta and the first column of the stoa. It is considerably higher in level than the other stylobate blocks of the south annexe and the original threshold and my estimates suggest that it is higher than the seat of the bench. In this way, the text of the *stelai* inserted in the block's slot would have been preserved from accidental damage done by individuals sitting on the bench.

[12] No capitals are preserved from these columns. The absence of bases for the columns in the north annexe suggests that they were Doric. In the south annexe, cuttings for empolia in the stylobate might suggest that these columns were Ionic; Shear, Jr 1971: 251. I find it hard to believe that different orders were used for different parts of the building's exterior.

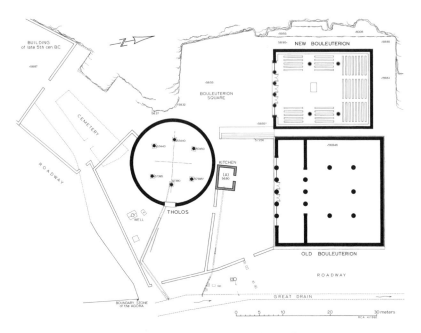

Figure 9   Restored plan of the Bouleuterion complex in the Agora in *c*. 405 BC.

While the annexes of the Stoa Basileios were under construction at the northwest corner of the square, a second and more extensive project was underway by the Bouleuterion where the Athenians were engaged in building a new council house to the west of the existing structure (fig. 9). This project involved a significant quarrying effort to cut back the Kolonos Agoraios and to make sufficient space for the new building. Perhaps because of the work involved, it was located on its own terrace reached by a set of stairs leading from the area in front of the original Bouleuterion below and to the east of the new project. Despite a difference of perhaps 1.10–1.30 m. in the ground level, the two structures were evidently conceived in relation to each other: the east wall of the new structure was parallel to the west wall of the old building and the south columnar façades of the two council houses were aligned (fig. 9).[13] As in the original structure, the new one contained a large chamber designed for the meetings of the *boule* and equipped with a flat floor and columns supporting the roof.[14] In their dimensions, the

---

[13] Shear, Jr 1995: 179. I have derived the figures for the elevations from the plan presented in H. A. Thompson, 1937: pl. VI with pl. VII section A-A.
[14] Shear, Jr 1995: 179–80.

two meeting chambers were quite similar in size and the same wooden benches could have been used in both structures.[15] In one respect, however, the two buildings differed significantly: while the council chamber in the Old Bouleuterion was reached by way of a vestibule, the chamber in the new council house was accessed directly from the terrace in front of the building without passing through any intermediate space.[16] In the New Bouleuterion, therefore, only grilles between the columns separated the *bouleutai* in their deliberations from spectators out on the terrace to the south.[17] This design afforded the councillors little privacy and anyone who wished could check on the doings of the *boule*, a situation not possible in the earlier council house. Just such a scenario is, in fact, envisioned at the beginning of Plato's *Menexenos* when Menexenos, despite not being a councillor, goes to the Bouleuterion in order to learn whom the *boule* will choose to give the funeral oration.[18]

The pottery evidence recovered from the construction fills for the New Bouleuterion shows that, like the annexes of the Stoa Basileios, the project must belong in the last decade of the fifth century.[19] Further evidence for the date is provided by Xenophon's description of the trial of Theramenes by the Thirty. We are told explicitly that it took place 'in the Bouleuterion' and a critical role is played by the Thirty's armed thugs.[20] Despite standing in 'the space in front of the Bouleuterion', these men are visible to the councillors sitting inside and their presence prevents the *bouleutai* from objecting as Theramenes is dragged away to his death.[21] Grilles (δρύφακ-τοι) alone separate the men inside from the thugs outside.[22] As several scholars have noted, such a setting is not possible in the Old Bouleuterion in which a lobby separates the council chamber from spectators outside the building (fig. 9).[23] This description, however, does fit the New Bouleuterion very well: Theramenes' trial must have taken place in this building and it must have been completed before 403 and presumably before the Thirty seized power in the previous year.[24]

The transfer of the *bouleutai* from their original meeting place to the new council house at some time between 410 and 404 left the Old Bouleuterion vacant. It was not, however, torn down and, by Demosthenes' day, the

---

[15] Interior dimensions: New Bouleuterion: 15.62 m. × 20.12 m.; Old Bouleuterion: 16.08 m. × 21.25 m.; Shear, Jr 1995: 180.
[16] Shear, Jr 1995: 180.　　[17] On the grilles, see Shear, Jr 1995: 185 with note 72.
[18] Pl. *Menex.* 234a1–b7.　　[19] Shear, Jr 1995: 180–4.
[20] Xen. *Hell.* 2.3.55.　　[21] Xen. *Hell.* 2.3.55.
[22] Xen. *Hell.* 2.3.55 with 2.3.50; for another description of the grilles, see [Dem.] 25.23.
[23] Roux 1976: 480–1; Shear, Jr 1994: 246–7 note 48; Miller 1995: 148, 151–2; Shear, Jr 1995: 184.
[24] Shear, Jr 1995: 184–5.

building was being used as the city's central archive.[25] In the fourth century, documents are often described as in the *demosion* (ἐν τῷ δημοσίῳ or ἐν τοῖς δημοσίοις), namely, in the city's archives, as the contexts make clear.[26] The earliest references to the *demosion* as the place in which the city's public documents are kept belong to 405/4. In Patrokleides' amnesty decree, one of the clauses requires the names of the men covered by the amnesty to be erased from the records in the *demosion*.[27] In the decree honouring the loyal Samians, the Athenian ships based at the island are to be handed over to the Samians and the names of the Athenian *trierarchoi* are to be erased from the records in the *demosion* so that they are not listed as defaulting on the return of their (state-owned) vessels.[28] In both examples, the term *demosion* is most easily understood as the city's archive, which must have been in existence when these two documents were proposed.[29] Andokides, however, in his speech about his return, which ought to date to soon after 410, refers to a decree of Menippos which is still in the Bouleuterion.[30] The city's archive cannot have been established when this particular speech was given, but it was in existence by 405, when the *boule* must have been comfortably installed in its new quarters.[31]

The dates for the establishment of the city's central archive are striking because they overlap quite closely with the period of the *anagrapheis'* first term in office and scholars have associated their activities with the creation of the archive.[32] Certainly, the compilation, organisation and republication of the laws must have produced a vast collection of documents which needed to be housed and which constituted an important archival resource. Housing the materials produced, however, need not have involved relocating the *boule* to a new structure. Instead, the Athenians could have created a purpose-built structure for the new archive and they could have chosen a location which did not involve significant cutting back of the Kolonos Agoraios. Placed in the Old Bouleuterion, however, the laws and decrees were conveniently available for the *bouleutai* to consult and the decision to place the laws and decrees in separate sections must have facilitated the process.[33]

---

[25] E.g. Dem. 19.129; Boegehold 1972: 28; Sickinger 1999b: 109.

[26] See e.g. Dem. 18.142; Aischin. 2.58, 89; and cf. Aischin. 2.32, 92, 135; 3.24, 75; Dem. 18.55; Shear, Jr 1995: 186–7; Sickinger 1999b: 109.

[27] Andok. 1.79; Sickinger 1999b: 110–11; Pébarthe 2006: 114–46.

[28] *IG* I³ 127.25–32. On this decree, see below chapter 8.

[29] Boegehold 1972: 23–8; Shear, Jr 1995: 186–7; Sickinger 1999b: 108–12. I remain unconvinced by the doubts expressed by Sickinger in connection with the honours for the Samians.

[30] Andok. 2.23.   [31] Boegehold 1972: 28, 30; Shear, Jr 1995: 189; Sickinger 1999b: 109–10, 111.

[32] E.g. Boegehold 1972: 29–30; Shear, Jr 1995: 188–9; Sickinger 1999b: 105–6.

[33] Separate sections: Sickinger 1999b: 105, 147–59.

THE AGORA AND THE *DEMOS*

In the period between 410 and 404, accordingly, the Agora was the site of significant construction located in the areas of the Stoa Basileios and the (Old) Bouleuterion (fig. 2). At one level, these projects had a practical function: the newly inscribed laws needed to be properly displayed and the archive had to be installed in a location where it could be easily consulted, particularly by the *bouleutai*. The new structures, however, also helped to display the control of the *demos* and the processes of its rule. In this way, they worked together with the inscriptions erected in and around these buildings. Like the texts, they further facilitated regaining the city's past for the *demos* because some of the structures were, in their original form, closely connected with Kleisthenes. The dynamics in the Bouleuterion complex helped in addition to define the relationship of the *demos* to the recent oligarchic past.

At a very basic level, the fact that the *demos* was able to build new structures in the Agora testified to its control of the space. Although Thucydides shows the Four Hundred trying to claim the market square, in his narrative, they do so by their physical presence and not through construction projects. Their control lasts only as long as they are physically present and, upon their departure, there is no evidence of their presence, except through memory, which is liable to forgetting. In contrast, the *demos* focused on the council house and the Stoa Basileios, structures housing the *boule* and the *basileus*, who were important for the running of the democratic city. In turn, the projects emphasised that importance and they made explicit what the rule of the *demos* entailed. Incorporating the laws into these dynamics through the inscribed display in the Stoa Basileios and the newly collected archives in the Old Bouleuterion showed clearly the relationship between the *demos* and the law: the laws made the rule of the *demos* possible. These structures certainly displayed the democrats' control of the city, and, like the inscriptions, they also wrote that control on to the very landscape itself. When the *bouleutai* were not meeting, when the *basileus* was not in his stoa, the structures still remained and reminded viewers that the city was now democratic. In this way, their physical presence nicely complemented the inscriptions which also insisted on democracy as the proper *politeia* for Athens and inscribed the *demos'* control on the cityscape.

The display in these buildings, however, was not limited to control of the city because the structures also put democracy itself on show. Recent discussion of the original Kleisthenic Stoa Basileios has stressed the public nature of this space and the lack of privacy which the *basileus* was afforded.[34] Despite the additions of the annexes, this official would have been no more shielded from public view in the last decade of the fifth century than he had been slightly more than 100 years before. Indeed, the installation of the newly inscribed laws must have encouraged more rather than fewer people to stop at the building; when they did so, they were in a perfect position to see what the *basileus* was doing. Similar dynamics also existed in the New Bouleuterion and we have already seen how, at Theramenes' trial, the Thirty and their adherents sitting inside the structure were very aware of the ruffians outside. Xenophon's description suggests the ease with which spectators looking from the outside could watch the *boule* on the inside. This external scrutiny was further aided by the absence of a lobby in the new council house, a design which emphasised the transparency of the proceedings. The situation in the New Bouleuterion also contrasted with the recent events under the Four Hundred. The oligarchs had used the original council house as the centre of their power which they maintained by excluding most Athenian citizens from the rule of the city. The *boule* of 500, however, now met in the most public council house possible, a design which invited external scrutiny, and they represented all Athenians through the tribes and the demes.[35] Brought together in this way, the democratic Athenians were unified by the very space itself, a dynamic which complemented the messages of the inscriptions and contrasted with the earlier lack of harmony under the oligarchs.

If the architecture of the Stoa Basileios and the New Bouleuterion opened up the interiors of the buildings to external scrutiny, it also displayed the activities of the Athenians using those spaces. Since the *boule* and the *basileus* were integral parts of the democracy, the structures themselves made the rule of the *demos* visible. As buildings continually present in the cityscape, their physical presence again reinforced the inscriptions' display of democracy as perpetually taking place. Individuals also took part in these dynamics. Every time a citizen consulted the inscribed laws in the Stoa Basileios or the written documents in the archive, his actions showed the documents' importance and emphasised their roles in making the rule of the *demos* possible. His activities were also a necessary part of the continued proper functioning of the democracy. Similarly, when the *anagrapheis* went to check or deposit documents in the archive or to inspect the inscribed

---

[34] Shear, Jr 1994: 239.
[35] For similar comments in connection with the Old Bouleuterion, see Shear, Jr 1994: 239.

versions at the Stoa Basileios, their actions involved the same dynamics. Meanwhile, their two collections of the laws were located at the north and south ends of the Agora's west side which they now stabilised (fig. 2). Together with the other inscriptions and the buildings, they emphasised that the Agora was now the space of *demos* which ruled through the very laws displayed in this space.

In the space of the Agora, the new buildings' importance was not limited to the ways in which they displayed democracy and its control because they also brought the past into the current dynamics. In their original form, both the Stoa Basileios and the Old Bouleuterion were constructed at the very end of the sixth century as part of the laying out of the new Agora and the provision of facilities for the new Kleisthenic democracy.[36] After the Persian destruction of 479, they were rebuilt to serve their original purposes.[37] Despite their reconstruction, there is no indication that the structures had lost their connections with Kleisthenes. Consequently, in the years after 411, the addition of the annexes to the Stoa Basileios will also have connected the current democrats with their forebears at the end of the sixth century. For several years, the *boule* must have continued to meet in the original council house while the new one was under construction and this meeting place will have made further associations between the present and the past. In addition, these connections allowed the *demos* to reclaim Kleisthenes from the oligarchs and to show that democracy had a proper past, one visible not just in the documents of the last chapter, but also in the monuments of the Agora. In this way, the system's roots in the *patrios politeia* were emphasised again in a very tangible way.

The past and the present come into play in a further way in the Bouleuterion complex and this interrelationship helps to explain both the new construction and the connection with the archives. Since the Four Hundred had used the (Old) Bouleuterion as the centre of their power, this structure became contested space. Upon the democrats' return, they had to contend with not only this memory, but also with the actions of the predecessors who had tamely taken their remaining pay from the Four Hundred and departed without protest. This behaviour is completely inconsistent with the models which we discussed in the previous chapter and it certainly was not an appropriate exemplum for future *bouleutai*. The presence of the oligarchs in the council house, accordingly, needed to be erased without a

[36] Shear, Jr 1994: 231–9; Shear, Jr 1995: 157–71; Shear, Jr 1993: 418–29, 472–7.
[37] Shear, Jr 1971: 250; Shear, Jr 1994: 240; Shear, Jr 1993: 402, 424, 426–7, 428–9, 459–60.

trace and their deeds had to be forgotten. In the face of these problems, these projects provided an excellent solution. The New Bouleuterion was fresh territory with no oligarchic associations at all and it was indubitably the space of the *demos*, now led by *bouleutai* who would not submit tamely to future oligarchs. The overall plan, the orientation, the aligned façades and possibly the design of the south side and the superstructure empha-sised the connections between the new building and the old Kleisthenic Bouleuterion so that the critical links to the democratic past were also maintained (fig. 9). Meanwhile, in the old council house, the oligarchs were not replaced by the democratic *boule*, but by the texts of the city's laws and decrees which made the rule of the *demos* possible and prevented any other type of *politeia*.[38] As documents produced by earlier generations of Athenians, they also served to link the present to the past and reinforced the idea that the democratic city did, indeed, have a suitable past. In this way, the oligarchs were erased from the Old Bouleuterion and no trace of their presence was allowed to remain. Now the past stretched without interruption from Kleisthenes through the city's laws and decrees to the present with the current *boule* in session next door. The removal of the oligarchs should also have reinforced the democratic nature of the spaces in the Bouleuterion complex.

In the context of the years after 411, accordingly, the construction projects in the Agora allowed the *demos* to gain control of this contested space and to stamp its possession visibly on to the square. These structures displayed the democratic system in operation and reinforced the dynamics which we have observed with the inscribed documents. Together, buildings and texts identified the Agora as a space now particularly associated with the rule of the *demos*. These developments mark a change in the nature and focus of the Agora: before 411, it had been multi-purpose space used in a variety of ways without one particular concentration, but, after 411, with its new focus on democracy, its documents and its processes, it was being turned into the space of the democratic citizen.[39] In this context, there is an especial concentration on the *boule* and the city's laws: in view of their manipulations by the Four Hundred, such an emphasis was necessary to redeem these important elements of the rule of the *demos*. The oligarchs, either the Four Hundred or the Five Thousand, are not, however, the particular focus of this space and its monuments: they and their presence are erased so that democracy, not the defeat of the oligarchs, is celebrated.

[38] Shear 2007a: 103.   [39] For these dynamics, see further Shear 2007a.

RECLAIMING THE AKROPOLIS

The Agora was not the only area in the city of Athens on which the struggles
for political control of the city were written. As we saw in chapter 2, both
the Four Hundred and the Five Thousand had inscribed documents and
erected them on the Akropolis. In the context of Athena's sanctuary, these
inscriptions bring out, especially for us, the ways in which the oligarchs
were using the city's traditions and offices for their own purposes. The
physical presence of these texts also allowed them to lay claim to the
sanctuary and to display their control of the space in a tangible fashion.
When the democrats came back into power, consequently, the Akropolis
was also an area of contestation and the *demos* needed to demonstrate its
control of the city's most important sanctuary. For the Athenians in 410,
the question must have been how to do so most effectively in a space
already crowded with buildings, dedications and inscriptions of all kinds.
Here, circumstances came to their aid: the new temple of Athena Polias
lay unfinished and had not been touched by the oligarchs (fig. 10, no. 9).
Finishing this building would demonstrate the power and control of the
demos. Since the temple had been begun in the mid to late 420s when
Athens was under democratic rule, completing it would also allow the
demos to make further connections with the city's democratic past.

The start of construction on the new temple must belong to some time
in the middle or later 420s. The karyatids are usually dated on the basis of
style to about 420 and the project must have been well along when they
were set in place.[40] The structure does not take its alignment from the
Propylaia and the Parthenon and, therefore, it cannot have been included
in the Periklean plan for the Akropolis (fig. 10).[41] Both the decision to
build and the start of the project ought to belong to the 420s. At some later
time, however, work ceased, as we know from the inscribed description
of the building which was produced in the first prytany of 409/8.[42] This
detailed document indicates that construction had reached the level of
the Ionic frieze except at the southwest corner where parts of the wall,
epikranitis and epistyle had not yet been put in place (fig. 11).[43] On the
west side, the four columns were in place and, on the south side, most

---

[40] Date of karyatids: see e.g. Hurwit 1999: 206; Stewart 1990: 167–8; Rolley 1999: 115, 117; Boardman
1985: 148.
[41] Shear 2001: 798. Contra: e.g. R. F. Rhodes 1995: 42; Camp 2001: 74, 100; Pedley 2005: 194–5; cf.
Hurwit 1999: 206.
[42] *IG* I³ 474 + *SEG* xxxIII 22.
[43] *IG* I³ 474 + *SEG* xxxIII 22.8–43; Paton and Stevens 1927: 301–8, 453, fig. 180.

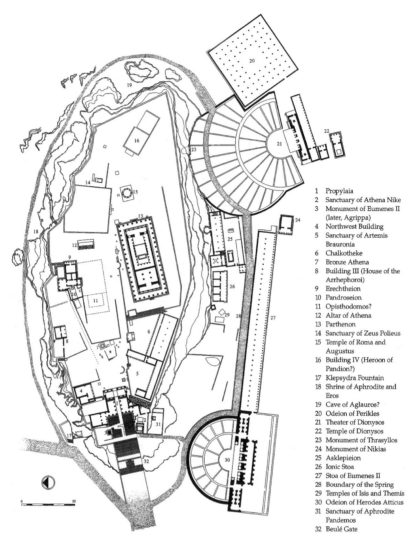

1   Propylaia
2   Sanctuary of Athena Nike
3   Monument of Eumenes II
    (later, Agrippa)
4   Northwest Building
5   Sanctuary of Artemis
    Brauronia
6   Chalkotheke
7   Bronze Athena
8   Building III (House of the
    Arrhephoroi)
9   Erechtheion
10 Pandroseion
11 Opisthodomos?
12 Altar of Athena
13 Parthenon
14 Sanctuary of Zeus Polieus
15 Temple of Roma and
    Augustus
16 Building IV (Heroon of
    Pandion?)
17 Klepsydra Fountain
18 Shrine of Aphrodite and
    Eros
19 Cave of Aglauros?
20 Odeion of Perikles
21 Theater of Dionysos
22 Temple of Dionysos
23 Monument of Thrasyllos
24 Monument of Nikias
25 Asklepieion
26 Ionic Stoa
27 Stoa of Eumenes II
28 Boundary of the Spring
29 Temples of Isis and Themis
30 Odeion of Herodes Atticus
31 Sanctuary of Aphrodite
    Pandemos
32 Beulé Gate

Figure 10   Restored plan of the Athenian Akropolis.

of the blocks were still covered with their working surfaces; in contrast,
the south porch with the maidens was almost complete.[44] Many blocks in
various stages of completion also lay around the structure.[45] Since much

---

[44] *IG* I³ 474 + *SEG* XXXIII 22.44–76, 83–92; Paton and Stevens 1927: 308–14, 453.
[45] *IG* I³ 474 + *SEG* XXXIII 22.93–237; Paton and Stevens 1927: 314–15.

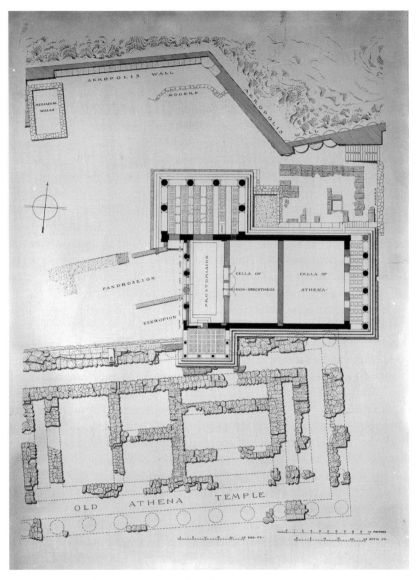

Figure 11   Plan of the Erechtheion and the foundations of the late sixth-century Temple of Athena on the Akropolis.

of the material needed to finish the project was already at hand, completing the temple must have seemed like a relatively manageable undertaking to the Athenians and so it proved to be: the project was brought to an end a few years later, probably in 406/5.[46]

The prescript of the inscription records that 'the *epistatai* (overseers) of the temple on the Akropolis in which the ancient image (is/will be)' presented their report in the first prytany of 409/8.[47] Their work had been authorised by a decree of the *demos* which had been moved by a certain Epigenes. This important detail indicates that the situation was discussed in the *ekklesia* and the proposal was subsequently approved by the *demos*. We are not told how long it took the *epistatai* to draw up their report, but, since there were only four meetings in each prytany or four meetings in every thirty-six-day period, it is very likely that the discussion had begun before the beginning of 409/8.[48] Chronologically, then, discussions about the possibility of continuing the temple must have been underway at the same time as the *demos* was considering how to respond to the oligarchs and the project needs to be understood in this larger context.

Completing the temple may have been particularly attractive because much of the necessary material was already at hand, but it was also extremely visible and, finished or unfinished, it could not have been overlooked (fig. 10). In contrast, a smaller monument might have been taken as a dedication and an inscription would not have stood out from among the many others already in the sanctuary. The project, however, also stressed the differences between the oligarchs and the democrats. With all of that available material, the oligarchs could have undertaken the project themselves, but they chose not to do so; in contrast, the *demos* did decide to finish the temple. In this sacred space, this opposition suggests implicitly that the Athenians were concerned about their relationship with Athena and the ways in which that relationship was made visible. Like sacrifices, offerings to the gods created and maintained a reciprocal relationship between humans and the divine.[49] The bigger and more elaborate the dedication, the greater the chances of further divine favour. In this dynamic, the Erechtheion was ideal: constructed of white Pentelic marble with dark Eleusinian limestone for the background of the frieze, the building was richly decorated with elaborate mouldings, a sculpted frieze running on

---

[46] This date is often given; see e.g. Hurwit 1999: 206; Stewart 1990: 167; Lawrence and Tomlinson 1996: 120; Pedley 2005: 194; cf. Camp 2001: 99; Wycherley 1978: 146.

[47] *IG* I³ 474 + *SEG* XXXIII 22.1–7.

[48] Meetings: Arist. *Ath. Pol.* 43.3; Mikalson 1975: 182–6; P. J. Rhodes 1981: 521.

[49] Parker 1998.

all four sides and the maidens of the south porch. Finishing the temple suggested a desire on the part of the *demos* to rebuild its relationship with the goddess in a conspicuous way. By implication, the oligarchs, who had left the structure alone, did not have such an association with Athena. The reciprocity of dedications, however, also functions at the level of display because the object makes the relationship visible in concrete terms. The temple, accordingly, displayed the reciprocity between the *demos* and the goddess, a dynamic which emphasised its piety and respect for the gods; the oligarchs, by contrast, lacked these important qualities. In addition, the project was undertaken by the whole *demos* and it brought the Athenians together both when they passed Epigenes' decree and when the newly finished temple was formally given to the goddess. Inscribing the document on stone further served to memorialise these dynamics.

For the *demos*, the links between itself and Athena were not the only benefits which finishing the temple brought because the structure also served to connect the democrats with the city's past. On the building's south side, the steps supporting the south wall and the south porch rest directly on the foundations of the archaic temple of Athena (fig. 11).[50] The overlap between the two structures is not very large, but its significance should not be underestimated: the Athenians had chosen deliberately not to rebuild the archaic temple after it was sacked by the Persians and the area had been left open and untouched. Moving the Erechtheion slightly to the north would have avoided this overlap with the ruined monument. That such a design was not chosen suggests that the connection between the two temples was deliberately sought. Of course, by 409/8, the new temple's plan was fixed and changes to it were no longer possible. The connection with the past, however, was still important. It allowed the democrats to link themselves with various points in the city's earlier history: the moment in the 420s when the new temple had been begun and the history of the archaic temple itself with its destruction by the Persians. Through the completion of the Erechtheion, these pasts were recovered for the *demos*. The 420s were important because, at that time, the city had been under democratic rule. The archaic temple is also significant because recent work has shown that its construction must date to about 500 BC[51] and it must belong to the extensive building undertaken at that time by the newly democratic Athenians. Consequently, in the years after 411, to finish the Erechtheion

---

[50] Paton and Stevens 1927: pl. 1. The archaic foundations are the ones frequently known in the scholarly literature as the 'Dörpfeld foundations'.

[51] Stähler 1972: 101–12; Childs 1994; Moore 1995: 633 with note 4; Stewart 1990: 129–30; Shapiro 1998: 128–9; Hurwit 1999: 121.

was to associate the *demos* with the democracy of Kleisthenes who was, therefore, reclaimed in much the same ways as were being done in the contemporary Agora. As in the market square, these associations indicated that the city had a good democratic past. The temple's connections also served to obscure the existence of the oligarchs because the city's history was construed as a direct line passing from the present to the 420s to the Persian destruction in 480 to the time of Kleisthenes. In this sequence, there was simply no room for any groups of Athenians who were not democrats and the enemies of the city were identified as foreigners and barbarians and not as Athenian oligarchs.

Elsewhere in the sanctuary, the Athenians faced a more visible oligarchic presence, a problem which required slightly different tactics. As we saw in chapter 2, the oligarchs erected a number of inscriptions on the Akropolis. Set up in sacred space and, in some cases, concerning the affairs of the goddess, these documents could not simply be removed and destroyed. They could, however, be de-emphasised. In the cases of the accounts for the Pronaos, the Hekatompedon and the Parthenon, the documents of the treasurers of 410/9 start either on a new *stele*, as in the case of the Pronaos and apparently the Parthenon, or on the reverse of the existing *stele*, as it appears with the Hekatompedon.[52] In either situation, the accounts were entered on a fresh and unused expanse of marble. Of course, these layouts may have been forced on the *tamiai* by lack of space under the existing accounts of the oligarchs. The absence of the oligarchs' entries above these texts, however, suggests that the accounts of 410/9 should be understood as marking a fresh start for the *demos*: these documents are not being related to the immediate past of the previous year. Meanwhile, the location of those texts on other *stelai* meant that their existence could be de-emphasised. Except in the case of the Hekatompedon accounts, however, this new start also meant that the activities of the treasurers of 410/9 could not be brought into relationship with the actions of the democratic *tamiai* from the period before 411.

Despite the erection of inscriptions in the Agora, the Akropolis contin-ued to be the primary location in the city for inscribed documents. From 410/9 alone, three inscriptions honouring the peoples of Neapolis and of Halikarnassos and Thrasyboulos the assassin of Phrynichos are preserved and similar documents are known from the following years.[53] In contrast

---

[52] *IG* i³ 338; 359; W. E. Thompson 1966: 286, 288–90. The *stele* for the accounts of the Pronaos in 410/9 is not preserved.

[53] 410/9: *IG* i³ 101–3. For subsequent years, see e.g. *IG* i³ 106; 108–10; 113–17; 119; 123–7.

to the documents in the Agora, these inscriptions on the Akropolis focus on foreigners and they do not concern Athenians, except in so far as the *demos* approved the honours. In this sense, these inscribed texts represent the continuation of earlier practices.[54] The accounts of the treasurers of Athena and of the loans of Athena Polias and Nike from 410/9 also were erected on the Akropolis. Since they concerned Athena and her sanctuary, the Akropolis was the appropriate place for them and their erection again followed earlier practices.[55] Their inscription, like the inscribing of the accounts for the renewed construction on the Erechtheion, permitted scrutiny and testified to the accountability of the *demos*, dynamics also at work in the Agora.[56] Continuing to erect decrees of the *demos* and other documents produced by the democracy on the Akropolis did provide continuity with the previous practices of both oligarchs and earlier democrats. The increasing numbers of inscriptions, however, continued to fill the space of the sanctuary and, as more *stelai* were erected, it must have become increasingly difficult to focus on specific earlier documents, unless, like the first inscription of (Athena's share of) the tribute, their physical appearance set them clearly apart from the mass of other documents.[57] Under these crowded conditions, the new *stelai* set up by the *demos* in the years after 411 will also have helped to obscure the documents of the oligarchs so that their desire to present themselves as legitimate now made it easier to render them inconspicuous. Although the oligarchs could not be completely erased from the documentary record, their memory could certainly be obscured so that it was not immediately apparent to visitors to the sanctuary. The texts of their inscriptions further aided this strategy because they do not use the terms oligarchs and oligarchy. Consequently, once readers had noticed these particular *stelai*, they would have to examine them quite closely, and to remember their archon years and secretary cycles, in order to work out the particular circumstances.

This reluctance to focus directly on the oligarchs appears even in the honorary decree for Thrasyboulos, the assassin of Phrynichos, a text which we might well have expected to focus directly on the Four Hundred and its members. Instead, Thrasyboulos is honoured with a gold crown simply because 'he is a goo[d] man [towards the *dem*]*os* of the Athenians

---

[54] On this pattern, see also Shear 2007a: 93–4, 99–100.

[55] *IG* i³ 338; 359; 375. For subsequent years, see e.g. *IG* i³ 314–16; 339–42; 376–9.

[56] Erechtheion accounts: *IG* i³ 476–9.

[57] First inscription of (Athena's share of) the tribute, known as the *Lapis Primus*: *IG* i³ 259–72. Meritt and McGregor in *IG* i³ estimate its minimum height as *c.* 3.583 m., a not inconsiderable inscription; Stroud 2006: fig. 1b.

and eager t[o do whatever] good he [can]'.[58] Without the literary sources about the assassination, we simply would not know why the Athenians were honouring Thrasyboulos at this moment.[59] Once the decree was inscribed and erected on the Akropolis, subsequent readers would have been equally uncertain about why the honorand merited such significant honours, which included citizenship and a gold crown announced at the City Dionysia, the first, as we shall see in chapter 5. Such a strategy may simply be about not singling out one particular individual from all the others and de-politicising the honours and circumstances,[60] but it also very neatly ignores the oligarchs, who remain unremembered in the gaps between the assassination, the passing of the decree, and its inscription and erection on the Akropolis. That this text reflects a deliberate decision is brought out by the slightly later honorary decree for Epikerdes of Kyrene, a document which also awarded a gold crown announced at the City Dionysia to the honorand. In this case, the reasons behind the document were stated explicitly and the text also mentioned his earlier honours.[61] Epikerdes' deeds, however, were financial: he aided the Athenians captured on Sicily and he donated a talent to the city for the war against the Spartans. These benefactions involve the Athenians and external enemies and they contrast with Thrasyboulos' action against an Athenian oligarch, an internal problem. Epikerdes' decree indicates that, on at least some occasions, the Athenians were willing to remember the honorand's benefactions in detail. To do so, however, required the circumstances to be presented in the text so that readers would know exactly what those benefactions had been. Such a strategy was not suitable in all situations and particularly not in Thrasyboulos' case when the details would allow the oligarchs to be remembered forever.

Since the Akropolis was also contested space in 410, the democrats needed to reclaim the sanctuary from the oligarchs. As in the marketplace, one of their strategies involved construction: finishing the incomplete new temple of Athena Polias. Through this project, the *demos* was able to rebuild its relationship with Athena, which had been ruptured by the oligarchy, and to create further links to the past. Its physical relationship to the sixth-century temple of Athena enabled the democrats to recover Kleisthenes yet again because that structure was part of the same construction project

---

[58] *IG* i³ 102.6–8.   [59] See above chapter 2.
[60] De-politicising: R. Osborne 1999: 354–7; not singling out individual: cf. Whitehead 1993: 47.
[61] *IG* i³ 125.6–17 and cf. 25–9 and Dem. 20.42.

as the Old Bouleuterion and the Stoa Basileios in the Agora. Since the oligarchs had done no work on the new temple of Athena, the democrats' project effectively erased them. Removing all traces of the oligarchs from the Akropolis, however, was not so easy a task because their inscriptions, set up in the precinct of the goddess, had become her property. Counteracting these texts' presence required most of the city's inscribed documents to continue to be erected on the Akropolis, where their sheer numbers would have obscured the inscriptions of the oligarchs. In some cases, of course, the Akropolis was the most appropriate place in the city. In other instances, it might have been possible to locate the *stelai* elsewhere in the city, but the Athenians chose not to do so and the inscriptions served an important role in the sanctuary. Forgetting the oligarchs could require further measures, as the inscription for Thrasyboulos, the assassin of Phrynichos shows. In the city's usual location for inscriptions, erasing oligarchs was not as simple as it was in the Agora and different parts of the sanctuary required slightly different strategies.

THE *DEMOS* AND THE POLITICS OF SPACE

As we have seen in this chapter, the Athenian cityscape in 410 included two areas, the Agora and the Akropolis, in which the democrats particularly contested for power with the oligarchs. The oligarchs had used both of these spaces to make their claims to the city visible. Their interest seems to have been sparked by two factors: the Akropolis was the city's most important sanctuary and the normal location for inscribed documents, while the Agora offered them a suitable meeting place and a base for their power. In both cases, using these spaces allowed the oligarchs to demonstrate the legitimacy of their regimes and to establish important links with the city's past. Their actions also made these two areas places of contestation, as Thucydides' narrative makes clear about the Agora. The power of place, then, was a very real aspect of the events in 411 and 410 and ignoring it was to invite further problems. The democrats, consequently, had to engage the oligarchs visibly and tangibly in the city's spaces. In so doing, however, they changed the politics of the Agora and also the power of its space.

For the democrats, as for the oligarchs, the importance of the Akropolis lay in its status as the city's most important sanctuary and, therefore, the best place for (re-)establishing and (re)displaying their reciprocal relationship with Athena. Using the space in its traditional fashion also brought with it complications as the *demos* sought publicly to erase the memory of the oligarchs. The democrats, however, need not have used the Akropolis in this fashion. Had they wished, they could have ceased to erect documents unconnected with the goddess in her sanctuary and they could have placed them elsewhere in the city. Changing this pattern of use, however, would have eliminated the opportunities for making connections with the past and so for reclaiming it for the democratic city.

Considering the traditional ways in which the *demos* made use of the Akropolis also emphasises the very different decisions which it made about the Agora. Once inscriptions began to be erected in the Agora, the marketplace might have seemed like the ideal place for setting up all documents except those pertaining to Athena and her sanctuary. This scenario, however, ignores the focus of the documents in the Agora: they are directed mainly or entirely at citizens; in contrast, the inscriptions on the Akropolis concern foreigners or matters connected in one way or another with the divine. These dynamics emphasise that the marketplace was a suitable place only for certain sorts of documents and they bring out the ways in which space for citizens was now being divided off from other areas, like sanctuaries and the Peiraieus, where everyone was welcome. In the Agora, the inscribed texts now literally write citizens and their interests onto the landscape and they suggest that they possess the space. This focus was complemented by the building projects because they also served citizens. Only *bouleutai*, an office restricted to Athenian men, would use the New Bouleuterion; other people would stand outside and watch them through the grilles. The display of the laws in the annexes of the Stoa Basileios would primarily have been of interest to citizens who played an important role in seeing that the laws of the city were carried out. For this same reason, they would have been the primary consultants of the city's archives now located in the Old Bouleuterion. Every time a citizen went to one of these buildings in the Agora and every time he consulted a document, whether inscribed on a *stele* or in the archive, his actions reinforced the Agora's new status as space now orientated towards and focused on the democratic citizen. In this context, the new structures also emphasised that the individual Athenian was a democrat and a man, a person who would use these buildings. This vision of the proper citizen reinforced the image presented by the bronze statues of the Tyrannicides and the inscriptions. If this ideal Athenian both read the texts and looked at the statues, as we saw in the previous chapter, then he also used the buildings, particularly the New Bouleuterion. In this space, his actions reinforced the multiple images of the good Athenian now promulgated in three different media.

Like the inscriptions, the construction projects both in the Agora and on the Akropolis also allowed the *demos* to display its control in very clear terms. When they were completed, they emphasised the democrats' success and they stressed that their power had lasted long enough for the structures to be finished. Like the inscriptions, the buildings wrote the control of the *demos* visibly onto the topography of the city. The new structures further helped to recover the past and more specifically Kleisthenes. In this way, they complemented the strategies of the inscriptions which we discussed in the previous chapter. In the Agora, the links with the past also assisted in establishing Kleisthenes as a figure on a par with Drakon and Solon, the city's two primary lawgivers, whose documents were among the new inscriptions. Making this democratic past physically visible through buildings and inscriptions further ensured that it would not be forgotten and it would remain available to the *demos*.

Not all aspects of the past were brought into the present. Just as the inscriptions left out the oligarchy from the past, so also did the new buildings. This process is most conspicuous in the Bouleuterion complex where the city's archives ultimately replaced the Four Hundred in a very tangible way and the *boule* was given a new structure of its own. This focus on physical space for the councillors complements the attention devoted to them in the inscribed regulations for the *boule* and the location of Demophantos' decree in front of the Old Bouleuterion. None of this display and documentation, however, accounts for the focus on the *boule*. The explanation must lie in the actions of the councillors towards the Four Hundred: instead of resisting the oligarchs, they meekly took their pay and disappeared. These inglorious actions, so much at variance with Demophantos' decree, had to be forgotten so that future *bouleutai* would not be tempted to model themselves on these particular predecessors. At the same time, the buildings in the Agora, like the texts, give us no idea why they were built and, consequently, the oligarchies are erased from the space. Similar strategies were also at work in some parts of the Akropolis: the new temple of Athena Polias and the decree for Thrasyboulos served to efface the oligarchs from memory. In this setting, more inscriptions were certainly better and only a determined reader would find the oligarchs and their presence inscribed into the precinct.[62] The politics of space, accordingly, are intricately intertwined with the remembering and forgetting,

---

[62] In theory, the oligarchs' presence could have been erased entirely by taking down their *stelai*. As the property of the goddess, however, the stones would have needed to remain in the sanctuary. With such a mass of inscribed texts on the Akropolis, these actions may not have seemed worth the trouble and they were not necessary to enable the politics discussed here to function.

issues crucial to the different ways in which the Athenians responded to the oligarchs. Negotiating these complications could not be done simply through buildings and documents. As we shall see in the following chapter, ritual, and particularly rituals involving all the Athenians, also played an important role in remembering and forgetting the oligarchs.

CHAPTER 5

Remembering and forgetting: rituals and *the* demos

In the years after 411, the democrats focused on reclaiming Athens and visibly remaking her into the democratic city. At the beginning of 410, two areas in particular, the Agora and the Akropolis, remained sites of contestation between oligarchs and democrats. If Athens was to be truly democratic, then these two spaces had to be reclaimed for the *demos*. This process, as we saw in the previous chapter, involved displaying democracy, its practices and its control in the cityscape, dynamics which very much complemented the strategies of the inscriptions erected in the marketplace. In the Agora, responding to oligarchy also began the process of changing the identity of the marketplace itself into the space of the citizen. These decisions, however, did not address a further important consequence of the events of 411: the fractures created among the different groups of the Athenians. The strength of these problems is clear in Thucydides' narrative which emphasises the oligarchs' creation and exploitation of these divisions both before and during the regime of the Four Hundred. For the *demos*, consequently, unity was an element which needed to be recreated among the Athenians and it is a feature in the inscriptions set up in the Agora which focus on all the Athenians. Documents, however, can only create so much unanimity because reading is inherently an individual activity.

Unifying divisions across the *demos* needed strategies which did not rely on the individual acting alone. For these purposes, rituals at the level of the city were ideal for uniting all the Athenians. The existing possibilities, however, were not completely perfect and, consequently, the *demos* created new ceremonies in the form of Demophantos' oath and the announcement of gold crowns, which it added to the City Dionysia. The rituals' roles, however, were not limited to unifying the *demos* and they also focused on the proper behaviour for the democratic citizen. Since rituals play an important role in the creation of memory, the new ceremonies at the Dionysia served as a way of negotiating the public memories of the oligarchs. Set in the city's topography, these ceremonials played a further important role: they animated space, monuments and inscriptions which would otherwise remain inanimate and amnesiac and they turned them into places of memory for the *demos*. In this way, these new rituals were critical to the Athenians' responses to the Four Hundred, both at the level of the individual, as we have seen in the last two chapters, and at the level of the city.

SWEARING THE OATH OF DEMOPHANTOS

The first of the two new ceremonies which the *demos* introduced to the City Dionysia is the oath of Demophantos, which we have considered as a text and a monument set up in the Agora. As we shall see, however, its full power comes not from its status as text and monument, but from its nature as a speech act and a ritual reinforcing the images which we have already discussed in connection with the text and the Agora. Our document prescribes quite specifically how the oath which it contains is to be administered: all the Athenians assembled by tribe and by deme are to swear over adult sacrificial victims 'before the Dionysia'.[1] Framed in this way, the document emphasises how and when the Athenians are to be marshalled, the two most important aspects of the ceremony. As I have argued in greater detail elsewhere, in order for all the Athenians to swear 'by tribe and by deme', the ten tribes had to be assembled in one place at the same time.[2] The occasion is given as 'before the Dionysia' (πρὸ Διονυσίων), a more specific phrase than hitherto appreciated and one which points towards the days immediately before the festival itself; the most likely candidate is 9 Elaphebolion between the Proagon on the 8th and the start of the festival proper on the 10th.[3] In this way, the oath was closely associated with Dionysos' celebration and its ideology, but it was not incorporated into the festival proper; indeed, as a one-off event, it did not belong within the ritual time and space of the Dionysia itself. The close association of these two occasions also allowed the Athenians to resolve one of the great problems surrounding this unique event: ensuring that 'all' the Athenians actually swore the oath when many of them were with the fleet in the Hellespont and in the absence of records identifying each individual citizen. At the time of the Dionysia, however, many citizens would have been in town for the festival and its ideology assumes the attendance, at least

---

[1] Andok. 1.96–8.   [2] Shear 2007b: 153–5.

[3] Shear 2007b: 155–7; compare Wilson 2009: 24–6. In contrast, MacDowell understood this term to mean any time over the period of eight to nine months between the first prytany, when the decree was passed, and the beginning of the Dionysia on 10 Elaphebolion; MacDowell 1962: 136.

figuratively, of the whole citizen body displayed in its democratic divisions, hence the presence of 'all' the Athenians ready to swear Demophantos' oath.[4] These dynamics further ensured the figurative presence of the fleet without requiring it to return physically to the city.[5]

As the text of the document now stands, it does not indicate where the Athenians were to swear the oath. Any possible location would have needed to be large in order to accommodate so many citizens in their tribes and demes and it would have needed an altar for killing the necessary sacrificial victims.[6] The connection with the Dionysia might suggest the god's sanctuary (fig. 4), but this sacred space was not connected with the taking of oaths and, in the days before the celebration, it was not the focus of ritual attention. The theatre's use as a gathering place for citizens in this period seems to have been restricted to the context of the festival.[7] More importantly, the document has no discernible connection with this sanctuary. Instead, its associations are elsewhere in the city: as we have seen, it was set up in the Agora at the (Old) Bouleuterion (fig. 2).[8] Its text explicitly connects the document with this space through the invocation of the Tyrannicides Harmodios and Aristogeiton in the oath; in 410/9, their statues had been standing in the Agora for almost one hundred years (fig. 8). More generally, the Agora was the place in which the Athenians were accustomed to gather by tribe for military service and to vote for ostracism and it was the location of the *lithos*, the oath-stone, at the Stoa Basileios, the site of the archons' annual oath to uphold the laws.[9] The Agora even seems to have had connections with the Dionysia because the procession bringing the statue to the city apparently halted at the Eschara to allow

---

[4] Shear 2007b: 156. Ideology of Dionysia: e.g. Goldhill 1990: 97–114; Ober and Strauss 1990: 237–40, 248–9; Henderson 1990: 285–7; Griffith 1995: 62–5, 107–24; Sourvinou-Inwood 1994: 270–3; Goldhill 1994: 360–9; Goldhill 2000: 35, 42–7; Sourvinou-Inwood 2003: 71–2; Wilson 2009; contra: Griffin 1998; Rhodes 2003.

[5] Shear 2007b: 156. We should note that the text makes no provision at all for another oath-swearing in some other time or place, as it would have to do, if it was taken by Athenians abroad with the fleet, as Rhodes has suggested; P. J. Rhodes 2007: 221 note 26. In fact, such multiple swearings would have undermined the whole point of the exercise by demonstrating that the Athenians were *not* united. As we shall see below, the memory politics of this document easily allowed the inclusion of the fleet.

[6] I have discussed this problem at greater length in Shear 2007b: 157–8. I remain unconvinced by Wilson's association of the oath and the theatre; Wilson 2009: 18 note 40, 24 note 73, 26.

[7] Csapo 2007: 107 with further references; Hansen and Fischer-Hansen 1994: 44–5, 51–2; Kourouniotes and Thompson 1932: 136–8. This pattern of use changed with the construction of the stone theatre in the 340s and 330s.

[8] Above chapter 3.

[9] Military service: Andok. 1.45; Siewert 1982: 10–13, 142; Traill 1986: 112–13 with further references. Ostracism: Philoch. *FGrHist* 328 F30; Plut. *Arist.* 7.5–6; Poll. *Onom.* 8.19–20; schol. Ar. *Knights* 855b; Forsdyke 2005: 146–9 with further references. Archons' oath: above chapter 3, note 120.

various rituals to take place there.[10] Collectively, this evidence suggests that the Athenians swore Demophantos' oath in the Agora on the *lithos* located not far from the Altar of the Twelve Gods, where the victims could be killed. On the appointed day just before the Dionysia, accordingly, the Athenians assembled by tribe and by deme will have gathered in the marketplace to wait until their deme was called forward to the *lithos* to swear its oath. By this time, Demophantos' decree authorising the ritual must already have been inscribed and erected in front of the (Old) Bouleuterion; in this location, it also commemorated the event in the place where it had taken place.

Swearing this oath was a collective experience because all the Athenians were gathered together in the Agora, where they would have waited for their turns and watched their fellow citizens perform. Since the text of the oath was specified in Demophantos' decree and drafted in the first person singular, each man individually swore exactly the same oath as his fellow Athenians.[11] As he stood at the *lithos*, each man touched the adult sacrificial victims in exactly the same way as everyone else.[12] In and of itself, this collective experience will have created unity among the citizens of Athens and using exactly the same oath will have reinforced this dynamic. At that moment when they were all collected in the Agora, the fractures between individual men will not have been visible as they all stood together in one body. The very mass of this collective body should also have reinforced the impression that all the participants were the same, an idea picked up by the single form of the oath. The process, consequently, made Athenian unity tangibly visible to all participants.

In the event that this representation would not be sufficient, the text of the oath itself also aided the process because it specifically annulled and dissolved any oaths sworn 'in Athens or in the camp or anywhere else against the *demos* of the Athenians'. Without this clause, these earlier oaths would still have been binding and they would have continued to create divisions between different groups of Athenians. Releasing the individuals concerned from their earlier oaths not only broke the relationships created with the gods by these actions,[13] but it also allowed the men to take part in Demophantos' oath and it brought them together with their fellow

---

[10] Sourvinou-Inwood 1994: 278–88; Sourvinou-Inwood 2003: 89–99; Parker 2005: 318.
[11] Shear 2007b: 155; Loraux 2002: 142.
[12] Compare Burkert 1985: 251–2 with Cole 1996: 230–3. Both Burkert and Cole stress the importance of touching the victims while swearing. The necessity of this contact will have had important practical implications for taking Demophantos' oath.
[13] Rudhardt 1958: 210.

citizens. In this way, they participated in and helped to create the unity being established among the Athenians. Their past actions, i.e. swearing the earlier oaths, did not prevent them now from being good members of the *demos*. Of course, in 409, no man could admit to not swearing Demophantos' oath because to do so was to identify himself as an enemy of the *demos*; consequently, this clause was necessary to enable the participation of Athenians across all the various divisions created by the events of the oligarchies. Since the oath identified opponents of the *demos* as *polemioi*, as external enemies of the city, swearing the oath created further unity among the citizens by setting them in opposition to these external foes.[14]

In these specific ways, consequently, the very actions of swearing Demophantos' oath created unity visually and tangibly among the Athenians involved. Although these dynamics are especially clear here, they are not limited to this particular case because swearing oaths reaffirms the unity of the community involved and assures its permanence by the very nature of the process.[15] Choosing to use an oath to unify the citizens and to heal the divisions among them, therefore, took advantage not only of the specific circumstances of this particular situation, but also of the regular dynamics of this general ritual, which would have been familiar from serving in court and holding public offices. For the Athenians just before the Dionysia of 409, perceiving what was taking place and understanding how the unity was being created should not have been difficult. They should not have had any illusions about exactly what they were doing and how the oath was enabling their reconciliation after *stasis*.[16] Demophantos' choice of the oath was, accordingly, extremely good and it was a much more relevant ritual than it might first appear to modern eyes.

Swearing this oath also functioned to display democracy. In the Agora, the Athenians were arrayed by tribe and by deme, the hallmarks of the Kleisthenic system, so that, for this day, the rule of the *demos* was made visible in the multitude of the citizens.[17] Since all men swore exactly the same oath in the first person singular, they all behaved in exactly the same way and no one person was given special treatment; the united citizens formed a single body of exact equals, a situation replicating

[14] Rudhardt 1958: 207. On the dynamics concerning *polemioi*, see Shear 2007b: 150–1, 159 and above chapter 3.
[15] Rudhardt 1958: 212; Cole 1996: 241; Loraux 2002: 130; Shear 2007b: 148.
[16] For the roles of oaths in reconciliation after civil strife, see Loraux 2002: 138–41; P. J. Rhodes 2007: 20–1.
[17] Similar dynamics also existed when the Athenians voted to ostracise or exile one of their fellow citizens for ten years: they gathered in the Agora and voted by tribe so that the *demos* and its divisions were put on display; above note 9.

precisely the dynamics of democracy itself. Reciting the text of the oath, as each citizen did, should also have brought out its emphasis on democracy; the dynamics which we discussed in chapter 3 would have been no less visible for being spoken rather than being read. Democracy was continually juxtaposed against what it was not: oligarchy and tyranny. Under the gaze of the bronze statues of the Tyrannicides and in the context of the Agora (figs. 2, 8), swearing the oath should also have looked back to that seminal moment when Athens first became a democracy and the tyrant was overthrown.[18] Reciting the words of the oath will also have reinforced the relationship between the statues, the citizen and the democracy because the man actually swore to become a tyrant slayer: if circumstances demanded, he must imitate the deeds of the two heroes in reality and preserve the rule of the *demos*.

These dynamics had further consequences because they identified the citizen as a good Athenian and his opposite, the bad Athenian who, by overthrowing the *demos* or getting involved in tyranny, became a *polemios*. Articulated again and again as each man swore, these images will have been inescapable: by the end of this particular day, all Athenians will have received a very strong impression of what being a good democratic citizen entailed. In the context of the Agora, that vision will have been made concrete not only by the Athenians taking the oath, but also by the statues of the Tyrannicides, the very figures whom they swore to imitate (fig. 8). Through the anti-tyrannical nature of the figures, the juxtaposition should have brought out further the anti-tyrannical nature of the oath and, consequently, of the Athenians. Furthermore, in this context of the Dionysia of 409, these relationships also identified the ideal viewer of the statue group as the Athenian man who swore Demophantos' oath, just as a few years later, the ideal viewer would be the ideal reader of the inscription with the text of the oath, as we saw in chapter 3.

Since oaths not only create bonds between different men, but also between men and the gods,[19] the citizen who swore this oath was also assured of divine help as he carried out his speech act and protected the democracy; for him, there would be many good things, as the last clauses of the document stipulate. These bonds were not just between the individual and the gods, but also between the united citizens, the *demos* as a whole, and the divinities. In this context, then, swearing the oath visibly indicated that

---

[18] So the deed of the Tyrannicides entered the popular imagination; Harmodios *skolia PMG* nos. 893–6 = Ath. 15.695a–b, nos. 10–13; Ar. *Lys.* 626–35. Whether it was true or not was, by 409, beside the point.

[19] Gods and men: Rudhardt 1958: 208–10; Cole 1996: 230.

the gods were supporting the rule of the *demos* and they were not supporting tyrants and oligarchs, whose previous bonds were explicitly broken. In the coming years, this notion of divine support would be reinforced both by finishing the construction of the Erechtheion and by erecting the sacrificial calendar, an indication, as it were, of what the Athenians needed to do to maintain the divine relationships created by taking their oath in 409. Participating in that ritual had also firmly united the Athenians and had identified them all as good democrats willing to die to preserve the rule of the *demos*. That occasion derived its power from the mass display of the event and from the oath's nature as a speech act, the very characteristics which made it a public ritual of the democratic city.

ANNOUNCING GOLD CROWNS AT THE CITY DIONYSIA

The oath of Demophantos was not the only new ceremony which the *demos* added to the City Dionysia of 409 because it also took this opportunity to create new honours for some of the city's foreign benefactors: gold crowns announced at the dramatic contests in the theatre. Until this time, foreigners helping Athens had been listed as benefactors and, as *proxenoi*, they sometimes received a one-time invitation to hospitality in the Prytaneion, as well as rewards such as the right to own property (*enktesis*) and other protections.[20] From the 430s, Athenian benefactors were granted *sitesis*, as authorised by decree of the *boule* and *demos*, and, by 425, occasionally front-row seats in the theatre (*proedria*).[21] None of these worthy men were given crowns, much less ones announced publicly at the Dionysia. Attested for the first time in this year, these awards mark both a significant development in the city's honours for its important benefactors and the beginning of a tradition of recognising them at this festival. In the context of 409, this new ritual was not merely about presenting better rewards to a few men. Instead, it also provided the *demos* with another opportunity for displaying itself, its power and its control, just as it had a few days earlier when Demophantos' oath had been sworn. This focus on democracy must have been reinforced by the identify of the honorands: they included none other than Thrasyboulos of Kalydon and Apollodoros of Megara, the assassins

---

[20] Benefactors: [Lys.] 20.19; Gauthier 1985: 16–18, 22–4. Rewards for *proxenoi*: Walbank 1978: 3–8, 10–23; M. J. Osborne 1981: 153–8.
[21] *IG* i³ 131; M. J. Osborne 1981: 158; Gauthier 1985: 93–5. Kleon was certainly awarded both *proedria* and *sitesis* after his victory at Sphakteria in 425; Ar. *Knights* 573–6 with 280–1, 702–9, 766, 1404–5; Gauthier 1985: 95–6. Crowns for citizens do not appear until the fourth century; for the epigraphical evidence, see Henry 1983: 23, 29–30.

of the oligarch Phrynichos. This new ritual presented an image of the ideal benefactor and his relationship to Athens, a role which complemented the ideal citizen displayed in the oath-taking in the Agora.

Although in the fourth century, Aischines and Demosthenes discuss the award of crowns and their announcements very forcefully, they are not concerned with the origins of a ritual which for them was an accepted part of public life in the city.[22] Its early history emerges through the epigraphical records which show that the custom was not as old as Aischines and Demosthenes may have supposed: the announcement of gold crowns is first attested in the inscription honouring Thrasyboulos of Kalydon in 410/9 and it next appears in 405/4 in the very fragmentary decree for Epikerdes of Kyrene. Passed by the *boule* and the *demos* in the eighth prytany of 410/9, the text honouring Thrasyboulos praises him for being a good man towards the *demos* of the Athenians and for being eager to do whatever good he can; in return, he is to be crowned with a gold crown and the herald is to announce at the contest of the Dionysia the reasons why the *demos* crowned him.[23] Two amendments follow. The first makes Thrasyboulos an Athenian citizen and provides him with further honours; it also identifies certain other men as benefactors of the *demos* and provides them with various lesser honours.[24] The second amendment requires the *boule* to investigate bribery connected with the passing of an earlier decree for Apollodoros, the other assassin of Phrynichos.[25] The honours for Thrasyboulos and Apollodoros are also explicitly mentioned by Lysias who states that both men were given Athenian citizenship and quotes from two of the decrees in question.[26] That the honours were contested by different participants and alleged participants emerges clearly from both the decree for Thrasyboulos and Lysias' remarks.[27] Despite the second amendment of Thrasyboulos' decree and all the wrangling which it implies, Thrasyboulos' and Apollodoros' rewards were upheld, as Lysias makes very clear; elsewhere, he also refers to the property which the *demos* gave to Apollodoros.[28] The second amendment requires that Apollodoros' honours were approved before those for Thrasyboulos. In Lysias' description, both men are described as receiving the same rewards and it is hard to believe that Apollodoros received less than Thrasyboulos.[29] We must imagine,

---

[22] Dem. 18 and Aischin. 3; Goldhill 1990: 104–5; Goldhill 2000: 44–5.

[23] *IG* I³ 102.1–14. For the date when Hippothontis was in prytany in 410/9, see *IG* I³ 375.27.

[24] *IG* I³ 102.14–38.   [25] *IG* I³ 102.38–47.

[26] Lys. 13.71–2; M. J. Osborne 1981–2: II, 17–19.   [27] Lys. 13.70–3; M. J. Osborne 1981–2: II, 20.

[28] Lys. 7.4.   [29] Compare M. J. Osborne 1981–2: II, 20.

therefore, that gold crowns for both men were announced at the City Dionysia of 409.

As far as our epigraphical evidence indicates, this honour was not awarded again until 405/4 when it appears in the very fragmentary decree for Epikerdes of Kyrene.[30] The text rewards him for donating a talent to the city for the war against Sparta and it orders him to be crowned. The crown is to be announced at the up-coming games in the *astu*, a phrase which ought again to refer to the City Dionysia.[31] At that time, the herald is to say that the *demos* had previously crowned Epikerdes for his earlier benefaction.[32] That this old crown is to be mentioned here suggests that it was not announced when it was originally awarded. The announcement for the new crown ought to guarantee that it was gold because only gold crowns are known to have been announced at the festival of Dionysos.[33]

These gold crowns announced at the City Dionysia are the earliest known examples. That they mark the introduction of a new ritual is suggested not only from their earlier absence in decrees for the city's benefactors, but also by the ways in which the two decrees describe the crowns: the relevant passages have not yet reached the canonical forms used in later documents.[34] Thrasyboulos' decree specifies:

Erasinides propos[ed to prai]se Thrasyboulos since he is a goo[d] man [towards the *dem*]os of the Athenians and eager t[o do whatever] good he [can]; and, in return for the good which he ha[s done both to the city] and to the *dem*[o]s of the Athenian[s, to crown him with a gol]d c[r]own [and] to mak[e the crown from one thousand *dr*]*achmai*; [let] the [*hellenotamiai* provide the fund]s; and [the herald is to announce at the] contest [of the Dionysia] the reasons w[hy the *demos* crowne]d [him].[35]

These instructions might not seem unusual at first sight: we are told why and how the man is to be honoured. They contrast, however, with later usage. For the clause of commendation, one of two canonical forms is

[30] *IG* i³ 125; for his benefactions, cf. Dem. 20.42.   [31] *IG* i³ 125.17, 23–9.

[32] On the two crowns, see MacDowell 2004: 131, 133. It is not at all clear to me when this first crown was awarded and whether we must imagine it being approved before 411; for the reasons outlined above, a date before 410 seems unlikely to me. MacDowell places it without explanation in 412; MacDowell 2004: 130 with note 14; see also Wilson 2009: 14 note 29.

[33] On the material of the second crown, see Henry 1983: 30–1; MacDowell 2004: 131; contra: Meritt 1970: 113.

[34] So also Wilson 2009: 10, 17–18, 20; cf. R. Osborne 1999: 354.

[35] *IG* i³ 102.5–14. For some other proposals for the fragmentary line 13, see Wilson and Hartwig 2009: 17–22. I am not quite sure that the herald, present in other early examples, should be eliminated. Their restorations do not greatly affect my argument.

used: either to praise so-and-so on account of his good deeds, or something similar, towards the *demos* and to crown him or to praise so-and-so and to crown him on account of his good deeds, or something similar, towards the *demos*.[36] In Epikerdes' inscription, this part of the text is too fragmentary to restore, but the remains suggest again that the later canonical form was probably not used here. We know more about the proclamation clause which seems to read:

[The herald is also] to announce proclaiming [in ad]dition a[t the contest] quite [dir]ectly in the *astu* [that previously Epike]rdes of Kyrene [contri]buted [one hundred *mnai* to] the Athenians [for their safety, in return for which they a]lso cro[wned] him [on] account of [his being a good man] and his good [will towards the Athenians].[37]

The inscription is quite specific about what exactly the proclamation is to say and when it is to be made. Both this clause and the parallel passage in Thrasyboulos' decree contrast with the later canonical form: to announce the crown at the contest of the City Dionysia.[38] The more elaborate formulations found in the documents for Thrasyboulos and Epikerdes suggest that the process of awarding and announcing crowns was new at this time and, consequently, the procedures needed to be spelled out in rather more detail than they would be in the later fourth century and in the Hellenistic period, when the formulae are extremely regular.

The terms used to described the honorands in these two inscriptions are also significant because they present a specific image of the benefactors. Thrasyboulos is described as an *aner agathos*, a phrase which at first sight appears rather aristocratic and perhaps recalls the term *kalos k'agathos*.[39] The proposer Erasinides, however, has been more specific because he has qualified the clause so that Thrasyboulos is 'a good man towards the demos of the Athenians'. This addition is crucial because it removed the word *agathos* from its traditional elite setting and made it firmly democratic.[40] This phrase, 'a good man towards the *demos* of the Athenians', is attested in honorary decrees by about 430 and it may have been used as early as the middle of the fifth century; by 410/9, it was part of the proper

---

[36] E.g. *IG* ii² 657.58–62 (honours for Philippides of Kephale of 283/2 BC); *Agora* xvi 187.26–30 (honours for the *taxiarchoi* of 271/0 BC). For further examples, see Henry 1983: 22–4.

[37] *IG* i³ 125.23–9.

[38] E.g. *IG* ii² 657.58–62 (honours for Philippides of Kephale of 283/2 BC). For further examples, see Henry 1983: 28–33.

[39] *IG* i³ 102.6–7. The phrase *aner agathos* has its origins in elite contexts and is then taken over by the Athenian *demos* for its own purposes, including the funeral oration; Sourvinou-Inwood 1995: 170–2; Whitehead 1993: 44–5; Loraux 1986: 98–109.

[40] Whitehead 1993: 47.

and accepted way of describing a man honoured by the democratic city.[41] In the years after 411, Thrasyboulos was not the only honorand to be so described. At the beginning of Epikerdes' decree, we learn that he, too, is to be praised for being a good man, but lack of space on the stone suggests that the *demos* was not mentioned at this point. His quality as *aner agathos* is apparently picked up later in the document in the specifications for the proclamation which seem to have mentioned not only his *eunoia* (good will), but also his *andragathia*. This term *andragathia* first appears in honorary inscriptions in the last twelve years of the fifth century when it seems to have been used precisely to avoid the aristocratic term *arete* which we might otherwise expect to be paired with the adjective *agathos*.[42] In the context of Epikerdes' document, consequently, the word stressed the text's democratic nature as an honorary decree approved by the *boule* and the *demos*; the term *aner agathos* also performs a similar function in both inscriptions. These words also serve to illuminate further the nature of the honorands and their benefactions on behalf of the democratically ruled city.

Together, the documents and the rituals at the Dionysia create and display relationships between the *demos* and the honorands and they also put forth specific images of those involved. The inscriptions particularly bring out the ways in which the Athenians honour their benefactors appropriately and later honorary decrees will articulate explicitly that the Athenians have acted so that they will be seen to reward those doing good for the city.[43] If the city has obligations to her benefactors, then they also have responsibilities towards her. This dynamic comes out very clearly in the honours for Epikerdes who is thanked for both his recent and his earlier benefactions. Having been honoured once, he needed to keep showing his good will towards the Athenians and these actions led, in turn, to his second round of honours. At the Dionysia, the form of his announcement with its recitation of his earlier benefactions and honours will have made this dynamic extremely clear.

More than displaying this reciprocal relationship was at work here, however. For the *demos*, honouring these men showed its power: it had

---

[41] *IG* I³ 17.7–9 (traditionally 451/0; Rhodes: 418/7?); 30.4–5 (*c.* 450?); 43.4–5 (435–427); 65.10–11 (*c.* 427/6); 96.16 (412/1); 101.9–10 (410/9); 227.13–14 (424/3); cf. *IG* I³ 73.24–5 (424/3); 92.7–9 (422/1); Whitehead 1993: 44–7; on the problems of dating fifth-century Athenian inscriptions, see P. J. Rhodes 2008; for the date of *IG* I³ 92, see Develin 1989: 429.

[42] Whitehead 1993: 47–50, 55–62; on the term *andragathia*, see also Whitehead 1983: 61, 69–70; Whitehead 2009: 50–5. The first occurrence is in *IG* I³ 97, dated to 412/1.

[43] Of the earlier examples, see e.g. *IG* II² 222.11–16; 223.13–14; 300.2–5; 448.16–19; 487.10–12; 505.41–3; 555.9–11; 657.50–2; *SEG* xxviii 60.83–6; RO 95.65–6, 76–8.

enough control that it could reward benefactors who had helped it. In the context of the Dionysia of 409, adding the new announcements of crowns to the other pre-play rituals should particularly have brought out this display of power because to augment or otherwise to change a festival is to demonstrate control of the event. The proclamation in the theatre will have shown the democracy in action as the *demos* honoured its benefactors. This process will have looked back to the moment in the *ekklesia* when the decrees were approved by the people, while the inscribed texts will have conveyed the sense that this activity was continuing because each reader repeated the proclamation used at the festival, dynamics familiar to us from the inscriptions erected in the Agora. In this setting with its emphasis on the rule of the *demos* and its power, the terms *aner agathos* and *andragathia* become significant as markers of what it means to be democratic: to serve the city in a way beyond the ordinary. These phrases also serve to characterise the honorands as democrats and supporters of the *demos*. They are men who use their qualities as *andres agathoi* to benefit the democratic city. In the case of Thrasyboulos and Apollodoros, their identity as the assassins of Phrynichos will have brought out further their associations with the *demos* and their opposition to oligarchy.

When the crowns were announced in the theatre, the herald will have announced the men's names and their ethnics, as the specifications about the proclamation in Epikerdes' decree indicate. At that moment, these ethnics will have identified the honorands as non-Athenians, albeit non-Athenians who cared enough about the democratic city to do good deeds on her behalf. Epikerdes' inscription further suggests, however, that rewards other than the gold crown were not mentioned in the proclamation so that spectators in the theatre would not know that both Thrasyboulos and Apollodoros had become Athenians by virtue of their benefactions. Consequently, the new ritual of announcing crowns presented a very specific image of the ideal honorand: he was certainly a democrat and a supporter of the *demos*, but he was also not Athenian. In this way, the *demos* retained power over its benefactors, the *andres agathoi* who could only become citizens through its gift. These announcements further served to display the democracy's power, particularly in 409, when this ritual was added for the first time to the festival. The ability to change the Dionysia in this way will also have served as a further testament to the control which the *demos* had over the city. The announcement of crowns at the Dionysia, consequently, very much complemented the dynamics visible elsewhere in the city, particularly in the Agora with its display of the *demos* and its power.

THE DIONYSIA OF 409

The addition of the oath of Demophantos and the announcements of gold crowns must have made the City Dionysia of 409 a particularly charged event for the Athenians as they celebrated the first festival for Dionysos since the *demos* regained power. In the context of this international setting, both these new additions and the existing rituals of the libation of the generals, of the presentation of the tribute and the war-orphans and of the proclamation against tyrants served to display the power and control of the *demos*. They worked together within the context of the overall festival and they also presented a series of ideal images, of the good Athenian, of the good benefactor and of the good colonist and ally. All of these individuals had a fixed role to play in the proceedings and the rituals will have reinforced those roles. The ceremonies by their very nature will have served to unify the divisions among Athenians who participated together in these events. Doing so will have created a particular set of memories about what it meant to be a democratic Athenian citizen at this precise moment.

Swearing the oath of Demophantos in the Agora was the first in this series of rituals and it established the focus on the power of the *demos* and the role of the proper Athenian citizen. He was identified as a male Athenian prepared to defend the democratic city against oligarchs and tyrants. Swearing the oath made him not merely an imitator of the Tyrannicides Harmodios and Aristogeiton, but it recreated him as a potential tyrant slayer. Arrayed by tribe and by deme, all the Athenians took part in this ritual and it further served to heal the divisions among them. Now, they were all identified as democrats and they were shown to be exactly equal. In contrast to this good Athenian, the occasion also identified the bad Athenian, the man who overthrows the democracy and replaces it with oligarchy or tyranny. In the course of the ritual, not only was the power of the democratic city prominently displayed, but it was actually recreated by the actions of the Athenians. The mass nature of the event must have increased this sense of the display of the power of the *demos*, while it must also have added a powerful stimulus to conform to and follow the model of the good citizen which was being presented. For the participants, subsequent visits to the Agora will have recalled this important moment when the Athenians brought together again in one body swore to be tyrant slayers.

This stress on democracy, unity and identity also appears in the various pre-play rituals which marked the important moment before the dramatic contests began. Although some of the generals were on campaign at the time of the festival, Thrasyllos and others seem to have been in Athens; they presumably offered their customary libation.[44] As elected officials of the *demos*, their presence on this particular occasion ought to have reminded spectators that the city was now democratically ruled. Their role as military leaders should have complemented the images of the Athenians marshalled by tribe and by deme, the same divisions in which they fought for the city, as they had sworn Demophantos' oath a few days earlier. The men offering their libation would lead the Athenians against the city's external enemies, the *polemioi* who figure in the text of the oath. This focus on the city's military strength may also have been picked up in our second ritual, the display of the tribute. Although the tribute was suspended in 413, it seems to have been reinstated towards the beginning of the final decade of the century, probably in 410/9, to which year a fragment of a decree assessing tribute has been assigned.[45] Once the tribute had arrived in Athens, displaying it in the theatre at the Dionysia was a very clear index of the power of the city which could compel this spectacle, as Isokrates makes clear for his own purposes in his description of the practice.[46] In describing the ritual, Isokrates sets up oppositions between the full theatre and the tribute, the allies and the other Greeks and the Athenians and everyone else. Who is looking and their relationship to what is seen is important: for the Athenians, looking at other cities' wealth brings out their superior status, but, for the allies, looking at their own wealth now in the hands of the Athenians stresses their inferior status; meanwhile, the other Greeks are located outside these dynamics as mere spectators without any connection to Athens. In this web of relationships, the power displayed is Athenian power; in 409, it reflected back on to the *demos* which had reinstated the tribute and still had the military might to compel its collection. These dynamics also emphasised the corporate nature of the

---

[44] Generals on campaign: Thrasyboulos, Theramenes and Alkibiades were in the Hellespont, but not official generals; of the official generals, Eukleides was at Eretria; Dexikrates, Pasiphon, Aristokrates and E[– 7 –] of Euonymon were on Samos; and Oinobates was on Thrace; *IG* i³ 101.47; 375.14, 16–18, 30–1, 35–6; Andrewes 1953: 2–8; Develin 1989: 165–6. Thrasyllos seems to have been in Athens between December 411 and April or May 409; Andrewes 1953: 2, 4–6. The names of three of the city's official generals are not known: presumably they were not on campaign at the time of the Dionysia of 409. Libation: Plut. *Kim.* 8.7–9; Goldhill 1990: 100–1; Goldhill 2000: 44.

[45] Suspension of tribute: Thuc. 7.28.3–4; Gomme, Andrewes and Dover 1970: 402, 408. Decree: *IG* i³ 100; contra: Mattingly 1967: 13–14. Reinstatement of the tribute: Xen. *Hell.* 1.3.8–9 (*phoros* collected from Kalchedon); Meritt 1936: 386–9; Meritt, Wade-Gery and McGregor 1950: 91–2, 363; Meiggs 1972: 438–9; Munn 2000: 156; Krentz 1989: 119–20; contra: Kallet 2001: 223–4; Hornblower 2008: 595–6 with further references. The evidence is admittedly not as certain as we would like.

[46] Isok. 8.82–3 with Raubitschek 1941b: 356–62; on the display of the tribute, see further Goldhill 1990: 101–4; Goldhill 2000: 45–6.

Athenians, who were treated as a single group set in opposition to everyone else; in this way, the ritual served physically to bring together again the divided Athenians. These images of Athenian collectivity and wholeness should have served to reinforce the unity which had been created by swearing Demophantos' oath. This spectacle of the tribute would also have recalled similar presentations of the tribute before its suspension and so the effect is also to reconnect the present with the past, a time when the city had also been ruled by the *demos*.

In his description, Isokrates links the display of the tribute with the presentation of the war-orphans, the sons of the war-dead who had been brought up at the city's expense and were now adults, ready to fight for Athens, as their armour indicated.[47] It is these young men, not the tribute, whom the other Greeks watch, an action which again emphasises their lack of relationship to the city. For the Athenians, however, these orphans were the sons of citizens who would now take their place as full members of the body politic. Dressed in armour donated by the city, these young men displayed its military might, an image which was reinforced by the presence of the generals, the men who would command the young men. Since the orphans were being formally presented to the Athenians at this moment, they were announced by the herald who gave their patronymics and, presumably, their demotics.[48] In Aischines' fuller version, the herald says 'that these young men, whose fathers died in the war as *andres agathoi*, the *demos* was bringing up until adulthood, but now, equipping them fully in these panoplies, the *demos* sends them out with good fortune to go their own ways and invites them to *proedria*' in the theatre.[49] Here, the stress is on the actions of the *demos*, which has been responsible for the orphans, while the young men are the recipients of its actions. In the context of 409, such an emphasis would have brought out the power of the *demos* and its control. The dead fathers are strikingly described as *andres agathoi*, the same phrase used in the honorary inscriptions for Thrasyboulos and Epikerdes. In this ritual, the *demos* is recognising not only the new adult status of the orphans, but also the *andragathia* of their fathers, and its acknowledgment further reinforces the democratic nature of the term *agathos* as it is used

---

[47] Isok. 8.82 with Aischin. 3.154; on the war-orphans, see further Goldhill 1990: 105–14; Goldhill 2000: 46.

[48] Lys. fr. LXIV.129 lines 30–8 (Carey).

[49] Aischin. 3.154; cf. Lys. fr. LXIV.129 lines 30–8 (Carey). In this more succinct version, Lysias says 'at the Dionysia, when the herald announces the orphans with their patronymics and he says by way of introduction that the fathers of these young men died in the war fighting on behalf of the fatherland as *andres agathoi* and that the city (*polis*) was bringing them up until adulthood'. On the term *andres agathoi*, see Loraux 1986: 98–101, 103–6.

in honorary inscriptions. This public recognition marks out the fathers' actions as the proper activities of the citizen. Fighting in *polemos*, external war, not *stasis*, internal conflict, they died on behalf of the city. They serve very clearly as a model for the sons, who should aspire to match their achievements; this exemplum, however, is also one for all the Athenian citizens sitting in the theatre and about to welcome the sons into their ranks.

In 409, this model of the good citizen who fights in external war and is an *aner agathos* linked the presentation of the war-orphans to two other rituals of this particular festival, Demophantos' oath and the new announcement of crowns. In the oath, the good citizen is presented as a democratic tyrant slayer who fights external enemies, *polemioi*, a term cognate with *polemos*, the war in which the orphans' fathers fought. Reframing this image in the rituals of the theatre will have reinforced its importance to the citizens and created another memory of what it meant to be a citizen of the city, an image complementing the one which, a few days earlier, they had sworn to put into action. The phrase *aner agathos* also links the orphans and the benefactors of the city. It suggests that these foreigners had achieved a level of attainment comparable to that of the war-dead, the ultimate model for the proper democratic citizen. That Thrasyboulos and Apollodoros had killed the oligarch Phrynichos, a man depicted by Thucydides in many ways as a tyrant, ought to have reinforced the connection and to have linked the announcement of crowns back to the oath and its imagery. For such benefactors, citizenship was an appropriate reward indeed.[50]

These announcements in 409 seem, however, to have been rather reticent, as further consideration of the details involved shows. When the moment came for this ritual to be performed for the first time, the herald must have risen and proclaimed that the *demos* of the Athenians crowned Thrasyboulos of Kalydon; as the inscription prescribes, he must have stated the reasons why. Perhaps he used the phrase from the beginning of the decree: 'because Thrasyboulos is a good man towards the *demos* of the Athenians and he is eager to do whatever good he can'.[51] Perhaps Thrasyboulos was described as a 'good man "towards the city and the *demos* of the Athenians"', as he is in the crowning clause of the inscription.[52] If, however, the herald said that Thrasyboulos was a 'good man towards the *demos* of the Athenians because he killed the oligarch Phrynichos', then he would have

---

[50] Thrasyboulos' and Apollodoros' status as foreigners presumably caused the Athenians to award these honours instead of the more generous ones specified in Demophantos' decree.

[51] *IG* I³ 102.6–8.   [52] *IG* I³ 102.8–10.

gone well beyond the rather bland phrases of the honorary inscription and he would have made explicit what is only implicit in the decree.[53] That more specificity could have been used in 409 is suggested by Epikerdes' decree which instructs the herald to announce the earlier honours bestowed on him by the *demos*. This passage also suggests, however, that such additional details needed to be added explicitly to the document, if they were to be included in the announcement in the theatre. The absence of such further details in Thrasyboulos' decree probably indicates that his actual deed was not described in any detail and that Phrynichos' name was not mentioned. Apollodoros' announcement was very likely parallel to Thrasyboulos' and, again, the details were probably missing. Of course, in 409, even if the herald did not make explicit that Thrasyboulos and Apollodoros were the assassins of the oligarch Phrynichos, the recent politics and contestation surrounding their honours probably ensured that the citizens in the theatre knew exactly why these men were being crowned by the *demos*: they were tyrant slayers.

The importance of their actions will have been reinforced by one further ritual, an announcement of a monetary reward to be given to any man who killed one of the (Peisistratid) tyrants. Although this practice is known only from Aristophanes' *Birds*, which was put on in 414, this ceremony was probably instituted much earlier, perhaps about 500 when the Peisistratidai were still alive.[54] The larger context of this passage suggests that this proclamation against the tyrants probably took place on the first day of the dramatic contests and it may have been connected with further announcements against other enemies of the city.[55] In 409, the pronouncement against the long-dead Peisistratidai will have reinforced this particular festival's specific focus on the importance of killing tyrants, while the *demos*' public offer of a reward for such actions demonstrated its power and control yet again. Since the announcement opposed individual tyrants with the corporate group of the democratically ruled Athenians, this strategy served both to unify them and to reinforce their new identity as tyrant slayers. Repeated in the different rituals, these dynamics will have been easily understood by the citizens in the theatre.

Whether the non-Athenian visitors realised what was going on is a very different question which brings out the ways in which these various rituals at the Dionysia of 409 were primarily aimed at the male citizens of Athens.

[53] Compare R. Osborne 1999: 354–6.
[54] Ar. *Birds* 1074–5; Dunbar 1995: 583–4; Wilson 2009: 26 with note 81; Seaford 2000: 35 with note 22.
[55] Ar. *Birds* 1072–84; Dunbar 1995: 581; Sommerstein 1987: 272.

They made up the *demos* which had decided in the assembly to make changes to this particular festival; even if individual men had not supported these actions, they now abided by the majority's decision and, therefore, they tacitly agreed to the principles of the democratic system. This political process, accordingly, helped to bring the Athenians back together and the unity which it created would have been reinforced and reaffirmed by the rituals at the festival. In the course of the ceremonies, the power of the democracy was presented repeatedly: in swearing Demophantos' oath, in the libations of the generals, in the presentations of the tribute and the war-orphans, in the announcement of crowns and in the proclamation against tyrants. That the *demos* had changed the festival made its power immediately clear and those decisions wrote its power into the ritual life of the city. Continuing earlier rituals also allowed the *demos* to connect itself to the past, to the democratically ruled city which had existed before the Four Hundred, the city for which the fathers of the war-orphans had died and which had begun to bring up the young sons. There was, indeed, a past for the democratic city and it was still relevant in 409. The ceremonies further served to unite the previously fractured city. Since oaths perform this function by their very nature, Demophantos' oath was a very important element in unifying the *demos*, as I argued earlier. The rituals in the theatre also played an important role in this dynamic because they required an audience of citizens who sat together and watched as one body seated in the same space. As a whole, they received the tribute and benefited from it; brought together as one group in the *ekklesia*, they approved the honours for the benefactors, a dynamic mirrored in their presence in the theatre itself.[56] The libations offered by the generals and the proclamation against tyrants were also made on behalf of the whole city which participated as a single group in the process. This unity would have been reinforced by the great sacrifice of oxen before the dramatic contests because sacrifices by their very nature mark out the members of the sacrificial community from spectators and they create unity within that select group which participates and, therefore, receives a share of the meat.[57] Unifying the *demos* and displaying its power, accordingly, were important aspects of these rituals which linked them together within the overall context of festival so that the later rites reinforced the earlier ones.

---

[56] On the relationship between the assembly and the theatre, see Goldhill 1994: 363–8.

[57] Oxen: *IG* II² 1496.80–1, 111–12; Parker 2005: 317. Nature of sacrifice: Detienne 1989a: 3–4; Detienne 1989b: 131–2; Durand 1989: 104; Rudhardt 1958: 289–90; Jameson 1998: 178; R. Osborne 2000: 311–12; Parker 2005: 37, 42–5; cf. Bruit Zaidman and Schmitt Pantel 1992: 34, 36.

If citizens and their collective power were the focus of these ceremonies, then their identity was also at the centre of the ideal images displayed in these different events. As the oath of Demophantos made clear, the good Athenian was a male citizen who was prepared to slay tyrants in order to protect the democratic city. The emphasis on his opponents as external enemies linked the oath with the military imagery clearly displayed by the generals and in the presentation of the (armed) war-orphans. This last ritual displayed the ideal citizen as a democrat and *aner agathos* who fought and, if necessary, died for the democratic city: the war-dead were the ultimate model for the *polis* ruled by the *demos*. When combined with the good Athenian of the oath, the composite image indicated to what lengths these citizens ought to go to defend the democratic city. Meanwhile, the announcement of crowns established a model for the good benefactor: as an *aner agathos*, he supported the *demos* through his actions which might require him to kill tyrants like a citizen. In return, the grateful city would award him a gold crown announced at Dionysos' festival. The allies were also not left out of this image-making and the tribute clearly displayed their role: to bring the funds which had been assessed and to present them to the watching Athenians. In return, they would watch the Athenians themselves perform for the god in the dithyrambic choruses and the dramatic contests. Those allies which were also colonists of the city had a further role: bringing a *phallos* to display in the procession.[58] In this way, they were differentiated both from Athenian citizens who carried jugs of wine and from the allies who brought only tribute to the theatre.[59] Participation in this festival was not equal[60] and how an individual took part in this international setting displayed very clearly his relationship to the city and its citizens who participated most extensively. Collected together in the procession, these citizens were shown to be well ordered and harmoniously participating together without divisions. The focus on making Athenian unity visible at the Dionysia served the important purpose of displaying the united city not only to itself, but also to its external enemies, who had not seized the opportunity offered by the oligarchy, and to its restive allies, who would now realise that there was no chance of revolt.

Embedding these images in ceremonies served a further function because rituals create memories of the events celebrated and those memories are activated when the rituals are performed again.[61] When the Athenians held

---

[58] *IG* i³ 46.15–17; RO 29.4–6.
[59] Citizens with jugs: *Suda* s.v. ἀσκοφορεῖν; Pickard-Cambridge 1988: 61 with note 6; Parker 2005: 317.
[60] Parker 2005: 317. [61] Above chapter 1.

the City Dionysia in the years after 409, their various ritual actions recalled the earlier festival which had been particularly focused on the power, unity and identity of the *demos*. Remembering summoned to mind the honours for Thrasyboulos and Apollodoros and made the citizens recall again what actions might be needed in defence of the democratic city. Repeating the rituals also reinforced these memories and the images which were conveyed by the actions. These dynamics ensured that the Dionysia of 409 and the rhetoric which it disseminated would not be forgotten with the passage of time. They also help to explain why a festival was considered an appropriate venue for responding to the events of 411. The important role which ritual plays in creating memory, however, does not explain why the Athenians chose the Dionysia; indeed, the emphasis on unity might have been considered more appropriate for the Panathenaia, the 'all-Athenian' festival held in 410/9 in its grand penteteric form. This inclusive celebration, however, does not distinguish between different participants with quite the same fine calibrations as the Dionysia nor does it particularly stress displaying the *demos* in its divisions.[62] Its focus was on participation rather than sitting and watching in the theatre. Of all the great Athenian festivals, the City Dionysia most closely mirrored the *ekklesia* and its politics most closely insisted upon the divisions between Athenian citizens and everyone else. Already the occasion for presenting the war-orphans and the proclamation against tyrants, there could be no more appropriate venue for announcing gold crowns for benefactors, especially those men who were, at the same time, made into Athenian citizens, or for swearing Demophantos' oath. These rituals and the images and memories which they created could only be properly accommodated in the City Dionysia with its extensive focus on the *demos* displayed in its democratic divisions.

SOPHOKLES' *PHILOKTETES* AND THE DIONYSIA OF 409

As I have been arguing, the Athenian democrats used the Dionysia very extensively in creating their responses to the oligarchies of 411. In the context of this festival, the *demos* as a whole is presented as addressing the issues and problems raised in a very clear and unambiguous manner, as if responding to these events was unproblematic. That the situation was not necessarily so clear is suggested by one other aspect of this festival, Sophokles' winning play *Philoktetes*. Placed against the backdrop of this particular festival for Dionysos and its specific ceremonies, both Demophantos' oath and the

---

[62] On the politics of the Panathenaia, see briefly Shear 2010: 147–50.

pre-play rituals, the play suggests that responding to oligarchy is not as simple as Demophantos' oath and the other rites imply and it asks its audience to think about complications and difficulties of creating unity. Since Demophantos' decree authorising the oath was passed in the first prytany of 410/9, the unusual context of this particular celebration was known well in advance and we should not be surprised that Sophokles seems to have addressed the issues involved in his play. Set in the tenth year of the Trojan War, *Philoktetes* tells the story of how Odysseus and Neoptolemos, the son of Achilles, attempt to bring Philoktetes back to Troy from the island of Lemnos where the Greek army abandoned him ten years earlier after he had been terribly wounded by a sacred snake. To take Troy, the Greeks must have the participation of both the son of Achilles and Philoktetes and his famous bow, hence Odysseus' determination to take Philoktetes to Troy by any means possible. Neoptolemos, however, becomes friendly with Philoktetes; he returns the bow which he has stolen and decides to take the older man not to Troy, but back to his home. Only Herakles' (divine) intervention ensures that all participants return to fight the Trojans.

From the beginning, the play confronted the Athenians with an all-too-familiar scenario: a war fought for so long that the sons of the fallen are now adult, divisions among the army, critical members of that army separated from the rest, the taking of oaths, trust and deception and the problems of allegiance. Despite the play's location on the deserted island of Lemnos, the indications in the text suggest that the focus is on Athens and that we are meant to take what transpires as a commentary in some sense on the city.[63] Particularly important in making this association is Odysseus' invocation of Athena Polias who is also Nike, the primary divinity of the Akropolis.[64] In this context, the play is going to ask its spectators to read its problems and its questions back on to the city around them. For these dynamics, the figure of Neoptolemos is particularly important. He is presented at the opening of the play as a war-orphan himself who is about to become an adult and to fight in the war.[65] He is also, it seems, without the arms of his famous father.[66] His status as orphan is brought out already in the opening lines of the play when Odysseus addresses him as Neoptolemos, the son of Achilles, and this phrase will appear repeatedly throughout the play.[67] When he meets Philoktetes, he will explicitly present himself

---

[63] Mitchell-Boyask 2007: 87–95; Mitchell-Boyask 2008: 155–62.
[64] Soph. *Phil.* 133–4; Mitchell-Boyask 2007: 89–93; Mitchell-Boyask 2008: 157–61.
[65] Goldhill 1990: 119.   [66] Soph. *Phil.* 58–64, 359–73.
[67] Soph. *Phil.* 4; other examples in 57, 240–1, 260, 542, 582, 940, 1066, 1237, 1298, 1433.

as an orphan without his father's arms.[68] Neoptolemos' status as child is further brought out by the other characters who regular call him *pais* and *teknon*, most certainly not the markers of the adult male.[69] Only three times is he called *aner*.[70] In the context of this Dionysia, the emphases on Neoptolemos' status as child and orphan recall the Athenian war-orphans who, like Neoptolemos, were presented to the Athenians in the theatre with their patronymics. Just as they were now given their arms, so also arms are at issue in the play, both the arms of Achilles, which lie in the background, and the arms of Philoktetes, his famous bow. This bow is called the *hopla* of Herakles, the same term regularly used for the weapons of the hoplite.[71] Philoktetes' questions about the great warriors at Troy also link back to the ritual: most of these men are dead.[72] In this context, references to the *aner agathos* also recall the use of that term to describe the war-dead.[73] Neoptolemos, consequently, seems to be looking particularly towards the war-orphans, those young men newly acknowledged as citizens not long before the play was performed. Educating Neoptolemos, an issue on which critics have focused, is also about educating the war-orphans.[74]

The play further links into the situation in 409 through the repeated references to oaths.[75] There is the oath which Neoptolemos did not swear before sailing to Troy, unlike Odysseus and the participants in the original expedition.[76] Philoktetes asks the merchant if Odysseus has sworn an oath to retrieve him from Lemnos.[77] When his sickness returns, he does not make Neoptolemos swear to return: his pledge (*pistis*) is enough.[78] According to Philoktetes, Neoptolemos swore an oath to take him home.[79] After returning the bow, Neoptolemos calls on Zeus Horkios, the guarantor of oaths.[80] Oaths, then, are very much at stake in this play. Neoptolemos' oath to take Philoktetes home brings out particularly well the problems of oaths. We first learn of it when Philoktetes accuses Neoptolemos of breaking it; later he will beg Neoptolemos to honour it.[81] Honouring this

---

[68] Soph. *Phil.* 354–81.
[69] παῖς: Soph. *Phil.* 79, 96, 201, 242, 260, 315, 372, 478, 533, 578, 589, 620, 628, 750, 776, 782, 804, 864, 869, 889, 896, 967, 981, 1008, 1072; τέκνον: Soph. *Phil.* 130, 141, 210, 236, 249, 260, 276, 284, 300, 307, 327, 337, 466, 468, 484, 635, 658, 662, 733, 742, 745, 747, 753, 799, 805, 807, 811, 833, 843, 845, 855, 875, 878, 879, 898, 914, 932, 1295, 1301, 1310, 1367, 1399; Avery 1965: 285–6; Vidal-Naquet 1986: 172.
[70] Soph. *Phil.* 531, 910, 1423.   [71] Soph. *Phil.* 262; cf. 802, 1292.   [72] Soph. *Phil.* 403–55.
[73] Soph. *Phil.* 456, 1050; cf. 119 where Neoptolemos is offered the opportunity to be *sophos k'agathos*.
[74] Educating Neoptolemos: Goldhill 1990: 121–3; Rose 1992: 288–327; cf. Vidal-Naquet 1986: 172–80 with Goldhill 1990: 122–3.
[75] Compare Mitchell-Boyask 2008: 181–2.   [76] Soph. *Phil.* 72–4.   [77] Soph. *Phil.* 622–3.
[78] Soph. *Phil.* 807–13.   [79] Soph. *Phil.* 941, 1367–8.   [80] Soph. *Phil.* 1324.
[81] Soph. *Phil.* 941, 1367–8.

pledge means not returning to Troy, as Achilles' son eventually resolves to do. This particular oath points up the problems of swearing oaths and the difficulties of keeping them. Similarly, at the beginning of the play, Odysseus claims that Philoktetes will not believe him because he had sworn the oath to Tyndareos. Here, an oath sworn long ago is said to prevent Odysseus from getting what he wants in the present. Swearing oaths, it seems, is a tricky business and they may come back to haunt a man in the future.

Deception, trust and lack of trust are also important themes.[82] Odysseus initially instructs Neoptolemos on how to deceive Philoktetes and Neoptolemos subsequently describes himself as having been tricked by Odysseus at Troy.[83] This play's use of deceit and trickery is just beginning . . . and the issue of whom one can trust appears repeatedly: Philoktetes thinks that he can trust Neoptolemos who is then persuaded to follow Odysseus, only to change his mind again and agree to take Philoktetes home. Even the audience is caught up in these webs and spectators do not always know what to believe, what statements are true and what statements are false;[84] in 409, this situation must have been uncomfortably familiar to viewers. Indeed, Odysseus, with his repeated deceptions and threats and his embassy to Neoptolemos, is just a little too reminiscent of Thucydides' portrayal of Peisandros and the oligarchs' behaviour before the *ekklesia* at Kolonos.[85] In this light, Odysseus is not a good person for Neoptolemos to believe or to obey, but whom is Neoptolemos to obey? Should he blindly follow those in authority or should he exercise his own judgment?[86]

Nor is Neoptolemos the only character for whom trust and deception are issues. Philoktetes trusted his fellow Greeks, but they still abandoned him on the island.[87] Although Neoptolemos has agreed to take Philoktetes home, he has actually deceived Philoktetes and intends to bring him to Troy. Philoktetes makes his fear of betrayal explicit and, when he discovers Neoptolemos' plan, he specifically accuses the young man of betraying him.[88] Later, when Neoptolemos offers to give back the bow, Philoktetes fears that he is being tricked a second time.[89] These deceptions and betrayals bring out Philoktetes' anger which is directed not only at the two sons of Atreus and at Odysseus, but also at the young Neoptolemos.[90] Even the city

---

[82] For deception in this play, see Hesk 2000: 188–99.   [83] Soph. *Phil.* 55–131, 343–84.

[84] Compare Easterling 1978: 29–31.

[85] Deceit and violence: Easterling 1978: 31; Garvie 1972: 214–22. Embassy: Soph. *Phil.* 343–53.

[86] E.g. Soph. *Phil.*, 925–6, 1222–58, 1291–4; cf. 54, 121–2; Goldhill 1990: 120–1.

[87] E.g. Soph. *Phil.* 268–84, 598–600, 1026–8, 1390; cf. 314–15.

[88] Soph. *Phil.* 910–11, 923–4, 947–9.   [89] Soph. *Phil.* 1268–9, 1288.

[90] Soph. *Phil.* 927–62, 986–94, 1001–39, 1197–9, 1280–6.

of Troy bears the verbal brunt of Philoktetes' rage.[91] This anger dominates the second part of the play and it shows very clearly the destructive effects of deception and betrayal. These actions have also made Philoktetes resolutely unwilling to go to Troy and no human is able to persuade him to change his mind.[92] Through their past actions, the thing which both Odysseus and Neoptolemos, in their different ways, most want is now impossible. They are faced with the problem of trying to rebuild their relationships with Philoktetes after his trust in them has been shattered.

The difficulty of this process is brought out by the ways in which the word *philos* or friend is used in the play. Although when Philoktetes meets the Greeks, he asks them to speak, if they come as friends, he usually uses this word for those not present.[93] In the first half of the play, Neoptolemos, in contrast, describes Philoktetes as his friend and, when he speaks to the merchant, Philoktetes is his great friend (φίλος μέγιστος);[94] his subsequent actions will throw these easy assurances of friendship into doubt. Once Neoptolemos has returned the bow and is trying to persuade Philoktetes to sail to Troy, he will have recourse to the word *philos* again, but now he uses it to describe himself and his relationship to the other man.[95] This shift points to the difficulties of repairing the relationship after it has been damaged, as well as the lengths to which Neoptolemos is willing to go. On his own, however, he is not able to persuade Philoktetes and their friendship seems at this point to have been irreparably destroyed.

In the context of the Dionysia of 409, this play forces the audience to ask about the consequences of division and what it does to human relationships. Should the war-orphans, should the Athenians, trust those in positions of leadership or are they being deceived, as Neoptolemos, the prototype for the war-orphans, was by Odysseus?[96] If Neoptolemos maps on to these new citizens, then Philoktetes and Odysseus, separated in different ways from the main army at Troy, provide ways of thinking about the actions and feelings of other Athenians, citizens involved in different ways in the events of 411.[97] That the army and the Athenian *demos* map on to each other is suggested by the specific reference to the sons of Theseus

---

[91] Soph. *Phil.* 1200–2.   [92] Soph. *Phil.* 628–34, 999–1000, 1275–6, 1348–72, 1392.
[93] Meeting: Soph. *Phil.* 229; not present: Soph. *Phil.* 421 (Nestor), 665 (friends at home). On friendship in this play, see Rose 1992: 290–305.
[94] Soph. *Phil.* 586, 671.   [95] Soph. *Phil.* 1375, 1385.
[96] See also Goldhill 1990: 121–3; cf. Rose 1992: 306.
[97] Philoktetes' separation from the army is particularly brought out by his first long speech to Neoptolemos, Soph. *Phil.* 253–316; for Odysseus, see e.g. Soph. *Phil.* 1293–8. I am not suggesting that some Athenians may not also have seen aspects of Alkibiades in one or both of these characters, but I would stress that he was probably not their most pressing worry in 409. On hunting for Alkibiades (and others) in this play, see Bowie 1997: 56–61 with further references; Mitchell-Boyask 2007: 86–7; Rose 1992: 329.

with the Greeks at Troy.[98] A divided army far from home will also have been very familiar in 409: without official generals, much of the fleet was in the Hellespont and not far from Troy, while the city's generals were on Samos; in 411, the fleet on Samos had been divided from the city. Furthermore, at Troy, the leaders' oath did not prevent division and, despite swearing his oath, Philoktetes was still abandoned. Nor does Neoptolemos' oath to return Philoktetes create unity and it is repeatedly under threat of being ignored. Indeed, at the end of the play, it will be broken by Herakles' command that Neoptolemos take Philoktetes to Troy and not to his home. This oath, it seems, was sworn in vain and it takes a divinity to solve the problems which it presents. That divinity is also instrumental in reuniting the army at Troy and in assuaging Philoktetes' anger so that he can finally describe the Greeks as his friends.[99] In the context of 409, this play poses important questions about the efficacy of oaths: can they really create unity or are they dangerous speech acts which one lives to regret? Could the oath of Demophantos really unite the Athenians into one harmonious body or is divine intervention necessary? What happens to the anger generated by division? If Demophantos' oath and the pre-play rituals create a specific and positive image of the Athenians and of how they are being reunited, then this play seems to throw all of those images into doubt. It suggests that the oath may not be enough to bring unity and friendship back to Athens and to diffuse anger; instead, this process may require divine intervention. In this way, Sophokles' *Philoktetes* responds not only to the events of 411, but also to the events of 410/9, both to oligarchs and to democrats. It asks its viewers to think more deeply about the problems of the democrats' particular, and public, collective responses to oligarchy and it suggests that the process may not be as easy as simply taking an oath. Sophokles, accordingly, is presenting a reaction both to oligarchy and to the subsequent responses to it.[100]

THE POLITICS OF MEMORY

For the Athenians, the combination of the rituals and their imagery and of the plays and the ways in which at least the *Philoktetes* brought those

---

[98] Soph. *Phil.* 561–2.   [99] Soph. *Phil.* 1467.

[100] Although scholars have concentrated on this play's ritual and intellectual setting, little work has been done to set it in its specific context of the Dionysia of 409; Goldhill 1990: 95–115, 118–29; Rose 1992: 266–327. Much more could be said than Rose's brief account indicates; Rose 1992: 327–30. By focusing on the private cult of Asklepios rather than the politics of this particular Dionysia, Mitchell-Boyask seems to me to imply a very optimistic reading of the play and of the ease with which Athens may be unified or, in his terms, healed; Mitchell-Boyask 2007; Mitchell-Boyask 2008: 153–82.

images into question must have made the Dionysia of 409 a particularly memorable celebration for Dionysos. Incorporating these models of the good Athenian, the good benefactor and the good colonist into the rituals caused them to be recalled every time the rites were performed. These reperformances allowed the participants to remember the original occasion when these images were first promulgated and the repetition reinforced the memories. These dynamics, however, required the presence of the individuals at the Dionysia of 409 and individuals not in Athens or too young to have been present or to have sworn Demophantos' oath would not have been able to recall events in which they had not participated. The Dionysia, however, was not the only context in which these memories were created because the rituals had been authorised by the inscribed documents which were also monuments in their own right. In and of themselves they could not remember because, like all such structures, they were inert and amnesiac.[101] For the creation of memory, they relied on viewers and readers whose actions served to animate them, a process which enabled remembering through the interactions between the memorial and viewers/readers. Since the monuments in the Athenian context included inscriptions, reading was just as important to these dynamics as viewing. The very process of reading not only activated the documents, but it also created memories for the readers of the critical moments in the Athenians' responses to the oligarchies of 411. In this way, individuals not present at the Dionysia of 409 could remember what it meant to be Athenian and the ways in which Athens had been made democratic again.

In discussing the dynamics of the inscriptions erected in the Agora, we saw that reading the texts was an important part of the process of recreating democracy. In the case of Demophantos' decree, reading the inscription required the individual to repeat the oath in the same setting in which the Athenians had originally sworn it (fig. 2). In this way, he reperformed the text, a process which was inevitably inexact because he was alone without the sacrificial victims, tribes and demes so necessary to the original performance. Who were these readers? In the years immediately after the Dionysia of 409, they would have been men who had actually sworn the oath. For them, the process of reading would have recalled their participation in that important festival. For Athenians abroad with the fleet and later generations which had not sworn the oath, reading the inscription would have given them access to the images of the text, the models for their behaviour. We can still see this process at work in 330 when Lykourgos

---

[101] Above chapter 1.

describes the document and emphasises the ways in which it provided a model both for the *bouleutai* and for his contemporaries who were listening to his speech as members of the jury; his description, however, also recalls the taking of the oath itself and it creates a memory of that event for his audience whom he describes as having taken the oath.[102] In the same way, reading the *stele* in front of the (Old) Bouleuterion provided a memory of taking the oath which the readers, belonging to subsequent generations, would not otherwise have had. For Athenians with the fleet in Elaphebolion of 409, these dynamics were particularly important because they provided a memory of an event in which these men had not literally participated. The memory politics, however, ensured that they were included and so shown to be good democrats. Since the oath-taking was not specifically commemorated in an annual ceremony, memories of it could only be created by reading the inscription. These processes forced the reader to reperform, however incompletely, the original ritual and to swear to be a good Athenian. Located in the Agora, the inscription was available to all citizens for memory-making and it created a single memory of what it meant to be Athenian: to kill oligarchs and tyrants. Since this single memory was the same for all citizens, it served as a 'national' memory which brought the Athenians together so that, in remembering the events, they were unified once again.[103]

These politics of memory were not limited to the *stele* with Demophantos' decree and they formed an important element of the dynamics of the honorary decree for Thrasyboulos and, we must imagine, his accomplice Apollodoros. In this case, to read the inscription was to remember the process which brought the text into being, the moment in the *ekklesia* when the citizens decided to honour this man. The details of the amendments, meanwhile, also recalled the ways in which those honours were contested when they were proposed. In this sense, Thrasyboulos' decree functions no differently from any other Athenian decree, including the others which we have discussed, and it shares the same politics of remembrance. To read this particular decree, however, was also to repeat again the herald's

---

[102] Lykourg. *Leok.* 126–7: 'These words, gentlemen, your fathers inscribed on the *stele* and they set it up at the Bouleuterion as a reminder to those meeting each day and deliberating over the business of the fatherland of how they should treat such men . . . Therefore, consider deeply, gentlemen, this foresight and their deeds . . . You have sworn in the decree of Demophantos to kill the man who betrays his fatherland by word and by deed and by your hand and by your vote. For do not think that you have inherited the wealth which your ancestors left behind, but not the oaths and the pledge which your fathers gave to the gods as a security and so shared in the common prosperity of the city.'

[103] Above chapter 1.

announcement of the honours at the Dionysia of 409 and to remember Thrasyboulos as an *aner agathos* towards the *demos* of the Athenians; Apollodoros' inscription ought to have functioned in a similar way. Together, the two documents created memories for subsequent generations of the moment when these two men were honoured for their good deeds. The actual details of what Thrasyboulos did, however, were carefully not mentioned and the name of Phrynichos can have appeared nowhere in the inscription. Readers, consequently, remembered the exemplum provided by the honorand rather than the specific details of his deeds, which were consigned to the gaps of memory and not preserved for future generations which were not present.

In these ways, then, the inscriptions picked out significant moments in responding to oligarchy for the Athenians to remember in the future. Demophantos' oath is very clearly one such point, but so, too, is the decision to reinscribe Drakon's law on homicide. Since every Athenian inscription memorialises the circumstances around its approval and publication, the opening formulae play an important role in the *stele*'s memory politics. For this reason, it seems very likely that the documents concerning the *boule* and the first *stelai* of both the laws and the sacred calendar contained authorising decrees parallel to the one at the beginning of Drakon's law. In this way, the different inscriptions with the laws memorialised the Athenians' decisions to collect and inscribe them and they created memories for subsequent Athenians who were not present in the *ekklesia*. Similar dynamics are at work in the decree for Thrasyboulos which also recalls the moment in the theatre when his honours were announced by the herald. These inscriptions all reminded the readers of what it meant to be Athenian and what being democratic entailed, while Thrasyboulos' *stele* added the image of the good benefactor of the city. Located in two of the city's most important memorial spaces, the Akropolis and the Agora, these monuments together perpetuated the memory of these events and made them always present for the Athenians. Since the images presented in the different texts complement each other, only a single image is presented so that all Athenians will remember the events in exactly the same way. The memory created, consequently, will function as a 'national' memory to unify them.

While these monuments serve very well to commemorate what being democratic entails and they memorialise the moment which brought each text into being, they also erase the larger context. The term oligarchy is missing entirely from Demophantos' decree and there is no mention of the Four Hundred. Similarly, in Thrasyboulos' document, the details, even the fact of his assassination of the oligarch Phrynichos, are carefully glossed over. On the basis of these inscriptions, we would not know that there had been an oligarchic revolution when the Athenians were heavily divided. Only democracy is to be remembered, while oligarchy and the Four Hundred are to be erased from the public sphere, as if they had never been. As Demophantos' decree makes clear, there is no room in the democratic city for oligarchs (and tyrants), who are *polemioi* and to be killed with impunity, and, consequently, they are not to be remembered. These moves, however, had consequences, as Lykourgos makes clear. Without any reference to the Four Hundred, the context of Demophantos' document is lost to him and so he conflates his oligarchs and associates the *stele* with the Thirty.[104] Similarly, he remembers Phrynichos as a traitor, but not as an oligarch.[105] By 330, the erasure of the earlier oligarchs had evidently been all too successful and only the democrats and their actions were now being remembered.

CONSEQUENCES

Ritual and memory were extremely powerful tools which allowed the *demos* to demonstrate its control of the city and to promulgate a specific image of the good Athenian: the male democrat who killed tyrants and oligarchs and modelled himself on the Tyrannicides Harmodios and Aristogeiton. Now embedded in the rituals of the Dionysia and the city's memorial landscape, this image was remembered both in the context of later celebrations of the festival and by readers of the texts in the Agora. At the Dionysia of 409, this image complemented the existing pre-play rituals, particularly the presentation of the war-orphans. A new rite, the announcement of gold crowns for benefactors, was also added to the existing ceremonies. It provided a new image, the good benefactor, who was identified as an *aner agathos* and so placed on a par with the war-dead. In 409, the identity of the first honorands as the assassins of Phrynichos also complemented the image of the good citizen and it showed the lengths to which one might have to go to defend the rule of the *demos*. Since these rituals focused on all of the Athenians, they also served to unify the divisions created by the events in 411. The oath of Demophantos was particularly important in this regard because of the ways in which oaths by their very nature unite the people swearing them. That this process was not necessarily as simple

---

[104] Lykourg. *Leok.* 124–5. For a similar conflation, see [Dem.] 58.67 with Thomas 1989: 132–8.
[105] Lykourg. *Leok.* 112–15.

as Demophantos thought was also powerfully suggested by Sophokles in his *Philoktetes*, but his individual reaction did not change the Athenians' public, collective actions. In this context, the focus on all the Athenians in their civic divisions explains why these rituals were added to the City Dionysia and not to some other important city festival, such as the Great Panathenaia or the Eleusinian Mysteries.

The image of the good citizen which was promulgated by the rituals and the related memory-making very much complements the ways in which the inscriptions and monuments in the Agora together presented the good Athenian. This focus was enhanced by an emphasis on democracy which was shown both as the proper *politeia* for the city and as perpetually functioning. Together, the texts, monuments and rituals emphasised that the rule of the *demos* was the only possible constitution for Athens. Swearing the oath of Demophantos, the actual decree and the display of the laws also made *isonomia* (equal political rights), a central tenet of that *politeia*, physically visible through their presentation of all citizens as exactly equal and subject to precisely the same rules. Erecting inscriptions and buildings in the contested spaces of the Agora and the Akropolis allowed the *demos* to display its control of the city and to write it quite literally onto the cityscape; in the context of the Dionysia, the new rituals worked in very much the same way. Focusing on the Agora and erecting Demophantos' decree and the laws here had further consequences because it created a new memorial space concentrated particularly on the *demos*; in this way, the process of turning the marketplace into the space of the citizen began as part of the response to oligarchy.

Together, these actions of the *demos* also reclaimed the past for the city and showed that democracy did have a history. The *patrios politeia*, Drakon, Solon and Kleisthenes were all shown to belong to the past of the democratic city. Not all elements of the past were brought into the present, however. Most conspicuously, the oligarchs and their actions were forgotten. They are not mentioned in the inscriptions, even in the decree for Thrasyboulos, a document extremely reticent about exactly what the honorand did to become an *aner agathos* towards the Athenian *demos*. Similarly, the actions of the *bouleutai* in 411 and the presence of the Four Hundred in the (Old) Bouleuterion were erased by providing the councillors with a new meeting place, together with proper models of behaviour, and by placing the archives with the city's laws and decrees in the existing council house. Even in the sacred space of the Akropolis, the documents of the oligarchs were obscured by other inscriptions. In the public sphere, the oligarchs and the events of 411 were ostentatiously forgotten and consigned to the gaps of memory:

in a sense, there was a response without an immediately obvious cause. In contrast, in the courts, individual Athenians could remember the oligarchs and their deeds in detail, as the pseudo-Lysianic speech for Polystratos clearly shows.[106] Their responses, however, were those of individual men, just as Sophokles' *Philoktetes* was his own reaction to the actions of the *demos* in 410/9. These men (and their anger) did not visibly influence the imagery of the public, collective sphere where the unified Athenians remembered democracy and its past and forgot oligarchy. In these ways, by 405, Athens had been remade into the democratic city and her past had been recovered for the *demos*; oligarchy, meanwhile, had been publicly forgotten.

---

[106] [Lys.] 20; see also above chapter 2.

CHAPTER 6

The Thirty and the law

By the eve of the Athenians' defeat by the Spartans in the Peloponnesian War, Athens had been fully remade into the democratic city and the rule of the *demos* was prominently displayed in texts and monuments located in the cityscape. The New Bouleuterion had been in use for some time and the city's archives had been moved into the older council house. Meanwhile, at the other end of the west side of the Agora, the laws and the sacrificial calendar were prominently displayed in and around the Stoa Basileios. Together with the inscribed texts, the monuments had also reclaimed the city's past for the *demos*. Its rule was shown to be *patrios* and the iconic figures of Drakon, Solon and Kleisthenes had been recovered as important founders of the current system. These results of the responses to the Four Hundred must have gladdened the heart of many a democrat, but, for oligarchs and would-be tyrants, they presented problems: they were an unwelcome reminder that the city was now democratic. Once the Thirty gained power, all of this democratic imagery was singularly inappropriate and it suggested that their regime was not legitimate. For them, a pressing issue was what to do about democratic Athens. Leaving the city in its current form was simply not an option because the cityscape and its monuments continually undermined their regime. In the face of the democrats' activities between 410 and 404, the Thirty had no choice: they had to claim Athens as their own and make her into the oligarchic city.

At the beginning of their regime, accordingly, one of the Thirty's important goals was to solidify their claim to power by all possible means. Doing so initially meant embarking on a significant campaign of political reform to remake the city's *politeia* into a form more congenial to oligarchs. As we shall see, our evidence for this process is quite significant and it suggests that, at the beginning, there was widespread support for this process among the different members and factions of the Thirty. Such unanimity, however, did not last and very quickly fissures developed between the different factions. At this point, some members of the Thirty began resorting to violence and it very quickly became the only way for them to retain their power. Violence was met with violence and *stasis* developed between the oligarchs within the city and the exiled democrats outside of it. This cycle was only broken through the intervention of Pausanias, the king of Sparta, who was instrumental in reconciling the different factions.

Like the Thirty themselves, modern scholarship has generally taken two approaches to these tyrants. The traditional view identifies any talk of constitutional reform as a cover intended to lull the unsuspecting Athenians; maintaining power by any means possible was always the Thirty's real intention.[1] More recently, scholars have begun to focus on the evidence for constitutional reform. This process is sometimes seen as a 'good period' at the beginning of the regime before the (inevitable) 'oligarchy and repression', but it generally does not take the efforts at constitutional reform seriously.[2] For these scholars, Theramenes and his moderate associates are the only Athenians who were interested in such matters.[3] More recently, Robin Osborne has focused in greater detail on the evidence for constitutional reform and has argued that at least some members of the Thirty were serious about the process.[4] Building on his arguments, we shall see that the evidence is more extensive than scholars have generally thought and that it presupposes a broader context. Indeed, it suggests that changing the constitution and returning to the *patrios politeia* must initially have received general support among the members of the regime and this process has left visible traces in the physical record. The extent of the Thirty's actions also required a subsequent response from the *demos* when it regained power and returned from exile. Whether the city was visibly oligarchic or democratic was a serious business irrespective of one's political allegiances.

THE *PATRIOS POLITEIA* AND THE ATHENIANS

When the *demos* returned to power in 410, it embarked on a substantial programme of responding to oligarchy, as we have seen in the previous three chapters. The Athenians, however, do not seem to have made changes to the city's *politeia* and evidence for political reform is strikingly absent from the period between 410 and 404. Certainly, the democrats were intent on

---

[1] E.g. Cartledge 1987: 281; Lewis 1994: 30; Wolpert 2002a: 16–24; Hornblower 2002: 211; cf. R. Osborne 2003: 262. Note that, for Wolpert, the violence was systemic; see also Wolpert 2006.
[2] E.g. Ostwald 1986: 475–81; Fuks 1953: 52–79, 110–11; Hignett 1952: 288–9.
[3] E.g. Ostwald 1986: 471–2; Fuks 1953: 52–79; cf. Finley 2000: 39.
[4] R. Osborne 2003: 262–6; cf. now Phillips 2008: 138–41.

recovering the past for themselves and they made large efforts to show that the democratic city did, indeed, have a past, but such activities were not political reform. In the aftermath of the defeat by the Spartans, however, constitutional issues once again came up for debate in Athens. As in 411, constitutional issues were an important part of the events which brought the oligarchs to power and our sources further indicate that the *patrios politeia* was again the subject of debate in the city by individuals from different parts of the political spectrum.

The debate over the constitution had certainly begun by the time when the peace terms with the Spartans were concluded. At this point, according to the *Athenaion Politeia*, the democrats were endeavouring to preserve the *demos*, those men belonging to the *hetaireiai* and the exiles who returned after the peace were eager for oligarchy and a third group of men who were not members of the *hetaireiai* wanted the *patrios politeia*; this last group is said to have included Theramenes, Archinos, Anytos, Kleitophon and Phormisios.[5] In its three different views on government and the invocation of the ancestral constitution, this description recalls the situation before the Four Hundred gained power. A slightly different version is presented by Diodoros who describes the oligarchs as wanting the ancient constitution (παλαιὰν κατάστασιν) and the democrats, the majority, as championing the constitution of their fathers (πατέρων πολιτείαν), which they agreed was democracy.[6] Since these two sources use slightly different terms and ascribe them to different groups, they should be independent of each other. The slight variations in the terms, however, suggest that they have not been invented by the two authors and they probably represent various slogans being bandied about in 404.[7] In 403, the use of the term *kata ta patria* in the reconciliation agreement and in Teisamenos' decree to describe how the Athenians are to be governed suggests that the democrats were not adopting the phrase for the first time;[8] very likely, democrats had been among those using the term *patrios politeia* in the previous year. After the defeat, accordingly, the city's constitution seems to have once again become the subject of debate, during the course of which the term *patrios politeia* was seized and used by various different factions, just as it had been in 411.

The importance of these debates about the constitution is further brought out by the existence of one tradition that the peace terms included the specification that the Athenians be ruled according to the *patrios politeia*; this version is preserved by the *Athenaion Politeia* and by

---

[5] Arist. *Ath. Pol.* 34.3.   [6] Diod. 14.3.3.
[7] P. J. Rhodes 1981: 427–8; contra: Fuks 1953: 64–8.   [8] Arist. *Ath. Pol.* 39.2; Andok. 1.83.

Diodoros.[9] Another tradition, however, does not include the *patrios politeia* clause among the peace terms.[10] Since some of these sources provide much more detail about the different terms, it seems odd that the condition about the ancestral constitution has been omitted. Andokides evidently knew the *stele* on which the terms were inscribed and Xenophon's authority as a contemporary source could also be invoked to argue that no such clause was ever included.[11] Since the *patrios politeia* is such a nebulous phrase, it seems like a strange addition to what is otherwise quite a concrete list of requirements which the Athenians must meet in order to have peace. If it is correct that the ancestral constitution was not mentioned in the peace,[12] then the version including it may well have originated as a way of explaining how the debate over the constitution began in Athens in 404. Alternatively, it may come out of a tradition eager to exonerate Theramenes for his membership in the Thirty.[13]

Further evidence for debates over how Athens should be governed is suggested by the circumstances surrounding the installation of the Thirty. In the version presented in Xenophon's *Hellenika*, the *demos* chose thirty men to draw up the ancestral laws, the *patrioi nomoi*.[14] Lysias also speaks of an *ekklesia* concerning the *politeia* which led to the appointment of the Thirty.[15] In describing the actions of the Thirty after they came to power, the *Athenaion Politeia* states both that they ignored what had been decreed about the constitutional issues and that they pretended to be pursuing the *patrios politeia*.[16] These versions consistently link the constitution with the Thirty and they identify it as the reason for the mandate which they received from the Athenians. The terms *patrioi nomoi* and *patrios politeia* reappear here in this context and they recall our other evidence for the on-going debates about the city's constitution. Collectively, then, our sources for the aftermath of the defeat point towards a period of debate over the city's constitution. At this time, various different groups, not just the moderates led by Theramenes, were invoking terms like the ancestral constitution and ancestral laws as the ways in which the city ought to be governed.[17]

---

[9] Arist. *Ath. Pol.* 34.3; Diod. 14.3.2.

[10] Xen. *Hell.* 2.2.20; Diod. 13.107.4; Andok. 3.11–12; Plut. *Lys.* 14.8.

[11] Andok. 3.12; Fuks 1953: 54, 58. Note also that Plutarch quotes the *dogma* of the Spartan ephors.

[12] As e.g. P. J. Rhodes 1981: 427; Hignett 1952: 285; Fuks 1953: 52–8, 62; contra: Ostwald 1986: 457–8 with note 165; Krentz 1982: 42; McCoy 1975: 133–9.

[13] Fuks 1953: 62. For other explanations, see Fuks 1953: 60–1.

[14] Xen. *Hell.* 2.3.2. This passage seems to be interpolated; Krentz 1989: 189–90.   [15] Lys. 12.72–7.

[16] Arist. *Ath. Pol.* 35.1–2. On the problems of the text of 35.2, see P. J. Rhodes 1981: 439–40.

[17] Notice that schol. Aischin. 1.39, to be discussed in more detail below, describes the Thirty as overthrowing the *patrios politeia* of the Athenians.

From our perspective, these discussions and issues seem very similar to the debates which preceded the appointment of the Four Hundred by the *demos* in 411. That the circumstances of 411 appear to have been repeated in 404 shows how the democrats' responses to oligarchy had not removed opposition to the rule of the *demos*. Conjuring again with the *patrios politeia* further indicates how little had changed: the constitution, its form and the city's past continued to be critical issues which could be used by groups on all parts of the political spectrum.

THE THIRTY, THE *POLITEIA* AND THE CITY

This debate about the *patrios politeia* must have combined with the visibly democratic city to bring to the surface questions for the Athenians: not only how the *polis* should be ruled, but also what sort of city were issues at stake in these debates. They were particularly important for the oligarchs who could not have approved of the *demos*' earlier actions. The city's constitution and laws also played a direct role in the circumstances surrounding the Thirty's ascent to power. Once these men gained control, consequently, they needed to address both the issues surrounding the *politeia* and the problem of the democratic city. Their initial solution was to take seriously the mandate which brought them to power and they embarked on an extensive project to remake the city's laws in a suitable fashion. In addition, they began to make changes to the city's physical appearance so that she was no longer visibly democratic.

Our sources for the Thirty's advent to power are explicit about the circumstances. They were elected by the *demos*, that is by the *ekklesia*, and, in Diodoros' words, the people, compelled by necessity, dissolved the democracy.[18] The necessary decree was moved by Drakontides, who was presumably a member of the Thirty, and its text seems to be reflected in part of Xenophon's account.[19] While the use of the *ekklesia* to create the new regime is very reminiscent of the rise of the Four Hundred in 411, our sources stress the important role which Lysandros played in the proceedings: his presence forced the *demos* into its actions. The decree authorising the Thirty not only brought them to power, but it also provided them with their orders; they were to draw up the (ancestral) laws for the city, a process which the *Athenaion Politeia* specifically links with the term

---

[18] Xen. *Hell.* 2.3.2, 11; Arist. *Ath. Pol.* 34.3–35.1; Lys. 12.72–3; Diod. 14.3.5–7; for modern discussions, see Krentz 1982: 48–50 with further references; Ostwald 1986: 475–8; Munn 2000: 219–22; P. J. Rhodes 1981: 433–7.

[19] Xen. *Hell.* 2.3.2; Arist. *Ath. Pol.* 34.3; Lys. 12.73. Drakontides: P. J. Rhodes 1981: 434.

politeia.[20] Changing the city's laws, consequently, was at the very heart of the Thirty's mandate and the reason for their power. Both Xenophon and the *Athenaion Politeia* quickly state that the Thirty delayed addressing these constitutional matters and focused on other issues. Their actions, however, are significant because they show the Thirty focusing on the rule of the city, a process which they carried out using traditional forms.

The Thirty's appropriation of the city's political past comes out very clearly in their initial actions. According to the *Athenaion Politeia*, they appointed a council of 500 *bouleutai* and other magistrates.[21] Xenophon does not give the number of councillors involved, but he describes the body as the *boule*.[22] A council of 500 is, as we have seen in the previous chapters, one of the hallmarks of the Kleisthenic system. Nothing would have stopped the Thirty from constituting themselves as the council and there was no apparent need to bring other men into this body. The Four Hundred provided a model for just such a move. Their number, however, matched the number of members of the Solonian *boule* so that it was easy for these oligarchs to use the connection to legitimise their actions. In contrast, such an option was not possible for the Thirty, whose number could in no way be described as *patrios*. If they wanted to claim the sanction of the past for their actions, then they had to add men to their number to make up a proper council. Alternatively, they could simply have not had a council at all, but such a move would have emphasised their rejection of the city's political traditions; evidently, they were not prepared to go so far. Their decision to have a council of 500 must have had wide support within the ranks of the Thirty because, otherwise, it is difficult to see how thirty men could have maintained control over the other 470. The Thirty's use of the city's traditions did not stop with the appointment of the *boule* because they used the New Bouleuterion as the seat of their power: it was the site both of Theramenes' trial, as we saw briefly in discussing the building's architecture, and of the trial of some of the generals and *taxiarchoi* (tribal commanders of hoplites) very soon after the oligarchs came to power.[23] By using this space, the Thirty were able to take over a location closely associated with the rule of the *demos* and to make it their own. They could also cite the city's traditions as the reasons for their actions, which would,

---

[20] Xen. *Hell.* 2.3.2, 11; Arist. *Ath. Pol.* 35.1; cf. Diod. 14.4.1; Fuks 1953: 75–6; Ostwald 1986: 477–8; cf. Hignett 1952: 287–8; Cecchin 1969: 74.

[21] Arist. *Ath. Pol.* 35.1.

[22] Xen. *Hell.* 2.3.11; cf. Diod. 14.4.1; Andok. 1.95; *IG* I³ 380.27. Xenophon will call this body the *boule* again in connection with Theramenes' trial and death; Xen. *Hell.* 2.3.23, 24, 50, 51, 55.

[23] Theramenes: Xen. *Hell.* 2.3.23–55; above chapter 4. Generals and *taxiarchoi*: Lys. 13.36–8.

therefore, appear as legitimate and not the deeds of usurping oligarchs or tyrants. These connections with the Kleisthenic past served to legitimise their regime and to begin the process of erasing the rule of the *demos* from some parts of the city. Once again, the Agora had become contested space between democrats and oligarchs.

The Thirty's adoption of the city's political traditions was not limited to a *boule* of 500 because some of the other traditional magistracies are also attested. As was to be expected, there was an eponymous archon for the year, Pythodoros, and he seems to have been chosen by the Thirty.[24] His name came to be closely associated with the Thirty and 404/3 was subsequently considered a period of anarchy in which there had been no archon to give his name to the year.[25] A *basileus*, Patrokles, is also known for this year.[26] Although Isokrates describes him as holding office when the Ten ruled after the Thirty fell from power, it seems likely that he was in office for the whole year and so was selected by the Thirty.[27] Treasurers of Athena and the Other Gods were chosen and they seem to have handed their inventory lists over in the normal fashion to their successors in 403/2.[28] They also made loans from the funds of Athena Polias and Nike to the *hellenotamiai*, as their fragmentary accounts show.[29] *Hipparchoi* are attested, and the Thirty also chose generals, who are mentioned by Xenophon only in connection with events at Eleusis; perhaps *strategoi* were not among the magistrates immediately appointed.[30] As with the oligarchs in 411, the Thirty clearly appointed many of the city's traditional magistrates and the records of the treasurers show them carrying out their regular duties. Taking over these offices allowed the Thirty to co-opt the city's past for their own use and these offices will have served to legitimate their regime and to emphasise its quality as *patrios*.

The Thirty's interest in regulating the city's legal affairs was not limited to the selection of magistrates. Despite comments in both Xenophon's account and the *Athenaion Politeia* that the Thirty were ignoring the constitutional issues which they were supposed to be addressing, we also know that they took a particular interest in the city's laws. The *Athenaion Politeia* records that they took down from the Areiopagos the laws of Ephialtes and Archestratos concerning the Areopagites and they also removed the

---

[24] Xen. *Hell.* 2.3.1; Arist. *Ath. Pol.* 35.1; P. J. Rhodes 1981: 436–7; Krentz 1982: 58; Develin 1989: 183; Todd 1985: 117.

[25] E.g. Xen. *Hell.* 2.3.1; Diod. 14.3.1; cf. [Plut.] *X orat.* 835F.   [26] Isok. 18.5.

[27] Krentz 1982: 58; Develin 1989: 183; Todd 1985: 117.

[28] *IG* I³ 380.1–4; *SEG* XXIII 81.1–8; cf. *IG* II² 1498.20–2; Lewis 1993: 226–9.

[29] *IG* I² 380; the *hellenotamiai* appear in lines 6–7 and 11–12.   [30] Xen. *Hell.* 2.4.8, 24, 26, 43.

ambiguous clauses from the statutes (*thesmoi*) of Solon.[31] Eliminating Ephialtes' and Archestratos' laws would cleanse the *politeia* of later accretions promulgated by the more radical democrats and it would allow a return to a more ancestral form of constitution. These actions fit with the pattern which we have already observed with the magistracies and, indeed, the *Athenaion Politeia* reports that they claimed to be restoring the constitution by these actions. That the Thirty may have had more radical plans is suggested by the scholia on Aischines' speech against Timarchos which report that, 'when they had overthrown the *patrios politeia* of the Athenians, they maltreated (ἐλυμήναντο) the laws of both Drakon and Solon'.[32] This information must come from a different source than the *Athenaion Politeia* because here the ancestral constitution is firmly associated with the rule of the *demos* and Drakon is mentioned in connection with these changes.[33] The strength of the terms used shows that the source of these remarks was certainly hostile to the Thirty. This description of the changes suggests that more was going on than simply removing the laws of Ephialtes and Archestratos from the Areiopagos and the combination of Drakon and Solon implies more substantial developments. Xenophon also seems to indicate that the Thirty were promulgating new laws: in the course of Theramenes' trial, Kritias refers to the 'new laws', one of which prevents anyone of the Three Thousand from being killed without the vote of the *boule* and allows the Thirty to kill anyone not among this number.[34] Elsewhere, Xenophon reports that Kritias was writing laws, one of which is specifically aimed at Sokrates.[35] Collectively, this evidence suggests that the work of the Thirty was rather more far reaching than simply removing laws promulgated by the more radical democrats during the fifth century.[36] Instead, the Thirty seem to have undertaken a significant attempt to reform the city's constitution.

Further evidence for this process is found in the measures which the Thirty took against the courts and sycophants. The *Athenaion Politeia* reports that the sovereignty of the courts was abolished and passes on to the ways in which Solon's law on bequeathing property was amended.[37] Until this time, his legislation invalidated a will made by someone who was mad,

---

[31] Arist. *Ath. Pol.* 35.2.
[32] Schol. Aischin. 1.39. On the meaning of the term ἐλυμήναντο, see the discussion below.
[33] Its source may be Lysias' speech written against an unknown man for his *dokimasia* and cited later in the entry as the source for the figure of 2,500 killed by the Thirty. All the detailed information which precedes this section is consistent with such a source, which seems to be very well informed about events under the Thirty.
[34] Xen. *Hell.* 2.3.51; cf. Arist. *Ath. Pol.* 37.1.   [35] Xen. *Mem.* 1.2.31.
[36] Removing laws: e.g. Ostwald 1986: 479–80; Krentz 1982: 61–2.   [37] Arist. *Ath. Pol.* 35.2.

senile, or under the influence of a woman; now, this clause was removed, and any such document was absolutely valid. The Thirty's change, we are told, was intended to remove opportunities for sycophants, presumably to use the various conditions to overturn the will.[38] Consequently, the only question for the courts was whether a will was genuine or not.[39] No other issues were involved and this particular law exemplifies the ways in which the powers of the courts were curtailed by the Thirty. This legislation is connected with the sycophants who are described as exploiting the existing system, a process which they could only carry out in the courts.[40] Eliminating the sycophants, consequently, was part of a larger process of bringing the democratic courts under control and removing the possibilities for their exploitation, as had been done under the rule of the *demos*. A further part of the process was the reforms to Solon's laws, including the one about wills. As Robin Osborne observes, such detailed changes to the laws indicate that the Thirty were serious about reforming the laws and producing a new *politeia* for the city.[41]

Collectively, our evidence suggests that the Thirty engaged in a considerable programme of reforming the city's laws and her constitution from the beginning of their regime. As part of this process, they retained the traditional magistracies and so they could claim to be adhering to the ancestral constitution, an appeal which would also confer legitimacy on their rule. As part of the procedure of changing the city's laws, the Thirty very likely appealed to the *patrios politeia* for authority and, in the *Athenaion Politeia*, the account of their legislative activities is prefaced by the statement that they claimed to be pursuing the ancestral constitution.[42] Just as the oligarchs in 411 had appealed to the city's past in order to legitimise their regimes, so now, in 404/3, the Thirty were employing the same tactics. On this occasion, however, they did more than simply invoke the ancestral constitution and they engaged in a serious programme of legislative reform. In its initial outlines, this project appears ambitious and, had it been completed, it would have remade the constitution in a very significant way. Such an undertaking would only have been possible with the support of the majority of members of the Thirty. Some of these men may have been more eager for the project to succeed than others, but, at the beginning, it must have had broad support. Had it been completely carried out, this reform of the city's laws would also have superseded the democrats' own

---

[38] R. Osborne 2003: 263.   [39] R. Osborne 2003: 263.
[40] Arist. *Ath. Pol.* 35.3; R. Osborne 2003: 264. For a different explanation of the attacks on the sycophants, see Xen. *Hell.* 2.3.12.
[41] R. Osborne 2003: 264.   [42] Arist. *Ath. Pol.* 35.2 with note 16 above; R. Osborne 2003: 265.

reorganisation and revision of the laws. Replacing that project with their own allowed the Thirty to erase the democrats' earlier actions and to make the city a more suitable place for their own regime. The reorganisation of the laws under the *demos* was very probably an important reason for the Thirty's own project for the city's legislation.

PHYSICAL EVIDENCE

Further evidence for the Thirty's project of reforming the city's laws comes from the physical remains, both inscriptions and monuments. This material suggests that the scale of the Thirty's reform was more extensive than our literary sources indicate. It also shows that the oligarchs were alert to the necessity of remaking the city so that it demonstrated their control of the physical space. Had the project been completed, it would have undone in some significant ways the democrats' earlier responses to the oligarchies of 411. Even in its incomplete state, their plans signal for us the ways in which particular spaces of the city again became sites of contestation between oligarchs and democrats, as both groups struggled to make their claims to Athens visible in the topography.

As with the oligarchs in 411 and the democrats' subsequent responses, inscribed material provides us with important traces of the Thirty's actions. In discussing the preserved fragments of the laws in chapter 3, we noticed that two fragments from the sacrificial calendar are now opisthographic with the later text of side A inscribed in an erasure (table 6: frs. 2, 3; fig. 6). This evidence can best be explained if, in the first period between 410 and 404, both faces of the *stelai* were inscribed; otherwise, the slabs could simply have been turned over when the later text was inscribed.[43] The most likely setting for these two fragments is the south annexe of the Stoa Basileios (fig. 7). These observations, however, raise a further problem: how did these two *stelai* erected in the south wing of the Stoa Basileios come to be available for re-use? The most likely explanation is that damage occurred to some of the inscribed slabs in the stoa during the Thirty's time in power. Such a scenario would be consistent with our written sources which indicate that the Thirty had embarked on a significant process to change the city's laws. It would also fit with our evidence that they 'maltreated' (ἐλυμήναντο) the laws of Drakon and Solon. The verb in question here (λυμαίνομαι) is a strong one which can be used both of physical damage up to and including destruction and metaphorically, as

---

[43] Above chapter 3.

in the case of Oedipus' anger which destroys him.[44] It can also be used in allegations about the laws: Lysias claims hyperbolically that Nikomachos 'maltreated' the laws of Solon, while the rest of the Athenians were out of the city on naval expeditions.[45] The damage done to the laws by the Thirty was great enough that they are subsequently described as having been destroyed (διεφθαρμένους, ἀπολωλότων). In the context of this passage in the scholia, these terms suggest that significant physical damage was done to the laws, an explanation which is compatible with the indications of our physical evidence.

These texts of the laws in the Agora were not the only inscriptions with which the Thirty were concerned. Although not so described by the *Athenaion Politeia*, the laws of Ephialtes and Archestratos on the Areiopagos must have been written on a *stele* or *stelai* which were removed by the Thirty. Other inscriptions also felt the wrath of the oligarchs. In the early fourth century, at least six proxeny decrees were reinscribed because the original documents had been taken down by the Thirty, as the texts take great care to tell us.[46] If the decree honouring the loyal Samians in 405/4 was inscribed before the *demos* lost power, then this document may also have suffered a similar fate.[47] These examples represent only the minimum number of *stelai* which the Thirty removed and other inscriptions may have been destroyed, but not subsequently reinscribed. On the surface, such destruction might seem like petty vandalism rather than a concentrated effort to eliminate laws. All the documents certainly involved, however, are proxeny decrees, texts which display the honours accorded by the (democratic) city to her *proxenoi* abroad.[48] They attest to a relationship both between the city and the honorands and between Athens and the honorands' cities. Removing the *stelai* visibly breaks these bonds which the documents had created and it signals that no such relationship exists between the honorands and their cities and the Thirty and oligarchic Athens. In a very powerful way, the removal of the inscriptions demonstrates the changed nature of the regime and of the city: such relationships were not appropriate for the Athens of the Thirty. As decrees for non-Athenians, these documents would originally

---

[44] Physical damage: e.g. Hdt. 5.33.3; 8.28; Dem. 23.33. Oedipus: Soph. *OC* 855.

[45] Lys. 30.26; cf. Dem. 18.312, an allegation in connection with the trierarchic law.

[46] *IG* i³ 229; *IG* ii² 6; 13 + addenda p. 655 + *SEG* xl 54; 52; *Agora* xvi 37; Walbank, *Proxenies* 26. The very fragmentary *Agora* xvi 39 may represent the remains of another such *stele*. On the Thirty's possible motives for taking down one of these decrees, see Avery 1979: 241; cf. Culasso Gastaldi 2003: 244–5. We shall discuss these inscriptions further in chapter 8.

[47] *IG* i³ 127 + RO 2 (= *IG* ii² 1); M. J. Osborne 1981–2: ii, 25; Rhodes and Osborne 2003: 15; Blanshard 2007: 35. For further discussion of these honours, see chapter 8.

[48] *Proxenoi* officially looked after Athenian interests in their own cities.

have been erected on the Akropolis; by removing them, the Thirty were also able to show their control of the city's most important sanctuary.[49] For us, these *stelai* also testify to the Thirty's particular interest in inscriptions and, together with our other evidence, they suggest a larger pattern of activity intended to change the ways in which inscribed texts fit into the city's topography.

The removal of these inscriptions also emphasises that the spaces in which the *stelai* were erected had become contested space, areas in which the Thirty needed to demonstrate their control. In view of the democrats' response to the events of 411, the focus on the Agora and the Akropolis should not surprise us: the Thirty needed to claim these spaces as their own (fig. 4). Their interest in the Areiopagos fits into a larger pattern of undoing the changes made by the *demos* to the city's *politeia*. The Thirty's focus on the spaces of the city, however, was not limited to these three areas and they also embarked on an ambitious project to change the orientation of the Pnyx by 180 degrees, as we learn from a comment by Plutarch.[50] He explains the project as intended to modify the orientation of the speaker's platform or *bema* so that it faced inland, rather than towards the sea, a more appropriate direction for an oligarchy. While the veracity of Plutarch's comments have been called into question, archaeological excavation has shown that the meeting place of the *ekklesia* was rebuilt at just this time and the orientation of the structure was reversed (figs. 12–13).[51] This new design required a significant retaining wall to be constructed on the north side of the slope and the pottery found in the fill dumped behind this wall at the time of its construction belongs to the very end of the fifth century BC.[52] By Plutarch's day, the second phase of the Pnyx had long since been obliterated by the rebuilding and expansion of phase three in the years after about 340 BC.[53] It is this version which Plutarch would have known and his comments about its earlier state at the end of the fifth century cannot have been based on autopsy. As excavation has shown, he was correct about the overall project and, consequently, it is difficult to believe that he made a mistake about the group responsible for rebuilding the Pnyx. In their original report, the excavators noted the 'hasty, careless workmanship'

---

[49] The decision to station the Spartan forces on the Akropolis may also represent an attempt by the Thirty to demonstrate their control of the sanctuary; Arist. *Ath. Pol.* 37.2; Lys. 12.94; 13.46; cf. Plut. *Lys.* 15.6 who attributes the decision to Lysandros.
[50] Plut. *Them.* 19.6.
[51] Veracity questioned: Moysey 1981; Hansen 1986: 97–8; archaeological evidence: Kourouniotes and Thompson 1932: 113–36; H. A. Thompson 1982: 138–40.
[52] Kourouniotes and Thompson 1932: 128–36; H. A. Thompson 1982: 139.
[53] Rotroff and Camp 1996.

Figure 12   Model of the Pnyx, period 1, from the northwest; built *c.* 500 BC.

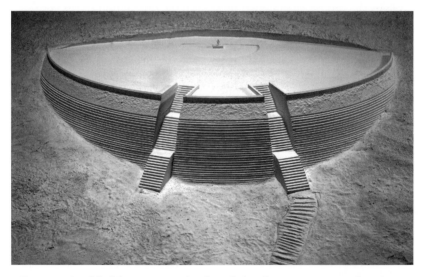

Figure 13   Model of the Pnyx, period 2, from the northwest; project started 404/3 BC.

evident in the construction of the second phase;[54] their observation fits well with Plutarch's comment that the Thirty were responsible for the project. It is less easy to explain, if the construction was done by the *demos* upon its return in 403, when such haste would not have been needed.

[54] Kourouniotes and Thompson 1932: 135.

An interest in the Pnyx also fits with the Thirty's focus on the city's laws. As we have seen, they were actively engaged in changing the laws and producing an appropriate constitution for the now oligarchic city. What the final form of these revisions would have been is difficult to know, but the emphasis on the *patrios politeia* and on establishing links with the political past suggests that there would have been some larger body than the *boule*, perhaps the Three Thousand which appear in our literary sources.[55] Such a body would have needed an appropriate place in which to meet, a function which the rebuilt Pnyx would certainly have provided. In addition, the project would have allowed the Thirty to lay claim to one of the locations in the city which was most closely associated with the *demos*: in Thucydides' narrative of the events of 411, the *demos'* first meeting on the Pnyx under the Four Hundred signals the demise of the oligarchs who were removed from power at that *ekklesia*.[56] Nor is the Pnyx the only place in which we see the Thirty trying to gain control of the city's spaces. Very much the same dynamic exists with the New Bouleuterion in the Agora which they were using as the centre of their power (fig. 2). Here, their presence together with that of their *boule* allowed them to make the space into their own and it made the building's democratic origins less noticeable. In the Stoa Basileios, damaging at least some of the great *stelai* with the inscribed laws may have been intended as a first step towards displaying their new lawcode,[57] but these actions certainly allowed the Thirty to demonstrate their power over another building closely associated with the *demos'* responses to the events of 411. On the Akropolis and the Areiopagos, taking down *stelai* with proxeny decrees and with the laws of Ephialtes and Archestratos allowed the Thirty to claim these spaces as their own. Their actions further served to begin to erase the control of the *demos* from the topography. Their project for the Pnyx performed much the same function of visibly removing the *demos* from this space.

The remodelling of the Pnyx, accordingly, fits in very well with the Thirty's other activities and particularly with their focus on creating a new lawcode for the city. Their work here, in the Agora, on the Areiopagos and on the Akropolis also marked out these four spaces as areas of contestation between themselves and the democrats (fig. 4). Controlling these places

---

[55] E.g. Xen. *Hell.* 2.3.18–19, 51, 2.4.2; Arist. *Ath. Pol.* 36.1–2, 37.1–2; Lys. 25.22.

[56] Thuc. 8.97.1; above chapter 2.

[57] It is impossible to know if the erasures on frs. 2 and 3 of side A of the sacrificial calendar were done by the Thirty, as Fingarette suggested, or by the *demos* in 403, as Clinton prefers; Fingarette 1971: 333; Clinton 1982: 32. Logically, such a step would come immediately before text was to be inscribed and, by that time, the laws must have been finalised so that the mason could copy them on to the stone.

meant that the Thirty could lay claim to the principal areas of political and memorial activity. They could begin to undo the *demos'* response to the events in 411 and to remake the city into an appropriate space for their rule. Their activities also allowed them to claim the city's political past which was now being visibly purified of the excesses of the people through the writing of new laws and the destruction of existing ones. In this way, the Thirty could take back the *patrios politeia* and use it as the basis for their own power. Their activities, consequently, very much represent a response to the earlier actions of the democrats. As part of this process, the Thirty took over and re-used many of the same strategies which the *demos* had itself used and they focused on much the same areas of the city. These plans for recreating Athens as the oligarchic, not democratic, city were ambitious and they could only have been implemented with extensive support from a large number of the Thirty themselves, and not just the so-called moderates, whom scholars have associated with the *patrios politeia*.[58] Since Kritias was one of the main leaders of the Thirty, his support of this project would have been crucial. That he was involved in these various activities is made clear by Xenophon who describes him as a lawgiver (*nomothetes*) and as writing laws when the Thirty were in power.[59] This broad support explains the impressive scope of the Thirty's plans; had they been completed, the city would have been substantially changed and she would have become a very different place than she had been under the rule of the *demos*.

VIOLENCE AND THE THIRTY

This project of replacing democracy with oligarchy and creating the oligarchic city was, however, never completed and now we can only see its broad outlines. At some point, support swung away from the project and the constitution and the laws became less important than maintaining power in any way possible and most especially through violence. Part of the difficulty in identifying the moment of this shift lies with our sources and their focus. None of our literary sources fully lays out the Thirty's plans for responding to democracy and, as we have seen, the situation has to be pieced together from different types of evidence. While the sources focus much more on the violence which took place, they also do not agree completely on the chronology of the events.[60] From our

---

[58] E.g. Fuks 1953: 64–7, 79, 110–11; Finley 2000: 39–40; Ostwald 1986: 469–72; R. Osborne 2003: 465; see also above chapter 2.

[59] Xen. *Mem.* 1.2.31.

[60] On the chronological problems, see P. J. Rhodes 1981: 415–22; Hignett 1952: 378–89; Krentz 1982: 131–52; Ostwald 1986: 481–4; Todd 1985: 221–33.

perspective, these differing accounts make it difficult to know when and why this project about the laws and the city came to a halt. Nevertheless, it is very clear that there was a shift to a much greater use of violence and the leaders of the project are unlikely to have been the same men who pushed violence as a solution to the Thirty's problems. Violence and terror were very much among the arsenal of weapons which the Thirty used to maintain their control of the city.

For Xenophon, the violence begins almost immediately: the Thirty's first act is to arrest and to kill the sycophants and this action is followed by a request to Sparta for a garrison.[61] Its arrival leads to a reign of terror during which Kritias is depicted as eager to kill people, while Theramenes objects and counsels moderation.[62] The unjust deaths of many individuals lead to unrest among the people and further objections from Theramenes; the Thirty's solution is to select the Three Thousand and to disarm all the other Athenians.[63] There follows a second period of terror in which the Thirty kill many people from personal enmity and to gain their money; each member of the oligarchy also kills a metic.[64] Once again, Theramenes objects to these actions and there follows his trial, one of the high points in Xenophon's narrative.[65] Theramenes' death frees the Thirty to act tyrannically and they expel the unprivileged citizens from the *astu* and then from the Peiraieus.[66] At this point, Thrasyboulos occupies Phyle (fig. 1) and, except for the Thirty's arrest and slaughter of the Eleusinians after their defeat near Phyle, the narrative concentrates on the military events.[67] For Xenophon, accordingly, the violence and terror begin immediately and they get progressively more severe. Theramenes' trial forms an important moment in the Thirty's evolution and his death marks a turning point for the regime: only at this point do they act tyrannically without fear (τυραννεῖν ἀδεῶς). When Kritias instructs the Three Thousand to approve the arrest and slaughter of the Eleusinians after the fact and states that the *politeia* which they are establishing is as much for them as for the Thirty, he is very clearly using constitution-making and the laws as an excuse, not as a serious process.

Diodoros presents a similar impression of these same events.[68] For this period, he differs from Xenophon in placing the killing of the metics in the period of terror after Theramenes' death, the sending forth of the unprivileged after Thrasyboulos' occupation of Phyle and the condemnation of

---

[61] Xen. *Hell.* 2.3.12–13.   [62] Xen. *Hell.* 2.3.14–16.   [63] Xen. *Hell.* 2.3.17–20.
[64] Xen. *Hell.* 2.3.21.   [65] Xen. *Hell.* 2.3.22–56.   [66] Xen. *Hell.* 2.4.1.
[67] Thrasyboulos and Phyle: Xen. *Hell.* 2.4.2; Eleusinians: Xen. *Hell.* 2.4.8–9.
[68] Diod. 14.4.1–6.3, 32.1–33.1; see also the helpful chart in P. J. Rhodes 1981: 416–19.

the Eleusinians (and Salaminians) before the Thirty's defeat at Acharnai.[69] Theramenes' trial, in contrast, does not have as prominent a place in the narrative as it does in Xenophon's account and it appears to be less of a significant point in the events described. Placing the arrest of the metics after his death, however, does mean that the violence continues to increase as time passes. This sense is increased in this section by the focus on the Athenians' reaction to the death of the blameless Nikeratos, the son of the general Nikias; their shared grief and their tears for the dead man contrast with the Thirty's lawlessness and madness.[70] The death of sixty blameless metics is balanced by the daily killing of citizens and the Thirty's destruction of the city (κατέφθειραν τὴν πόλιν), a strong phrase, leads to the flight of more than half the Athenians. The emphasis on the deaths of Nikeratos and Autolykos, both prominent citizens, gives the violence a focus on the individual, rather than on the mass of the nameless victims as in Xenophon's account. For Diodoros, the atrocities appear to be more important than the trial of Theramenes, who, unlike the other victims of the Thirty, is at least awarded a trial before his death.

In contrast to these two accounts, the *Athenaion Politeia* gives us a version which presents a different focus and sequence of events. The opening sections are concerned not so much with violence, but with constitutional matters and the ways in which the Thirty are going to govern Athens.[71] Getting rid of the sycophants also takes place at this time, but it is not until they have greater control over the city that they start putting citizens to death; not less than 1,500 is the estimated number of dead.[72] Theramenes' objections lead to the selection of the Three Thousand, but this move does not prevent Theramenes from expressing his disapproval.[73] The next event in the narrative is Thrasyboulos' seizure of Phyle and the defeat of the Thirty's forces.[74] At this point, the oligarchs decide to get rid of Theramenes, a process which entails two new laws, but apparently no trial.[75] Only then do the Thirty disarm all Athenians except members of the Three Thousand and request a garrison from the Spartans.[76] The disarming is accompanied by much more savageness and wickedness, but no specific details are provided. This version of the events focuses much less on violence and terror and it keeps the personalities involved to a minimum: only Theramenes, Thrasyboulos and Kallibios, the Spartan governor, are

---

[69] Diod. 14.5.6, 32.4–33.1.   [70] Diod. 14.5.5–7.
[71] Arist. *Ath. Pol.* 35.1–2; see also the helpful chart in P. J. Rhodes 1981: 416–19.
[72] Arist. *Ath. Pol.* 35.3–4. On the numbers, see P. J. Rhodes 1981: 447 with further references.
[73] Arist. *Ath. Pol.* 36.1–2.   [74] Arist. *Ath. Pol.* 37.1.
[75] Arist. *Ath. Pol.* 37.1.   [76] Arist. *Ath. Pol.* 37.2.

named. Theramenes is never explicitly described as a member of the Thirty and the altered order of events places the request for a Spartan garrison after his death: he cannot be responsible for these actions.[77] By not naming any members of the Thirty, the focus remains on Theramenes who is presented in a positive light which contrasts with the negative presentation of the Thirty.[78] Although violence is not emphasised in this version, we cannot forget the 1,500 estimated dead who are mentioned early in the narrative.

For all three of these accounts,[79] violence is a very real aspect of the Thirty's regime and they agree that it became much more pronounced as time passed. Theramenes is also an important figure, but his trial is a pivotal moment only in Xenophon's narrative; in contrast, the version of the *Athenaion Politeia* never mentions a trial. These different presentations of Theramenes have been influenced by subsequent attempts to defend or to attack his memory: the positive depiction in the *Athenaion Politeia* contrasts with Xenophon's apparently more measured account, while Lysias' denunciation in his speech against Eratosthenes represents the opposite extreme.[80] Even Xenophon, however, makes it clear that the situation deteriorated significantly after his death. Our sources' general focus on Theramenes and Xenophon's and Diodoros' particular emphases on violence make it difficult to know how we should connect these narratives with the project to remake the constitution and to claim the city from the *demos*. If we want to believe that it was the work of Theramenes, then his trial must mark the end of the process. As we saw earlier, however, this project was extensive and it must have required broad support from among the members of the Thirty. Certainly, it must have been more important and more popular at the beginning of the regime and, inevitably, it could not compete with the necessity of staying in power: maintaining control required violence and so force, rather than the *politeia*, became the order of the day.

The Thirty's decisions to use violence and exile against the Athenians and to involve the Spartans had important further consequences: military

---

[77] Compare P. J. Rhodes 1981: 422; Keaney 1992: 143.

[78] This depiction fits very well with Theramenes' positive presentation elsewhere in the *Athenaion Politeia*, for which, see Keaney 1992: 133–48.

[79] Since Justin's summary of Pompeius Trogus largely follows Diodoros, I have left his version out of consideration here; see further P. J. Rhodes 1981: 416–20.

[80] Lys. 12.62–79; in this very hostile account, violence is pervasive. The so-called Theramenes Papyrus (*P. Mich.* 5982) also seems to be presenting a positive view of Theramenes, but this fragmentary text concerns only the peace negotiations with the Spartans, rather than events under the Thirty; Merkelbach and Youtie 1968; Henrichs 1968; Andrewes 1970; Engels 1993. Theramenes' memory: R. Osborne 2003: 266; see also P. J. Rhodes 1981: 21–2; Ober 1998: 360–1; Wolpert 2002a: 10–11; Wolpert 2006: 219.

force would be used by Athenians against other Athenians and the Spartans would be further involved in internal Athenian affairs.[81] These developments made the end of the Thirty very different from the end of the Four Hundred in 411. Now military force was important and the situation was not to be resolved simply by deposing the oligarchs in the *ekklesia*. The Spartan contribution was also significant in bringing the conflict to an end and, without their intervention, it is difficult to see how the Athenians' problems could have been solved. These events also affected how they would be publicly remembered after the *demos* returned to power, as we shall see in the following chapters.

Violence and exile are presented as important factors leading to the democrats' seizure of Phyle (fig. 1). In Xenophon's account, the exiling of the Athenians not among the Three Thousand is immediately followed by Thrasyboulos' departure from Thebes and capture of Phyle.[82] It provokes an immediate response from the Thirty who send out the Three Thousand and the *hippeis*. This description brings out the ways in which the Athenians are now divided and the narrative moves forward to the democrats' capture of Peiraieus and defeat of the forces of the Thirty at Mounichia (fig. 3). Similarly, in Diodoros' account, the Thirty are said to exile and put to death Athenians daily, a process which again leads directly to Thrasyboulos' seizure of Phyle.[83] In the *Athenaion Politeia*, as in Diodoros' version, Thrasyboulos is accompanied by men exiled by the Thirty.[84]

For the democrats, seizing Phyle was only the first step in their attempts to return to Athens. When their forces had grown large enough, Thrasyboulos led them from Phyle to the Peiraieus.[85] According to Xenophon, the Thirty immediately led out their own forces.[86] The subsequent battle was fought in Mounichia itself and the oligarchs were convincingly defeated; among the dead were two members of the Thirty, Kritias and Hippomachos, and one member of the Ten in Peiraieus, Charmides, the son of Glaukos.[87] With the democrats in control of the Peiraieus, divisions broke out among the Three Thousand in the city and they deposed the Thirty, who departed to Eleusis (fig. 1).[88] Violence had not succeeded in keeping them in power. The Thirty were replaced by ten men elected, according to the *Athenaion Politeia* and Diodoros, specifically to bring

---

[81] For discussion of the military situation, see Krentz 1982: 69–101 with further references.
[82] Xen. *Hell.* 2.4.1–2.   [83] Diod. 14.32.1.   [84] Arist. *Ath. Pol.* 37.1.
[85] Xen. *Hell.* 2.4.10; Diod. 14.33.1–2.   [86] Xen. *Hell.* 2.4.10.
[87] Xen. *Hell.* 2.4.10–22; Diod. 14.33.2–3; Arist. *Ath. Pol.* 38.1; Krentz 1982: 90–2.
[88] Xen. *Hell.* 2.4.23–4; Arist. *Ath. Pol.* 38.1; Diod. 14.33.5.

the war to an end, something which they did not, in fact, do.[89] While the democrats controlled the Peiraieus, the oligarchs held the city (*astu*), but neither side had enough power to defeat the other decisively (fig. 3). At this point, the oligarchs and, according to Xenophon, the Thirty at Eleusis, appealed to the Spartans for help.[90] The Spartans' first move was to send off a force under Lysandros who planned to besiege the men of the Peiraieus by land and by sea.[91] Jealousy of Lysandros prompted King Pausanias to act: after persuading the ephors, he led the Spartan army to Athens.[92] His presence provoked a military engagement with the men of the Peiraieus and the Spartan dead were subsequently buried in a tomb near the Dipylon Gate (fig. 4).[93] According to Xenophon, however, the king's real aim was to reconcile the warring Athenian factions.[94] To this end, he gave secret instructions to the envoys of the men of the Peiraieus, created divisions within the city and encouraged men in Athens to ask for reconciliation.[95] He then sent the delegation from the Peiraieus to Sparta along with private individuals from the city, while an official delegation also set out from the city.[96] In response to these various groups of Athenians, the Spartans sent fifteen men to Pausanias in Athens with instructions to make a reconciliation among the warring Athenians.[97]

The Thirty's violence and the exiles which they created, consequently, led directly to the military confrontation between the different Athenian factions. That conflict, in turn, made a peaceful, internal solution, such as occurred in 411, unlikely. In 403, in contrast, an external power, Sparta, was needed to arrange a settlement between the two sides. Without such an arrangement, armed conflict was likely to break out again very quickly between the different factions. How to reconcile the Athenians and to heal their divisions was a critical question at this moment. As we shall see in the following chapter, the process itself was an important factor in addressing the fractures among the Athenians and it also marked the first step in responding again to oligarchy.

---

[89] Xen. *Hell.* 2.4.23–4; Arist. *Ath. Pol.* 38.1; Diod. 14.33.5; Lys. 12.54–7.

[90] Xen. *Hell.* 2.4.28; Diod. 14.33.5. On the problems of second Ten reported by Arist. *Ath. Pol.* 38.3, see P. J. Rhodes 1981: 459–60. Rhodes gives good reasons for denying their existence; contra: Krentz 1982: 97; cf. Loening 1987: 45–6.

[91] Xen. *Hell.* 2.4.28–9; Diod. 14.33.5; Plut. *Lys.* 21.3–4.

[92] Xen. *Hell.* 2.4.29–30; Diod. 14.33.6; Plut. *Lys.* 21.4–5. On the king's motives, see Krentz 1982: 98–101; Todd 2000: 192–3.

[93] Xen. *Hell.* 2.4.30–5. Spartan dead: Xen. *Hell.* 2.4.33; Lys. 2.63; *IG* II² 11678; below chapter 10.

[94] Xen. *Hell.* 2.4.31, 35.

[95] Xen. *Hell.* 2.4.35. For one delegation of individuals from the city, see Lys. 18.10–12.

[96] Xen. *Hell.* 2.4.36–7.

[97] Xen. *Hell.* 2.4.38; cf. Arist. *Ath. Pol.* 38.4; Diod. 14.33.6; Plut. *Lys.* 21.6.

THE THIRTY AND THE CITY

Although the regime of the Thirty came to use violence to solve its problems and it ended in armed confrontation with other Athenians at Mounichia, the Thirty did not originally gain control through violence. Instead, their rise to power comes out of debate over the proper constitution for the city and calls for the implementation of and/or the return to the *patrios politeia*. In our sources, resolving the constitutional issues are an important part in the Thirty's mandate and the reason why they were elected by the *demos*. Reforming the constitution and remaking the city's laws was a serious undertaking for the Thirty and the overall project must have enjoyed wide support in its initial phases. As part of this process, the oligarchs used the city's political past for their own ends; the *patrios politeia* was very probably invoked to make their plans acceptable. Claiming the past for themselves conferred legitimacy on their regime. In this regard, the dynamics at play were no different than they were under the oligarchs in 411 or the *demos* in 410.

As part of this process, the Thirty also began to remake the democratic city so that she would be a suitable place for oligarchs. They focused particularly on the previously contested spaces of the Agora and the Akropolis and they also added two new areas of contestation between oligarchs and democrats, the Areiopagos and the Pnyx (fig. 4). In the Agora, the Thirty focused particularly on the New Bouleuterion and the Stoa Basileios (fig. 2). In so doing, they followed the lead of the *demos* and their actions constitute a reaction to the democrats' own responses to oligarchy. The Thirty's overall project of remaking the *politeia* and the city, consequently, very much belongs in the context of the ways in which these issues had already been used during the previous decade by both oligarchs and democrats. Their actions represent a particularly Athenian response to Athenian problems. This local context also provides the best argument that the Thirty were not trying to remake Athens as an imitation of Sparta.[98]

Nevertheless, the Thirty's interest in remaking Athens did not prevent them from using force to achieve their own ends; in due course, violence dominated issues about the constitution and the city. At that point, factions must have developed among the different oligarchs, divisions which may, perhaps, be reflected in the circumstances around Theramenes' trial. Their

---

[98] For this argument, see Krentz 1982: 63–6; Ostwald 1986: 484–7; Whitehead 1982–3; Munn 2000: 218, 225–7; Wolpert 2006: 221. Against this argument, see also the comments of Cartledge 1987: 282; Lewis 1994: 34–5; Forsdyke 2005: 199 note 270.

recourse to violence and exile as means to ensure their continued power led to military confrontation with the democrats and eventually to Spartan intervention. As in 411, the *patrios politeia* and displaying the oligarchs' control of the city were not enough to keep the Thirty in power. Meanwhile, the ways in which the Thirty used both the past and the cityscape would prove significant for the newly returned democrats: once again, they would have to remake Athens as the democratic city and to reclaim her past for the *demos*. As we shall see, achieving these aims was to absorb much of the Athenians' energy during the next decade or so, but they were also able to make important constitutional changes which would prevent another recurrence of oligarchy.

CHAPTER 7

Reconciling the Athenians

In 403, the *stasis* between the Athenians dramatically exposed the rifts between different groups, first between the exiled *demos* and the Thirty in the city, and later between the *demos* in the Peiraieus, the more oligarchically minded Athenians in the city (*astu*) and the Thirty and their supporters now ensconced in relative safety at Eleusis. Events escalated so that military action took place and blood was shed between Athenians and Athenians. In the city, the Thirty began the process of remaking Athens into a place suitable for oligarchs: work started on a new constitution and the Thirty attempted to write their claim on the cityscape by taking over significant spaces, the Agora, the Areiopagos, the Akropolis and the Pnyx, as their own. When Pausanias, the Spartan king, appeared outside the city with an army, a fresh defeat must have seemed likely to the Athenians;[1] their most pressing need was to recover from their differences. Neither the Athenians in the Peiraieus nor the Athenians in the city (*astu*) were strong enough to deliver a decisive defeat in battle and fighting would only lead to further bloodshed as the victors seized the territories and persons of their opponents. Such actions might also lead the defeated party to appeal again to Sparta and so *stasis* would continue. Guided by Pausanias and a delegation from Sparta,[2] the different Athenian factions were able to find another solution for resolving their differences: an agreement of reconciliation between the warring groups.

That agreement, however, was only the beginning of resolving the Athenians' problems. Without further steps, the agreement might not hold and factions might never go away. There also remained the important question of how to respond to the Thirty. Their actions showed the power of the *demos*' earlier responses to oligarchy and their own appropriations of the

---

[1] Compare Xen. *Hell.* 2.4.28–9: Lysandros certainly planned on military action to put down the democrats.

[2] For the importance of Pausanias' role, see Todd 1985: 176–91; Loening 1987: 14–15; cf. Krentz 1982: 107.

city's monuments, spaces and past could not be allowed to remain. Once again, the city needed to be made visibly democratic and the past needed to be recovered for the *demos*. Overthrowing the Thirty had been far more violent than removing the Four Hundred and Five Thousand from power and individual Athenians had been much more personally involved and affected. At this moment, the Athenians also had to ask how they would remember these events, the *stasis* and fighting.

How the Athenians reconciled themselves and responded to the Thirty is the subject of the next four chapters. Our discussion must begin with the reconciliation agreement and the ways in which it worked to bring the Athenians back together and to reunite them again. This document and its associated rituals form the foundation of the Athenians' responses to the Thirty: without them, the responses to the Thirty, which we shall discuss in the following three chapters, simply would not have been possible. The reconciliation agreement in and of itself, however, was not a sufficient reaction to oligarchy. The process was far more extensive and encompassed some of the vital areas of the city: democracy and law (chapter 8), monuments and topography (chapter 9) and ritual and remembrance (chapter 10). As we shall see, the Athenians remade Athens as the democratic city and they recovered the space of the Agora for the *demos*. Through monuments and rituals, they selectively remembered the events of 404/3 and the oligarchy. This difference between the responses to the Thirty and the earlier reactions to the oligarchs of 411 shows that the process in 403 was not simply the blind continuation of the *demos'* earlier programme, but a new undertaking which responded to the different circumstances and events.

In 403, however, these actions and issues still lay in the future and the Athenians' most pressing task was to reconcile their warring factions. For this purpose, the reconciliation agreement was to prove a perfect solution for their problems. In addition to solving such basic issues as places of residence, the future of the surviving oligarchic leaders and the return of confiscated property, the document also had to prevent further unrest and to unite the fractured community. These ends were achieved both through the terms themselves and also by the ritual associated with the document. As in 410/9, all the Athenians again swore an oath, in this case to uphold the terms of the agreement. This process played an important role in reconciling the Athenians and in helping them to negotiate the events of the oligarchy. This process was not finished when the oath was taken because the Athenians then used the courts as a place for working out how the new rules of engagement, which the agreement put in place, would work in practice. Despite the importance of these processes and their roles in creating unity among the Athenians, scholars have not particularly concentrated on how the agreement functioned. Instead, they have focused on establishing the terms of the agreement, the extent to which it was actually followed in the courts and individual men's use and abuse of the document.[3] The injunction not to remember past wrongs (*me mnesikakein*) has also been discussed in the context of remembering (and forgetting) the Thirty.[4] Underlying all of these discussions is the basic assumption that the agreement actually did reconcile the Athenians, but, in 403, the Athenians could not assume that the document would successfully bring the warring factions together: reconciliation and unity had to be created. Then the details could be negotiated in the courts by individuals.

THE RECONCILIATION AGREEMENT

To bring the *stasis* and fighting between Athenians to an end, Pausanias and envoys from Sparta brought representatives of the two Athenian sides together, a process which led to the reconciliation agreement.[5] Although there was significant Spartan involvement in the proceedings,[6] the resulting document is focused on Athenians and their concerns and issues. The terms were well enough known that the speaker of Isokrates' speech against Kallimachos could have them read out at the trial and, in the years after 403, other speakers in the courts often allude to certain of the clauses, particularly the stipulation not to remember past wrongs.[7] This familiarity indicates that the terms must have been published and erected in a public setting. Despite this publication, we do not possess a full text of the document and the terms must be reconstructed from our various sources.

Fourth-century authors usually describe the agreement as 'the covenants and the oaths' (αἱ συνθῆκαι καὶ οἱ ὅρκοι)[8] and these two sections were read separately in this order at Kallimachos' trial; the document must have fallen into two separate parts in much the same way that Demophantos' decree gives the text of the decree proper and then the text of the oath which the

---

[3] Terms: e.g. Loening 1987: 19–58; Todd 1985: 61–70; Krentz 1982: 102–8; Ostwald 1986: 497–9; Carawan 2006. Courts: Loening 1987: 59–146; Todd 1985: 73–128, 154, 196–7; Munn 2000: 279–80; Wolpert 2002a: 84–6, 91–118. Use and abuse: e.g. Loening 1987: 69–84, 88–146; Todd 1985: 73–154; Wolpert 2002a: 48–71, 84–6, 91–129; Wolpert 2002b: 111–14, 118; Quillin 2002: 84–98; cf. Krentz 1982: 114–20.

[4] Loraux 2002, especially 94–169, 229–64; Wolpert 2002a: 119–36; cf. Lévy 1976: 214–16.

[5] Xen. *Hell.* 2.4.35–8; Arist. *Ath. Pol.* 38.3–4.

[6] [Lys.] 6.38 and 40 may refer to the Spartans' role; Todd 2007: 464, 465.   [7] Isok. 18.19–20.

[8] E.g. [Lys.] 6.39, 45; Lys. 13.88; 25.23, 28, 34; Isok. 18.19–21, 67.

Athenians are to swear. Our fullest summary of the document is provided by the *Athenaion Politeia*, but it is certainly an abridged version rather than the complete text (table 10).[9] The text of the oaths is not included and two other clauses are provided by Lysias and Isokrates (table 10).[10] In the *Athenaion Politeia*, the agreement is introduced by the statement that the reconciliation took place in the archonship of Eukleides, the archon of 403/2.[11] The first part of the summary concerns the Athenians of the city who wish to migrate to the oligarchic enclave at Eleusis and the relations between this autonomous community and the Athenians in the city (table 10; fig. 1). A special clause concerns the control of the sanctuary of Demeter at Eleusis which is to be common to both parties. Procedures are established for registering those men migrating to Eleusis, as well as the conditions upon which a man may return to the city. Additional clauses focus on matters of concern to all Athenians. For killing by wounding with one's own hand, homicide trials are to be conducted according to ancestral custom (*kata ta patria*), but, otherwise, no one is to remember past wrongs (*me mnesikakein*) except those of the Thirty, the Ten, the Eleven and the Ten in Peiraieus, i.e. the leaders of the oligarchs.[12] Should any of these men go through the process of *euthuna*, the scrutiny held after being in office, however, the amnesty clause will apply to them; these oligarchs are also apparently given the right to emigrate to Eleusis.[13]

As presented in the *Athenaion Politeia*, the terms of the agreement largely concern the individuals joining the oligarchic enclave at Eleusis. The document, however, seems not to have been quite so focused on the men emigrating to Eleusis. Xenophon's description begins with the statement that there is to be peace between the two sides and they are all to return to their homes except for the Thirty, the Eleven and the Ten

---

[9] Arist. *Ath. Pol.* 39.1–6. I am unpersuaded by Carawan's argument that this document is actually an amalgamation of two separate reconciliation agreements of 403/2 and 401/0; Carawan 2006. How this amalgamation came to be attached to the archonship of Eukleides (403/2) needs explanation, as does the document's location at *Athenaion Politeia* 39.1 rather than 40.4.

[10] Lys. fr. LXX.165 lines 34–48 (Carey); Isok. 18.20.

[11] Eukleides cannot have come into office until after the reconciliation was made and the *demos* returned to Athens, but the whole year seems to have been known by his name; see further P. J. Rhodes 1981: 462–3; Loening 1987: 21–2.

[12] Following Chambers' Teubner text: αὐτόχειρ ἔκτεινεν τρώσας. For the textual and other problems, see P. J. Rhodes 1981: 468; Chambers 1990: 318; Phillips 2008: 142–3 note 23; Loening 1987: 39–40. For Carawan, the clause about past wrongs must belong in 401/0 because such hostility to the Thirty is inappropriate for 403/2; Carawan 2006: 65–8. That the Athenians were confiscating and selling the property of the Thirty and their main supporters in 402/1 suggests otherwise; *SEG* XXXII 161 = *Agora* XIX P2 + LA2; below chapter 8.

[13] For the problems of this passage, see P. J. Rhodes 1981: 470–1; Loening 1987: 47–50; Carawan 2006: 66–7.

Table 10   *The reconciliation agreement of 403*

Aristotle, *Athenaion Politeia*	Clause	Other Reference	Clause
39.1	The reconciliation took place in the archonship of Eukleides.		
		Xenophon, *Hellenika* 2.4.38	There is to be peace between the two parties.
		Xenophon, *Hellenika* 2.4.38	They are to return to their own homes except for: the Thirty; the Eleven; the Ten in Peiraieus.
39.1	Athenians who remained in the city and wish to emigrate are to have Eleusis.	Xenophon, *Hellenika* 2.4.38	If any in the city (*astu*) are afraid, they may live at Eleusis.
39.1	They retain their full citizen rights with full power and authority (κυρίους καὶ αὐτοκράτορας) over themselves and they are entitled to draw on the revenues of their property.		
39.2	The sanctuary of Demeter at Eleusis is to be common to both parties and under the control of the Kerykes and the Eumolpidai according to ancestral custom (κατὰ τὰ πάτρια).		
39.2	It is not permitted for those in Eleusis to go to the city (*astu*) and those in the city to go to Eleusis except for the Mysteries.		

Table 10 (*cont.*)

Aristotle, *Athenaion Politeia*	Clause	Other Reference	Clause
39.2	The Athenians at Eleusis are to contribute funds to the alliance just like the other Athenians.		
39.3	If any of those departing take a house at Eleusis, they are to persuade the owner; if they cannot come to terms with each other, each party is to choose three assessors and to accept whatever they assess.		
39.3	Those of the people of Eleusis whom the new settlers are willing to accept are allowed to stay there.		
39.4	Registration for those migrating: residents in Athens and Attica: within ten days of swearing the oaths; their migration within twenty days; residents abroad: similarly from the date of their return.		
39.5	Anyone living at Eleusis is not to hold office in the city (*astu*) before he is re-registered as living in the city (*astu*).		
39.5	Homicide trials are to be in accordance with ancestral custom (κατὰ τὰ πάτρια), if someone has killed by wounding with his own hand (αὐτόχειρ).[a]		

(*cont.*)

Table 10   (*cont.*)

Aristotle, Athenaion Politeia	Clause	Other Reference	Clause
39.6	No one is to remember the past wrongs (μὴ μνησικακεῖν) of anyone else except: the Thirty; the Ten; the Eleven; the Ten in Peiraieus.	compare Xenophon, *Hellenika* 2.4.38 compare Andokides 1.90	except: the Thirty; the Eleven; the Ten in Peiraieus. except the Thirty and the Eleven.
39.6	If any of those listed above undergo an *euthuna*, they are also to be covered by this amnesty clause.		
39.6	Those ruling Peiraieus are to appear before courts in Peiraieus; those in the city before courts of men with a property qualification.[b]		
39.6	Or, if they wish, they may emigrate.[c]		
39.6	Each party is to repay separately its loans for the war.		
		Lysias fr. LXX.165 lines 34–48 (Carey)	The agreement orders that purchasers are to possess items already sold, but those returning are to recover what is unsold. Land and houses are to be returned without payment.
		Isokrates 18.20	The terms of the agreement specifically acquit anyone who has informed against someone or denounced someone or done any other similar thing.

Table 10   *(cont.)*

Aristotle, Athenaion Politeia	Clause	Other Reference	Clause
		Xenophon, *Hellenika* 2.4.43	They swore oaths not to remember past wrongs (μὴ μνησικακήσειν).
		Andokides 1.90	'And I shall not remember the past wrongs (οὐ μνησικακήσω) of any citizen except the Thirty and the Eleven and not of anyone who is willing to undergo an *euthuna* of his magistracy.'

[a] On the textual problems of this passage, see Rhodes 1981: 468; Chambers 1990: 318.

[b] For the problems of this clause, see Rhodes 1981: 470–1; Loening 1987: 47–9; Carawan 2006: 66–7.

[c] On the problems of this passage, see Rhodes 1981: 471; Loening 1987: 49–50.

in Peiraieus (table 10).[14] He then adds that anyone who was afraid could live at Eleusis.[15] Although Xenophon gives no further details about the enclave at Eleusis and the rights of those moving there, these clauses presumably lie behind his brief reference at the end of his description. It seems likely, therefore, that Xenophon has preserved for us the opening clauses of the agreement which the *Athenaion Politeia* has omitted and that his final sentence reflects in abbreviated form the opening clause of the version in the *Athenaion Politeia*.

Two further clauses are preserved by Lysias and Isokrates (table 10). According to Lysias' fragmentary speech against Hippotherses, the reconciliation agreement specifically stated that purchasers were allowed to keep what had been sold, while the returning exiles were allowed to recover anything which was unsold.[16] Land and houses were to be given back to those returning, apparently without payment, and, at this point, the text becomes extremely fragmentary.[17] While a clause concerning property recalls the entitlement of men at Eleusis to draw on the revenues of their

[14] Xen. *Hell.* 2.4.38; for the peace, cf. Arist. *Ath. Pol.* 38.4: Pausanias brought peace and reconciliation.

[15] I am unpersuaded by Carawan's suggestion that these two sentences may refer to two different documents; Carawan 2006: 58–9.

[16] Lys. fr. LXX.165 lines 34–48 (Carey).

[17] Sakurai 1995: 179; Carawan 2002: 7; contra: Loening 1987: 52–3.

property, the focus of the two passages is quite different: the former concerns those returning from exile, i.e. the democrats, while the latter applies only to the men going to Eleusis, i.e. oligarchs. These two passages, consequently, seem unlikely to refer to the same clause in the agreement and the information provided by Lysias further suggests that, just as a whole section of the document concerned primarily oligarchs going to Eleusis, another section focused on the returning democrats. Isokrates in his speech against Kallimachos reports that informers were also specifically covered in the agreement.[18] Perhaps this clause belonged with the section about not remembering past wrongs, as Rhodes suggests.[19] Since, however, the Thirty also took measures against the sycophants, the clause might fit better into the part which focused primarily on the returning exiles. Our evidence seems to indicate, accordingly, that the reconciliation agreement included one section concerning those wishing to emigrate to Eleusis and a second concerning the returning exiles. Another portion of the document also focused on matters relevant to both sides, such as the repayment of loans for the war, and, most importantly, on the amnesty provision.

Originally, the document must have given both the clauses of the agreement (αἱ συνθῆκαι) and the oaths (οἱ ὅρκοι) which the Athenians were to swear; Demophantos' decree provides us with an analogous format.[20] Of our sources, only Andokides quotes the oaths which he gives as 'and I shall not remember the past wrongs (οὐ μνησικακήσω) of any citizen except the Thirty and the Ten and not of anyone who is willing to undergo an *euthuna* of his magistracy'.[21] His list of exceptions contrasts with the version of the *Athenaion Politeia*, which also includes the Eleven and the Ten in Peiraieus (table 10), and various proposals have been made to amend the texts in question.[22] It may be that Andokides simply quoted the text incorrectly. In Demophantos' decree, however, the terms of the decree and the oath are not identical, and there could easily have been a similar situation here, that the agreement provided more detail than the oath or vice versa. Certainly,

---

[18] Isok. 18.20.

[19] P. J. Rhodes 1981: 463, 469; Carawan 2002: 7–8; cf. Todd 1985: 62. I remain unconvinced by the objections of Loening 1987: 56. Against his arguments, note that Isokrates specifically mentions this clause in connection with the agreement and not the oaths.

[20] For fifth-century epigraphical parallels, see e.g. *IG* I³ 37; 62; 75; 86; cf. *IG* I³ 76.

[21] Andok. 1.90; cf. Xen. *Hell.* 2.4.43, where the oaths are placed in 401 after the destruction of the oligarchic enclave at Eleusis.

[22] See e.g. MacDowell 1962: 130–1; P. J. Rhodes 1981: 469–70; Krentz 1982: 104–5; Loening 1987: 42–3. Xenophon's clause allowing everyone to return home except for the Thirty, the Eleven and the Ten in Peiraieus has also been brought into these discussions, but, as I have suggested, this specification belongs to a different part of the document and it should not have any bearing on the amnesty provision and its exclusions.

the clauses about the courts for the *euthunai* require the Ten in Peiraieus to have been included among the exceptions in the amnesty clause.

In his quotation, Andokides begins with the word 'and', an unlikely beginning for the oath. It should indicate that the clause quoted was preceded by at least one other specification, as MacDowell observes,[23] but it is difficult to know what else was included. Some variation between the oaths and the agreement is certainly possible, as Demophantos' decree shows. That document, however, is shorter and less complicated than the reconciliation agreement, as reconstructed here, and it is hard to believe that the oaths repeated all the details. Xenophon certainly presents a very abbreviated version including most of the main points except for the amnesty provision, which, apparently for his own purposes, he has held back until after the destruction of the oligarchs at Eleusis.[24] Perhaps his source is not the text of the agreements, but of the oaths which the overall document included. If this suggestion is correct, then we might expect some variation between the two texts, but the provisions described by Xenophon should also have been in the agreement and not just in the oaths.

On this reconstruction, accordingly, we have a document in two parts, the longer and more detailed section of the agreement proper and the shorter section of the oaths which the Athenians swore. In both sections, the injunction not to repeat past wrongs is important, but it is one of a series of clauses. The availability of the document for consultation and presentation in court must indicate that it was published. Although Isokrates does not use the term *stele* in connection with this request, such an inscribed stone was a common way of making a document public. That this text was described as *sunthekai* (συνθῆκαι), both an agreement and an alliance, brings it into the class of treaties between cities, documents which were regularly published and erected by all participating parties.[25] This model further suggests that the reconciliation agreement will have been inscribed and erected; another copy will also have existed in the city's archives. The form of this document has remained problematic for scholars. Xenophon's narrative makes it clear that the reconciliation agreement belongs to the period before the *demos* formally returned to the city on 12 Boedromion, i.e. before the democracy was re-established.[26] This chronology has led to the conclusion that the agreement was never part of a decree or a law.[27]

---

[23] MacDowell 1962: 130.
[24] Xen. *Hell.* 2.4.43; Krentz 1995: 155; Loening 1987: 25; Todd 1985: 171–2.
[25] Of the better preserved fifth-century examples, see e.g. *IG* i³ 11; 75; 76; 83.
[26] Xen. *Hell.* 2.4.38–9; cf. Andok. 1.81. Date of return: Plut. *De glor. Ath.* 349F.
[27] Loening 1987: 28–30; Krentz 1982: 107–8.

These observations, however, do not explain how the text was inscribed and what precise form it may have taken.

The term *sunthekai* (συνθῆκαι) is sometimes used in the inscribed texts of alliances between Athens and other cities in the fifth century and these inscriptions give us one possible model open to the Athenians when they came to inscribe the reconciliation agreement.[28] For our purposes, the two most useful parallels are the alliances between Athens and the people of Halieis in 424/3 and between Athens and the Bottiaians in 422.[29] Both situations involve oaths sworn by representatives of the two parties and, in both documents, the oaths are provided along with the names of the men who will swear them. In this sense, these two documents are analogous to the reconciliation agreement. In the case of the alliance with Halieis, the beginning of the inscription is preserved and it proves instructive: the alliance is presented as a decree of the *demos* and the *boule* and the text of agreement proper is preceded by the usual preamble of an Athenian decree.[30] The beginning of the alliance with the Bottiaians is not preserved, but it presumably began the same way. In fact, it is the normal format for recording alliances between Athens and other cities, even when the term *sunthekai* is not used. The inscribed version of the alliance between Athens, Argos, Mantineia and Elis of 420 seems to be an exception to this pattern because the remains list the cities in the first line and the second begins immediately with the text of the document.[31] In the earlier fourth century, inscriptions recording alliances also follow the format of the fifth century with a decree of the Athenians before the terms of the alliance.[32] This epigraphical evidence shows that alliances are normally presented within the context of a standard Athenian decree and it would be extremely unusual not to present the document in such a way. In 403, consequently, not to present the reconciliation agreement as a decree would certainly signal the unusual status of the document and mark it out as quite different from other similar texts. Since the *demos* was not yet back in power, it is also difficult to imagine the form of the text preceding the reconciliation agreement proper. Despite the use of the term *sunthekai*, alliances between Athens and other cities may not provide the best model for understanding the inscribed text of the agreement.

Another possible solution is suggested by the *stele* with the reinscription of Drakon's law on homicide.[33] In this case, an earlier document, which

---

[28] Examples: *IG* i³ 31.2; 75.5, 29; 76.21–2, 26–7; 89.26, 34.   [29] *IG* i³ 75; 76.
[30] *IG* i³ 75.1–6.   [31] *IG* i³ 83.
[32] Compare e.g. *IG* ii² 44; RO 6; 41; Rhodes and Osborne 2003: 40–1.   [33] *IG* i³ 104.

was not originally approved by the *demos* and the *boule*, is preceded by a decree of the standard sort which enjoins its publication. It provides a model of how the *demos* and the *boule* could publish a text which they had not originally approved, exactly the situation which we must have with the reconciliation agreement. This format also emphasises the sanction of the *demos* and the *boule* for the earlier document. Restoring a clause authorising publication of the reconciliation agreement would create a document which made it clear how it came to be authorised by the democracy which had not been in power when it was agreed and why it was being published. It would also allow the agreement to fall within the usual norms for Athenian documents of the period. Restoring the text in this fashion, furthermore, would explain both why contemporary authors describe it as the agreement and the oaths and why Plutarch, Dionysios of Halikarnassos and several other later sources describe it as a 'decree' or a 'law'.[34] Following the usual form for Athenian decrees, the authorising decree would have included the archon's name, hence the association of the reconciliation agreement with a specific archon in the *Athenaion Politeia*. Using the republication of Drakon's law on homicide as a model, accordingly, allows us to restore a document which is consistent with our extant inscriptions of the late fifth and earlier fourth centuries and it avoids creating a text which would otherwise be without parallel in our Athenian material.

Collectively, our evidence allows us to reconstruct the reconciliation agreement as a document containing a series of clauses prescribing how the Athenians are to reconcile themselves after *stasis*. This text was followed by the oaths which all the Athenians were to swear. Only the clause about not remembering past wrongs is known, but the oaths originally included further specifications; they need not, however, have been as complicated and detailed as the agreement itself. The whole document was published, almost certainly in the form of an inscribed *stele*. Existing inscriptions indicate that the agreement must have been preceded by a preamble, very probably in the form of a decree authorising publication of the document. In this way, the reconciliation agreement could be brought within the conventions of Athenian public documents.

---

[34] Plut. *Prae. ger. reip.* 814B; Dion. Hal. *Lys.* 32; schol. Aischin. 1.39; schol. vet. Ar. *Wealth* 1146a; schol. Tzet. Ar. *Wealth* 1146; schol. rec. Ar. *Wealth* 1146b; Val. Max. 4.1.ext. 4; Vell. Pat. 2.58.4; Nep. *Thras.* 3.2; Loening 1987: 28. This reconstruction may be supported by Andokides' description that 'it was decided (decreed?) not to remember wrongs against one another for what had happened' (ἔδοξε μὴ μνησικακεῖν ἀλλήλοις τῶν γεγενημένων), but it is difficult to be certain that the verb ἔδοξε is being used here in a technical sense; Andok. 1.81; cf. Joyce 2008: 508.

THE STRATEGIES OF ATHENIAN UNITY

As reconstructed here, the text of the agreement focuses on different groups of Athenians, an inevitable situation after the violence and *stasis* of 404/3. The references to the city (*astu*) and the settlement at Eleusis together with the form of the document as treaty have made it tempting to understand it as separating the Athenians into two divided communities.[35] Concentrating on the agreement as a treaty or alliance, however, focuses on a single word which probably appeared only once or twice in the text and it neglects the rest of the surviving text and its dynamics. In 403, the Athenians did not need further divisions because they would cause the *stasis* to continue. Instead, the Athenians very much required strategies which would bring them together again as a single community, but the difficulty was to create the necessary unity which would allow them all to live in harmony. How was it to be done and what would it entail? In this fractured society, agreeing on political issues was not going to be easy, but both the men of the city and the men of the Peiraieus could see the need for healing the divisions: the very existence of the reconciliation agreement presupposes just such an implicit agreement. The lack of explicit articulation also removes the possibility of difference and so it contributes to the unity of the community. Repairing the fractures among the Athenians needed more than a tacit agreement and it had to be carried out in the rhetoric of the document. Bringing the citizens back together would also entail forgetting some events which took place under the oligarchy, while remembering others. Unity, as we shall see, is also about exclusion. The strategies of the text were only the first step in the process of removing division from the city and they needed to be reinforced by the swearing of the oaths and the inscribing of the text.

The importance of bringing the Athenians back together as one community appears already in what seem to be the opening clauses of the agreement: the Athenians on both sides are to return home with the exception of the leading members of the Thirty (table 10).[36] Neither side is singled out for special treatment and no distinction is made between those who stayed in the city and those who were in exile. The only exceptions mentioned here, the Thirty, the Eleven and the Ten in Peiraieus, form a special group of particularly culpable individuals who are singled out elsewhere in the document. Otherwise, all the Athenians are treated the same way, just as they had been previously when the *demos* was still in power. By

---

[35] Wolpert 2002a: 31; Forsdyke 2005: 203; cf. Todd 1985: 67–8, 183.   [36] Xen. *Hell.* 2.4.38.

returning home, these Athenians through their actions physically reconstitute the community previously fractured by violence and *stasis* which led to the departure of the *demos* for exile. Furthermore, not singling out different members of the re-united city also demonstrates that Athens will be a place in which everyone is treated equally, i.e. it will be democratic.[37] Since this rhetoric is implicit, it precludes division and provides the Athenians with a clause on which they can all agree.

Contrary to what we might expect, the creation of the Eleusinian community does not mark the division of the Athenians (table 10). The section about Eleusis began with the establishment of the settlement, but immediately we are told that those emigrating will retain their full citizen rights (ἐπιτίμους ὄντας).[38] Since these men will remain citizens, and so Athenians, this clause presupposes their return to the city at some later date without any loss of status. This possibility of return to the city is further picked up in the registration clauses which allow a man to hold office in the city once he is re-registered as resident in the *astu*.[39] While these men are in Eleusis, they will be entitled to draw on the revenues from their property. On a practical level, this clause about their funds ensures that these men will be able to live without recourse to violence and confiscation and that they will be able to pay for their houses at Eleusis. This specification, however, marks these men out very clearly as not being in exile, as not having had their property confiscated upon their departure. Instead, like the other Athenians, they may continue to benefit from their property, albeit not directly by living on it.[40] As in the opening clauses, no one is particularly singled out and so their equal treatment is apparent. They are also not being treated less well than the Athenians who chose to stay in the city. Similarly, the men at Eleusis and in the city are equally forbidden to go to the other settlement except at the time of the Mysteries when both communities may visit the other.[41] Repeatedly, then, we see that unequal treatment of some members will not be allowed to create further divisions among the Athenians, as it did under the oligarchy; instead, treating all

---

[37] Equal treatment for all cannot imply a moderate oligarchy because such a *politeia* only treats some Athenians equally, as Phormisios' proposal to restrict the franchise to those citizens owning property shows; Dion. Hal. *Lys.* 32; below chapter 8.

[38] Arist. *Ath. Pol.* 39.1.   [39] Arist. *Ath. Pol.* 39.5.

[40] These requirements are very similar to the penalties of ostracism: the man's property remained unharmed and he was allowed to draw on the revenue; Plut. *Arist.* 7.6. An ostracised man, however, had to leave Attica, unlike the Athenians who went to Eleusis. Like the agreement, ostracism also seems to have played an important role in defusing *stasis* and in creating Athenian unity; Forsdyke 2005: 144–79.

[41] Arist. *Ath. Pol.* 39.2.

Athenians in the same way serves to bring out what they share in common and the issues on which they have decided to agree in order to prevent further fractures.

The requirements concerning the funds for the alliance with the Spartans make use of this same rhetoric and emphasise that the Athenians at Eleusis are no different from other members of the community (table 10). They are to contribute in exactly the same way as the other Athenians.[42] This clause is important because it signals that the men in Eleusis are also allies of the Spartans, just like the rest of the city. They will not have fewer benefits because they are not resident in Athens nor will the burden of the alliance fall on them more than it falls on the rest of the citizens. Mandating the same financial contributions for everyone erases the distinctions between these two groups of Athenians who are now physically separated. The lack of explicit differences brings them together and makes them into one group, the unity of which is reinforced because they are all members of the same alliance. By not singling out any individual, whether he is resident in Eleusis or in Athens, the clause also tacitly acknowledges that they all live under the same political system and in the same *polis*. Once again, the equality of treatment implicitly marks that system as democracy.

The document's rhetoric of equal treatment for all Athenians irrespective of their deeds under the Thirty requires sections concerning other groups besides the men at Eleusis. Only by including returning exiles and informers, presumably those active under the Thirty (table 10), can the divisions which led to *stasis* be erased. Since complaints about unequal treatment of other groups would undo the language of equality used to heal the divisions, we must imagine that these sections were originally more extensive than they are now preserved. By making provision for the exiles to recover some of their property, a potential source of discontent, and so disunity, is addressed: these men cannot complain that they have been treated less well than other Athenians. Through restrictions on what can be reclaimed and under what conditions, the provisions do not create further discontent on the part of the other parties in these transactions. As with the men at Eleusis, so also the possessions, the property and, in the case of informers, the actions of different men under the Thirty will not be allowed to continue to create dissension and division in the city. Enshrined in this way in this document, these clauses bring out a decision to make re-uniting the Athenians as a single group more important than rewarding or punishing individual men for their earlier activities. Since all

---

[42] Arist. *Ath. Pol.* 39.2.

members of the community would benefit in some way from these terms, they would not in and of themselves be a cause for further dissension.

These rhetorical strategies rely on the tacit assumption that the deeds of the individual Athenian must be forgotten so that the community may be made whole again. This decision is made explicit in the clause prohibiting the remembering of past wrongs (table 10). Both the version presented by the *Athenaion Politeia* and Andokides' quotation of the oath stress that no one (μηδενὶ πρὸς μηδένα and τῶν πολιτῶν οὐδενί) is to remember the terrible deeds of the past.[43] This clause treats all the Athenians equally and without regard to whether they were men of the city or men of the Peiraieus. They are juxtaposed with the small group of exceptions: the Thirty, the Ten, the Eleven and the Ten in Peiraieus in the *Athenaion Politeia* and the Thirty and the Eleven in Andokides' version. As at the beginning of the document, singling out these men as exceptions to the rule brings out the further politics of unity: excluding this small group of men allows the rest of the Athenians to agree to come back together again and to forget their deeds against their fellow citizens. Blame for what happened in 404/3 is shifted to a small group of men who are officially identified as the extreme oligarchs responsible for what took place.[44] That some of these men were already dead and most of the rest had probably already fled to Eleusis will have made agreeing on this process easier. Nevertheless, a mechanism is still provided for reintegrating them back into the community: if they wish, they may rejoin the united Athenians, either by passing an *euthuna* or by emigrating to Eleusis.

The document further envisions that the unity created through exclusion will also be prominently displayed in the sanctuary of Demeter at Eleusis and reinforced by its rituals (table 10). Even though Eleusis is clearly marked out as the territory of the men of the city who, perhaps out of fear, do not wish to stay in Athens, they are not allowed to control the sanctuary. Instead, by the decision of the Athenians, it is to be common to both parties and to remain under the control of the Kerykes and the Eumolpidai, its ancestral overseers, who will not be required to remove themselves from the city in order to carry out their ritual functions in the sanctuary. That moving to Eleusis might not have seemed desirable to these two *gene* is suggested by the presence of Kleokritos, the herald of the initiates and a member of

---

[43] Arist. *Ath. Pol.* 39.6; Andok. 1.90. On the term *me mnesikakein*, see Loraux 2002: 145–69; Phillips 2008: 142–5, 192–4; Todd 1985: 43, 69–70; Carawan 2002: 2–12 with Joyce 2008: 507–15; cf. Lévy 1976: 214–16.
[44] Loraux 2002: 152–3.

the Kerykes, on the side of the democrats at the battle of Mounichia.[45] If, however, the Eumolpidai and the Kerykes were not allowed any access to the sanctuary, the rituals, and particularly the Mysteries, would not have been carried out and the (divided) Athenians would have run the risk of angering the gods through their neglect.[46] Making the sanctuary common to all the Athenians, consequently, allowed the appropriate rites to be celebrated and it physically created one group out of several by bringing them together in one worshipping community, the Athenians without any further distinctions. This process was reinforced by the very nature of the rituals which separate out the worshipping community from everyone else present.[47] Celebrating their rites together in this sanctuary served very powerfully to erase the visible fractures among the Athenians and to display their status as a single *demos.*

These dynamics require a festival rather than unlimited access to the sanctuary, a situation which would also have increased the potential for conflict between the two formerly hostile groups of Athenians. Consequently, the men in the city may visit it only for the Mysteries, the only time when the men at Eleusis may go into the city. At one level, this festival is one of the city's most important and most international celebrations: like the sanctuary in which it takes place, it cannot be controlled only by the men at Eleusis. The Mysteries, however, also rely very heavily on the linkages between the city and the sanctuary at Eleusis (fig. 1). In order to be a candidate for initiation at the Great Mysteries, an individual was normally first initiated at the Little Mysteries in the sanctuary of Meter in Agrai just outside the city walls, the sphere of the men of the city (fig. 4).[48] Only then was the person ready to be initiated at the Great Mysteries, the territory of the men of Eleusis.[49] The necessary rituals for this process, however, took place both in the city and at Eleusis so that initiands needed to be in both locations sequentially (fig. 1).[50] The two places were also connected by the formal movement of people and objects from one to the other. Before the rituals could begin, the sacred objects needed to be brought from Eleusis to the City Eleusinion in the *astu.* Subsequently, those objects were returned to the sanctuary at Eleusis in a procession which included the initiands and the other participants.[51] Marching from the *astu* to the sanctuary visibly

---

[45] Xen. *Hell.* 2.4.20–2.
[46] For the problems involved with not holding a festival, see briefly Shear 2010: 141–7.
[47] Above chapter 5.   [48] On the relationship, see Parker 2005: 343–6.
[49] These ritual complexities require the reference to the Mysteries in the agreement to include both the Great and the Little Mysteries and not just the former, as has sometimes been suggested; Loening 1987: 33 with further references; cf. P. J. Rhodes 1981: 465–6.
[50] Parker 2005: 346–50.   [51] Parker 2005: 348–50 with further references; Graf 1996: 61–3.

connected both the two locations[52] and the Athenians in the city and at Eleusis (fig. 1); the process also made visible the reciprocal relationship of the two communities because only by going from one to the other could the rituals be carried out properly. When the participants reached Eleusis, their divisions were eliminated and their resulting unity was stressed and created by the sacrifices which took place at Demeter's sanctuary.[53] Dividing up the sacrificial meat will have emphasised not only who did and who did not belong to the sacrificial community, but also that this community included all the Athenians present, both those from the *astu* and those from Eleusis. The rituals of the Great Mysteries, accordingly, brought the divided Athenians together and they emphasised what the two groups had in common, rather than their differences. These rituals visually displayed the resulting unity both to the citizens of the *polis* and to the international audience. In this setting at Eleusis, the warring Athenian factions were physically shown to be reconciled and their lack of division was displayed. The success of the agreement was made tangible to all.

The reconciliation agreement, consequently, has very clear strategies for re-uniting the Athenians after *stasis*. Repeatedly, the warring groups are treated equally so that the supporters of the oligarchs are not singled out for punishment and the process is made explicit by the clause not to remember past wrongs. Since unequal treatment would lead to complaints and potentially further divisions, all the Athenians can agree that this situation is preferable; in 403, dissent from this general position is hard to imagine. Giving them something very broad on which they can all agree creates the unity which the city badly needs. By incorporating the Mysteries and the sanctuary at Eleusis into this process, the rituals physically recreate the Athenians as one city and their existing dynamics are co-opted for the larger process of reconciliation. Singling out the Thirty, the Ten, the Eleven and the Ten in Peiraieus shifts blame on to them and excludes them from the Athenians so that unity in the document is also created through exclusion. In combination with the explicit prohibition of past wrongs, the document creates new rules of engagement to which the different groups have explicitly agreed and through which they can also be re-united again.

Agreeing to forget is not limited to the clause about past wrongs because the agreement is very reticent about the events which led to its drafting and to the earlier rupture of the community. As reconstructed here, the term 'peace' appears in the opening clauses, but there is no further reference to

---

[52] Graf 1996: 63.   [53] Parker 2005: 351; Clinton 1988: 69–72; Burkert 1983: 292–3.

peace in the extant fragments and, quite probably, in the missing sections; war appears only in connection with repaying the loans incurred in the process. The word *stasis* is also conspicuously absent from all our preserved sections nor are forms of its cognates used. These linguistic omissions may simply be due to the ways in which our sources have reported the various clauses. The *Athenaion Politeia*, however, introduces the section with the specification that the reconciliation was made 'according to the following agreements' (κατὰ τὰς συνθήκας τάσδε), a phrase suggesting that what follows adheres fairly closely to the original text; it is likely that our other sources have also taken their vocabulary from the document. The agreement, accordingly, seems specifically not to use the regular terms for *stasis* and the fighting which accompanies it or military terms; even the word oligarchy is absent. It seems likely that the missing sections also avoided these various words. Not emphasising these issues makes them implicit rather than explicit and so the reasons for the *stasis* cannot now be used to create further dissension. Had they been explicitly stated, then they would have created disunity and so undermined the strategies and rhetoric of the document.

Equally implicit in the text is the decision over the political system which the newly reconciled Athenians will use. The strategy of treating different groups of men in the same way and of singling out only the leading oligarchs mirrors the workings of the democracy in which no man is considered politically better (or worse) than his contemporaries. In the context of the reconciliation agreement, this emphasis on equality of status identifies the community being healed as the city ruled by the *demos*. The provision of *euthunai* for members of the groups excluded from the amnesty clause also alludes to the democratic city because her officials must undergo the same procedure on completion of their offices. The judgment of peers, which is part of the procedure laid out in the agreement, is a further hallmark of the democratic system. If, as I argued earlier, the inscribed version of the agreement was preceded by an authorising decree passed by the *demos* and the *boule*, then it will have reinforced the agreement's implicit construction of the city as democratically ruled. That the political system is not specifically delineated in the document is extremely important because it makes it impossible for anyone to disagree on this issue;[54] instead, the Athenians are agreeing not to disagree, a move which in and of itself also creates unity. Since division is an inherent part of democracy,[55] the

[54] In view of these strategies, the absence of any evidence for such a clause should not cause surprise; see, however, Wolpert 2002a: 30.

[55] Compare Loraux 2002: 70.

Athenians are not agreeing that they will not differ at all, but rather that they will disagree within the rules of this particular system, an implicit strategy which, in turn, reinforces the agreement's overall rhetoric of unity among the Athenians. Since the system of democracy is implicit rather than explicit, anyone who cannot agree to it must leave the community, just like the extreme oligarchs, and their exclusion also serves to reinforce the unity of the rest of the Athenians, whose new harmony will be displayed at and further constructed by the rituals in the international setting of the sanctuary at Eleusis.

SWEARING THE OATHS

In so far as we can reconstruct its clauses and strategies, the reconciliation agreement focused on unifying the Athenian factions created by *stasis*. The dynamics at work were not limited to this text because it also contained a series of oaths and, like Demophantos' decree, it must have specified the ways in which the Athenians were to swear them. The very nature of this process will have reinforced the strategies of the agreement and it will have brought the warring Athenians together as a single group for the first time since the *ekklesia* at which they voted the Thirty into power. Their participation will have marked their assent to the provisions and strategies of the document and their agreement to the new rules of engagement which it creates. This process will have made their unity concrete and visible to all and it will also have reinforced it further.

Apart from general references to the agreement and its oaths, our evidence for the details of the oaths is limited (table 10). When Andokides quotes the clause concerning the amnesty, his language indicates that he is giving us merely a part of the larger oath.[56] In introducing this passage, he describes the oath from which he is going to quote: it is the oath 'common to the whole city, which you all swore after the reconciliation'. That all the Athenians were involved in this process is also presupposed by the clauses concerning registration of men wishing to go to Eleusis and they make clear that the oaths are to precede recording the names of the men leaving the *astu*. When Xenophon comes to describe the oaths, he adds that the *demos* still abides by them, a statement which also suggests that the Athenians swore en masse. Otherwise, we are given no further details about the process.

---

[56] Andok. 1.90.

That all the Athenians swore the oaths of reconciliation immediately recalls the oath of Demophantos which the Athenians took some six and a half years before at the Dionysia of 409. This earlier occasion forms the most likely parallel for the events in 403.[57] Consequently, when the Athenians came to swear their oaths of reconciliation, they were very probably arrayed by tribe and by deme, as they had been in 409. This arrangement would have allowed the greatest number of citizens to participate and it would have ensured that their presence was known to the people most likely to recognise them: their fellow demesmen and tribesmen. Including all the Athenians in the process would have contrasted significantly with the Thirty's restriction of citizen numbers and their exclusion of most of the citizens from the political process. The participation of all the Athenians would also have given the agreement and the oaths the best possible chance of success: they could only function properly if all citizens participated and demonstrated their agreement with the document's strategies.

The parallels with Demophantos' oath do not explain when and where the Athenians swore their oaths of reconciliation. Although this information was presumably originally incorporated in the agreement, it is not preserved in our surviving sources. Our evidence, however, suggests both the sequence and timing of the events and the probable location for the swearing. Xenophon's narrative is very clear on the order in which events surrounding the reconciliation took place: negotiations led to the reconciliation agreement; Pausanias then disbanded his army and the men from the Peiraieus went up to the Akropolis where they sacrificed to Athena; afterwards, they held an *ekklesia* and they appointed magistrates.[58] Although less detailed, the version of the *Athenaion Politeia* supposes a similar sequence: Pausanias' arrival, the agreement, its terms, reconciliation accomplished and the resumption of political life.[59] The text of the agreement as presented here presupposes that swearing the oaths was part of the process of reconciling the Athenians. Lysias also describes the democrats' procession to the Akropolis, an event which he places immediately after the reconciliation, and he makes it clear that the men of the Peiraieus went up to the *astu* which they entered through one of the city's gates before they came to Athena's sanctuary.[60] The date for this procession and sacrifice is given by Plutarch as 12 Boedromion.[61] Agreeing on the terms of the reconciliation and then swearing the oath must both precede the democrats' sacrifice on

---

[57] Above chapter 5; see also Shear 2007b: 153–8.
[58] Xen. *Hell.* 2.4.38–43. For the sacrifice, see below chapter 10.   [59] Arist. *Ath. Pol.* 38.4–40.1.
[60] Lys. 13.80–1.   [61] Plut. *De glor. Ath.* 349F.

12 Boedromion. Until the oaths had been sworn, the reconciliation was not in force and the men of the Peiraieus and the men of the city could not go to the *astu* and Peiraieus respectively, as Lysias' description of the procession and sacrifice brings out. Consequently, swearing the oath must have taken place very shortly, if not immediately, before 12 Boedromion. A likely date for the swearing is 11 Boedromion.[62]

This date, however, does not initially seem to fit with our other evidence and the additional events which must have taken place in Boedromion of 403 (table 11). The reconciliation agreement specifies that registration for those men going to Eleusis must take place within ten days of swearing and their migration within twenty days; whether the twenty days is calculated from the taking of the oath or from the individual's registration is not clear.[63] More importantly, the celebration of the Great Mysteries does not leave very much time in the ten days after 11 Boedromion for registration (table 11).[64] Some of the events, such as the transportation of the sacred items from Eleusis and the initiates' trip to the sea, however, would not have required general participation. Similarly, the announcement of the Mysteries (*Prorrhesis*) probably did not take a full day and it need not have prevented other activities from happening. In the fourth century and the Hellenistic period, meetings of the *ekklesia* are attested for 14, 16 and 18 Boedromion;[65] in 403, rituals on the 14th and 16th need not have precluded registrations from taking place. Registration could have taken place, accordingly, on 12–16 and 18 Boedromion. A further chronological problem is raised by the report in the *Athenaion Politeia* that the men who fought on the side of the Thirty put off their registration to the last days and, when Archinos focused on their delay, he terminated the registration period early.[66] Although we are not told the context in which this episode took place, a meeting of the *ekklesia* seems the most probable occasion. The most likely day is 18 Boedromion, i.e. the day immediately before the procession to Eleusis and the beginning of the Mysteries proper

---

[62] And so assumed without discussion by Loening 1987: 38, 68–9.

[63] P. J. Rhodes 1981: 467; Loening 1987: 37–8.

[64] For the events of the Mysteries, see Parker 2005: 346–51, 486. In the following discussion, I have assumed that the *stasis* did not curtail the various rituals in Boedromion. Certainly, the Little Panathenaia was celebrated as expected in late Hekatombaion of 403; Lys. 21.4. The complexities created by the different rituals of the Mysteries are not discussed by Loening; Loening 1987: 38, 68–9.

[65] Mikalson 1975: 54–5, 216 with further references.

[66] Arist. *Ath. Pol.* 40.1. Since only ten days after swearing the oath were allocated for registration, Archinos' actions cannot have taken place 'within the first few months', as Carawan suggests; Carawan 2006: 69. His chronology would rather implausibly require hostilities with Eleusis to start within ten days of swearing the oaths and to continue until 401/0; Carawan 2006: 68–9, 75–6.

Table 11 *Events in Boedromion*

Boedromion	Religious rituals[a]	Political activities (years other than 403)[b]	Events of 403[c]
1			
2			
3	Sphragitic nymphs?		Sphragitic nymphs?
4		meeting of *boule* known	
5	Genesia		Genesia
6	Artemis Agrotera	meeting of *boule* known	Artemis Agrotera
7	Boedromia?		Boedromia?
8	Kybernesia?		Kybernesia?
9		meeting of *ekklesia* known	
10		meeting of *ekklesia* known	
11		meeting of *ekklesia* known	swearing of oaths of reconciliation?
12	Thanksgiving for freedom		Democrats sacrifice to Athena; registration for Eleusis begins?
13			
14	Eleusinian sacred items brought to Athens	meeting of *ekklesia* known	Eleusinian sacred items to Athens
15	*Prorrhesis*		*Prorrhesis*
16	Initiates to the sea (ἅλαδε μύσται)	meeting of *ekklesia* known	Initiates to sea
17	Epidauria (or 18th)		Epidauria
18		meeting of *ekklesia* known	meeting of *ekklesia*?
19	Iakchos procession (or 20th)		procession to Eleusis

Table 11   (*cont.*)

Boedromion	Religious rituals[a]	Political activities (years other than 403)[b]	Events of 403[c]
20	Initiates at Eleusis?		Mysteries
21	Initiates at Eleusis		Mysteries registration for Eleusis ends?
22	Initiates at Eleusis		Mysteries
23	Plemochoai?: end of Mysteries	meeting of *boule* known	Plemochoai?
24		meeting of *boule* known	
25		meeting of *ekklesia* known	
26			
27		meeting of *ekklesia* known	
28			
29			
30		meeting of *ekklesia* known	

[a] From Parker 2005: 346–8, 486.
[b] From Mikalson 1975: 47–65.
[c] I have assumed that the rituals were not curtailed by the *stasis* in the city.

in the sanctuary there. With these rituals taking place, large numbers of men were probably not likely to have been registering themselves. Putting this chronological data together shows that there would have just been enough time for the registration to have taken place between 12 and 21 Boedromion and for the Mysteries to have been celebrated in the normal way without the two hostile groups coming into contact during the festival. The eleventh day of Boedromion remains the most plausible date for the process of swearing the reconciliation oaths. This restored chronology also suggests that the Athenians strongly desired to make as much progress as possible towards resolving the conflict before the celebration of the Mysteries; otherwise, they could have waited until after the Mysteries to start the process. That they chose not to do so brings out the importance of the festival and the opportunity which it presented for showing the Athenians' newly created unity in an international setting.

Our sources do not record where the Athenians swore their oaths of reconciliation. Since the men of the Peiraieus and the men of the city had not yet reconciled, the location must have been outside of both places. The text of the agreement certainly focuses on Eleusis, Demeter's sanctuary and the Mysteries, but Eleusis at that moment was under the control of the surviving members of the Thirty and their associates; it was no more suitable a place for taking the oath than a location in the city or the Peiraieus (fig. 1). The reference to the Little Mysteries in the document suggests a possible venue for the swearing of the oaths: the sanctuary of Meter in Agrai where these rituals took place (fig. 4). Not controlled by any party, it was neutral ground for all Athenians with the necessary altar for slaughtering the sacrificial victims and then for swearing the oath. It also fits very well with the focus on Eleusis and the Mysteries both in the agreement and in the ways in which the process seems to have interlocked with the city's ritual calendar. Since the sanctuary was located just outside the city on the southeastern bank of the Ilissos River, there should have been plenty of room in which to marshal the Athenians by tribe and by deme. They may have assembled in the Kynosarges, located apparently not far away, or they may have waited northeast of the sanctuary in the open area created by the bend of the river to the northwest (fig. 4).[67] On the specified day, very probably 11 Boedromion, accordingly, the Athenians will have gathered at the sanctuary of Meter in Agrai, where assembled in their civic divisions they will have waited for their turn and watched their fellow citizens perform.

Swearing the oaths of reconciliation will have been a collective experience as the Athenians as a group made peace with their fellow citizens and renounced *stasis*. Since the oath was written in the first person singular, each man must have sworn it individually as he touched the sacrificial victims.[68] That every man used exactly the same formulation indicated that there was no difference between any of these citizens, irrespective of whether they had been among the men of the city or the men of the Peiraieus. The continual repetition of the same words and actions as each tribe and deme came forward would have reinforced exactly this point. The uniformity of the process will also have unified the men who had previously been divided.

---

[67] Travlos 1971: 291 fig. 379, 340. For further discussion of the location of the Kynosarges, see Morison 1998: 144–5 with further references; Wycherley 1978: 229–30.

[68] Loraux 2002: 141, 149, 167–8; cf. Cole 1996: 236.

The text of the oath itself with its small, but significant, exceptions to the amnesty clause explicitly pointed to the culprits of the *stasis* which had engulfed the city. This focus on individuals who were probably not present made the individual men of the city or men of the Peiraieus, who were actually swearing the oath, not responsible for the events; through this exclusion, unity was created again. Of course, the effect would have been very different for members of the Thirty, the Ten, the Eleven and the Ten in Peiraieus; perhaps there was no expectation that they would be present and participate.

As with the oath of Demophantos, the divisions among the citizens would not have been visible as they stood gathered together in one body by tribe and by deme, an organisation which mixed up men from the different political factions. The cohesion created by this experience will have complemented the strategies of the document's and oaths' texts, while the Athenians' new harmony would have been visibly displayed by the whole process. That the text was an oath further unified the citizens because oaths regularly create unity in the community which swears them and affirm its permanence, as we saw in chapter 5. In the face of their recent defeat by the Spartans and their allies in the war and the *stasis*, reinforcing the stability of the city was an important part of the process. In this context, the oaths signalled that the Athenians would survive and prosper.[69] Incorporating these strategies, the oaths should also have signalled that *stasis*, i.e. divisions between citizens, was a thing of the past.

Swearing the oaths of reconciliation also served to display the democracy implicit in the document's text. Since each man used exactly the same words as every other citizen, they all performed in the same way and no one was singled out. In this way, their actions reinforced the document's implicit emphasis on democracy. Marshalling the Athenians by tribe and by deme will have reinforced this display because the tribes and demes were the markers of the rule of the *demos*. The process also brought out each man's implicit assent to this system of government for the city and his implicit identity as a democrat, while agreeing not to disagree on this issue performed a now familiar function in bringing the Athenians back together again. Arraying the Athenians in their tribes and the demes will have further identified democracy as the proper political system for the city and the display should have left no ambiguity about the *demos'* power over Athens.

---

[69] Compare Lysias' description of the agreement and oaths which bring 'a constitution (*politeia*) lasting for the longest time'; Lys. 25.28.

The process of taking the oaths of reconciliation in the sanctuary of Meter in Agrai on 11 Boedromion showed very clearly what recovering from *stasis* entailed. It required citizens to forget wrongs committed against them during the civil strife and to recreate themselves as a united community. This process was aided both by the text of the document and by the oath-taking which it stipulated. By their nature, the oaths formed a single community out of the divided Athenians and affirmed its permanence. In this way, the actions of the citizens made concrete and reinforced the dynamics of the document's text. The process itself served to heal the divisions created by *stasis* and it displayed the Athenians as a single body made up of men who were shown to be exactly equal as citizens of the democratic city. Taking the oaths also recreated the relationship between the reunited Athenians and the gods, a relationship which had been ruptured by the Thirty's actions. Some days after swearing the oaths, these bonds with the gods and with their fellow citizens would have been (re)created and displayed again in the course of celebrating the Great Mysteries at Eleusis. Presented on this occasion not just to themselves, but also to an international audience, the Athenians indicated through their actions that they had put an end to *stasis* and had reconciled with one another.

REMEMBRANCE

For Athenians standing in the sanctuary of Meter in Agrai on 11 Boedromion, taking the oaths of reconciliation created a memory of the process of re-uniting the city after *stasis* and the procedures themselves emphasised what needed to be done to protect that unity: except in certain very specific cases, past wrongs committed against other Athenians were to be forgotten and the Athenians tacitly agreed on democracy as the appropriate *politeia* for the city. Every time these men visited this sanctuary, as they would have done annually for the Little Mysteries, they would have remembered the occasion and what resolving their differences entailed. These dynamics, however, required the citizens to have taken part in the reconciliation in Boedromion of 403. Not all Athenians were present at that time: the agreement specifically provides a registration process for citizens abroad at the crucial time.[70] This clause indicates that these men were not exempt from the process simply because they were not present to take part. Other Athenians were not yet citizens and so they were too young to take part, but they also needed to remember what it meant to reconcile from *stasis*. For these

---

[70] Arist. *Ath. Pol.* 39.4.

individuals, the presence of the document published in an inscribed form was critical: without it, there would be no memories for them of reconciling from civil strife and they would not be included among the reunified Athenians. The physical presence of the document in the city's topography, accordingly, was vital to the continuing process of remembering the reconciliation.

Since the agreement and oaths were published, they will have been inscribed on a stone *stele* and erected in an appropriate place in the same way as other Athenian documents. Although our sources do not indicate where it was set up, Athenian publication practices in the fifth century suggest two possible locations. Before the return of the democrats in 410, such documents were erected either on the Akropolis or, if they concerned sacred matters, in the relevant sanctuary (fig. 4).[71] For Demophantos' decree, the Agora was particularly appropriate because it memorialised the oath-taking in the place in which the event had been held. For the other inscriptions in the marketplace, the square was an especially suitable place for them because they were closely linked to the democracy. Democracy, however, was not a particular concern of the reconciliation agreement and, for this reason, it is unlikely to have been erected in the Agora. Two more appropriate locations exist. The sanctuary of Meter in Agrai was eminently suitable because the oaths had been sworn there; in this location, the *stele* would memorialise the reconciliation where it had taken place. Alternatively, for Athenian documents, the Akropolis would always remain a proper place for their erection.[72] Which location we choose depends on what aspects of the agreement we decide to privilege: if it is reconciliation and unity, then the Metroon is the logical spot; if it is the physical form of agreement and treaty, then the *stele* belongs on the Akropolis with the alliances between Athens and other cities. In the latter case, the parallels of foreign relations suggest that a second copy ought to have been erected at Eleusis in the sanctuary of Demeter (fig. 1). In the precinct in Agrai, the *stele* with the reconciliation would probably have been more visible than on the Akropolis where it would have been lost among many other inscribed documents. For this reason, as well as the text's emphasis on unity, reconciliation and the Mysteries, the sanctuary at Agrai seems to be the most appropriate place for the *stele* to have been erected.

Visiting the precinct and examining the document were important elements in the continuing process of reconciling the Athenians. Reading the document required the individual to say the oaths aloud, most probably

---

[71] Above chapter 4; Shear 2007a: 97–8. [72] Liddel 2003: 79–81.

where they had been taken in Boedromion of 403, and these dynamics will
have been similar to those of reading Demophantos' decree.[73] Although it
did not replicate exactly the situation in 403, the reader did have to utter
the oaths again, to repeat *me mnesikakein*, and to agree anew to the clauses
and strategies which had brought the Athenians back together. For original
participants, reading the *stele* would have caused them both to remember
their reconciliation with their fellow citizens and to resolve their differences
anew. For individuals absent from Athens or too young to take part in 403,
reading the documents created a memory of this important occasion when
all the Athenians agreed to reunify the city and to renounce discord. If
any of these men were also jurors, then they may additionally have recalled
swearing the dikastic oath with its new clause not to remember past wrongs
so that their different memories will have reinforced each other.[74] Reading
the *stele*, consequently, created memories which would otherwise not have
existed and it required individuals to retake, however imperfectly, the oaths
which re-united the Athenians. As with Demophantos' oath, the process of
reading created for all Athenians a single 'national' memory of reconciling
which served to unify them not only in fact, but also in memory.

This display visibly kept the oaths in front of the Athenians and continually reminded them of their agreement. It also indicated in perpetuity
the consequences of not adhering to the oath: the return to Athens of the
divisions and fractures which the agreement had healed. The memories
which the document created, however, were selective: although the Thirty
and their close associates were mentioned on several occasions, their deeds
apparently were not, and oligarchy and *stasis* and its cognates also seem
to have been avoided. *Stasis* was remembered only indirectly by what it
created: the divisions among the Athenians who, consequently, need reconciling. Instead, the events are described as war, a war for which both the
men of the city and the men of the Peiraieus took out loans, now to be
repaid separately. Peace, the opposite of war, is also mentioned: it is what
the agreement creates and it brings together the divided Athenians. Listing
specifically the Thirty, the Ten, the Eleven and the Ten in Peiraieus makes
them, and only them, responsible for the discord which occurred. The roles
of the ordinary Athenians, the men who actually swore the oaths and read

---

[73] See above chapter 5.
[74] Andok. 1.91: 'and I shall not recall past wrongs (οὐ μνησικακήσω) nor will I be persuaded to do so
by another, but I shall vote according to the established laws'. On this oath, see Mirhady 2007: 48–53
with further bibliography; Hansen 1991: 182–3. We do not know how long this clause remained in
the oath. At this time, the bouleutic oath was augmented by a new clause concerning denunciation
and summary arrest because of past events, but the term *me mnesikakein* was not used; Andok. 1.91;
P. J. Rhodes 2007: 12–14; P. J. Rhodes 1972a: 194–5.

the text, are forgotten along with the terms *stasis* and oligarchy. So, too, are the names of the leaders of the men of the Peiraieus and of the city who, in the memories created by this document, will remain anonymous. In contrast, what is remembered is the reconciliation and the resulting unity of all the Athenians.

These dynamics of remembering and forgetting bring out the ways in which the document and the oaths need to be read repeatedly: each reading (re)creates reconciliation and (re)unifies the Athenians. The process of bringing the citizens back together as one people cannot be done only once in Boedromion of 403. Instead, reconciliation is a fragile process which needs to repeated frequently so that memory is continually refreshed. Each time the reader swears *me mnesikakein* and the other terms, his resolve to abide by the oaths should be renewed and strengthened. This process of remembering further brings out the importance of the publication of the reconciliation: without a text inscribed on a *stele* and set up in public, the document remains inert without the ability to create memories in its readers. Indeed, like the *stasis* which it ignores, the whole agreement is liable to be forgotten, as if it had never been made. Reading and display, consequently, are integral to the proper functioning of the agreement and to its lasting effects on the Athenians.

THE DIFFICULTIES OF RECONCILIATION

Even with repeated readings and the memories which they created, reconciling the Athenians was not so easily achieved because they had to work out exactly how their new rules of engagement would function. What precisely did it mean not to remember past wrongs in democratic Athens where division was an essential part of the political process? What would happen when specific clauses of the agreement were put into effect? The primary venues for answering these questions were the city's lawcourts, places of contestation and division within the democratic system.[75] In them, individual men contested and assented to the agreement, an inherently fragile process kept in check by the implicit general acknowledgment that democracy required abiding by the decision of the majority. Through a series of trials and *dokimasiai* or scrutinies for office, the Athenians began to work out the answers to these questions. As they quickly discovered, reconciliation was an on-going and continual process. It had to be worked out both in cases explicitly concerning events in 404/3 and in situations which

---

[75] Loraux 2002: 231–8; Todd 1985: 37; Gernet 1955: 69.

ostensibly had nothing whatsoever to do with deeds under the Thirty. Both actions and the reconciliation agreement could be invoked to harm one's opponent or to aid oneself and men who had been on the same side in the fighting might end up on different sides in court.

Cases directly concerning events under the Thirty brought out the problems and difficulties which the Athenians faced. Lysias' thirteenth speech brings Agoratos to trial for the murder of Dionysodoros by the Thirty. As we are told, Dionysodoros along with some of the generals and *taxiarchoi* was denounced by Agoratos shortly before the Thirty gained power; they were tried under the Thirty in the Bouleuterion and sentenced to death.[76] The defendant asserts several times that Agoratos killed Dionysodoros and he describes Dionysodoros' final instructions to his apparently pregnant wife: if she bears a son, he is to be told that Agoratos killed his father.[77] The case is not strong: since Agoratos did not kill his victims with his own hand, as required by the agreement, the trial should not have taken place at all.[78] Indeed, the Eleven were apparently concerned about the legality of this case because they required the phrase 'in the act' (ἐπ' αὐτοφώρῳ) to be added to the charge.[79] The speaker also anticipates that Agoratos will invoke the agreement to protect himself and he argues (speciously) that it only applies to men who were on opposite sides, while he and Agoratos were both men of the Peiraieus.[80] As the prosecutor attempts to gain revenge on Agoratos, he must negotiate the new rules created by the reconciliation agreement: what exactly does the prohibition on past wrongs mean and what constitutes murder by one's own hand?[81] Who exactly is covered by the terms of the document? As part of his case, he also creates a particular image of Dionysodoros: the good democrat killed by the minions of the Thirty.[82] In contrast, Agoratos is characterised as a man who helped to overthrow democracy and a known informer; when he changed sides and went to Phyle, no one would have anything to do with him.[83] In this way,

---

[76] Lys. 13.12–42.   [77] E.g. Lys. 13.2, 41–3.

[78] Todd 2000: 139. Phillips argues that the agreement did not apply because Agoratos was not a citizen; Phillips 2008: 192–8. Since Agoratos was present at Phyle (Lys. 13.77–9), he should have received citizenship through the decree RO 4, on which see below chapter 8.

[79] Lys. 13.85–7 with the helpful comments of Todd 2000: 139; Todd 1993: 275–6. On the term ἐπ' αὐτοφώρῳ, see Todd 1993: 80–1 with further references; Phillips 2008: 186–91.

[80] Lys. 13.88–9. For such creative uses of the agreement, see Todd 2007: 17 note 65. Agoratos was at Phyle and Peiraieus; Lys. 13.77–82.

[81] Definition of murder: cf. Todd 1985: 92.

[82] He and other men killed by Agoratos are specifically called *andres agathoi* towards the *plethos*, i.e. *demos*, at Lys. 13.2; on the term *plethos*, see Todd 2007: 620; Wolpert 2002a: 129–33.

[83] Lys. 13.17–18, 65, 77–9.

the prosecutor negotiates his own memories of this death which he shares with his listeners: they, too, will not forget.

In this case, the recrimination is specifically about events during the *stasis*, but deeds done at that time could be at stake without being explicitly mentioned, as Sokrates' trial in 399 makes abundantly clear.[84] He was charged by Meletos, Anytos and Lykon with impiety: not believing in the city's gods, introducing new ones and corrupting the young.[85] On the surface, these issues do not appear to be relevant to recovering from the *stasis*, but Sokrates' real problem was his close connection with known oligarchs, particularly Kritias and Charmides, both members of the Thirty now dead and beyond reach of vengeance.[86] As Aischines put it in 346/5, the Athenians put Sokrates to death 'because he was shown to have educated Kritias, one of the Thirty who had overthrown the *demos*'.[87] He could not, however, be charged in this fashion because of the reconciliation agreement's clause against remembering past wrongs. As Lysias 13 indicates, however, the terms apparently did not prevent speakers from discussing events committed by their opponents under the Thirty and the charge as preserved would have allowed the prosecutors to bring up Sokrates' actions in 404/3. He would not have been able to deny either his connections with the oligarchs or his residence in the city at a time when good democrats had fled. If Mogens Hansen's suggestion is correct, Anytos focused on the political dimensions of the case, an appropriate role since he was one of the leaders of the Athenians at Phyle.[88] In this context, he could continue to pursue dead oligarchs and the trial provided a venue for continuing to fight against oligarchy. Anytos' role as prosecutor created a stark contrast between his actions and those of Sokrates, between a good democrat who had gone into exile and a closet oligarch who had stayed in Athens; Meletos and Lykon also had the opportunity to burnish their own political credentials.[89]

---

[84] Date: Diog. Laert. 2.44. For a helpful introduction to the trial, see Millett 2005.

[85] Diog. Laert. 2.40; Xen. *Mem.* 1.1.1; Todd 1993: 309; Parker 1996: 201; Hansen 1995: 16–17. On the religious dimensions, see Parker 1996: 199–217; Connor 1991. On the prosecutors and their roles, see Hansen 1995: 16–17, 33–4.

[86] Charmides, Kritias' cousin, was one of the Ten at Peiraieus; Xen. *Hell.* 2.4.19; Krentz 1982: 59. Sokrates' associates included a significant number of oligarchs and men involved with the profanation of the Mysteries and/or the mutilation of the Herms; Hansen 1995: 27–8; Millett 2005: 38–9.

[87] Aischin. 1.173.

[88] Hansen 1995: 16–17. Anytos and Phyle: Lys. 13.78–9; Isok. 18.23; cf. Xen. *Hell.* 2.3.42, 44; Strauss 1987: 94–6.

[89] This Meletos has been identified as the Meletos who prosecuted Sokrates and took part in the arrest of Leon of Salamis under the Thirty; Andok. 1.94; Todd 2007: 409; Edwards 1995: 180; Blumenthal 1973; Dover 1968: 78–80; Todd 1985: 47–8; Ostwald 1986: 495; contra: MacDowell 1962: 208–10; cf. Hansen 1995: 16; Millett 2005: 52 note 37. If this identification is correct, then he will particularly have needed to improve his image. That Sokrates refused to participate in arresting Leon might

Personal gain was very much at stake. Prosecuting Sokrates, accordingly, was a way of punishing oligarchs and their supporters without overtly contravening the terms of the agreement. Reconciliation did not preclude vengeance for past wrongs.

Sokrates' trial was not the only major impiety case in Athens at this time and two other men, Nikomachos and Andokides, also faced prosecution on religious issues.[90] The reconciliation agreement was brought into play in relation to both men, although it was irrelevant to the case against Nikomachos and it probably did not apply to Andokides.[91] The surviving speeches from these trials show how the document's terms needed to be continually negotiated even in cases in which it was not obviously relevant. Nikomachos, the *anagrapheus* involved in the reorganisation of the laws, was brought to court on very unclear charges connected with his office.[92] The speaker against him, indignant at the accusation of membership in the Four Hundred, expresses his incredulity that his opponent should be allowed to remember past wrongs (*mnesikakein*), an obvious allusion to the clause *me mnesikakein*.[93] The speaker seems to be trying to divert the jurors in a weak case against an opponent with good democratic credentials: he was in exile under the Thirty.[94] This passage, however, also calls into question exactly what it means to remember past wrongs and when, if ever, it is appropriate to do so.

Andokides must have been a notorious figure in Athens at the time of his trial, probably soon after the Mysteries in 400, because he had been an informer in connection with the profanation of the Mysteries and the mutilation of the Herms in 415 on the eve of the Sicilian Expedition.[95] Soon afterwards, he went into self-imposed exile in order to avoid the strictures of the decree of Isotimides which prohibited those having admitted impiety from entering sanctuaries or the Agora;[96] despite his various attempts to return, he remained in exile until soon after the restoration of democracy in 403. In this case, he was accused of breaching the terms of the decree of Isotimides by attending the Mysteries and also of illegally placing an

---

explain Meletos' prosecution, but Meletos would also have needed to distance himself from the Thirty; Pl. *Ap.* 32c3–d7; Xen. *Mem.* 4.4.3.

[90] Nikomachos: Lys. 30; Andokides: Andok. 1 and [Lys.] 6. For the identification of [Lysias] 6 as a court speech, see Todd 2007: 403–8.

[91] Andokides: Todd 2000: 62–3; MacDowell 1962: 201–2; Todd 1985: 64. Nikomachos: Todd 1996: 120.

[92] On the difficulty of determining the charges, see Todd 1996: 108–15; Todd 1985: 87–9.

[93] Lys. 30.7–9; Todd 1996: 120.   [94] Lys. 30.15–16.

[95] For the date of the trial, see MacDowell 1962: 204–5; Todd 2007: 409–10. For the events in 415, see Thucydides 6.27.1–29.3, 53.1–2, 60.1–61.7; Andok. 1.11–70.

[96] Andok. 1.71; [Lys.] 6.9, 24.

olive branch on the altar in the Eleusinion at the time of the Mysteries. The reconciliation agreement ought not to apply because the events in question took place after 403. Andokides, however, places the issues in a much larger context from events in 405 to the reorganisation of the laws after 403 in order to show that the decree of Isotimides was no longer valid.[97] These efforts suggest his doubt about whether the agreement alone was enough to protect him.[98] The speaker of the sixth Lysianic speech certainly thought that Andokides was covered by the reconciliation and he attempts to argue it away on the grounds that it was made between the men of the city and the men of the Peiraieus, groups which did not include Andokides.[99] Andokides also argues that the case actually concerned whether the agreement and its oaths would be upheld or not.[100] For us, it brings out the ways in which reconciliation had constantly to be negotiated in the courts and it complements the dynamics which we have seen with Lysias 13.

The politics of the situation are further brought out by the individuals involved. Although the real enmity was between Andokides and Kallias, who were at odds over an heiress, the main prosecutor was Kephisios, allegedly in Kallias' pay.[101] He was aided by Meletos, Epichares and Agyrrhios.[102] Agyrrhios was one of the leaders of the *demos* in the years after 403, but both Meletos and Epichares were tainted by the events in 404/3: Epichares had been a *bouleutes* under the Thirty and Meletos had arrested Leon of Salamis.[103] Prosecuting such a notorious individual allowed these men to create new images of themselves as supporters of the democratic city. Meanwhile, Andokides had important Athenians on his side as well because Anytos was one of his supporters.[104] The image of the good democrat, consequently, was brought into play by both prosecution and defence, as both sides sought to manipulate the same imagery.

These cases all belong in 400 or 399, not very long after the reconciliation agreement was made.[105] In the years immediately following 403, the evidence for negotiation over the terms and their consequences is to be expected as the Athenians put them into practice. Contestation over the events and individuals' roles in them, however, continued as late as 383/2 when the *dokimasia* of the (eponymous) archon was the setting

[97] Andok. 1.71–91.   [98] Todd 2000: 62 note 2.
[99] [Lys.] 6.37–41; Todd 1985: 84; on this tactic, see Todd 1985: 137–8; Todd 2007: 464–5.
[100] Andok. 1.105.   [101] Andok. 1.121.   [102] Andok. 1.94–5, 133–5; Edwards 1995: 15.
[103] Andok. 1.94–5. Epichares is probably not the same man as Epichares of Lamptrai, a member of the Ten; MacDowell 1962: 133; Todd 2007: 401 note 10; Németh 2006: 126.
[104] Andok. 1.150; Todd 2007: 402–3.
[105] Todd 1985: 11–12; Todd 2007: 102–3, 118–20; Phillips 2008: 184 with note 1; above notes 84 and 95.

for disputes involving alleged activities under the Thirty.[106] The original candidate, Leodamas, was rejected at the instigation of Thrasyboulos of Kollytos apparently because his name had been inscribed on a *stele* on the Akropolis and then was removed by the Thirty.[107] Leodamas was evidently not a good democrat and he may have been a supporter of oligarchs. His replacement, Euandros, was subsequently accused at his own *dokimasia* of having been a member of the cavalry and also a *bouleutes* under the Thirty.[108] In contrast, his opponent, the speaker of Lysias 26, notes that he was too young to have been active in the oligarchy.[109] He also anticipates that Euandros will appeal to the agreement and so he divides the men of the city into good and bad men; Euandros, of course, falls into the latter category and, therefore, he should not pass his scrutiny.[110] As this strategy suggests, the accusations being made against Euandros are vague and he did, indeed, become archon for 382/1.[111] The strategies used here are not specific to this particular scrutiny and, in Lysias' speeches for *dokimasiai*, what the candidate did or did not do under the Thirty is regularly at issue, as is his presence in or absence from Athens.[112] In a *dokimasia* after 394, Mantitheos, for example, had to explain why he came back to Athens five days before the democrats returned to the Peiraieus and he stresses that he did not serve in the cavalry under the Thirty.[113] Since the date of his return is obviously suspicious, Mantitheos diverts attention from it by concentrating on his earlier absence. To bolster his case, he focuses most of his speech on his image as a good citizen who provided dowries for his sisters despite his (relative) poverty and who fought for the city.[114] He stresses that he performed his military duties enthusiastically and he contrives to emphasise his ancestors' continuous political activity on behalf of the city.[115] In this way, Mantitheos' actions in 403 are counterbalanced by his later activity and the image of him as a potential supporter of oligarchy is replaced by the good (democratic) citizen. Scrutinies seem to have been particularly good opportunities for accusing opponents of oligarchic deeds and, in response, the past of both the city and individual had to be carefully (re)constructed.

Being in Athens at the wrong time was an issue which the speaker of Lysias 25 also had to confront at his *dokimasia* at some time after 401/0.[116]

---

[106] On the process of the *dokimasia*, see with further references Todd 1993: 287–9; Wolpert 2002a: 67–9.

[107] Lys. 26.13–15, 21–4; Arist. *Rh.* 2.23.25; Todd 1993: 286–7.   [108] Lys. 26.10.

[109] Lys. 26.21.   [110] Lys. 26.16–20.   [111] Todd 1993: 285–6.

[112] Todd 1993: 289; Todd 2000: 177–8.   [113] Lys. 16.4–8; date: Lys. 16.15–17; Todd 2000: 179.

[114] Dowries: Lys. 16.10; fighting: Lys. 16.13–18.   [115] Lys. 16.17, 20.

[116] Date: Lys. 25.9; Todd 2000: 260–1.

As his opening sentence makes clear, he was in the city under the Thirty and he emphasises several times during the speech that he is not guilty of the deeds of the Thirty, as alleged by his opponents.[117] He also stresses that he was not a member of the Four Hundred and nor was he a *bouleutes* or a holder of any other office under the Thirty.[118] He was, so he would have us believe, simply in Athens at the wrong time and, indeed, he is the same sort of man 'as the best man of those in the Peiraieus would have been if he had stayed in the city'.[119] In contrast, he describes his opponents as exiles, saved by other people, who have now become sycophants and he imagines their behaviour if they had been in Athens under the Thirty: they would have acted no differently.[120] Physical location under the oligarchy is apparently not an indication of a man's behaviour and the connection is not as simple as we might suppose. That feelings were running high is further brought out by the first sentence: 'I easily forgive you, gentlemen of the jury, for being equally angry against all those who remained in the city when you hear such speeches and remember what has happened.'[121] In response to what was presumably an impassioned speech by his opponents, the speaker legitimises the jury's anger at men like himself. He will go on to refer to the jury's anger against the Thirty and he will tell them that they should not hate men like himself when they can vent their spleen against individuals who committed offences against the *demos* as he describes.[122] The speaker seems to be deliberately inflaming the situation and feeding the anger of his listeners. Swearing oaths of reconciliation did not immediately create harmony and men's rage was liable to erupt in *dokimasiai* and trials which then became venues for negotiating the anger created by remembering.[123] These occasions also provided opportunities for working out exactly what reconciling from *stasis* entailed at the level of the individual and for asking what precisely it meant to be a citizen of democratic Athens. As the speech against Euandros shows, even twenty years after the fact, reconciliation remained an on-going process in need of repetition and reinforcement.

Reconciling the Athenians, accordingly, could not simply be done by swearing a shared oath and later reading the document on the *stele*. Instead, the process also had to be carried out on the level of the individual as the Athenians worked out how the city would now function under its new rules. In the courts, the speakers negotiated where and when the terms of the

---

[117] Lys. 25.1–2, 5, 15–16, 18.   [118] Lys. 25.14.   [119] Lys. 25.2.

[120] Lys. 25.29–31. The opponents were apparently not with the exiled democrats.   [121] Lys. 25.1.

[122] Thirty: Lys. 25.5, 16, 19; democracy: Lys. 25.18–19 and compare 27.

[123] For further discussion and examples, see Wolpert 2002a: 84–6.

agreement would be applied. As they did so, they created memories of the difficult events under the Thirty and they shared them, and their anger, with their listeners and judges, who, in their dikastic oaths, had agreed not to remember past wrongs. In stark contrast to the agreement, these legal processes distinguished sharply between different parties and their actions under the Thirty. In this way, good democrats, closet oligarchs and open supporters of the Thirty were all brought on stage as political careers were burnished and damaged and, at least in Sokrates' case, strife was continued by other means. A trial like Andokides' might see leading democrats on opposite sides and also co-operating with known oligarchs. Indeed, Archinos even prosecuted Thrasyboulos for illegally proposing to award citizenship to all the foreigners who aided in the return from Phyle.[124] In contrast, Theozotides was able successfully to defend his decree honouring the sons of the dead democrats against a lawsuit.[125] In this charged atmosphere, democrats were also targets. This divisiveness spilled over into the political sphere, which was rife with factions and changing political allegiances,[126] but *stasis* did not return to the city. Instead, the Athenians tacitly agreed both to use the courts as one of the main spheres for negotiating their differences and also to abide by the decisions of the majority. Unity was to be found in division.

THE CONSEQUENCES OF RECONCILIATION

Reconciling the Athenians and healing their divisions was a complicated and on-going process which required a series of measures: the agreement, its oaths, their publication and the contestation in the courts. Collectively, they brought the Athenians back together and began the process of healing their divisions. Recovering from civil strife, however, was not a neutral operation. While individual men could remember the events in the courts, in the agreement and its oaths, *stasis* was forgotten and war was remembered, a strategy which was to be repeated in other monuments connected with the Athenians' response to the Thirty, as we shall see in chapter 10. Through the document and its rituals, the Athenians tacitly agreed on the sort of *politeia*

---

[124] Arist. *Ath. Pol.* 40.2; cf. Aischin. 3.195; below chapter 8.
[125] *SEG* XXVIII 46; Lys. fr. LXIV.128–50 (Carey); below chapter 8. His decree was attacked by a *graphe paranomon*. That the decree was inscribed indicates that Theozotides won his case; Todd 2000: 383; Stroud 1971: 300–1; cf. Ostwald 1986: 507; contra: Sartori 1983: 67–9, who disassociates the decree and speech.
[126] Strauss 1987: 89–163. On the term 'faction', see Strauss 1987: 11–36. Against the idea of parties and the use of the terms 'radical' and 'moderate', see also Todd 1985: 45–51.

which the city would have: treated equally throughout the agreement and arrayed by tribe and by deme to take the oaths, the citizens were now all democrats and oligarchy was consigned to the gaps of memory. If the inscribed *stele* included a decree authorising the publication of the agreement, then this imagery would have been made more explicit, but no more open to debate.

Taking the oaths was an important part of the reconciliation process and, as texts sworn by all the Athenians, they invite comparison with the oath of Demophantos on which they seem to have been modelled. On both occasions, oaths were used to reconcile the Athenians and to strengthen the democracy after *stasis*, which is carefully ignored in both texts. The oaths, however, differ significantly in the image created of the Athenians. In Demophantos' oath, that vision is uncompromising: the good Athenian is a democrat and male citizen who has sworn to kill tyrants and oligarchs. Swearing the oath in the Agora under the gaze of the bronze statues of Harmodios and Aristogeiton reinforced the power of this stern image. There is no indication that any other behaviour is appropriate and certainly no hint at all of reconciliation. In contrast, the oaths of 403 focus closely on reconciling the Athenians and healing their divisions, but their image is left relatively undefined. They are all democrats, but the proper behaviour is not clearly articulated beyond reconciliation and forgetting of past wrongs. Creating an image of what it means to be Athenian was left to the courts and to the public monuments, as we shall see in the following chapters. In contrast to 410/9, the Athenians appear to have realised that reconciliation must precede the (re)construction of the citizen's identity and that both of those steps could not be achieved at once as part of the same process.

Like Demophantos' oath, the oaths of reconciliation created a specific set of memories which were shared by all Athenians and were reinforced by the inscribed document. As such, they were very much collective memories and they contrast strongly with the ways in which individual Athenians negotiated the events of 404/3. In court, these men argued over terms, described past events and invoked the agreements and oaths to help themselves and to harm their opponents. The debate not permitted by the document and its rituals was carried out here as the Athenians negotiated and contested the details of the agreement's terms and worked out how the new rules of engagement would function. Despite all these individual strategies of remembering, forgetting and (re)creating the past, the Athenians did make the reconciliation agreement work and it was so remembered in antiquity.[127] Although modern scholars often have focused on the ways in which the Athenians failed to adhere to the agreement, they, too, have emphasised its success.[128] They have explained rather less well why it succeeded. The actions of individual men were balanced by the very process of swearing the oaths among all the Athenians in the sanctuary at Agrai and by the collective memories which were created there. That remembering was reinforced by reading the inscribed text on its *stele* in the precinct. Each time the oath was read, the blessings of the gods were called down on the Athenian keeping his oath and their wrath on the man breaking it. Rituals and their memories, therefore, were an integral part of the success of the reconciliation. The agreement and oaths also marked the beginning of responding to the Thirty, a process which, in and of itself, was also instrumental in the success of the reconciliation. These responses would both reinforce and add to the images created in the agreement and oaths so that they truly became the safeguard (*phulake*) of the democracy, as Lysias described them.[129]

---

[127] E.g. Arist. *Ath. Pol.* 40.2; Xen. *Hell.* 2.4.43; Andok. 1.140; Isok. 18.45–6; Wolpert 2002b: 109–10 with note 3.

[128] E.g. Krentz 1982: 119–20; Wolpert 2002a: 137–8, 140–1; Loening 1987: 147–9; Quillin 2002: 71–105; Loraux 2002: 248, 256–60.

[129] Lys. 25.28.

CHAPTER 8

Recreating democracy: documents and the law

In Boedromion of 403, the Athenians faced a series of pressing problems as a consequence of the Thirty's period in power and the resulting *stasis*. Most immediately, they had to reconcile the warring factions of the men in the Peiraieus and the men in the city. As we saw in the previous chapter, bringing the Athenians back together and re-uniting the divided groups was done through the reconciliation agreement and its oaths which were sworn by all the Athenians. It constituted their first step which, in contrast to the situation in 410/9, they undertook immediately, before they began to create a full response to the Thirty. The agreement and oaths also mark the beginning of reacting to the oligarchy. Since the Thirty had appropriated both the city's past and her spaces, particularly the Agora and the Akropolis, for themselves, the Athenians needed to make the city democratic again. They also had to consider how the past might be reclaimed from the oligarchs and how the events of 404/3 should be remembered, if at all.

As products of the *demos*, the laws and decrees discussed in this chapter played an important role in this response which they show started almost immediately. During this process, the Athenians needed to address issues raised by the Thirty's efforts to create a new constitution for the city and their maltreatment of the city's laws. What constituted the city's laws, how they were displayed and their relation to the rule of the *demos* were all issues which needed to be resolved. Reinforcing the legal basis of the city, however, was not concerned simply with statutes. The Thirty's response to democrats' earlier use of the physical and symbolic properties of laws and decrees showed the power of this approach. As in the years after 411, the Athenians once again needed to recreate the rule of the *demos* visibly and tangibly by taking advantage of the documents' qualities as commemorative monuments to (re)display the democracy as it functioned and to (re)write its control on to the city's (contested) topography. Bringing into the process honorary decrees for Athenians, the first time such documents seem to have been inscribed, allowed the identity of the democratic Athenian to be recreated and displayed. Inevitably, these documents also required the Athenians to grapple with their memories of the oligarchy and the ways in which it would be remembered. As we shall see, those memories were to be selective as they were used for the purposes of recreating democracy and the democratic city.

Despite the importance of these issues and the clear links between the documents' practical, visible and symbolic aspects, scholars have concentrated on them only in practical terms. For them, they are important in so much as they represent the Athenians' attempts to improve their political system.[1] That simply approving laws and decrees was not enough to recreate the rule of the *demos* has not become the focus of discussion. Similarly, work on the revision of the laws has also concentrated on the practical aspects of the project.[2] The extant inscribed fragments of the laws have also been considered in this context,[3] but, just as scholarly treatments of these remains are unsatisfactory for the period between 410 and 405, so also are their discussions of the second period between 403 and 399. Reconsideration of the fragmentary *stelai* shows that the display of the laws was significantly changed at this time and, in particular, the sacrificial calendar was reinscribed and erected in a new and different setting in the Stoa Basileios. As these remains of the calendar demonstrate, the texts both of the laws and the other documents, their form as inscribed monuments and their setting cannot be separated;[4] brought together, they allow us to see the ways in which the Athenians recreated both the rule of the *demos* and the democratic city. Through these documents, they wrote their control on to the cityscape and provided models for the proper behaviour of citizens.

DATES, DOCUMENTS AND RESPONSES

In the previous chapter, we saw that the reconciliation agreement did not focus explicitly on democracy, but its procedures and the ways in which it treated all men equally tacitly presuppose the system of the rule of the *demos*. Swearing the oaths would have reinforced this image because the Athenians seem to have been marshalled by tribe and by deme. Dated to early Boedromion in 403 and negotiated before the men of the Peiraieus

---

[1] See e.g. Ostwald 1986: 500–24; Krentz 1982: 109–24; Wolpert 2002a: 35–47; Munn 2000: 250–72.
[2] See e.g. P. J. Rhodes 1991; Robertson 1990; Todd 1996; Ostwald 1986: 510–24; Dow 1960; Clinton 1982; Sickinger 1999b: 93–105; Wolpert 2002a: 35–42.
[3] Dow 1961 and Lambert 2002a are crucial for understanding the material; see also e.g. Dow 1941; Dow 1953–7; Fingarette 1971.
[4] Compare Wolpert 2002a: 88; Hobden 2007: 169–70.

returned to the city, the reconciliation agreement constitutes our earliest evidence for the democrats' response to the Thirty. The evidence of the laws, the decrees and the documents recording the sales of the property of the Thirty shows that the process continued after the return of the *demos* on 12 Boedromion in 403, but it also indicates that responding to oligarchy could not be completed quickly: the consequences were still playing out in the late 390s, at least ten years after the return of the democrats from exile.

Just as the events of 411 led to the reorganisation of the laws and their display and inscription, so also the actions of the Thirty in 404/3 resulted in another period of work on the city's laws. Some of the same personnel were involved, including Nikomachos, whose term as *anagrapheus* between 410 and 404 and trial have already been discussed. The Lysianic speech against him reports that Nikomachos took four years to write up what could actually have been done in thirty days.[5] Although the prosecutor has clearly made an effort to be as hostile as possible, he does not say that Nikomachos was appointed by the Thirty and he admits that his opponent was in exile; consequently, Nikomachos should have been appointed by the *demos* soon after its return.[6] His term in office ought to have run from 403/2 to 400/399.[7] In describing the length of his office and his mandate, the speaker uses the verb to write up (ἀναγράφειν), a usage which should indicate that Nikomachos held the office of *anagrapheus*, as he had during his first term.[8] Further evidence for work on the laws is provided by the decree of Teisamenos, which Andokides quoted in the course of his speech on the Mysteries.[9] The text as quoted does not contain the name of the archon or any other dating material, but Andokides describes its context in introducing the text: after the reconciliation was made, twenty men were elected to oversee the city and the laws of Drakon and Solon were to be used; once the *boule* was chosen and *nomothetai* were elected, conflicts were discovered between the laws of Drakon and Solon and the reconciliation agreement and so an *ekklesia* was held to consider the situation.[10] At that meeting, Teisamenos proposed his decree. This sequence presupposes that these events took place very soon after the return of the *demos* and they should belong early in the official year. This process is also described

---

[5] Lys. 30.4.   [6] Todd 1996: 103.
[7] Todd 1996: 103; P. J. Rhodes 1991: 88; Dow 1960: 271–2; Ostwald 1986: 511; Lambert 2002a: 354.
[8] Lys. 30.4. Note also chapter 17, where the project is described as an ἀναγραφή, a process of writing up. On Nikomachos' title, see Todd 1996: 109; Dow 1960: 271; P. J. Rhodes 1991: 88; Robertson 1990: 52.
[9] Andok. 1.83–4. I remain unconvinced by Carawan's arguments that the decree at 82–3 was not the text read out at the trial; Carawan 2002: 19–23.
[10] Andok. 1.81–2.

by the scholia on Aischines: 'when the *demos* had recovered its freedom, twenty citizens were appointed to search out and write up (ζητήσοντας καὶ ἀναγράψοντας) the laws which had been destroyed. And they decreed that they propose new laws in the place of the destroyed ones in the archonship of Eukleides, who was the first archon after the Thirty'.[11] This passage shows that work on the laws certainly began in 403/2 and it corroborates the evidence provided by Andokides and Lysias 30.

In addition to the laws, the documents from the Agora consist of the accounts of the sale of the property of the Thirty, Theozotides' decree concerning the orphans of the dead democrats and honorary decrees for the Athenians returning from Phyle, for Euagoras of Cypriot Salamis and for Konon (table 9). Since the inscriptions are all fragmentary and their opening preambles are only partially preserved, they cannot all be precisely dated. For the documents recording the sale of the property of the Thirty, the archon's name is still visible on the heading of the first *stele* and they certainly date to 402/1 BC.[12] The rewards for the Athenians returning from Phyle have traditionally been dated to 403/2 BC, but the archon's name is not preserved.[13] The recent identification of a new fragment of the decree shows that Eukleides cannot have been archon when the decree was passed and the honours must belong slightly later.[14] Theozotides' decree is also missing its archon and the fragmentary preamble does not fix the date with certainty.[15] The original editor dated it to 403/2 and he rightly stressed that the situation described in the text is relevant to the events in 404/3, but not in 411.[16] Changing the date of the honours for the Athenians from Phyle, however, may also require moving Theozotides' decree slightly later. As we shall see in this chapter, the politics of this decree fit very well with the other

---

[11] Schol. Aischin. 1.39. This passage does not seem to have been brought into discussions about the reorganisation of the laws after the Thirty. Since it differs both from Andokides' and Lysias' (tendentious) accounts, it must represent an independent tradition which may be derived from a Lysianic speech mentioned later in the entry. The passage quoted here comes immediately after the destruction of the laws of Drakon and Solon; above chapter 6. The twenty men are also described by Poll. *Onom.* 8.112.

[12] *SEG* XXXII 161 = *Agora* XIX P2 + LA2.

[13] *SEG* XXVIII 45 with Aischin. 3.187, 190–1. For the traditional date, see Raubitschek 1941a: 285–6, 295; M. J. Osborne 1981–2: II, 30.

[14] *SEG* LII 45.   [15] *SEG* XXVIII 46.

[16] Stroud 1971: 285–7, 297–301; contra: Calabi Limentani 1986. She objects that the events in 404/3 were war, not *stasis*, and so fit poorly with this decree. Lysias and Xenophon, however, do use the term *stasis* in connection with these events; Lys. 2.61, 63, 65; Xen. *Hell.* 3.1.1. As we shall see in chapter 10, the literary sources are in part responding to the response to the Thirty. I understand that Angelos Matthaiou will also opt for an early date in a forthcoming publication. Such a date implausibly requires a man with the rare name of Theozotides to have intervened on two separate occasions in matters connected with the war-orphans.

documents responding to the Thirty, but they differ significantly from the response to the events in 411. The two honorary decrees for Euagoras and for Konon belong after the battle of Knidos, very probably in 394/3; in neither case, however, is an archon date preserved and Konon's document is known only from Demosthenes' quotation from it.[17] Nevertheless, these other documents from the Agora complement the evidence of the laws and they show that, in the years immediately after the democrats' return, the Athenians' response to the Thirty was well underway. The later documents also demonstrate that the effects of this activity continued for at least ten years after the return and related material was still being added as late as 394/3.

Documents connected with the Athenians' response to the Thirty were also erected on the Akropolis. The earliest of them is the fragmentary decree providing rewards for the non-Athenians who participated in the return from Phyle.[18] The preamble is again only partially preserved and only the last two letters of the archon's name are preserved; they are consistent with the archon Xenainetos who held office in 401/0 and the document should belong in his year.[19] Some of the proxeny decrees which the Thirty destroyed were also reinscribed and re-erected, as their texts specifically record.[20] Of them, only one preserves an archon date, so we can be certain that it was approved in 399/8.[21] A second document specifies that it is to be set up 'on the Akropolis', rather than 'in the *polis*'; since the term Akropolis first appears in publication clauses in 386/5, it is likely that this inscription dates to around this time.[22] The honorary decree of 405/4 for the loyal Samians may also have been part of this process;[23] enough of the archon's name is preserved to show that the extant document was inscribed in 403/2.[24] The material from the Akropolis covers a similar range of years as the documents from the Agora. Collectively, this evidence indicates that the Athenians began constructing their response almost immediately after their return in 403/2. Their activities were on-going and the Athenians were still responding to the Thirty in 394/3; at least one of the proxeny decrees was probably inscribed even a few years later.

---

[17] Euagoras: RO 11; date: Lewis and Stroud 1979: 184–8; Funke 1983: 152–61; Rhodes and Osborne 2003: 55. Konon: Dem. 20.69–70.

[18] RO 4.

[19] M. J. Osborne 1981–2: 11, 30 with note 81; Rhodes and Osborne 2003: 26; cf. Krentz 1986: 201 note 1; contra: Krentz 1980: 299–301; Karamoutsou-Teza 1990: 266–73.

[20] *IG* I³ 229; *IG* II² 6; 13 + addenda p. 655 + *SEG* XL 54; 52; *Agora* XVI 37; Walbank, *Proxenies* 26; above chapter 6.

[21] *IG* II² 13 + addenda p. 655 + *SEG* XL 54.   [22] *IG* I³ 229.5–6; Henry 1982: 95–6, 98, 117.

[23] *IG* I³ 127 + RO 2 (= *IG* II² 1).   [24] RO 2.57.

DOCUMENTS AND CONTENTS

As with the Athenians' response to the events of 411, the texts of inscriptions provide important evidence for the city's reactions to the Thirty and its focus on democracy. Of the laws, only fragments of the sacrificial calendar inscribed in Ionic letters are preserved (table 6: frs. 1, 2, 3, 5, 6, 7, 8, 9, 12; fig. 6). The entries record the date of the sacrifice, the name of the divinity or hero, the animal to be sacrificed, any extras and, as necessary, payment to the officials involved. Although the dates of the offerings are specified by day and month, the names of the festivals are not given. On fragments 2 and 3, headings in the fascia at the top of the *stelai* specified the frequency of the sacrifices listed below (fig. 6); in this case, the offerings are made in alternate years or biennially. Although no other such headings are preserved, originally there must have been further headings for annual and quadrennial festivals and perhaps others.[25] As with the earlier sacrificial calendar inscribed between 410 and 405, when this version in the Ionic alphabet was completed, it would have laid out very clearly exactly what offerings were to be given to a particular divinity or hero on which occasion. This project was apparently not limited to the sacrificial calendar. In Lysias' speech against Nikomachos, we are told that Nikomachos was an *anagrapheus* of both secular and sacred matters (καὶ τῶν ὁσίων καὶ τῶν ἱερῶν).[26] Although there is no specific term of office mentioned here, this passage comes in a section discussing Nikomachos' second term and it seems likely that this passage should refer to the period after 403. Since the Thirty took down the laws of Ephialtes and Archestratos and damaged at least some of the laws of Solon and Drakon, and the *demos* subsequently chose men to replace this destroyed legislation, the *anagrapheis* must have been working on both sacred and secular laws during their second term in office.

Of the decrees, three record honours related to the return of the *demos* from exile. As it is now preserved, the fragmentary honours for the Athenians returning from Phyle consist of a two-line heading in larger letters followed by the names of the men honoured, a four-line epigram and the beginning of their honorary decree, the first such document rewarding Athenians and known to be inscribed (fig. 14).[27] The names of the men with patronymics and demotics are arranged in two columns in official

---

[25] *SEG* LII frs. 2A.1; 3A.30; Lambert 2002a: 356, 371, 376; Dow 1960: 285–7, 289; Dow 1953–7: 10–14.

[26] Lys. 30.25.

[27] *SEG* XXVIII 45; Raubitschek 1941a: fig. 1. Honorary decrees for Athenians were not regularly inscribed until the 340s and the earlier examples are all exceptional; Lambert 2004: 86–7; Lambert 2005: 125.

Figure 14   *SEG* xxviii 45: honours for the Athenians who returned from Phyle.
The outlines mark the preserved sections of the inscribed face rather than the outlines
of the fragments.

tribal order, while the heading, now largely restored, probably read 'the following men, having seized Phyle, brought back the *demos*'.[28] Only a few words of the epigram and the beginning of the decree are preserved, but Aischines' description provides us with further information. He reports that Archinos of Koile proposed the decree which awarded the honorands 1,000 *drachmai* for a sacrifice and offerings and crowned them with olive

[28] Since the non-Athenians were honoured in a separate decree, RO 4 to be discussed below, it is implausible that some of them were also honoured here, as Taylor suggests; M. C. Taylor 2002a: 379–95. Her scenario requires some foreigners, but no Athenians, to be honoured twice and ignores the stress in this document on bringing back the *demos* and the role of the *boule*, both of which are absent from RO 4.

crowns;[29] the *boule* was to conduct an examination to make sure the men were actually at Phyle when the Lakedaimonians and the Thirty attacked. Aischines also provides us with the text of the epigram: 'these men the Athenian *demos*, ancient inhabitants of this land, honoured with crowns on account of their valour; they first began to depose those ruling the city with unjust statutes (ἀδίκοις θεσμοῖς) and hazarded their bodies'.[30] Since he reports that the sum of money awarded came to less than ten *drachmai* per man, there ought originally to have been 100 or so names in the list.[31]

A second very fragmentary decree honours the non-Athenians involved in the return of the *demos*.[32] The fragments show that the *stele* was originally opisthographic and they preserve part of the decree and some of the names of those honoured. The decree mentions three different classes of individual: those who joined in the return from Phyle, those who joined in the fighting at Mounichia and those who remained with the *demos* in the Peiraieus when the reconciliation took place.[33] The men in the first group get Athenian citizenship, while those in the second two groups seem to get *isoteleia*, equality with citizens for taxation and military duties, a reward which Xenophon says was promised to those men joining after the battle of Mounichia.[34] The names of the men were divided into three corresponding groups, each with its own heading, and the names were listed in tribal order. According to Michael Osborne's estimates, about 70–90 men returned from Phyle, about 290 were at Mounichia and about 560–580 were with the *demos* at Peiraieus.[35]

The third decree concerning the return from Phyle was moved by a certain Theozotides who, as we saw briefly in chapter 1, specifies that

---

[29] Aischin. 3.187.

[30] Aischin. 3.190. His quotation forms the basis for the restoration of the epigram at lines 73–6 of the inscription and the identification of the subject of the text; Raubitschek 1941a: 287, 291, 294–5.

[31] In view of the very fragmentary nature of the remains, we simply cannot guess how many names went under each tribal heading. Consequently, there are no grounds for Raubitschek's assumption that the names were divided into two lists inscribed above and below the decree respectively; Raubitschek 1941a: 294; Taylor 2002a: 392–5. Contrast RO 4 with the lists placed after the decree. Autopsy reveals that the text was inscribed, not on a standard *stele*, but on a large block more than 0.30 m. thick. Although the back of the monument is not preserved, portions of both sides are; they were smoothly polished, but not inscribed. These physical details mean that the decree's overall dimensions (and text) cannot be restored on the basis of contemporary *stelai*, as Taylor wished to do; Taylor 2002a: 386–95.

[32] RO 4. Walbank associated *SEG* XLIV 34, a small fragment of a very damaged list of names, with this inscription; Walbank 1994: 169–71, no. 2.

[33] The last group is partially restored on the basis of lines 56–7 of column 6; contra: Krentz 1980: 302.

[34] Xen. *Hell.* 2.4.25; M. J. Osborne 1981–2: ii, 32–5; Rhodes and Osborne 2003: 25–6; contra: Krentz 1980: 302–4; Whitehead 1984; Krentz 1986; Harding 1987: 176–81.

[35] M. J. Osborne 1981–2: ii, 35–42.

the sons of 'as many of the Athenian[s] as, [co]mi[ng] to the aid of the democracy, d[ie]d a [v]iolent death in the oligarchy' are to be honoured on account of the *euergesia* (good deeds) and *andragathia* of their fathers toward the *demos* and they are to receive public maintenance just like the war-orphans.[36] This striking description of the fathers' deaths brings out the violence involved without using either the term *stasis* or words connected with war.[37] The end of the decree is now illegible and we do not have its full text (fig. 15). The names of seven sons with patronymics and demotics are inscribed on the left side of the *stele*; since they seem to have been added at a later date, the names must originally have begun on the front below the end of the decree in the now illegible lower part of the stone.[38] If the names were given in tribal order, there is no indication of the appropriate headings in the text on the left side of the *stele*.

The reinscribed proxeny decrees also show the Athenians responding to the Thirty.[39] In all cases, the texts refer to earlier honorary decrees which the Thirty had taken down and these actions are explicitly given as the reason for erecting the new *stelai*.[40] In one case, the text of the earlier decree was also reinscribed on the stone.[41] In three cases, the preserved texts indicate that an older relative had previously been *proxenos*, while two of the inscriptions invite the current honorand to dinner (*xenia*) in the Prytaneion.[42] The terms used to describe the honorands are not preserved, but, in two cases, the phrase *aner agathos* may be restored with some

---

[36] *SEG* XXVIII 46; the quotation is from lines 4–6. No evidence supports the suggestion that dowries were awarded to the daughters; Pomeroy 1982: 125–7. Note that female war-orphans were not so treated in Athens. Since this inscription is essentially an honorary decree, it will not have included Theozotides' provisions for changes to the pay for *hippeis* and mounted archers (*hippotoxotai*); Lys. fr. LXIV.130 lines 72–81 (Carey); Stroud 1971: 297–8; contra: Hansen 1978: 320 note 18.

[37] There are no good parallels for this entire phrase. In Lysias' funeral oration, the dead foreigners came to the aid of the *plethos* (*demos*) and relatives of Nikias' nephew died on behalf of the democracy under the Thirty, while living men brought aid to the fatherland in 404/3; Lys. 2.66; 18.24; 31.8. The phrase βιαίωι θανάτωι ἀποθάνει occurs in some fifth-century proxeny decrees, but these texts concern individual (non-Athenian) men and the situation is not otherwise described; *IG* I³ 28.14; 57.9–10; 91.15–16; 227.22–3. The term βιαίωι θανάτωι is also used with the form ἀποκτείνει in proxeny decrees; *IG* I³ 161.5–6; 162.9–10; 164.24–5; 179.6–7; 228.11–12. The phrase is not used by either Thucydides or Xenophon to describe the events in 411 or 404/3. None of this evidence provides support for Calabi Limentani's date of the decree; above note 16.

[38] Stroud 1971: 283, 295–6.

[39] *IG* I³ 229; *IG* II² 6; 13 + addenda p. 655 + *SEG* XL 54; 52; *Agora* XVI 37; Walbank, *Proxenies* 26. The small fragment *Agora* XVI 39 may originally have been part of a similar proxeny decree.

[40] In the case of *IG* II² 13 + addenda p. 655 + *SEG* XL 54, the text is very fragmentary and the relevant section is now mostly lost. Such a clause should lie behind the reference to earlier *stelai*.

[41] *IG* I³ 229.

[42] Previous *proxenoi*: *IG* II² 13 + addenda p. 655 + *SEG* XL 54; 52; *Agora* XVI 37. Xenia: *IG* II² 6; 13 + addenda p. 655 + *SEG* XL 54.

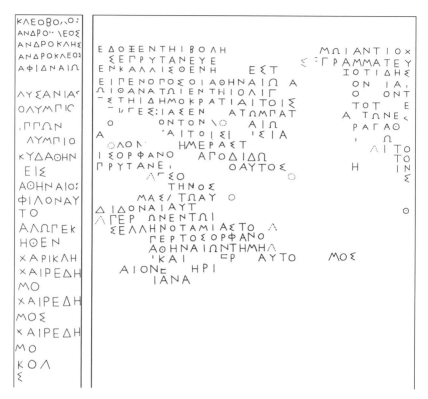

Figure 15   *SEG* xxviii 46: the decree of Theozotides honouring the sons of the dead democrats. The lower part of the *stele*, where no text is preserved, is not shown in this drawing.

certainty.[43] A similar history may lie behind the great inscription for the loyal Samians.[44] The original decree was passed in 405/4 to honour the Samians still loyal to Athens with citizenship and other benefits. In 403/2, this grant was reaffirmed by another decree of the *demos* and *boule* and honours were also voted for Poses, the Samian ambassador, and his sons. All three documents were inscribed in this order on a great *stele* under the heading: 'Kephisophon of Paiania was secretary. For the Samians who were with the *demos* of the Athenians'.[45] Since Kephisophon is listed as the secretary of the third decree, there could be no doubt that all the

---

[43] *IG* II² 13 + addenda p. 655 + *SEG* XL 54; 52. In a third case, the term *philos* has been restored; *Agora* XVI 37.

[44] *IG* I³ 127 + RO 2 (= *IG* II² 1).

[45] *IG* I³ 127.1–4 (= *IG* II² 1.1–4); photograph: Rhodes and Osborne 2003: pl. 1.

texts were inscribed at the same time. Both in the original decree and in the documents of 403/2, the Samians are praised for being *andres agathoi* towards the Athenians, while Poses is commended both for being an *aner agathos* and for his *andragathia*.[46]

The honorary intentions of both the inscription for the Athenians returning from Phyle and Theozotides' decree emphasise the unusual nature of these two documents and link them to two further such texts which were also set up in the Agora. Since the decrees for Euagoras of Cypriot Salamis and Konon, the victors at the battle of Knidos in 394/3, developed out of the Athenians' reactions to the events of 404/3 and formed the logical extension to them, they need to be discussed in this context. The very fragmentary remains of Euagoras' *stele* show that the document was originally of some considerable length, while the references to Konon and Euagoras connect the text with the battle of Knidos.[47] Euagoras was evidently awarded a gold crown to be announced at the tragedies at the City Dionysia and the inscription should also have recorded the award of his bronze statue in the Agora in the now missing portions.[48] The text also specified the herald's announcement which included the information that Euagoras had acted as 'a Hellene on behalf of Hellas', a striking phrase for a sea battle won with a Persian fleet; he is also connected with the Greeks earlier in the decree in a context which cannot now be recovered.[49] Although the relevant section of the beginning of the decree is not preserved, it is likely that Euagoras was described as an *aner agathos* towards the Athenians.[50] Unlike Euagoras' document, Konon's honorary decree is now known only through Demosthenes' brief description of it in his speech against Leptines.[51] He quotes it as saying 'since Konon freed the allies of Athens', a clause which must come from the beginning of the document when the proposer explains why the honours are being awarded. Demosthenes also reports that Konon was awarded *ateleia*, immunity from liturgies, military service and certain other duties, and a bronze statue, the first man to receive this honour after Harmodios and Aristogeiton, the Tyrannicides.[52] Since Demosthenes refers to the *stele*, we can be sure that this document was, in fact, inscribed and erected.

---

[46] Samians: *IG* I³ 127.7–9, 36–7; RO 2.43, 71; Poses: RO 2.58, 64–5, 71–2.

[47] RO 11. On the location, see the discussion below.

[48] Crown: Lewis and Stroud 1979: 189–90. Statue: Lewis and Stroud 1979: 192; Rhodes and Osborne 2003: 53–4; below chapter 11.

[49] RO 11.12–13, 17; Lewis and Stroud 1979: 190–1.   [50] RO 11.5–6.

[51] Dem. 20.69–70. On the location of the decree, see below. For its honorary character, see Lambert 2004: 86.

[52] For the benefits conferred by *ateleia*, see MacDowell 2004: 127–9.

The subject matter of the *stelai* recording the sales of the property of the Thirty and their supporters clearly identifies them as part of the Athenians' response to 404/3.[53] The entries all concern real property taken from the Thirty, the Ten, the Eleven and the Ten in Peiraieus, the same men excluded from the amnesty clause of the reconciliation agreement. Each entry identifies the man from whom the property was confiscated, its location, the purchaser, price and sales tax. At the top of the first *stele*, a heading provides the relevant information about the prytany, secretary and archon.[54] It also specified the source of the property and mentioned both the Thirty and oligarchs; the titles of their other followers presumably followed the reference to the Thirty and the Eleven appear in a heading in the text.[55] The extant fragments of the text now represent at least three *stelai* and perhaps as many as six.[56] The documents involved in the Athenians' response to the Thirty, consequently, included a variety of subjects: honours for both Athenians and non-Athenians, the sales of the property of the oligarchs and the city's laws, now physically represented by the sacrificial calendar.

(RE)WRITING THE LAWS

Further evidence for the project of collecting and writing up the laws comes from our literary sources. The speaker of Lysias' speech against Nikomachos is particularly incensed about his opponent's work on the city's sacrifices and he alleges that, through Nikomachos' omissions and inclusions, three talents worth of traditional rites were not celebrated, while new rituals worth six talents were.[57] This emphasis has suggested to scholars that, in their second term, the *anagrapheis* concentrated on the sacrificial calendar and were not working on secular laws.[58] As we saw earlier, however, the scholia on Aischines show that they were working on both types of law.[59] Moreover, this passage, which is apparently derived from a contemporary source, provides us with further important, but neglected, information about the *anagrapheis'* duties in their second term. As described here, the project falls into two parts: first discovering and writing up laws to

---

[53] *SEG* XXXII 161 = *Agora* XIX P2 + LA2.   [54] *SEG* XXXII 161 *stele* 1.1–5; Walbank 1982: 91.
[55] Eleven: *SEG* XXXII 161 *stele* 3.7.
[56] Lalonde, Langdon and Walbank 1991: 74; Walbank 1982: 74–5.
[57] Lys. 30.17–25 and especially 20.
[58] See e.g. Todd 1996: 109–10; MacDowell 1962: 198; Clinton 1982: 34–5; cf. Robertson 1990: 65–6; Ostwald 1986: 512, 520; Pébarthe 2006: 135; Volonaki 2001: 153–6.
[59] Schol. Aischin. 1.39.

replace the ones destroyed by the Thirty, i.e. at least part of the project carried out by the *anagrapheis* in their first term, and then the proposing of additional laws as required. A similar division also appears in Diokles' contemporary legislation concerning which Athenian laws are to be in force: both laws enacted under the democracy before the archonship of Eukleides in 403/2 and laws enacted in Eukleides' archonship and written up (ἀναγεγραμμένοι) are to be valid.[60] These two categories correspond to the material destroyed by the Thirty[61] and the new legislation, as described in the scholia. In Diokles' law, these terms further exclude any legislation made by the Thirty.

This evidence also elucidates the context of Teisamenos' decree. This document specifies that the Athenians are to govern themselves *kata ta patria* and to use the laws of Solon and the statutes (*thesmoi*) of Drakon.[62] The text then proceeds to stipulate how additional laws are to be made: written up on boards (*sanides*) by the *nomothetai* elected by the *boule*, the new laws are to be displayed in front of the eponymous heroes; they are to be examined by the *boule*, the 500 *nomothetai* elected by the demesmen and anyone who wishes; once they have been passed, the *boule* of the Areiopagos is to see that they are used. Finally, the laws which are being ratified are to be written up on the wall where they were before. As described in this document, the process is about the creation of new laws[63] in addition to the laws of Solon and Drakon. This latter legislation should be equivalent to the laws destroyed by the Thirty, as reported by the scholia on Aischines, and it ought to refer to the corpus of laws produced by the *anagrapheis* in their first term.[64] When Teisamenos specifies that the new laws are to be written up where they were before, he must mean the place where these destroyed laws were originally erected. In introducing this document, Andokides mentions an assembly in which it was voted to examine 'all' the laws and to inscribe those approved in the stoa.[65] As we saw in chapter 3, the information presented by Andokides and the physical evidence in the Agora require that the location of the earlier inscribed laws is the annexes of the Stoa Basileios (fig. 7). Since Teisamenos is described in Lysias 30 as one of Nikomachos' colleagues, it seems likely that the *anagrapheis* realised fairly

---

[60] Dem. 24.42. Diokles also provides for laws to be made in the future after the archonship of Eukleides. For further discussion of this law, see Hansen 1990.

[61] I.e. the work of the *anagrapheis* in their first term; see Ostwald 1986: 522.   [62] Andok. 1.83–4.

[63] As various scholars have noted, e.g. Robertson 1990: 60; P. J. Rhodes 1991: 97, 99; Ostwald 1986: 515–16; Carawan 2002: 21; Volonaki 2001: 157; Gagarin 2008: 183–4; contra: Joyce 2008: 514–16.

[64] For the laws of Solon and Drakon and the work of the *anagrapheis*, see e.g. P. J. Rhodes 1991: 98; Robertson 1990: 63; Todd 1996: 128; Sickinger 1999b: 100.

[65] Andok. 1.82.

quickly that new laws would be needed in addition to the ones destroyed by the Thirty, hence this decree which represents the second part of the process outlined in the scholia on Aischines and in Diokles' law.

The project concerning the laws, consequently, consisted of two parts. The laws destroyed by the Thirty needed to be located, reinscribed and the new *stelai* erected in the annexes of the Stoa Basileios. These documents will certainly have included both sacred and secular matters. Additional laws also needed to be made, perhaps, as Andokides says, because of conflicts created in existing laws by the reconciliation agreement.[66] The actual process of making this new legislation was done by the *nomothetai*, as Teisamenos specified, but they will have needed to work closely with the *anagrapheis* who were probably responsible for overseeing the inscribing of the laws in the Stoa Basileios. Teisamenos' decree seems to envision a very short period of time for the creation of these new laws and Andokides' text implies that the process happened quite quickly. Nikomachos, however, was in office for four years and the speech against him alleges that he actually could have completed his work in thirty days, had he done what he was supposed to do and no more.[67] As in the *anagrapheis'* first term, it appears that the project turned out to be more complicated than it was originally thought. Part of the problem may simply have been the amount of destroyed material which needed to be reinscribed: on our current evidence, it is impossible to know the extent of the destruction and the difficulties in locating the texts in the archives.

PRESENTING THE LAWS

For the project of reinscribing and updating the laws, further evidence is provided by the extant remains both of the sacrificial calendar and of the Stoa Basileios. The details of this material show that the setting of the calendar was radically changed at this time and it was now displayed in a new location inside the stoa. Our evidence, however, does not allow us to estimate the extent of the Thirty's damage. The extant state of fragments 2 and 3 of the calendar can best be explained if they were originally erected in the south annexe and then damaged by the Thirty, but it is impossible to tell whether all the *stelai* in this wing were so treated. Similarly, we do not know if Drakon's law, inscribed on its own stone and erected in front of the stoa, was a victim of their violence. The very worn state of the text, however, suggests that it probably remained standing in front of the stoa and so

---

[66] Andok. 1.82.   [67] Above note 5.

continued to be exposed to the weather (fig. 5).[68] Demophantos' decree is unlikely to have been destroyed by the oligarchs because Andokides describes it as standing in front of the (Old) Bouleuterion.

Of the replacement *stelai*, our only extant fragments belong to the sacrificial calendar. Six fragments are opisthographic and preserve text from both the earlier (Attic) and later (Ionic) versions (table 6: frs. 1, 3, 5, 8, 9, 12; fig. 6), while the backs of three other inscriptions are broken away so that only the later calendar is extant on their front surfaces (table 6: frs. 2, 6, 7; fig. 6). A tenth stone preserves an uninscribed section from below the bottom of the text, as well as the earlier calendar on its reverse (table 6: fr. 4; fig. 6). On fragments 2 and 3, the later calendar is inscribed in erasures and, at the top of the *stelai*, both stones preserve part of the fascia with headings for the two biennial sequences of sacrifices. The remains of a single clamp cutting on the top of each *stele* indicate that, in this phase, these two blocks must have been clamped to their neighbours (fig. 6). That the *stelai* of the calendar stood next to each other is also shown by the anathyrosis on the preserved sides of five fragments (table 6: frs. 1, 2, 3, 5, 8; fig. 6). On fragments 1 and 8, this anathyrosis is unusual because only one band adjacent to side A is preserved.[69] Although two bands are preserved on fragment 3, the anathyrosis, like the clamp cutting, only functions with the later side A.[70] On fragment 5, the band adjacent to face A is considerably wider than its mate and the anathyrosis should have been designed to work with the later side.[71] Consequently, it is only in the second phase when the Ionic calendar was inscribed on side A that the *stelai* with the calendar were clamped together. Further evidence that the inscribed blocks were joined together in this phase is provided by the relationship of the text to the stones. On fragments 2, 3, 5 and 8, the edges of the *stelai* cut through the text in the middle of the lines;[72] the text must have continued on to the adjacent blocks and it ought to have been inscribed once the *stelai* were *in situ*. Where the original surface is preserved on fragments 1, 3, 4 and 9, it has been very carefully smoothed and beautifully polished (table 6). The appearance of this treatment on fragment 3 shows that the smoothing and polishing occurred after the erasure was made and so it must belong with the second phase. The treatment of the worn surfaces of fragments 2, 5 and 8 is consistent with this same treatment (table 6). In this way, the working of

---

[68] For the worn state of the inscription, see Stroud 1968: 1, pls. 1–2.
[69] Above chapter 3 with note 68.   [70] Above chapter 3 with note 69.
[71] Width of band adjacent to side A: 0.036 m.; width of band adjacent to side B: 0.020 m.; Gawlinski 2007: 38 fig. 1. On a normal architectural block, the anathyrosis bands are usually the same width.
[72] Lambert 2002a: 355, 361; Gawlinski 2007: 42.

the inscribed surfaces differs quite noticeably from the first phase when the remains preserve a variety of surface treatments. At this time, accordingly, the *stelai* of the sacrificial calendar were clamped together to form a single unit, the earlier texts on fragments 2 and 3 were erased and the surface of the whole unit was carefully smoothed and highly polished.

This monument is highly unusual: a whole series of *stelai* clamped together to form a great polished surface on which to inscribe an extensive text. There remains the problem of how and where it was erected. Quite clearly, this monument will not fit into the *stelai* slots in either the north or the south annexes of the Stoa Basileios (fig. 7). Those slabs were also opisthographic, but, in its second phase, the calendar will not have been; any surviving texts on the reverse of the *stelai* will have been obsolete, hence the availability of the slabs for re-use. In addition, the annexes were the location of the laws and the replacements for the *stelai* damaged or destroyed by the Thirty will have been erected here. In terms of their erection, we might have expected the entire creation of the clamped *stelai* to be treated as a single huge slab and inserted with lead into a great long rectangular base; such a design would differ from other Athenian inscriptions only in dimensions and scale. The evidence of the fragments, however, shows that they were not set up in this way. Fragment 4 currently preserves a flat bottom worked with a fairly fine claw-toothed chisel (fig. 6); this fragment was evidently not set into a slot in the usual fashion of Attic inscriptions, but it rested on a flat surface in exactly the same way that a statue base does.[73] At the junction with the earlier side B, the edge is worn and rounded, but, on the uninscribed side A, the junction is crisp, sharp and unworn. Exactly the same treatment is found on the bottom of the very small fragment 10 which now only preserves the earlier side B; as on fragment 4, the junction between the bottom and side B is worn and rounded (fig. 6). A close parallel for the working and treatment of the bottom of fragment 10 is provided by the pieces from the bottom of the general Chabrias' statue base which was erected in the Agora in or just after 375.[74] In 403 or a little later, the *stele* now represented by fragment 10 must

---

[73] This side shows very clearly on the photographs on the catalogue card in the Agora Excavations, which I have been allowed to examine through the kindness of K. Clinton who is to publish the fragment.

[74] *SEG* xix 204; see briefly below chapter 9 and Shear 2007a: 110–11. As autopsy of these fragments together shows, there is no reason to believe that the bottom of fragment 10 does not represent the bottom of the inscription in the second phase. Lambert was, therefore, correct to say that this working is not original, i.e. it does not belong to the first phase, but Dow rightly realised that it belonged with the calendar and not to some later use as Lambert seems to imply; Lambert 2002a: 70–1; Dow 1961: 68–9, pl. 9e.

also have been re-used to form part of the great marble slab on which the calendar was inscribed, but this face has not been preserved.

Our evidence suggests the following situation. Either through the tender mercies of the Thirty or through the obsolescence of the earlier text, the *stelai* with the sacrificial calendar, as well as at least two slabs of the laws from the south annexe, were available for re-use in 403. If the text on side A of fragments 2 and 3 had not previously been erased, it was erased now. These blocks together with the calendar *stelai* were cut down to have flat bottoms, as on a statue base,[75] anathyrosis was cut on their vertical sides and the slabs were clamped together to form a great marble sheet. It was smoothed and polished in preparation for receiving the new text and, presumably, a fascia matching those of fragments 2 and 3 was cut across the top of the whole slab. Since side A was the front of the monument, care was lavished on this side as it was not on the unimportant and superseded side B, hence the chipping and wear visible at the junction between side B and the (new) bottoms of fragments 10 and 4. This monument, consequently, was extremely unusual and it did not appear like any other inscription in the city, hence the scholarly perplexities which the remains have created.

DISPLAYING DOCUMENTS IN THE CITY

Reconstructing the physical appearance of the sacrificial calendar in its second phase brings out its unique aspects and helps to locate the structure in the cityscape of Athens. It was erected in the Agora in a novel location, but it was also part of a series of documents which were erected in the square at this time. Not all of our inscriptions, however, were placed in the marketplace and another group was set up on the Akropolis. Where specific documents were erected brings out the different ways in which these two areas were being conceptualised at this time and how the spaces themselves contributed to the responses to the Thirty. The standard form and location of some of these inscriptions also emphasises the unusual character of the sacrificial calendar.

As part of the project of restoring the damaged and/or destroyed laws, at least two of the marble slabs in the south annexe of the Stoa Basileios were replaced and reinscribed; these damaged *stelai*, now represented by fragments 2 and 3, became available for the sacrificial calendar. In its new form, the calendar would also have been erected somewhere in the Agora,

---

[75] Hence on fragment 10, the text now seems to run to the bottom of the block, as Lambert notes; Lambert 2002b: 70–1.

as it had been in its first incarnation in the years after 411. Now, however, it required a very specific setting: it needed to rest on a flat surface like a statue base and it had to be placed so that the obsolete sections at the back were not visible. We might imagine the proper support for the monument as a long stone platform with a tall wall behind it, ideally in the area of the Stoa Basileios, the location of the monumental display of the city's laws. Such a setting is hard to come by in the market square and the only suitable place for the laws is in the stoa itself, as the remains indicate.

The stoa's north wall is particularly well preserved and it reflects the complicated history of the structure. Particularly important for us is its evidence for repairs after a terrible fire which severely damaged this north wall.[76] Subsequently, the heavily calcined surface required extensive restoration; as part of this process, the section immediately adjacent to the top of the back wall's second course was patched with a small stone block and, when the repairs were completed, the whole north wall was covered with stucco.[77] For us, this patch is important because it marks the east edge of the two lowest courses of the back wall, which is now only preserved at the level of the lowest foundations, and it provides the thickness of the wall in the bottom two courses above the floor (0.718 m.).[78] A small stump of the third course of the back wall now projects from the north wall and so the thickness of the third course above the floor is also known (0.535 m.).[79] It shows that there was a difference in thickness of some 0.183 m. between the thicker lower two courses and the narrower third course; there was very clearly a ledge in the back wall of the stoa (fig. 16). Furthermore, the traces of burning on the north wall show that whatever stood on the ledge protected the north wall of the stoa and caused a very clear vertical line of burning on course 3 of the north wall. Where the north wall was protected, the original finish of the wall is still visible: whatever stood on the ledge was clearly uninflammable and solid.[80] The ledge's width of 0.183 m. is slightly wider than fragment 2 of the calendar, the thickest piece with a preserved thickness of 0.144 m. (table 6; fig. 6). This ledge provides a suitable location for the sacrificial calendar which could stand on its flat base on the ledge and the back, now necessarily uneven, would not have been

---

[76] On the fire, see also Shear, Jr 1971: 252.   [77] On the repairs, see also Shear, Jr 1971: 252.

[78] This block is clearly visible in Shear, Jr 1971: pls. 48a, b.

[79] For this block, see the very clear photographs of Shear, Jr 1971: pls. 48a, b.

[80] Compare on the basis of the excavator's notes, Fingarette 1971: 335 note 22. Any suggestion that wooden boards or *sanides* with temporary texts of the laws stood here is, therefore, impossible; Kuhn 1985: 216–18. Similarly, the laws cannot have been written up on plaster on the back wall of the stoa; Ostwald 1986: 519; P. J. Rhodes 1981: 134–5.

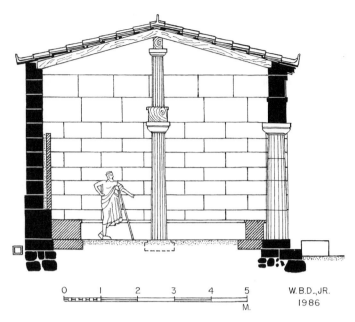

Figure 16   Restored section of the Stoa Basileios. Note the ledge in the back
wall of the building.

visible. This indoor setting also explains why the well-preserved fragments
are in such good condition: inside the stoa, they were protected from the
weather, unlike most *stelai* which were erected out of doors. In 399, at
the end of the project of recollecting and restoring the laws, accordingly,
the little Stoa Basileios contained vast amounts of inscribed text: great *stelai*
with the texts of the laws stood once again between the columns of the
two annexes, while the sacrificial calendar now covered the back wall of the
building.

The laws were not the only documents erected in the Agora at this time.
The great inscription honouring the Athenians returning from Phyle was
also located in the square. When Aischines comes to describe the monu-
ment in 330 BC, he places it 'at the Metroon beside the Bouleuterion'.[81]
The building which he and his listeners knew as the Metroon is the Old
Bouleuterion, the focus of so much activity in the years after 411; here, too,

---

[81] Aischin. 3.187: ἐν . . . τῷ Μετρώῳ [παρὰ τὸ βουλευτήριον]. Since the manuscripts' texts make
perfect sense, it is not clear why we should follow Bake and delete παρὰ τὸ βουλευτήριον; see
Wycherley 1957: no. 466.

were found the published fragments of the document (fig. 2).[82] Setting
up inscriptions at the Old Bouleuterion and in the Stoa Basileios in
the years after 404/3 maintained the democrats' particular focus on these
two areas because the rest of the Agora remained without inscribed texts
(table 9). This epigraphical activity suggests that we should locate two
further documents in these two areas. The *stelai* recording the sale of the
property of the Thirty and their supporters were probably set up in the
Bouleuterion complex; the inscriptions produced by the fourth-century
poletai, the sellers of state contracts, seem to have been erected in front of
the new council house and this court may also have been the location for
the inscriptions concerning the Thirty's property.[83] Equally, they would not
have been out of place in front of the earlier council house. Theozotides'
decree very probably was set up in front of the Stoa Basileios, hence the
discovery of the great *stele* re-used as a cover-slab for the Great Drain not
far away (fig. 2).[84] In 394/3, inscriptions began to be set up in a third area
of the Agora in front of the Stoa of Zeus (table 9). Euagoras' inscription
preserves a fragmentary publication clause specifying that the document is
to be set up next to the *agalma* or statue of a divinity, almost certainly the
statue of Zeus in front of his stoa where the statue of Euagoras was also
erected (fig. 2).[85] Konon's figure was also set up here and it seems likely
that his inscription was located next to the statue.[86]

During the ten or so years after the return of the *demos*, other inscriptions
were set up not in the Agora, but on the Akropolis, the city's regular place
for documents of all kinds;[87] the rest of our documents seem to have
been located here. The fragments of the honours for the non-Athenians
returning from Phyle were found scattered as far away as Aigina and
Peiraieus, but the fragment with the beginning of the decree was discovered
on the Akropolis;[88] since it is easier for fragments to travel down from the
Akropolis rather than up to it, the other pieces presumably were dispersed
from there. The decrees for the Samians also belong on the Akropolis,

---

[82] Raubitschek 1941a: 287.
[83] *SEG* xxxii 161; Lalonde, Langdon and Walbank 1991: 66–7, 74; Shear 2007a: 99. Among other
tasks, the *poletai* were responsible for the sale of confiscated property; for their duties in the fourth
century, see Arist. *Ath. Pol.* 47.2–3; see more generally Lalonde, Langdon and Walbank 1991: 57–65.
[84] *SEG* xxviii 46; Stroud 1971: 280; Shear 2007a: 99.
[85] RO 11.20–1; Lewis and Stroud 1979: 191–3; Shear 2007a: 99, 107; contra: Lawton 1995: 122, no. 84.
Euagoras' statue: Isok. 9.56–7; Paus. 1.3.2–3; see also below chapter 9.
[86] Shear 2007a: 99, 107; cf. Wycherley 1957: 213, no. 261; Konon's statue: Dem. 20.69–70; see also
below chapter 9.
[87] Akropolis and inscriptions: Liddel 2003: 79–81.
[88] M. J. Osborne 1981–2: 1, 37–8; Rhodes and Osborne 2003: 20; Hereward 1952: 102; commentary on
IG ii² 10.

as the publication clause of the original decree specifies; the amendment to Poses' decree calls for all the documents to be published together on one *stele*.[89] Of the various reinscribed decrees, two preserve enough of the publication clause to be sure that they were erected on the Akropolis and a third can be easily restored with this location.[90] A fourth was found in Athena's sanctuary, where it was presumably set up.[91] Although the small fragment of the fifth inscription was found in the Agora, it probably rolled down off the hill; we should imagine that it, too, was originally erected on the Akropolis.[92] Consequently, by the late 390s, documents representing the Athenians' responses to the Thirty had been set up both in Athena's sanctuary and in the Agora, contested sites which they helped to recover for the *demos*. They were also instrumental in finishing the process of turning the square into the space of the citizen.

DOCUMENTS, DEMOCRACY AND THE CITY

Faced in 403 with many of the same general issues which had existed after the events of 411, the *demos* chose to continue the strategies which had successfully used inscriptions to display democracy and its control of the city. In responding to the Thirty, consequently, the inscribed texts and their nature as monuments again played important roles. With these different texts, the *demos* showed the importance of its rule and its status as the only proper *politeia* for the city. We see also a continued emphasis on displaying the functioning of the system in permanent monumental form which was activated by reading. Again, these documents helped to recover the city's past from the oligarchs for the benefit of the *demos* and to inscribe its control on the city's topography so that it visibly laid claim to areas which the Thirty had sought to make their own. While the overall strategies develop from the response to the events of 411, the specific ways in which they were implemented do not. The details of these texts reflected the current situation in Athens after the Thirty and their differences from the earlier documents particularly affected how the importance of democracy and its workings were displayed. In these ways, the inscriptions once again played a significant role in helping to remake the democratic city. They also complemented the dynamics of the new buildings and monuments, as we shall see in more detail in the following chapter.

---

[89] *IG* I³ 127.38–9 and RO 2.66–8.
[90] *IG* I³ 229.4–6; *IG* II² 13 + addenda p. 655 + *SEG* XL 54.8–11; 52.5–7.
[91] Commentary on *IG* II² 6.   [92] Woodhead 1997: 52 and cf. his comments on 3.

The three decrees connected with the return from Phyle bring out the new ways in which these strategies were applied. Their specific focus on the *demos* and its rule mark it as important for the city. In Theozotides' document, the opening lines of the decree proper signal the text's concern with the phrase 'as many of the Athenian[s] as, [co]mi[ng] to the aid of the democracy, d[ie]d a [v]iolent death in the oligarchy'.[93] It sets democracy clearly in opposition to oligarchy and it emphasises the importance of supporting the rule of the *demos*: in the next few lines, the sons will be honoured because of the fathers' good deeds. The rewards recorded here have been caused by the fathers' positive relationship with the *demos* and particularly their role in making its rule possible again. The *demos* is similarly the focus in the honours for the Athenians returning from Phyle. In the heading at the top of the block, the second line very probably began τὸν δῆμον, the *demos*, and the location of the word together with the larger letters of the heading would have emphasised its importance.[94] Below the lists of names, the epigram specifies clearly that the *demos* has voted the crowns for the honorands.[95] The importance of this body is further emphasised by its position at the beginning of the second line of the poem, while the slightly larger letters and the empty space above, below and on both sides of the epigram draw attention to it (fig. 14).[96] Designed in this way, the emphasis on the *demos* was easily apparent and could not be missed. As in Theozotides' decree, the *demos* is opposed with 'those ruling the city with unjust statutes', a group which the honorands first started to depose at their own peril. The *demos* is associated with justice, the proper rule of the city, while its opponents are not.[97] Very probably these same issues were originally brought out in more prosaic terms in the now lost decree. The list of names arranged in tribal order with demotics further stresses the importance of the democracy which is closely associated with these specific terms; in Theozotides' decree, the lists of names with patronymics and demotics serves the same function. Similar dynamics are also at work in the honours for the foreigners returning from Phyle. The larger heading above the main text gave the name of the secretary and the archon, officials integral to the proper functioning of the democracy; in the decree itself, this aspect is picked up with the specification that the

---

[93] *SEG* xxviii 46.4–6.
[94] Raubitschek 1941a: 289 fig. 1. In the heading, the nu is 0.023 m. tall, while the letters in the column below have a height of 0.011 m.
[95] *SEG* xxviii 45.73–6 with Aischin. 3.190.
[96] Raubitschek 1941a: 289 fig. 1, 290. Letter height of epigram: 0.0135 m.; contrast letter height of decree: 0.009 m.; of names: 0.011 m.
[97] Compare Hobden 2007: 160–5, who stresses the connection between democracy and the law.

first class of honorands are to be distributed among the tribes and, in the lists of names, by the tribal headings.[98] The *demos* itself is mentioned in connection with the foreigners who remained with it in the Peiraieus both in the text of the decree itself and in the heading above the third class of honorands on the back of the *stele*.[99] Since these men have helped to make democracy possible once again, their actions further bring out the importance of the *demos*.

In these texts, as in the inscriptions set up after 411, their form as decrees of the *boule* and the *demos* focuses attention on the rule of the *demos* which is shown to be functioning properly with all the necessary officials involved. The prescript of Theozotides' decree, for example, stresses the text's status as the product of the city under the rule of the *demos* and of Athenian citizens who, by voting, used their democratic power in the council and the assembly to decide on the best course for the city. These dynamics are also at work in the proxeny decrees and the inscription for the Samians. When the decree is preceded by a heading giving in larger letters the name of the secretary, as in the case of the Samians, or the secretary and archon, as in the case of the rewards for the foreigners from Phyle, the effect is intensified by the repetition, while the size of the heading makes it impossible to miss the document's status as the product of the democracy.[100] This treatment also brings out the special care devoted to inscribing these documents and their politics of display. In the case of the Samians, the third and fourth lines of the heading specify that it was for the Samians 'who were with the *demos* of the Athenians', a usage which gives particular prominence to the *demos*. This phrase recalls the foreigners who remained with the people in Peiraieus in the honours for the foreigners from Phyle. In the context of 403/2, the heading initially might suggest that the Samians really had a part in overthrowing the Thirty, even though the actual texts of the decrees make it clear that they aided and supported the Athenians in a different context. Later in the original decree, the specification that the Samians are to be assigned to demes and tribes, the constituent parts of the democracy, further reinforces the emphasis on the rule of the *demos*.[101]

The documents recording the sales of the property of the Thirty and their associates also focus on democracy. In them, an opposition is set up between the oligarchs and the *demos*: the property of the former is being sold, while the *demos*, through the *poletai*, is doing the selling. This situation shows

[98] RO 4.6, col. 5.45, col. 6.58, col. 7.10. For a photograph of the top front of the *stele*, see M. J. Osborne 1999: pl. 4 (and note that the captions for pls. 3 and 4 are reversed).
[99] RO 4.8, col. 6.56–7.   [100] *IG* I³ 127.1–2; Rhodes and Osborne 2003: pl. 1; RO 4.1–2.
[101] *IG* I³ 127.34.

the power of the democracy: not only can it seize and sell the property of these undesirable individuals, but it has also done so. At the top of the first *stele*, the authorising text mentions such markers of the *demos'* rule as the archon, the secretary and the tribe in prytany.[102] They serve to focus on the democratic process at work here and they bring out the importance of the people because the text, the *stelai* and the actions recorded here are the products of the Athenians' exercising their democratic power. These dynamics find a close parallel in the re-erected proxeny decrees: destroyed 'in the time of the Thirty', they are now reinscribed and set up again by the secretary of the *boule* at the orders of the council, that characteristic body of the democratic city.[103] The importance of the rule of the *demos* in both groups of documents is made very clear.

These inscriptions also bring out the ways in which the rule of the *demos* is the proper *politeia* for the city. This dynamic is particularly clear in the inscription for the Athenians returning from Phyle and in Theozotides' decree because the two texts set up an explicit opposition between the democracy and the oligarchy of the Thirty. The oligarchy, which had to be overthrown by violence and is marked as an inappropriate form of government, contrasts with the democracy, which passed the decrees and is the proper sort of rule for the city. In the honours for the foreigners, these dynamics are less explicit and the text emphasises to a greater degree than the other two inscriptions the process which led to the current rule of *demos*. The violence necessary is brought out by the verb to join in the fighting with (συνεμάχησαν), while the juxtaposition between the events narrated and the honours subsequently awarded by the *demos* and *boule* brings out the happy outcome: the return of the democrats. This positive result is further emphasised by the description of the first group of honorands who 'joined in returning' from Phyle. The extension of citizenship, that is the benefits of democracy, to these honorands also stresses the positive results of their actions because they are the gift of the restored *demos*. In this context, the reference to the return reinforces the stress on the rule of the *demos* as the proper form of government for the city.

In the immediate aftermath of the Thirty's rule, the identification of democracy as the correct *politeia* for Athens should also have been brought out by the re-erection of documents destroyed by the Thirty. In the proxeny decrees, the texts explain that the current *stele* is a replacement for one

---

[102] *SEG* XXXII 161 *stele* I.1–5.

[103] These dynamics appear mostly clearly in *IG* II² 6, the only complete decree in the group; cf. also *IG* II² 13 + addenda p. 655 + *SEG* XL 54; 52. In the last inscription, agency is directly assigned to the Thirty.

destroyed by the Thirty. Since that earlier inscription was the product of the *boule* and the *demos*,[104] the new *stele* connects the present rule of the *demos* with its earlier period of power and it denies the Thirty any legitimacy as the city's rulers. Consequently, democracy is presented as the only possible system of rule. The destruction and subsequent replacement of the laws also functioned to create a similar situation in the years immediately after 404/3. That the inscribed *stelai* in the annexes of the Stoa Basileios were reinscribed and re-erected testified powerfully not only to democracy's power, but to its status as the only appropriate *politeia*. They marked a concentrated effort to return to the situation before the Thirty's rule when the rule of the *demos* had been clearly identified as the only proper sort of rule. If these reinscribed laws or the sacrificial calendar were preceded by authorising decrees parallel to the one empowering the republication of Drakon's law, then they will further have emphasised the role and authority of the *demos*, now publishing the documents which gave it power. As in the period after 411, the reinscribed laws as a group presented clearly the legislation currently in force in the city, but now they also contrasted with the 'unjust statutes' marking the rule of the Thirty, as described in the epigram for the Athenians returning from Phyle. In the present situation, the laws not only made the rule of the *demos*, the current system, possible, but they also emphasised that other forms of government, such as oligarchy, were not possible; they further reinforced the dynamics at work in the various inscriptions concerning honours in connection with Phyle. The identification of the laws of Solon and Drakon in Teisamenos' decree as *kata ta patria* will also have reiterated democracy's status as the *politeia* historically appropriate for Athens, as will the process of locating the texts of the damaged laws. Since this process was both the replacement and, in some sense, the continuation of the earlier project of the laws, these activities will have linked the new documents with the earlier ones and their emphasis in the period between 410 and 404 that democracy was the only appropriate political system for the city.

The roles of these documents were not limited to bringing out the importance of the rule of the *demos* and its status as the historically correct *politeia* because, in their inscribed monumental form, they also served to display it in very much the same ways as the inscriptions did in the period after 411. Like them, the documents erected after the Thirty functioned as monuments to the democratic process itself and they made it permanently visible in the city. Displayed in this way, the prescripts of the decrees

---

[104] Seen most clearly in *IG* i³ 229 which preserves the beginning of the earlier decree.

showed off the proper functioning of the political process, which was now memorialised along with the texts themselves. The contents of these documents further served to show the *demos* in action. This dynamic is particularly clear with the sales of the property of the Thirty because these inscriptions record the *demos*' decision to seize and sell the oligarchs' property. In this way, the *stelai* served to commemorate not only the decision and the process of taking it, but also the sales themselves, transitory activities which would have been forgotten soon after they were finished. Instead, the *demos* is perpetually shown punishing its opponents. In the case of the various honours connected with Phyle and the honours for Konon and Euagoras, the inscriptions show in perpetuity the *demos*' gratitude and its response to these men's actions. These documents also bring out what the *demos* will do: it will award the honorands the specific rewards listed in the texts. This focus on the people's future actions is even clearer in the sacrificial calendar because this document records precisely and in exactly what ways the Athenians will sacrifice to the gods.

This stress on display is even more overt in the cases of documents like the honours for the Samians and *IG* I³ 229 when the new decree actually contains earlier documents produced by the *boule* and the *demos*. The repetition of the earlier material testified to the proper functioning of the democratic city, which made the necessary documents available for republication, while the inscribed text memorialises and displays the ability of the *demos* to do so. The earlier texts in the newly reinscribed laws will also have performed a similar function. These laws and proxeny decrees further served to display the *demos* and its actions because, without the necessary legislation, the reinscription would not have taken place, as the proxeny decrees clearly testify.[105] The inscriptions also show the *demos* perpetually recovering the city from the oligarchs and making it democratic once again. As in the period after 411, the very process of relocating and reinscribing the laws will have presented the democracy in action and, when these inscriptions were erected, their monumental form will have shown the *demos* as perpetually active.

As with the *stelai* set up after 411, reading the inscribed documents activated the democratic procedures and made the individual repeat the very process which brought them into being, yet another display of democracy. In the case of the honours for Euagoras, the reader spoke aloud again the herald's announcement at the Dionysia and, as it were, represented the

---

[105] *IG* II² 6 and 13 + addenda p. 655 + *SEG* XL 54 show these dynamics most clearly. The necessary legislation for the laws is represented in part by the decree of Teisamenos.

honours.[106] With the other honours, reading the text served to repeat the process by which the honours were originally conferred so that it was taking place continually. This dynamic not only showed the democracy forever in action, but it also served to honour the recipients perpetually. In the case of the sales documents, reading the text served to repeat both the process of the auction and the subsequent writing up of the accounts. In this way, the *demos* was shown to be continually selling the property of their opponents, the Thirty and their oligarchic associates. As we have already seen, reading, which involves one person, cannot be an exact reperformance of events which require many men such as participating in the *ekklesia* or auctions and swearing oaths. Nevertheless, even reading the texts imperfectly did continue to activate them and to display perpetually the democratic processes which had brought them into being.

The locations in which these inscriptions were erected also helped to show off the *demos* and its activities. In decrees, as we saw with the inscriptions responding to 411, the publication clauses recorded the approval of the *boule* and the *demos* for the settings in which the inscriptions were placed, the culmination of the entire democratic process. In these approved settings, the texts then interacted with the surrounding monuments. These dynamics are particularly important in the Agora where *stelai* were erected only in certain locations: at first, just at the Bouleuterion and the Stoa Basileios, but, later, also in front of the Stoa of Zeus (table 9; fig. 2). The decision to place the honours for the Athenians returning from Phyle and the sales documents in the Bouleuterion complex significantly brought these texts into relationship not only with the *bouleutai*, but also with Demophantos' decree with its specifications about how the Athenians were (and were not) to behave: the good Athenian is to oppose tyranny and oligarchy and to be rewarded accordingly, while the bad Athenian overthrows democracy and becomes a *polemios* of the city (fig. 9). These two formulations describe exactly the behaviour of the exiled democrats and of the Thirty and their supporters respectively. The treatment of the Thirty matched particularly closely Demophantos' prescriptions: their property was sold and a tenth given to the goddess. The Athenians were not killed and consequently did not merit the Tyrannicides' rewards, but, nevertheless, they were commended for their exemplary conduct. In this context, they were shown to have behaved as good democrats and their honorary inscription provided the *bouleutai* with another model on which to base their conduct. That this inscription was so interpreted is made clear by

---

[106] RO 11.14–17.

Aischines who uses it in 330 as a positive foil for Ktesiphon's bad decree, in his view, in honour of Demosthenes.[107] Meanwhile, in the Bouleuterion complex, the sales documents served as a warning about the consequences of bad conduct and their relationship with Demophantos' decree also functioned to justify the *demos'* confiscation of the property. Erecting these inscriptions near the council house reinforced the documents' stress on the importance of democracy. They also allowed the *demos* to reclaim the New Bouleuterion which the Thirty had used as the centre of their power and, by erasing the oligarchs' presence, to mark it once again as democratic space.

To the north, in the Stoa Basileios, the new installation of the sacrificial calendar made the city's laws omnipresent: in this building, it was not possible to escape from their presence as the documents which made the rule of the *demos* possible (fig. 7). The new setting for the calendar emphasised the *basileus'* role as the magistrate responsible for the ancestral sacrifices. Close perusal of the contents would have revealed that most of these offerings were not at all new, despite the claims made against Nikomachos: the activities of the old Solonian tribe Geleontes and trittys Leukotainioi at the Synoikia and of the tribe-kings (*phulobasileis*) at the Genesia were certainly not recent innovations.[108] Set up on the ledge along the back wall of the stoa, the calendar provided the backdrop for impiety trials, such as that of Sokrates, which now took place literally in its presence. There could be no escaping proper religious obligations clearly spelled out in the new inscription. These dynamics perhaps suggested to Plato that it was appropriate to bring the city's laws on stage in his dialogue *Crito*;[109] certainly, their behaviour in that text suggests the power of the display in the stoa. Anyone looking into the building would have gazed directly at the new calendar and its new, very intimate relationship with the *basileus* would have been immediately displayed.

Meanwhile, the *stele* with Theozotides' decree, very probably located here, ought to have interacted with this setting in quite a different way. If the inscription with Drakon's law also concerned voluntary homicides, then it would have formed a point of reference for the decree immediately in front of the stoa. More importantly, this location also linked Theozotides' document to the neighbouring Stoa Poikile where the Athenians had been commemorating the city's military victories against the Persians and the

---

[107] Aischin. 3.187–8.
[108] Synoikia: *SEG* LII 48 fr. 3A.31–58; Genesia: *SEG* LII 48 fr. 1A.6–22. For another occasion involving the *phulobasileis*, see *SEG* LII 48 fr. 7A.1–4.
[109] Pl. *Cri.* 50a6–54d1.

Spartans since the 450s (fig. 2).[110] Unlike the return from Phyle, those successes were achieved by the Athenians as a corporate group and they were so presented in the memorials which did not single out any particular individual.[111] The men honoured in Theozotides' decree were certainly the 'right' part of the Athenians: as the text says, they died a violent death helping the democracy against the oligarchy; they were, however, only a part of the city. The juxtaposition of the two monuments emphasised that the oligarchs were external enemies (*polemioi*) of the city and not Athenians.[112] In this setting, the dead Athenians were also equated with the war-dead, just as their sons were assimilated to the war-orphans in the text; their burial in the Demosion Sema will have reinforced the association.[113] These rewards, however, are not the Tyrannicides' benefits, as specified in Demophantos' decree. Setting up Theozotides' document in front of the Bouleuterion would have brought out the absence of the appropriate reward. In contrast, the location by the Stoa Basileios brought the Stoa Poikile and its memorialising functions into play and it obscured the difference between the reward prescribed and the one actually awarded. Since the victories commemorated in the Stoa Poikile were won by the democratic city, this setting also reinforced the emphasis on democracy in Theozotides' text.

If the inscriptions for Phyle in the Agora celebrated the achievements of a part of the Athenians, then the decrees for Konon and Euagoras carried the process one step further because they honoured individual men for their deeds against external enemies on behalf of the democratic city, a dynamic which we shall discuss further in the following chapter in connection with their statues. Set up in front of the Stoa of Zeus Eleutherios and near the statue of Zeus Soter, the inscriptions worked together with their setting to suggest that the two men had brought freedom to the democratic city, like the Athenians returning from Phyle, and that they were her saviours (fig. 2). The text of Konon's inscription reinforced this connection because it stated that he had freed the allies of Athens.[114] This context indicated that these men were deservedly rewarded by the city which had been kept democratic by their actions.

[110] Paus. 1.15.1–4; *IG* I³ 522. On the connections between the stoa and the Persian Wars, see Castriota 1992: 76–89, 127–33. On the date of the battle of Oinoe, see below chapter 11, note 7.
[111] Shear 2007a: 105–6. The same dynamics are at work in the earlier Eion herms; see Aischin. 3.183–5; Plut. *Kim.* 7.4–8.1.
[112] Compare Aischines' description of victory memorials: he passes from the Eion Hermes to the Marathon painting in the Stoa Poikile to the Phyle monument in front of the Bouleuterion; Aischin. 3.183–91.
[113] Lys. 2.64, 66; Loraux 1986: 35–6, 200.   [114] Dem. 20.69.

The erection of these decrees in the Agora also served to maintain the area's focus on the citizen of the democratic city, a development which began with the response to the Four Hundred. The citizen status of the individuals rewarded in the Phyle honours and Theozotides' decree is made clear by the names with their demotics and their tribes and the dead fathers are specifically described as Athenians. The Thirty and their followers were also citizens, as was Konon. Euagoras, although the king of Cypriot Salamis, had been awarded Athenian citizenship some years before, perhaps early in 407;[115] in this setting, he was identified as an Athenian, not a foreigner. Ensuring that the city's laws were properly carried out was the responsibility of citizens, not metics or foreigners, and so also the proper punishment of her enemies, in these cases the oligarchs and Spartans. That these documents were the products of citizens reinforced this focus on Athenians and their activities and complemented the stress on democracy in the texts. As monuments, they celebrated the rule of the *demos* and they allowed the democrats to write their control quite literally on the city. In this way, they helped to take back for the *demos* a space which the Thirty had tried to claim for oligarchy. Re-erecting the laws will have been a particularly important part of this process, especially when readers and viewers were still aware that the damaged *stelai* had been recycled for the new version of the calendar.

The inscriptions in the Agora with their focus on citizens contrast with the texts set up on the Akropolis. The documents in Athena's sanctuary focused on non-Athenians, whose honours were very much at home in this setting.[116] On the Akropolis, the stress on democracy emphasised the *demos'* power and its control of the city. Inscribed on stone *stelai*, the texts also displayed the authority of the democracy. Through this medium, the *demos* was able to demonstrate graphically its claim to Athena's sanctuary, the other area of the city which the Thirty had made into contested space. Here, the importance of these documents lay in their ability to help to reintegrate the precinct into the democratic city. In contrast, the inscriptions in the Agora had further tasks to perform: in addition to displaying the control of the *demos*, they also played a significant role in finishing the process of turning the Agora into space for the democratic citizen. In this context, they visibly displayed the democratic processes against the city's fabric so that they could continue indefinitely. The repetition of the same themes

---

[115] *IG* I³ 113 = M. J. Osborne 1981–2: D3; Isok. 9.54; for the date of the inscription, see M. J. Osborne 1981–2: II, 22–4.
[116] Shear 2007a: 99–100; cf. Liddel 2003: 79–80.

and issues in the inscriptions in the Agora and on the Akropolis united these two parts of the responses to the Thirty and they linked the two spaces. Now, both areas were equally important in a city which the inscriptions clearly showed to be democratic again.

THE *DEMOS* AND THE PAST

Set up in the Agora and in Athena's sanctuary, these decrees and the laws played an important role in the *demos'* display of its power and its control of the city and so in the ways in which Athens was remade, once again, into the democratic city. These documents also continued the earlier strategy of reclaiming the city's past which the *demos* now needed to take back from the Thirty. As in the years after 411, this process entailed recovering the iconic figures of Drakon, Solon and Kleisthenes once again for democracy, but now it also linked the present with the more recent past: the responses to the Four Hundred and the Five Thousand. In this way, the current actions of the *demos* were brought into the context of the past.

In this process, the reinscription and re-erection of the laws played an important role. Since the laws of Drakon and Solon had been destroyed by the Thirty, setting them up again allowed the democrats to show that these two men were part of their past and not the oligarchic past. These actions also linked the *demos* with its earlier project of collecting and displaying the laws in the period between 410 and 404. As long as the re-use of the damaged earlier *stelai* was common knowledge, the connections between the two phases will have been especially clear. In these ways, the new work was shown to be an extension of the *demos'* past actions. In the sacrificial calendar, the rubrics specifying the different sources of authority for the entries also served to link the present with the city's various pasts.[117] In at least one, if not two, instances, the heading specifies that the material came 'from the *stelai*'.[118] We do not know what exactly these *stelai* were, but the sacrifices were certainly established more recently and not included in the *kurbeis*; as such, they connected the city with the more recent, and inevitably democratic, past. The references to the tribe Geleontes and the trittys Leukotainioi in connection with the Synoikia and the involvement of the tribe-kings (*phulobasileis*) on at least two other occasions specifically

---

[117] Source rubrics: Lambert 2002a: 356–7; Dow 1953–7: 15–21.
[118] *SEG* LII 48 frs. 3A.77 and possibly 2A.8. On the restoration, see Lambert 2002a: 357, 378; P. J. Rhodes 1991: 94 note 40, 95; Dow 1953–7: 16, 19–20; contra: Robertson 1990: 70; Nelson 2006: 311. We may wonder if these *stelai* are not, in fact, the earlier version of the calendar from the period 410–404.

linked the present with the Solonian past. Setting the calendar up on the ledge in the back wall of the Stoa Basileios brought it into a structure originally built when the Kleisthenic democracy was instituted; in this way, Kleisthenes, too, was recovered for the democratic city.

Using many of the same strategies as the documents erected after 411, the laws served to recover a series of different pasts, but the various decrees focused more closely on the recent past. This strategy is particularly clear in the *stele* with the decrees for the Samians. Here, the repetition of the prescripts emphasises both the similarities of their form and their source as documents of the *boule* and the *demos*. This connection is reinforced by the second decree's explicit reference to the first one and the repetition of this information in the amendment for both this decree and the third one for Poses;[119] in all three instances, the passages state specifically that the earlier decree shall still be valid. Whatever circumstances caused the first decree not to be inscribed are carefully obscured and we are given no sense that the regime of the Thirty intervened between the first decree of 405/4 and the second and third decrees of 403/2. It is as if the *demos* had controlled the city for the whole time and so the two periods are directly linked. In the decree *IG* I³ 229, repeating the earlier document has a similar effect. The new text, however, also makes the circumstances of the destruction of the original text explicit: it was taken down 'in the time of the Thirty'. In this case, there is also a sense that history is being undone,[120] that the actions of the Thirty, while not forgotten, need to be reversed if the city is to be democratic. In the other proxeny decrees, this dynamic is particularly strong when the inscription to be replaced recorded the honorand's own proxeny rather than that of another relative.[121] In contrast, the proxeny of another relative brings out more strongly the links with the earlier actions of the Athenian *demos*.[122]

In the Agora, the inscriptions used a different strategy so that the present is connected to the recent past by the interactions between the monuments and their settings (fig. 2). In the case of the honours for the Athenians from Phyle and the sales documents, the two texts work closely together with Demophantos' decree, as we saw earlier. The effect is to connect together the two responses to oligarchy. Similarly, the interaction between Theozotides' decree and the nearby Stoa Poikile also served to link the new document to the Athenian past represented in the building. Since that monument commemorated both the recent past, e.g. Marathon and

---

[119] RO 2.43–4, 52–4, 66.   [120] Compare Wolpert 2002a: 88; Culasso Gastaldi 2003: 245, 262.
[121] See *IG* II² 6.   [122] E.g. *IG* II² 52; *Agora* XVI 37; cf. *IG* II² 13 + addenda p. 655 + *SEG* XL 54.

Sphakteria, and the deep past, i.e. Troy and Theseus and the Amazons, both periods were recovered for the *demos* through this relationship. Similarly, the decrees for Konon and Euagoras associated these documents with the earlier Stoa of Zeus and his statue. As we shall see in the following chapter, the statues of the two men formed an important part of these dynamics and set up further associations in the square and with the *demos'* past.

The documents and the laws, consequently, played an important role in recovering the city's previous history for the democracy and in demonstrating that there was, indeed, an appropriate history for democratic Athens. As with the response to the events of 411, recovering Drakon, Solon and Kleisthenes showed that these significant figures were part of the democratic city's past and they provided the *demos* with names for conjuring. There is also a very strong trend to making connections with more recent events and, particularly, with the responses to the earlier oligarchs. The effect is either to de-emphasise, if not to ignore, the Thirty, as with the decree for the Samians and the Agora decrees, or to undo the events of the immediate past, as with the proxeny decrees and, more generally, with the replacements for the destroyed laws. The result is a more nuanced engagement with recent events which contrasts with the strategy used after 411 when the oligarchs were ignored and their presence erased.

DEMOCRATS, OLIGARCHS AND THE ATHENIANS

In their settings in the Agora and on the Akropolis, the inscribed laws and the various different decrees began the process of remaking Athens as the democratic city and served to display the importance of the rule of the *demos*, the historically proper *politeia* for the Athenians. They also allowed the *demos* to recover the past for its own uses and they placed the *demos'* response to the Thirty in the context of its responses to the Four Hundred and the Five Thousand. In their physical form as marble *stelai*, these texts memorialised the very functioning of this political system. Reading and rereading the documents activated them so that the processes of democracy were shown to be continuously taking place in the present. As instantiations of the rule of the *demos*, the inscriptions also wrote its control on to the cityscape, now shown to be properly democratic, and they linked together the city's two most important memorial spaces, the Akropolis and the Agora.

The strategies of these documents and their location in the city also had further consequences because they recreated the image of the Athenians. As we saw earlier, Theozotides' decree explicitly places democracy and oligarchy in opposition to each other; in the sales documents the opposition is between the *demos* and the Thirty, while the rewards for the Athenians from Phyle contrast the democratic Athenians and those ruling with 'unjust statutes'. For the first time, oligarchy, not tyranny, is the focus of attention and, however imperfectly, that emphasis was displayed in monumental form. These decisions contrast significantly with the strategy of Demophantos' decree and its emphasis, through the invocation of Harmodios and Aristogeiton, on the opposition between democracy and tyranny. This new opposition also created a shift in what it meant to be Athenian: the good Athenian was still a democrat, but now he fought oligarchs in aid of the democracy. In the process, he certainly hazarded his life and he might die violently. As the inscriptions' placement in the Agora shows, Demophantos' decree was, not so much irrelevant, as in need of updating: the decree for the Athenians from Phyle and the sales document also functioned as tangible examples of the good and bad citizen as Demophantos had defined them. This new vision of what it meant to be Athenian was, in the aftermath of the Thirty, extremely partisan: only those fighting against the oligarchy were good citizens. It must have offered very cold comfort indeed to the men of the city. Despite the reconciliation agreement, recovering from the Thirty was no easy task.

Nor was working out what it meant to be Athenian a simple matter. These documents belong to a larger context where Athenian status was under both threat and redefinition.[123] The courts with their parade of good democrats, closet oligarchs and partisans of the Thirty provided one venue for this negotiation, as we saw in the previous chapter. The political sphere created another arena for this process. Soon after the reconciliation agreement was sworn, a certain Phormisios, who had fought for the *demos* at Peiraieus, proposed that Athenian citizenship should be limited to those possessing land and that the exiles, presumably the Thirty and their supporters in Eleusis, should be allowed to return; reportedly about 5,000 Athenians would have lost their citizenship.[124] Evidently not everyone was in favour of full democracy, but the proposal was unsuccessful. External politics in the form of the trial (and acquittal) of King Pausanias of Sparta were probably also at work here, hence the references to Spartan approval.[125] Thrasyboulos' attempt to grant citizenship to everyone who joined in the

[123] Ostwald 1986: 503–9; Krentz 1982: 109–13.
[124] Dion. Hal. *Lys.* 32. This proposal generated Lysias 34. Phormisios and Peiraieus: Lys. 34.2; Strauss 1987: 99.
[125] Spartan approval: Lys. 34.6; Dion. Hal. *Lys.* 32. Connection with Pausanias' trial: Todd 2000: 337–8; Todd 1985: 191–5.

return from the Peiraieus also failed: although it was approved by the *demos*, Archinos attacked the decree with a *graphe paranomon* on the grounds that it had not first been presented to the *boule*;[126] only later in 401/0 were some of these men honoured in the inscription set up on the Akropolis. In 403/2, Perikles' law on citizenship was also reintroduced. While the initial proposal seems to have made it retroactive, a further decree made it apply only from the archonship of Eukleides: men born before this year were exempt.[127] Similarly, only the legitimate sons of Athenians killed fighting the Thirty were eligible for reward in Theozotides' decree. Not everyone could be Athenian, even if they had helped to overthrow the Thirty, and the extension of this coveted status was to be limited to selected individuals. In terms of the image presented in the Agora, this aspect was brought out by the location: the documents in the Agora concerned only citizens, not all inhabitants in the city. These honorands had died a violent death aiding the democracy. In contrast, the foreigners on the Akropolis either joined in or remained with the *demos*, a less impressive achievement, but one still worthy of honours from the democratic city. More, however, was expected of the good citizen.

These documents are also much clearer than Demophantos' decree on the circumstances which generated them. Oligarchy is mentioned in Theozotides' decree and the sales documents refer to oligarchy, the Thirty and the Eleven. Unjust rule and fighting also both appeared. These texts indicate that all was not well in Athens and extreme measures were needed. In contrast, the decrees for non-citizens are more reticent. The rewards for the foreigners from Phyle focused on the honorands' actions, but ignored their opponents; we hear, therefore, about the battle at Mounichia, but not about the enemy. Similarly, only one proxeny decree specifies that the Thirty took down the earlier monument;[128] the other texts report simply that the earlier monuments were destroyed 'in the time of the Thirty'. The oligarchs, consequently, were remembered primarily in relation to citizens and even the proxeny decrees involved the actions of the Athenians who approved the replacements. If the identities of the Athenians and their supporters are specific, the oligarchs remain vague and ill-defined except when their properties are specifically described. In the years after 404/3, this move

---

[126] Arist. *Ath. Pol.* 40.2; cf. Aischin. 3.195. This proposal is thought to have been the same as that awarding citizenship to Lysias; [Plut.] *X orat.* 835F–836A; schol. Aischin. 3.195; P. J. Rhodes 1981: 474–7; M. J. Osborne 1981–2: II, 29–30; Ostwald 1986: 503–4; Todd 2007: 6 with notes 18 and 20.

[127] Karyst. fr. II = *FHG* 4.358 fr. II (= Ath. 13.577b); schol. Aischin. 1.39 = Eumelos, *FGrHist* 77 F2; cf. Dem. 57.30; Isai. 8.43; Ostwald 1986: 507–8; Patterson 1981: 145–7; Ogden 1996: 77–8.

[128] *IG* II² 52.4–5.

repeated the tactics of the reconciliation agreement by focusing attention on the chief leaders and exonerating the men of the city from complicity.[129] If they were excluded from the Athenian identity constructed in the Agora documents, at least they were not included among the oligarchs. As we shall see in the following two chapters, these decisions had further consequences for the ways in which the images of the Athenians would continue to be created in the Agora and the oligarchs would continue to be remembered and forgotten in the city.

[129] For the parallel strategy in the legal speeches, see Wolpert 2002a: 93–5, 111–15.

CHAPTER 9

The Agora and the democratic citizen

When the *demos* returned from exile on 12 Boedromion 403, they came back to a city which the Thirty had attempted to remake as oligarchic by changing her laws and legal procedures and by taking over specific areas of the cityscape, most importantly the Agora and the Akropolis. In the face of these actions, the democrats needed to remake Athens so that she was once again the democratic city. As we saw in the previous chapter, reinscribing the laws and decrees destroyed by the Thirty and erecting new documents associated with the return of the *demos* were important aspects of reclaiming Athens. Inscribed on marble *stelai*, these texts were also monuments which allowed the *demos* to write its claim on to the Akropolis and the Agora, areas made into contested spaces by the Thirty's actions. In this way, these two places were marked out as important parts of the democratic city.

Despite the oligarchs' attempts to control the sanctuary of Athena, the *demos* did not undertake any further projects on the Akropolis: in the early fourth century, it remained much as it had been in 405 (fig. 10). Similarly, the democrats did not focus on the Pnyx in any significant way. If the Thirty's construction was unfinished when they fell from power, then the *demos* completed the work, but they took no further action, as far as we know, and the Pnyx remained the home of the *ekklesia*.[1] The presence of the *demos* in its formal assembly was evidently enough to dispel any lingering pall emanating from the oligarchs' activities. In contrast, the Agora was the focus of the democratic attention as monuments and construction projects were used to reclaim the area which the Thirty's activities had made into contested space. The inscriptions' focus on displaying the *demos*, its functioning and its control was complemented by the construction of new structures, the city's first dedicated court buildings and a new

---

[1] The pottery evidence will not allow such a fine-grained chronology and we cannot distinguish between work done by the Thirty and any possible construction done by the *demos* after its return in 403.

mint, the first time such an industrial establishment had been built in the Agora. The courts reinforced the images of the Athenian citizen as presented by the inscriptions. The projects in the Agora also allow us to see how Athenian identity continued to develop after about 400. As we shall see, in 394/3, the Athenians set up bronze statues for Konon and Euagoras of Cypriot Salamis, the first figures in this medium to be set up after those of Harmodios and Aristogeiton, as Demosthenes says with respect to Konon.[2] The interaction between their honorary inscriptions, their statues and their setting built on and further developed the image of the Athenian citizen, who now not only fought for the city, but also brought freedom and salvation to her. These monuments, the first honorary statues for living men, marked the end of the process of turning the Agora into the space of the citizen. Now the civic heart of the city, the square was the place where citizens came to do their civic duty and the Athenians set up statues of their particularly accomplished citizen generals. By 330, Lykourgos could say in court, 'you alone of the Greeks, O Athenians, know how to honour *andres agathoi*: you will find that, in the *agorai* of other cities, statues of athletes are set up, but, in your own, good generals and the slayers of the tyrant'.[3]

CONSTRUCTING THE DEMOCRATIC AGORA: THE BUILDINGS

As we have seen in the previous chapters, the *demos* erected inscriptions only in certain locations in the Agora: before 394/3, they were placed in front of the Bouleuterion and in and around the Stoa Basileios, but nowhere else (table 9). In 410/9, when the democrats began the process of reclaiming the square from the oligarchs and making it into the space of the citizen, they focused on these two spaces as the sites of their new construction projects. While inscriptions continued to be located in these areas in the years following the overthrow of the Thirty, the *demos* evidently saw no need for further construction either in the Bouleuterion complex or in and around the Stoa Basileios. Instead, they focused on hitherto neglected areas: the northeast corner of the square on the east side of the Panathenaic Way and the southeast corner between the old Southeast Fountain House and the processional route (fig. 2).

The northeast corner saw the construction of two simple buildings now known as Buildings A and B. Both have been largely destroyed by later construction on the site and they are preserved only by scanty remains.

---

[2] Dem. 20.70.   [3] Lykourg. *Leok*. 51.

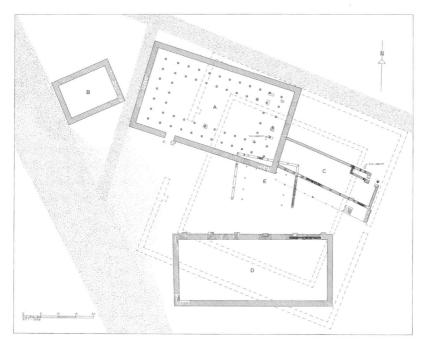

Figure 17   Restored plan of the buildings for the courts in the northeast corner of the
Agora in the fourth century BC.

The larger and better preserved Building A exists only at the level of its
foundations; enough remains to show that it was a rectangular building
with an entrance on the south side (fig. 17).[4] On the east and north sides,
it was bounded by two side streets, while the south side with its entrance
looked across an open space toward the Panathenaic Way. The interior
appointments consisted of a clay floor and, in the first phase, apparently
no interior supports.[5] Subsequently, in a later phase, a double colonnade
surrounding a court was installed in the interior; at this time, the building
was certainly roofed.[6] In its first phase, the large width to be spanned
suggests that it was probably unroofed and no remains of its superstructure
have been identified.[7] At the beginning of the fourth century, Building A
was an altogether simple structure. Across the north–south side street from

---

[4] Townsend 1995: 25–6.   [5] Townsend 1995: 26–7.

[6] The use of conglomerate blocks in the foundations for some of the piers which supported the
colonnade suggest that it is a later addition because conglomerate is not used extensively in Athens
until the second half of the fourth century BC; Townsend 1995: 26–7.

[7] Internal dimensions: *c.* 41 × 22 m.; Townsend 1995: 25.

Building A lies Building B, now preserved in even more exiguous fashion: only part of the foundation trench for the east wall is now extant (fig. 17).[8] The west side must have been limited by the Panathenaic Way, but the north side of the building has been destroyed by the Athens–Peiraieus railway and the building may perhaps have extended further to the north. No evidence exists to indicate whether it was roofed.[9] Since it seems to be sited in relation to Building A, it should be part of the same project.[10] Again, our evidence suggests that we have the simplest of structures. Evidence for the date of the two buildings is provided both by the fills used to level the site and by the fills associated with their construction. While the pottery contains earlier material, the latest fragments must come down to *c.* 400.[11]

The use of these buildings, as well as those constructed nearby later in the fourth century, is suggested by the discovery of dikastic equipment, particularly bronze tokens and ballots, in this area.[12] The excavations of the Agora have revealed a distinctive distribution of such materials: they are concentrated in two areas: the area of Buildings A–E and the later Square Peristyle in the northeast corner and the Tholos in the southwest part of the square (fig. 18).[13] Since the Tholos was the home of the *prutaneis*, the discovery of such materials here is presumably to be linked to their functions in the *boule*. For the structures under the later Square Peristyle, no such connection exists. Instead, the appearance of this material suggests that the buildings were used as the city's courts.[14] In the fifth century, the courts met in various 'borrowed' facilities at different places around Athens: there were homicide courts on the Areiopagos, at the Delphinion, Prytaneion and Palladion and in Phreatto, while popular courts are attested in the Odeion of Perikles and possibly at the sanctuary of Lykos.[15] It has

---

[8] Townsend 1995: 29.   [9] Townsend 1995: 29.   [10] Townsend 1995: 30.
[11] Townsend 1995: 139–42, 171–7.   [12] Townsend 1995: 40–3.   [13] Townsend 1995: 43, ill. 2.
[14] Townsend 1995: 40–1; cf. Shear 2007a: 104 note 49. Disassociating the courts from these structures, consequently, requires a convincing explanation for this distribution of material. At the same time, the absence of such material should suggest that certain other structures, such as the Rectangular Peribolos and the *poros* steps north of the New Bouleuterion on the west side, are best not identified as court structures, despite the attempts of various scholars; see: Boegehold 1967: 117–20; Thompson and Wycherley 1972: 62–5; Hansen and Fischer-Hansen 1994: 77; Boegehold 1995: 12–14, 93, 95; Blanshard 1999: 37–8; Millett 2005: 42–3. The Rectangular Peribolos is now identified as the Aiakeion; Stroud 1998: 85–104.
[15] Homicide courts: Andokid. 1.78; Isok. 18.52; cf. Dem. 23.65–78; Boegehold 1995: 43; popular courts: Ar. *Wasps* 389–94, 818–21, 1108–9; Boegehold 1995: 9; see generally Blanshard 1999: 18–59, 221–2, especially 41–2, 47. A court at the sanctuary of Lykos depends on how we interpret *Wasps* 389–94 and 818–21. It is very likely that the nomenclature of the popular courts changed with the construction of the facilities in the Agora and care is also needed to distinguish between the court and the place in which it met.

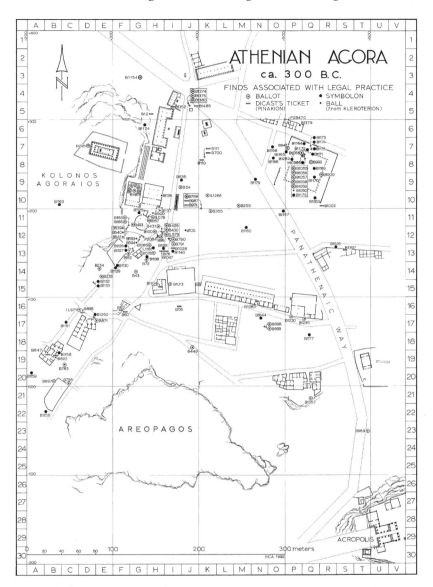

Figure 18   Restored plan of the Agora in *c.* 300 BC with the distribution of dikastic equipment.

been suggested that a court met at some location 'beside the walls', but the relevant passage in Aristophanes' *Wasps* does not support this interpretation and there is no other evidence for such a court.[16] The Agora, however, does not appear in *Wasps* as a place in which trials were accustomed to be held in the 420s and our earliest written evidence for courts meeting in specific buildings in the market square belongs to the middle of the fourth century, when they are found in the Stoa Poikile (fig. 2).[17] Antiphon's speech on the murder of Herodes shows that, in the fifth century, a trial could occasionally take place 'in the Agora', but no specific location is mentioned.[18] In contrast, the construction of Buildings A and B about 400 marks the first appearance of dedicated facilities both in the city and in the marketplace.[19] In fact, special structures designed specifically for court proceedings seem to be extremely rare in the archaeological record[20] and they are certainly not among the structures normally expected in a city's *agora*. Their construction in the Agora at Athens, consequently, marks an important development in the space and its use, as we shall see in more detail shortly.

The second structure built at this time is the Mint located in the southeast corner of the square (fig. 2). Slightly better preserved than Buildings A and B, the remains show that it was a large, almost square building with one large and two small rooms on its south side (fig. 19).[21] The northern half of the structure was poorly preserved and its interior arrangements are uncertain; at some period, it may have had a colonnade along its northern side.[22] It is restored with entrances on the east and west sides.[23] Evidence for its use is provided by the remains in the large room in the southwest corner of the structure. Excavation revealed ten pits and two water basins in the eastern part of the room; the remains in the pits together with lumps

---

[16] Ar. *Wasps* 1108–9; Boegehold 1995: 9, 93, 184. The word used for walls is τειχίον, normally used for the wall of a building, not τεῖχος, which is the wall of a city. For this reason, Starkie emended the text and his emendation has been followed by subsequent editors; Starkie 1897: 421; MacDowell 1971a: 275.

[17] Dem. 45.17; *IG* II² 1641.25–33; Blanshard 1999: 33–5; Shear 2007a: 104 note 49.

[18] Antiph. 5.10–11. The speech has been dated to either *c.* 420–417 or *c.* 417–414; Gagarin 1997: 174; Hansen 1976: 124. It is difficult to know where this trial took place; the obvious structures are the Stoa Poikile and the Stoa of Zeus because a trial would potentially have blocked access to the rooms in South Stoa I. The construction of these last two buildings is conventionally dated to the 420s, but the summary of the relevant deposit (O 16:1–2) suggests that South Stoa I might have been built a little later; Thompson and Wycherley 1972: 100; H. A. Thompson 1968: 53; Shear 2007a: 94; Sparkes and Talcott 1970: 392 (H 5–6, H 7:1), 396 (O 16:1–2).

[19] Compare Shear 2007a: 104.

[20] Hansen and Fischer-Hansen 1994: 76–9. They cite only one example outside of Athens.

[21] Camp and Kroll 2001: 131.   [22] Camp and Kroll 2001: 131.

[23] Camp and Kroll 2001: 131, 133 fig. 6.

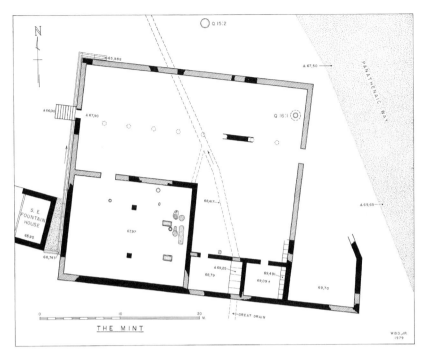

Figure 19   Restored plan of the Mint in the Agora.

of bronze and slag indicated that this room served a distinctly industrial function as the site of bronze working.[24] This room also produced an impressive array of unstruck coin blanks, as well as rods from which such blanks were cut.[25] This material allows the identification of the structure as the city's mint for bronze coins. Silver coinage, however, was never minted in this building; consequently, the silver mint, with its relevant decrees and laws, must have been located outside of the Agora and somewhere else in the city.[26] The construction fill associated with the building is dated by its pottery to about 400.[27] The earliest Athenian bronze coins are now also thought to begin about 400; it is very likely that this structure was

---

[24] Camp and Kroll 2001: 133–9, 142–4.   [25] Camp and Kroll 2001: 139–42, 146–60.
[26] Camp and Kroll 2001: 144; Shear 2007a: 104–5.
[27] The latest pottery in these fills, such as *olpai* of the type Sparkes and Talcott 1970: no. 273, must go down to *c.* 400 BC; Camp and Kroll 2001: 142 note 9. Since this pottery must have been made, used and destroyed before it ended up in this fill, the building cannot have been built much before 400 BC; Shear 2007a: 104 note 51. It is, therefore, not possible to date its construction to the last decade of the century, as Camp and Kroll would evidently like to do; Camp and Kroll 2001: 142, 144–5.

constructed as the city's mint for bronze coins, as it certainly was between the fourth and first centuries BC.[28] It may also have originally been connected with the manufacture of public weights, tokens and measures.[29] This building, consequently, was the site of production for items needed for the proper functioning of the (democratic) city.[30] This industrial structure was not necessarily an obvious addition to the Agora and its purpose and use contrast with the neighbouring buildings.[31]

DEMOCRACY, THE CITIZEN AND THE AGORA

About 400, consequently, the east side of the Agora was the site of significant building projects as the new structures for the city's courts and for making bronze coinage were erected. The construction represented important new developments for the city because hitherto the courts had met in various locations and no dedicated buildings existed for them, while manufacturing establishments had not previously been built in the Agora itself. Erecting them here would have required deliberate decisions of the Athenian *demos* and the locations, unlikely as they may seem, cannot have been chosen by chance. Certainly, these structures had practical functions and the courts in particular link closely to the project to collect and organise the laws and to the constitutional changes which we shall discuss in the next chapter. These buildings, however, also served to display the democracy at work and they allowed the *demos* to reclaim this contested space as its own. The courts played a further role because, as the spaces were used, they provided yet another image of the proper democratic citizen. In these ways, the new projects complemented the construction done between 410 and 404 and they helped to shift the focus of the space on to the citizen.

In these dynamics, the courts played a particularly important role. As we saw in chapter 6, the Thirty seem to have been particularly keen to dismantle the lawcourts as they functioned under the democracy.[32] In this system, the courts ensured that the city's laws were actually followed, a process in which the individual citizen played a crucial part. This relationship was made physically visible by erecting the new court buildings in the northeast corner of the Agora where they were juxtaposed with the Stoa Basileios

---

[28] Camp and Kroll 2001: 144–5; Shear 2007a: 105.   [29] Camp and Kroll 2001: 145.
[30] Shear 2007a: 105.
[31] Mints seem to be rare buildings: for some examples, see Camp and Kroll 2001: 144 note 12. At Halieis, the mint was constructed next to the city wall in an area otherwise taken up by houses and streets; Boyd and Rudolph 1978: 347.
[32] Above chapter 6; R. Osborne 2003: 263–4.

with its great display of inscribed laws (fig. 2). These permanent structures made the courts visible in the cityscape as they had never been before: now, a particular spot in the city was permanently associated with this important element of the rule of the *demos*. This prominent location also complemented the courts' new function as the venue in which Athenians negotiated their memories of the events of 404/3. Buildings A and B, consequently, provided a place in which an important part of the democracy could function regularly. As such, they served not only as markers of the system's health, but also as a means of displaying its operation. In addition, they acted as tangible symbols of the Athenians' tacit agreement to abide by the decisions of the majority and not to revert to civil strife. The courts, consequently, complemented the dynamics created by the inscriptions and also the earlier projects on the west side of the Agora. In the context of the overall square, their presence also suggested that the courts with their large numbers of citizen *dikastai* or jurors were just as important as the *boule* and the archons were for the democratic city.

The Mint also played a role in this display of democracy because it was producing bronze coins and perhaps weights and measures for the city. These items, and particularly the coins, were necessary for the proper functioning of the city. Without the money produced here, citizens could not be paid for doing their civic duties, particularly in the courts, in the Bouleuterion and, from the 390s, in the assembly.[33] Locating the manufacturing process in the southeast corner of the Agora along a major street made it particularly visible and it suggests that such dynamics were desirable (fig. 2). Here, it was easily accessible not only to the *boule* and the archons, but also to individual members of the *demos*. Operations going on in this structure, consequently, would have been surprisingly transparent and a desire for such oversight presumably outweighed the disadvantages of locating an industrial structure in the Agora. This location also brought the structure into the dynamics of the square and its emphasis on the display of democracy and its processes.

Like the inscriptions, these three buildings also allowed the *demos* to write its control of the city physically on the topography of the Agora through the construction of structures which it needed for its own use (fig. 2). Putting the city's courts into permanent facilities suggested not only the importance of their functions to democratic Athens, but also their longevity as institutions. Since they were expected to continue playing their roles in the city for a long time, it was worth the money, time and effort

---

[33] On assembly pay, see Arist. *Ath. Pol.* 41.3 and below chapter 10.

needed to construct these buildings. In turn, this situation suggested that the *demos* itself would not be replaced quickly, a message repeated by the display of the inscribed laws in the Stoa Basileios on the opposite corner of the Agora. With the construction of the buildings for the courts and the Mint, structures specifically associated with the rule of the *demos* and the proper functioning of the democratic city now anchored all four corners of the square and they visibly demonstrated the *demos*' control of the area.

Building these three new facilities also allowed the democrats to lay claim again to the Agora, a space which the oligarchs' actions had turned into an area of contestation. Buildings meant for the uses of the *demos* now stood in the square. As new structures, they had no connection at all with the oligarchs and so they also represented the undoing of the Thirty's actions. While the oligarchs had tried to restrict and emasculate the courts, the *demos* returned them to their earlier position of power and now gave them their own permanent location. While the Thirty were said in the epigram for Phyle to rule with 'unjust statutes', the *demos* followed the laws in a system requiring citizens to help with their enforcement by bringing lawsuits. For their own purposes, the Thirty had held a sham trial of Theramenes in the Bouleuterion, but, under the *demos*, trials were properly conducted in the new dedicated structures and they served the greater good of the city. Under the Thirty, money was something for which men were killed;[34] under the democracy, in contrast, money was produced for the benefit of the *demos*, which was very much alive. Previously, only a few men had profited from the money, but, under the democracy, the whole *demos* would. In this way, the court buildings and the Mint repeat some of the strategies which we saw in the proxeny decrees on the Akropolis. Juxtaposing the democratic present with the oligarchic past served to put the two systems in opposition to each other and it made use of a dynamic which we also saw in the Agora inscriptions. These strategies also tied the Mint and Buildings A and B more closely to the rest of the project of responding to the Thirty.

The Athenians' decision to locate the courts' new permanent facilities in the Agora had a further consequence because they now required large numbers of citizens to come to the square to perform their duty as *dikastai*, as members of juries.[35] In this way, the patterns of use in the Agora were radically changed so that a large portion of the *demos* regularly came to the Agora for civic reasons and democratic activities were no longer limited to the archons and the *boule*. This new pattern of behaviour brought out the

---

[34] E.g. Xen. *Hell.* 2.3.21–2, 40; Arist. *Ath. Pol.* 35.4; Lys. 12.6–23.   [35] Shear 2007a: 115.

importance of doing one's duty as a citizen, a process which helped to make the democracy function properly and also served to safeguard it. When the citizen came to the Agora to serve in the courts, he would have walked by other structures connected with the rule of the *demos*, particularly the Old Bouleuterion with the city's archives and the Stoa Basileios with the display of the laws (fig. 2). These structures and their connections with the city's laws should have brought out the importance of the role which the citizen was about to perform in the courts. In this setting, he may also have recalled his dikastic oath with its new clause requiring him to vote according to the established laws.[36] When the trial was finished and he came out of these buildings to go home, he will have looked across the Agora to the Tyrannicides, those models which the Athenians had sworn to follow just before the Dionysia of 409 (fig. 8). As he looked at the statues, our *dikastes* may have asked himself how their behaviour compared with what had been described in the trial. He may also have remembered that the text of Demophantos' decree stood not far away on the terrace in front of the Old Bouleuterion: now, its juxtaposition with the court buildings brought out the importance of using his vote to protect the democracy from being overthrown, an aspect of the decree which had not previously been stressed by the topography. These relationships suggested that the good Athenian citizen was not only required to kill tyrants, but also to protect the rule of the *demos* through his actions in court. Violent deeds were no longer the only way to ensure that Athens continued to remain democratic. As a member of a jury, a man had in addition to adhere to the new clause in the dikastic oath not to remember past wrongs[37] and so his service was linked to his memories of reconciling after *stasis*. Since participating in the courts was associated with the behaviour for the proper citizen, not to do so was to identify oneself as a bad Athenian, the kind of person who might overthrow the democracy in the future and who would remember past wrongs against fellow citizens.

In the years after the return of the *demos* from Phyle, the new court structures and the new Mint played an important role in helping to make the Agora into the space of the citizen, who now came regularly to this space to do his civic duty in especially designed facilities (fig. 2). These new buildings also served to display the democracy and to demonstrate its control over the cityscape; in this way, they complemented the inscriptions discussed in the last chapter. Like these texts, the structures also juxtaposed the democratic present with the oligarchic past so that the two systems were

---

[36] Andok. 1.91; above chapter 7 with note 74.   [37] Above note 36.

brought into opposition with each other. Meanwhile, the location of the courts near the statues of Harmodios and Aristogeiton also asked viewers to compare the Tyrannicides' actions with those of citizens in the courts. In this way, serving in court became another marker of the good Athenian, whose actions were no longer focused on violent deeds against external enemies and tyrants. This addition to the image of the good citizen had a further benefit in that it left open the possibility for the men of the city to perform according to this standard, an achievement which they could not match if being Athenian required a man to fight oligarchs, as it did in Theozotides' decree.

BRONZE STATUES AND THE AGORA

In the years immediately after 400, accordingly, the new structures worked together with the inscriptions and existing buildings to provide an image of the proper Athenian and how he should behave. Although the individual citizen was to follow these models, the imagery focused on groups of Athenians: all the Athenians of Demophantos' decree, the *boule*, the *dikastai*, the Athenians returning from Phyle and the dead citizens who did not. This emphasis on the corporate nature of the citizens was reinforced by the Athenian victories commemorated in the Stoa Poikile (fig. 2); those monuments celebrated the achievements of all the Athenians and no individual was singled out for special mention.[38] The only exception to this rule was the statue group for the Tyrannicides Harmodios and Aristogeiton, long since dead and turned into figures of cult (fig. 8). As I have argued elsewhere, this fifth-century pattern of commemoration began to change with the honours for the Athenians returning from Phyle and with Theozotides' decree because, for the first time, only a portion of the Athenians were honoured.[39] Both of these inscriptions were sizable monuments in their own right: the *stele* with Theozotides' decree may have been as tall as 2.00 m., while the remains of the block inscribed with the honours for the Athenians show that it clearly supported another object such as a statue, relief, or herm; both memorials would have been impossible to overlook in the Agora.[40] With their erection, commemoration of Athenian

---

[38] Shear 2007a: 105–6; above chapter 8.   [39] Shear 2007a: 106–7; see also briefly chapter 8.

[40] The *stele* with Theozotides' decree is 1.53 m. tall, but cuttings on its top surface indicate that a crowning member is now missing; Stroud 1971: 280. A document relief would bring the monument to about 2.00 m.; Stroud 1971: 285, 301; Lawton 1992: 246. The full width of the monument for the Athenians is not preserved, but it must have been more than 0.936 m., the total of the preserved width of the three largest, non-joining fragments (frs. a–c). The largest fragment (fr. a), which includes parts of the left column, the epigram and the decree, has a preserved height of 0.828 m.

valour in combat was no longer limited to the Stoa Poikile and the market square was clearly marked as an important location within the city for celebrating the exploits of citizens. These changes in commemoration opened the way for the memorialisation of individual victorious generals in the Agora, a decision which completed the development of the marketplace into an area now focused on the individual citizen. The earliest such monuments were erected in 394/3 when the Athenians decided to set up bronze honorary statues for Konon and Euagoras, the first time such honours had been awarded to anyone other than Harmodios and Aristogeiton, as Demosthenes stresses.[41] Now, for the first time, living men were publicly honoured in the Agora and their individual achievements were commemorated. In this setting, these figures interacted with the relevant inscriptions and other monuments to modify the image of the good citizen. As the first such statues, they also marked an important change in the uses of the Agora's space and the ways in which individual Athenians could be honoured.

Before 394/3, statues in the Agora had been extremely limited. The most well-known examples, the figures for Harmodios and Aristogeiton, were erected by the end of the sixth century as part of the process of creating the Agora as public space.[42] Replaced in 477/6 after the Persian Wars, they constituted a well-known monument for figures of cult (fig. 8).[43] The statue of Zeus Soter erected in the 420s also had a religious role as the god's cult image.[44] Other monuments of a sacred nature also existed in the Agora (fig. 2). Leagros' base, which was erected against the outside face of the barrier of the Altar of the Twelve Gods and so in contact with sacred space, is specifically described in the inscription as dedicated to these divinities by Leagros.[45] Onesippos' herm set up in the north annexe of the Stoa Basileios also specifies that it is a dedication (fig. 7).[46] That all these statues have cult functions, either as dedications or as representations of cult figures, brings

---

and the original monument must have been considerably taller. More of this fragment is preserved than the text suggests; for a photograph, see Raubitschek 1941a: 290.

[41] Dem. 20.70.

[42] Plin. *HN* 34.17; Shear 2001: 687–93. For the development of the Agora at this time, see Shear, Jr 1994: 228–45 with Shear, Jr 1993: 418–29.

[43] *IG* XII.5 444 = *FGrHist* 239, A54, lines 70–1.

[44] Shear 2007a: 96; Thompson and Wycherley 1972: 101.

[45] *IG* I³ 951. On the earlier history of this base, see Gadbery 1992: 473–4; on the statue, see Seaman 2002: 100–10. I would stress here the monument's status as a private dedication.

[46] *SEG* XXXII 239. This base, incidentally, cannot have been set up in 404/3 because we know that Patrokles, not Onesippos, was the *basileus* under the oligarchs; Isok. 18.5; above chapter 6. Edmondson would connect it with 403/2; Edmondson 1982. Since, stratographically, this base seems to belong with the first phase of this annexe, Edmondson's date is unlikely to be correct.

out for us the important role of the Eponymous Heroes, whose monument was set up in the southwest corner of the Agora soon after 430, as religious figures, as the heroic 'founders' of the ten tribes, rather than merely as democratic imagery available for manipulation (fig. 2).[47] As this survey of the known statues in the Agora before 394/3 brings out, sculpted figures were not common in this space and, when they were set up here, they were either of figures of cult or dedications to them. In contrast, the honorary statues of Konon and Euagoras had no religious role at all: their purpose was to honour the achievements of these outstanding men and Athenian citizens.

Now no longer preserved, these two monuments are attested by our written sources. Isokrates reports that the Athenians, in gratitude for Konon's and Euagoras' victory over the Spartans at Knidos, awarded them the highest honours and set up their statues next to the *agalma* of Zeus Soter and to each other.[48] In his description, these two figures very much form a pair, a single memorial 'both of the greatness of their benefactions and of their friendship for each other'. Some centuries later, Pausanias described them as standing with Zeus Eleutherios in front of that divinity's stoa in the Agora (fig. 2).[49] In the middle of the fourth century, when Demosthenes came to discuss Konon's honours, he stressed the unparalleled nature of the statue as the first bronze figure erected after those of the Tyrannicides.[50] Demosthenes does not specify its location and his text does not focus on the Agora; although the reference to the Tyrannicides immediately draws our attention to the market square, Demosthenes seems to have the larger setting of the city as a whole in mind.[51] His comments must apply not only to Konon's statue, but also to the figure for Euagoras. Consequently, when these two monuments were set up in the Agora, they were unique and their novelty would have been brought out by their medium, subject and location. Furthermore, despite extensive building work not far away in the early Roman period, Isokrates' and Pausanias' descriptions together show that these two statues remained where they were originally set up in front of the Stoa of Zeus. Erecting them together with their inscriptions in front of this particular building in the Agora not only made them players in the area's politics of space, but it also opened up a new part of the square for inscriptions and commemoration.

---

[47] Shear 2007a: 96. For the erection of the Eponymous Heroes, see Shear, Jr 1970: 203–22; contra: Kron 1976: 229–32; Robertson 1990: 50–2.

[48] Isok. 9.57.   [49] Paus. 1.3.2–3.   [50] Dem. 20.70.

[51] Statues of humans dedicated on the Akropolis, whether bronze or stone, were private monuments set up by individuals and not public ones erected by the *demos*; see Shear 2007a: 108.

In this setting in front of the Stoa of Zeus, the two statues complemented the existing monuments and their dynamics, but they also served to continue the creation of the image of the proper Athenian citizen and they provided him with further models of behaviour. The connection between Euagoras' statue and the image of the citizen is striking because he was the king of Cypriot Salamis. As we saw in the previous chapter, however, the Athenians had made him an Athenian in a decree passed perhaps early in 407.[52] His status was stressed by Isokrates when he, too, discussed Konon's and Euagoras' exploits at Knidos and their rewards from the Athenians.[53] When Pausanias came to describe the monument, he also emphasised that Euagoras acted as an Athenian when he persuaded the Persian king to give Konon the necessary ships and he explains Euagoras' lineage, which went back to Teukros and Kinyras' daughter. The prominence given to this information suggests that it came from the base of the statue.[54] If this inference is correct, then Euagoras' status as an Athenian will have been prominently displayed in the monument itself. It will have been reinforced by Konon's monument, on which he was presumably listed in proper Athenian fashion with patronymic and demotic, and it will have interacted with the other memorials celebrating the earlier exploits of Athenian citizens. The emphasis on Euagoras' citizenship should also have brought out the importance of citizenship in this space: despite the greatness of his benefactions, no excuse had to be made for him and this apparent exception actually proved the rule. In this way, the Agora continued to remain focused on the deeds of citizens, while non-Athenians were ignored in this space.

The Athenians' decisions to erect these two statues in front of the Stoa of Zeus had consequences for the image of the two men. As we saw in the previous chapter, the honorary decrees for Konon and Euagoras seem to have been set up next to their statues. Since Konon's inscription specifically said that he had 'freed the allies of Athens', the text configured the honorand as a bringer of freedom. This image was reinforced by the setting of the statue in front of the Stoa of Zeus because this divinity was both Eleutherios and Soter, the protector of the city's freedom and its saviour.[55] The juxtaposition of the decree, the building and the cult statue made this small area of the Agora into a space focused on the freedom of the city. The relationships will have emphasised Konon's role as the bringer of freedom to Athens, the reason for his statue. These same dynamics also constructed Euagoras as a citizen who ensured that the city remained

[52] *IG* i³ 113 = M. J. Osborne 1981–2: D3; above chapter 8.   [53] Isok. 9.54.   [54] Shear 2007a: 108.
[55] On Zeus Eleutherios and Zeus Soter, see Raaflaub 2004: 106–17; Parker 1996: 157.

free. The statues, consequently, identified both men as the liberators of Athens.[56]

At the same time, the statues of Konon and Euagoras, the bringers of freedom, were juxtaposed on the larger setting of the Agora and particularly on the statues of the Tyrannicides located not far away in the middle of the square (figs. 2, 8). As the other pair of figures in the relatively empty space of the early fourth-century Agora, they served as the only real points of comparison for these two new statues. Harmodios and Aristogeiton were also known as the liberators of Athens[57] and the relationship between the two sets of statues will have reinforced these dynamics. The interaction will also have encouraged viewers to compare the two pairs of individuals and the achievements of the honorands. Interestingly, when Demosthenes comes to describe Konon's statue, he reports the judgment of Konon's contemporaries that 'when he destroyed the empire of the Lakedaimonians, he, too, had ended no small tyranny'.[58] Since this information is immediately followed by Demosthenes' request that the decree be read out, the observation is probably based on the honorary text, in which case, Konon was already imagined as a killer of tyrants in his inscription. Certainly, the juxtaposition of his statue and the figures of the Tyrannicides will have reinforced this image: viewers will have been asked to compare the accomplishments of these different men. Zeus's role as saviour will have emphasised Konon's role as saviour of Athens through his actions as a tyrant slayer and liberator. Set next to Konon's figure, Euagoras' statue will have taken part in the same dynamics so that he, too, was constructed as a killer of tyrants. This image of the citizen as tyrant slayer should also have brought Demophantos' decree located on the terrace of the Old Bouleuterion into play. Since that text specified that the good citizen killed tyrants and, therefore, kept the city free for democracy, its relationship to the two statues both reinforced the image presented by the figures and made them into the newest example of the good citizen, a suitable model for other Athenians to follow. In these ways, the relationships constructed in the space of the Agora insisted on Konon's and Euagoras' status as saviours and bringers of freedom, a position hitherto reserved for the god and the cult figures Harmodios and Aristogeiton.

[56] Shear 2007a: 107; cf. G. J. Oliver 2007: 197.
[57] E.g. Hdt. 6.109.3–6, 123.2; Ar. *Lys.* 626–35; Demophantos' decree (Andok. 1.96–8); Dem. 20.69–70; 19.280–1; Lykourg. *Leok.* 46–51; Hyp. *Epit.* 34–9; M. W. Taylor 1991: 93–4 note 6, 96–7; Raaflaub 2003: 66.
[58] Dem. 20.70.

If the statues for Konon and Euagoras picked up on the Agora's images of the tyrant slayer, the liberator and the saviour, they also worked together with the military images present in Theozotides' decree and the Stoa Poikile.[59] The occasion for their honours, after all, was a military success in a naval battle. From Demosthenes' description, these circumstances appear to have come out in Konon's honorary decree and they were probably also mentioned in Euagoras' inscription; certainly, its remains suggest a longer explanation for his honours than a simple notice that he was an *aner agathos* towards the Athenians. Like the earlier monuments for Athenian military victory in the Stoa Poikile, the statues provided Athenians with a model of achievement which focused on destroying external enemies, *polemioi*, of the city. Unlike those memorials, however, the statues emphasised that the individual man, not just the corporate group, could receive rewards for his deeds in battle. These images of the citizen warrior and of the citizen tyrant slayer and saviour need not have been mutually exclusive and the statues ought to have engaged with both images and their representation in the Agora. The extent to which one or the other dominated will have depended on the appearance of the figures, information nowhere described to us by our ancient sources. If the figures were naked, then the resemblances to the Tyrannicides would have been pronounced; if they were carrying weapons and either wearing armour or a short chiton and chlamys, then the military image would have dominated. On contemporary gravestones, the two military versions are standard, but bearded, naked figures are extremely unusual.[60] In describing Konon's honours, however, Demosthenes stresses the parallels between the honorand and the Tyrannicides: he was the first to receive a bronze statue 'just like Harmodios and Aristogeiton' and, like the Tyrannicides, 'he, too, had ended no small tyranny'. These parallels together with the figures' location in front of the Stoa of Zeus, where they engaged with the god's roles as saviour and protector of freedom, suggest that the tyrant slayer was probably more evident in these figures than the military commander. For this reason, it remains more likely that these two special statues were shown naked and carrying weapons rather than clothed in armour or a short chiton and chlamys; no matter what they wore, the figures will not have imitated the pose of the Tyrannicides.

Irrespective of these details, the statues' location in the Agora, an overall space focused on the democratic citizen and the location of structures

---

[59] Above chapter 8.

[60] Military costume: Dillon 2006: 69–70, 107–8; Hallett 2005: 23–5; rarity of naked, bearded men: R. Osborne 1998: 95–100. Osborne stresses that nakedness goes together with beardlessness in this period; contrast Dillon 2006: 108–9; Hallett 2005: 26–9.

particularly connected with the rule of the *demos*, will have brought out the honorands' democratic connections. In 394/3, Konon's absence from Athens during the rule of the Thirty ought to have been well known and he owed his role in the victory at Knidos to his presence in Cyprus, rather than Athens, after the disaster at Aigospotamoi. He was certainly no oligarch and the use of his name, patronymic and demotic on the base and in his honorary decree should have reminded viewers and readers of this fact.[61] The decrees next to the statues should also have brought out the democratic credentials of the honorands: had they not been democrats, they would not have been honoured in this unprecedented fashion by the *demos*. The setting, accordingly, also brought out Konon's and Euagoras' status as good democrats. As tyrant slayers, they will also have appeared to live up to the stipulations of Demophantos' decree and this dynamic will have further emphasised their democratic credentials.

In the overall setting of the Agora, the statues of Konon and Euagoras provided another model of behaviour for the democratic citizen. The good citizen was shown to be a tyrant slayer who brought freedom to the city; in so doing, he served as her saviour. He also fought the city's external enemies in military conflict and was honoured for it. Slaying tyrants and killing *polemioi* were equated, much as they had been in Demophantos' decree. In addition, these honours for individual men mark an important development in the politics of the Agora and they signal the end of the process of turning the square into space focused on the citizen. That concentration was now quite literally on the individual Athenian: if he followed the models of behaviour promulgated in the square well enough, he, too, would be voted his own individual honours, including, perhaps, a bronze statue of his own.

CONSEQUENCES

In the Agora, consequently, Konon's and Euagoras' figures would have stood out as the only bronze statues for living men. The erection of the relevant honorary decrees next to the monuments ensured that there was no confusion about exactly what type of image was being presented here. They were certainly not figures of cult nor were they dedications.[62] These

---

[61] For Konon as the good democrat, see Dem. 20.72–4.
[62] Contra: Krumeich 2007: 163. He stresses the 'clear religious context' of these two statues and their location 'in the Shrine (*sic*) of Zeus the Liberator'. Strikingly, the statues are not described as dedications in our ancient sources. The stoa is also not normally called a shrine or *temenos*; see Wycherley 1957: nos. 24–46; *Agora* XVI 214 from the mid third century BC (archon: Philoneos) is

two statues introduced a new type, the honorary statue, and a new location for its display, the Agora. This setting emphasised their public character and it also brought out their novelty: they were invented specifically for this location in order to honour good democratic citizens.[63] This context, however, brings out only certain aspects of the victory at Knidos. It is very much constructed as an Athenian military success and the crucial role of the Persian fleet, without which no victory would have been won, is ignored. The sculpted monuments and the setting also de-emphasise the identity of the vanquished: there is no indication that it was the Spartans. These same strategies were also apparently at work in Euagoras' decree with its description of his activities on behalf of the Greeks and particularly as a Hellene on behalf of Hellas.[64] If the Persians and their satrap Pharnabazos were mentioned in the text, it is not evident from the remains. A similar strategy appears in our literary texts. Isokrates' description of the circumstances surrounding the battle privileges the Greeks and Euagoras' good deeds on their behalf; indeed, the king is said to have made the outcome possible and to have provided the greater part of the force.[65] Likewise, when Demosthenes writes about Konon's honours, the Persians are completely absent from the text and only the Spartans are mentioned. His description suggests that a similar strategy was also at work in Konon's decree. In the Agora, the inscriptions should have reinforced the statues' strategies and kept the focus clearly on the honorands' roles as tyrant slayers, liberators and saviours. The monuments further suggested that this victory concerned all of the Athenians, hence the honours. As such, they contrasted with the memorials for Phyle, which honoured only some of the Athenians, those men who were committed democrats. The victory at Knidos in 394/3, however, could be constructed as a success won by all of the Athenians irrespective of their actions ten years earlier. In this way, the whole *demos* together could celebrate the result and they could ignore the realities of the current situation: their own lack of power and their dependence on the Persians, that hated enemy of the fifth century.

If Konon's and Euagoras' statues provided a new way of commemorating the achievements of individual generals, they also began the process of transforming the Agora into a space in which honorary statues would be set up. Indeed, in the twenty or so years after the battle of Knidos, the *demos* erected three more honorary statues for generals: for Chabrias after

---

an exception with its reference to the *temenos* of Zeus. The modern tendency to elide the categories honorary, dedicatory, public and private serves to obscure rather than illuminate the differences between them.
[63] See further Shear 2007a: 107–9.   [64] Lewis and Stroud 1979: 190–1.   [65] Isok. 9.54–6.

his naval victory at Naxos in 376; for Iphikrates after destroying a Spartan division near Corinth in 390; and for Timotheos after his cruise around the Peloponnese to Kerkyra in 375.[66] The statues all seem to have been set up shortly after the military successes commemorated and they apparently all stood in the Agora.[67] Timotheos' figure was erected in front of the Stoa of Zeus along with the images of his father and Euagoras. This setting constructed Timotheos as a saviour and liberator, just like his father and the Cypriot king; like them, he, too, had achieved this position by virtue of his military success.[68] He could also be clearly seen to have imitated the example set by the earlier honorands. The literary sources stress the ways in which Timotheos' statue made a pair with that of his father; very likely, the figure derived its pose and perhaps its appearance from the two earlier images.

In contrast, Chabrias' monument was decidedly martial both in the design of the base and of the figure. As the extant fragments of the base show, the front and the left and right sides were decorated with citations and carved olive crowns which had been voted by the *demos* of Mytilene and various groups of soldiers, including those at Naxos, hence the identification of the honorand as Chabrias.[69] The crown voted to Chabrias by the Athenian *demos* is not preserved on the extant fragments, but there is room for it on the front of the monument where it should be restored.[70] Since some of the soldiers campaigned at Lesbos and in the Hellespont, the crowns seem to reflect Chabrias' activities in both 376 and 375.[71] This array of crowns voted for military success proclaimed the martial nature of the monument. The statue would have enhanced this sense because it showed Chabrias at ease with his spear upright and his shield leaning against one knee.[72] Since this pose depicts one of Chabrias' famous exploits, which took place during a land campaign in 378/7 in Boiotia, it is likely that the figure also wore a cuirass.[73] The image presented was not particularly appropriate for a naval campaign, like the battle of Naxos, but it certainly emphasised the martial nature of the honorand's achievements. Together

---

[66] Aischin. 3.234; Dem. 23.196–8; [Dem.] 13.21–2; cf. Dem. 20.75–86.
[67] Gauthier 1985: 97–103, 177–80; Krumeich 1997: 208–9; Shear 2007a: 110 with note 75; Dillon 2006: 102. For the location of Timotheos' and Chabrias' statues, see Paus. 1.3.2–3 and Nep. *Timoth.* 2.3 (Timotheos); Nep. *Chab.* 1.2–3 (Chabrias). The fragments of Chabrias' base, *SEG* xix 204, were also found in the Agora; Burnett and Edmondson 1961.
[68] Shear 2007a: 110.   [69] *SEG* xix 204; Burnett and Edmondson 1961: 77–9, figs. 1–3, pl. 12.
[70] Dem. 24.180; Burnett and Edmondson 1961: 80–7, 90–1; Shear 2007a: 110.
[71] Burnett and Edmondson 1961: 80–7.
[72] Diod. 15.32.5, 33.4; Polyainos 2.1.2; Nep. *Chab.* 1.2–3; J. K. Anderson 1963; Buckler 1972; Shear 2007a: 111; Dillon 2006: 107; contra: Tanner 2006: 113.
[73] Compare Dillon 2006: 107.

with the crowns and citations on the base, the overall monument, ostensibly for one naval battle, displayed a part of a larger military career. In the space of the Agora, this pronounced martial flavour contrasted with the very different image of the Tyrannicides: no one could mistake Chabrias for a tyrant slayer. It will also have complemented the earlier memorials for the city's military successes. It suggested that simply winning a military victory put a man on a par with these earlier citizens and their superior achievements and it provided yet another model of the proper conduct for the good Athenian.

These statues for Athenian generals mark the beginning of the process of turning the Agora into a space filled with figures of good generals and the Tyrannicides, as Lykourgos described it in 330.[74] They also served to identify the square as an important memorial space in the city, one which, by the early fourth century, had become second only to the sanctuary of Athena on the Akropolis. Since these monuments celebrated military victory, they worked together with the memorials in the Stoa Poikile to mark out the square as a place to celebrate Athenian martial triumphs.[75] Commemorating individual Athenians' achievements, in contrast to the corporate successes memorialised in the stoa, they also increased the Agora's focus on the citizen. Indeed, the decision to put up the statues of Konon and Euagoras in this setting, rather than on the Akropolis, already testifies to the way in which this focus was achieved. Had the figures been erected in Athena's sanctuary, they would not have been able to portray the honorands as tyrant slayers, liberators and saviours: these images were only possible in the Agora.[76] The statues' emphasis on the individual citizen was reinforced by the other structures focused on the male Athenian. This connection between monuments is brought out by the location of the courts: they are opposite the Stoa of Zeus so that these two areas particularly focused on the citizen were joined together by their place in the square (fig. 2). As monuments decreed and set up by the *demos*, the statues also continued the emphasis on democracy and its display which existed in the Agora from 410/9.

If the statues of the generals, the new structures for the courts and the Mint collectively served to focus attention on the individual citizen, they

---

[74] Lykourg. *Leok.* 51. It is to this time in the later fourth century that the dynamics discussed by Tanner properly belong; Tanner 2006: 109–40. With more attention to the chronological developments and the categories public, private, dedicatory, honorary and posthumous, see Dillon 2006: 101–6.

[75] See further Shear 2007a: 111–13.

[76] For this point, see further Shear 2007a: 108. Note also Oliver's stress that it was 'relatively unusual for *honorific* statues to be set up on the Akropolis' in the fourth century; G. J. Oliver 2007: 197.

also interacted with the other structures and inscriptions around them. In this way, these monuments built after 404/3 also established connections with the past, both the more distant past represented by the Tyrannicides and the more recent period of Demophantos' decree, and they mirrored the dynamics which we have already seen in the contemporary inscriptions. Together, the monuments and the *stelai* helped the *demos* to reclaim the city's past for its own uses and they set the current response to oligarchy in the context of the reaction to the events of 411. This relationship brings out the continuity between these two periods, the ways in which the Athenians continued to use the same strategies for controlling the space of the Agora. After both 411 and 404/3, it was important for the *demos* to display its processes and power and to inscribe its control on the landscape. Over this period, the monuments and texts focused increasingly on the individual citizen until, in 394/3, the first honorary statues of individual men were erected in the Agora.

This decision marks the culmination of the area's transition from being multi-use space to being the space of the democratic citizen. Now, the Agora focused on male Athenians who came to this part of the city to do their civic duty. Here, they were provided with images of exemplary individual citizens on whom they should model their behaviour. They were to be tyrant slayers, liberators and saviours, men who fought against the city's external enemies. In contrast, the Akropolis did not focus particularly on these democratic citizens and it remained the place for texts and monuments of all sorts, a multi-purpose memorial space available to citizens, other inhabitants of the city and foreigners. In this setting, statues had no particularly democratic resonances and they did not provide images for the good citizen. Those functions were now firmly established in the Agora with its close connections to democracy and civic buildings. In contrast, commercial structures were located outside the market square behind the Stoa Poikile, north of Buildings A and B and southwest of the Tholos where recent work suggests that the so-called Strategeion was, in fact, dedicated to commerce (fig. 2).[77] Their construction was relatively simple without the architectural elaboration of columns, colonnades and entablatures which

---

[77] Commercial building behind the Stoa Poikile (perhaps built *c.* 400 BC): Shear, Jr 1984: 43–8; Camp 1996: 236–8; Camp 1999: 274–9; Camp 2003: 247–50; Camp 2007: 642. Structures north of Buildings A and B (rebuilt after 479): Shear, Jr 1971: 265–6; Shear, Jr 1973: 138–42. So-called Strategeion (built in the second half of the fifth century): Thompson and Wycherley 1972: 78; Camp 2007: 657–60. For the general principle, cf. Camp 2007: 660. Houses in the area around the Agora were used both as workshops and as domestic spaces; see Tsakirgis 2005. Facilities focused on shopping only appear in the Agora itself in the middle of second century with the construction of the Stoa of Attalos.

marked out the larger public buildings nearby, particularly the four stoai and the two bouleuteria. In contrast, shopping inside the Agora itself took place in temporary facilities so that, when the market had ended, only the civic structures remained visible. In this setting, the icons of the democratic city resolutely proclaimed the importance of doing one's civic duty and the relative unimportance of other users and uses of the space, events which happened against the backdrop of these public monuments of the *demos*.[78]

[78] For the other uses of the Agora, see Millett 1998: 211–28; Vlassopoulos, 2007: 39–46. Note that, for both Millett and Vlassopoulos, the Agora is a 'neutral stage' for the activities of humans; Millett 1998: 220; Shear 2007a: 101 note 41.

Forgetting or remembering: oligarchy, stasis *and the* demos

In the aftermath of the official return of the *demos* on 12 Boedromion, the democrats faced the problem of the Thirty's attempts to claim Athens as their own. In response, they had to remake the city once again into the democratic *polis*. As we have seen in the previous two chapters, this process involved the erection and re-erection of inscriptions both on the Akropolis and in the Agora where they served to display democracy and its practices and to write its control on to these two contested memorial spaces. By about 390, further construction in the Agora had also completed the process of turning the area into space for the democratic citizen. These actions, however, did not fully address the issues of the memory of the Thirty, the ways in which the oligarchs were to be remembered (or forgotten). Since many citizens had been men of the city and, effectively, on the losing side of the resulting *stasis*, addressing these issues was not a simple matter to be resolved merely by setting up an inscription or two or constructing a few new monuments. These strategies ultimately focused on the individual readers and viewers and they might well have provoked very different reactions from the men of the city and the men of the Peiraieus. Such actions were, in fact, more liable to create further division and the possibility of renewed *stasis*, despite the terms of the reconciliation agreement.

Remembering the events on a collective level, however, solved these potential problems because the processes created the same memories for the whole *demos*. While public monuments and texts could certainly function in this way, they were insufficient on their own, even when reinforced by important changes to the city's constitution. Rather, they needed to work together with rituals to create for all the Athenians a specific set of memories and images of the events under the Thirty. The repetition of these ceremonies regularly reinforced these particular remembrances and prevented the formation of competing memories. For these purposes, the City Dionysia, with its display of the *demos* in its corporate divisions, once again proved ideal as the announcement of the war-orphans was put to a new use. The rituals for the war-dead and the Demosion Sema were also brought into this process. The existing rituals, however, were not completely sufficient, hence a new occasion for sacrificing to Athena on 12 Boedromion, the date of the return, was also instituted. As events for the whole city, these ceremonies created the same memories for all of the Athenians, whether they had been men of the city or men of the Peiraieus, and they recalled these important events for later generations. As we shall see, however, not all of the events under the oligarchy could be recalled. Only certain episodes could be remembered and only in specific ways: war rather than *stasis* proved to be a suitable memory for all of the Athenians. Forgetting was just as important as remembering.

RITUALS AND MEMORY

If rituals were to be used to create collective memories of the events of 404/3, then the occasions had to be carefully chosen. Since the Dionysia had already played a big part in the responses to the oligarchs of 411, this festival with its focus on the *demos* must have been an obvious choice. Deciding to emphasise war will have helped to select the ceremonies in the Demosion Sema. In both cases, the rituals' close connections with democracy also marked them as appropriate occasions for this memory-making. These associations also allowed the *demos* to display itself and its power to Athenians and to their visitors at the Dionysia. The presentation of democracy and its control, however, is even more pronounced in the new sacrifice which was instituted for Athena on 12 Boedromion. Our evidence shows that this event was very quickly modified to become more inclusive and these changes had important effects on the memories created by the rituals, a development not visible in the other ceremonies.

With the exception of the reconciliation agreement, the sacrifice on 12 Boedromion is the earliest evidence for the Athenians' responses to the Thirty and most of our information concerns the inaugural event, which clearly differed significantly from the subsequent celebrations. In his description of the events of 403, Xenophon reports that, after the reconciliation had been made, Pausanias withdrew his troops and the men of the Peiraieus went in arms to the Akropolis where they sacrificed to Athena.[1] A rather more colourful version is provided by Lysias in the course of his speech against Agoratos, with whose behaviour he is particularly concerned.[2] Like Xenophon, he places the occasion immediately after the

---

[1] Xen. *Hell.* 2.4.39.   [2] Lys. 13.80–1.

reconciliation; at that time, the men of the Peiraieus processed up to the Akropolis under the leadership of Aisimos, a leading democrat and associate of Thrasyboulos.[3] Bearing his arms, Agoratos joined in as they marched up to the *astu*, but, at the gates of the city, he was thrown out of the procession by Aisimos on the grounds that, as a murderer, he had no business taking part in a procession to Athena.

Both Xenophon and Lysias make it clear that only the men of the Peiraieus participated in this procession and sacrifice; despite the reconciliation agreement, the men of the city were not (yet) able to participate in the same ways as their democratic counterparts. This moment marks the democrats' formal entry into the *astu* when they marched up from the Peiraieus. That they did so in arms signalled their military success.[4] The fuss over Agoratos' participation brings out the importance of taking part in this particular procession: doing so identified a man as a member of the *demos* returning for the first time after its 'victory' over its opponents. By marching from their base in the Peiraieus to the Akropolis, the democrats visibly displayed their control of the city (fig. 3). Their presence in Athena's sanctuary allowed them to reclaim this contested space and to replace the Spartans' garrison with their own procession which had come in arms, but for the peaceful purpose of sacrificing to Athena.[5] Since offering victims to the goddess was the purpose of the whole event, the procession will also have included the necessary sacrificial beasts. At the moment when the sacrifice had been made and the resulting meat was divided among the participants, the ritual will have created unity among the men of the Peiraieus and identified them as members of the sacrificial community.[6] This process also showed that the men of the city were not members of this community; had they gone up to the Akropolis to watch, they would have been mere spectators, not participants. In this way, their status as not (yet) being proper democratic citizens would have been strikingly and unambiguously brought out. Despite the superficial resemblances to the procession of the Little Panathenaia,[7] the two events have very little in common: the Panathenaia, as its name suggests, was about unity, but this sacrifice to Athena was about division.

In Xenophon's version of events, immediately after the rituals on the Akropolis, the men of the Peiraieus went down from the sanctuary and the

---

[3] Little is known about Aisimos; see Strauss 1987: 96.
[4] Compare Strauss 1985: 70; Todd 1985: 152.
[5] Spartan garrison: Lys. 13.46; Arist. *Ath. Pol.* 37.2; Plut. *Lys.* 15.6; cf. Lys. 12.94.
[6] On these dynamics, see above chapter 5 with note 57.
[7] E.g. the armed procession through the city; for this comparison, see Strauss 1985: 70–1.

generals held an assembly.[8] As he presents it, both the men of the city and the men of the Peiraieus were present at this *ekklesia* which presumably began with the usual rituals: the purificatory sacrifice, the prayer and the curses.[9] In contrast to the earlier events on the Akropolis, these rituals required the participation of all present, both men of the Peiraieus and men of the city. Only at this point were the latter allowed to participate and to demonstrate their membership in the ritual community, the *demos* of the Athenians. If the sacrifice to Athena emphasised divisions, these rites in the assembly displayed Athenian unity and the re-incorporation of the men of the city into the democratic city. Now the Athenians were shown to be one *demos*, just as they had been when they all swore the oaths of reconciliation in the sanctuary of Meter at Agrai perhaps only a few days earlier: the oaths and the agreement had not been in vain.

Despite these ritual dynamics, this sacrifice to Athena was not a one-time affair, as we know from Plutarch. He reports that on 12 Boedromion the Athenians used to offer (ἔθυον) *charisteria* for freedom because they had returned from Phyle on this day.[10] These *charisteria* or thank-offerings allowed the Athenians to offer sacrifices to the goddess in return for her help in their return in much the same way that such sacrifices were offered after victory in battle. This description fits with our evidence from Xenophon and Lysias. Its most striking feature, however, is the verb θύω, sacrifice, used in the imperfect tense which must indicate regular repetition. The context in the *Moralia*, Athenian religious observances celebrating military successes, also demonstrates that this sacrifice cannot have occurred just once and this repetition presumably explains Plutarch's knowledge of the date and rites. What he does not tell us is perhaps the most important information: whether the second celebration happened in 402/1 and how long it continued to be held.[11] It certainly seems likely that the sacrifice took place annually on 12 Boedromion in the years immediately after 403/2. These occasions, however, must have differed significantly from the inaugural sacrifice: then, only the men from the Peiraieus took part, but, in subsequent years, it was a religious rite of the whole city, open to men of the

[8] Xen. *Hell.* 2.4.39–42. Unfortunately, he does not tell us where this *ekklesia* was held.
[9] For fourth-century procedures with copious references, both ancient and modern, see Strauss 1985: 73–5.
[10] Plut. *De glor. Ath.* 349F.
[11] This sacrifice to Athena may be the same as or may have been transformed into the sacrifice for Democracy known in the 330s; *IG* II² 1496.126–33, 138–42. The latter certainly occurs at the right time of year between the Eleusinia and the Asklepieia. An altar for Athena Demokratia, *IG* II² 4992, is attested on the Akropolis in perhaps the Augustan period. For further discussion, see Parker 1996: 228–9; Parker 2005: 466.

city and men of the Peiraieus alike. In the years after 403/2, consequently, the participation of all the Athenians in the sacrifice to Athena served to create unity within the city as all participants were identified as members of the single sacrificial community of Athens. Since this occasion celebrated the return of the *demos* from exile, taking part in this ritual identified a man as a democrat and displayed his membership in the *demos*. In this way, the men of the city were again brought back into the *demos* and transformed into democrats. Their participation created memories for them of the event in which they had certainly not participated, so that now the whole *demos* could together remember the return from Phyle. For the younger generations who were not old enough to have taken part in the actual events, these sacrifices created memories of them and they also kept the return from Phyle ever present as a foundational moment for the democracy. Celebrating this particular event demonstrated year after year the *demos'* power and control of the city both to Athenians and to any visitors.

This sacrifice to Athena was not the only ritual occasion which celebrated the return of the *demos*. As we know from Aischines, the Athenians who returned from Phyle were awarded money for a sacrifice and dedications.[12] This occasion will have been unique, but like the earlier sacrifice to Athena, participation was restricted: in this case, only the Athenians who had returned from Phyle, some 100 or so men, could take part. The process will have separated them out from the rest of the Athenians and identified them as the committed core which was most responsible for the return of the *demos*. The dedications of these men served as a marker of both the return and the rites; whenever the participants returned to the sanctuary, the dedications then served as a point of memory for them to remember taking part in this particular sacrifice. The recipient of the sacrifices and dedications is not specified, but Athena seems to be a likely candidate, especially since the returning democrats had already sacrificed to her. If this inference is correct, then the offerings will have been made on the Akropolis and the dedications will have been set up in that sanctuary. When citizens who had participated came to the Akropolis for the city's sacrifice to Athena on 12 Boedromion, they will have remembered both the original occasion of that ritual and the moment when they, as the hard-core of Thrasyboulos' companions, made offerings as a selected group. In this setting, their memories will again have set them apart from the (former) men of the city.

[12] Aischin. 3.187.

In addition to establishing new rituals which helped to create the proper memories for the Athenians, the *demos* also used existing rites for their own purposes. As one of the consequences of the decree of Theozotides, the announcement of the war-orphans at the City Dionysia became involved in this creation of memory. As we saw in chapter 8, Theozotides prescribed that the legitimate sons of the Athenians killed fighting for the democracy be supported by the city in the same fashion as the war-orphans.[13] Consequently, as we know from the irate speaker of the fragmentary Lysianic speech against Theozotides, the sons of the dead democrats were to be announced in the theatre at the Dionysia along with the war-orphans.[14] Strikingly, what is at stake in this fragment is not the inclusion of these orphans in this ceremony, but Theozotides' exclusion of the adopted and illegitimate sons.[15] In imagining what will happen, the speaker gives us the herald's announcement, which matches the version later reported by Aischines.[16] Importantly for us, this passage shows that the announcement was evidently not modified when the *boule* and the *demos* passed Theozotides' decree. Consequently, when the oldest of the sons of the dead democrats came of age and were announced in the theatre with the war-orphans, their fathers were publicly identified as *andres agathoi* who died fighting for the city in war, not as men who came to the aid of the democracy and died a violent death in the oligarchy, as they are described in the decree. In this way, the events of 403 and the return of the *demos* were both de-emphasised and recast as an ordinary military operation, rather than an extraordinary event. Certainly, the family and friends of the individual young men will have known the true circumstances, but many individuals in the theatre will have remained ignorant about the circumstances of particular fathers' deaths. Remembering these deaths as deaths in war, however, did not single out the sons as the progeny of special men who were more committed to democracy than many in the audience. This memory of the fallen as war-dead was also suitable for the men of the city whose actions against the *demos* were, therefore, ignored. This act of collective remembering provided the Athenians gathered in the theatre with only one memory of the events surrounding the overthrow of the Thirty and the

---

[13] *SEG* XXVIII 46; above chapter 8.
[14] Lys. fr. LXIV.129 lines 26–47 (Carey). On the ritual at the Dionysia, see above chapter 5.
[15] Since the sons of the war-dead ought to have been announced with patronymics and demotics, it is not at all clear to me that illegitimate war-orphans could ever have been included in this ceremony. At the same time, the extant text of *SEG* XXVIII 46 does not suggest that a boy previously adopted by an Athenian father was, in fact, to be excluded.
[16] Aischin. 3.154.

return of the *demos*. As a 'national' memory, consequently, it also served to unify the citizens, irrespective of their actions in 404/3.

In the years immediately after 403, the announcement of these young men, both the actual war-orphans and the sons of the men killed by the Thirty, also served to display the *demos* and its power. Without an on-going war and without allies, the Athenians could have decided to stop this ritual altogether, as they evidently had by the time when Isokrates came to write his speech on the peace in 355. That they did not suggests that the ideology displayed here, and particularly the image of the good citizen, continued to be relevant to the Athenians in the early fourth century. As in 409, the positive actions of the *demos* were being made visible and *andragathia* on its behalf continued to be rewarded, just as it had been in earlier years. Repeating ceremonies regularly performed at earlier celebrations of the Dionysia also connected the present with the democratic past of the city so that the current actions of the *demos* were shown to be the proper continuation of its earlier activities. In this way, too, the actions of the Thirty and the men of the Peiraieus were de-emphasised, if not ignored, just as they were in the announcement itself.

The strategies of selective remembering in the announcements for the sons of the democrats killed by the Thirty appear again in the circumstances of the burial of the dead fathers. In assimilating the sons of the dead democrats to the war-orphans, Theozotides assumes also the assimilation of the dead men to the war-dead. In addition, these dead democrats were actually buried in the Demosion Sema along with the dead from the city's other wars, as we learn from Lysias' funeral oration, which cites the Athenians from Phyle as a shining exemplum.[17] The dead citizens, however, were not interred alone because the foreigners who died fighting the Thirty were also buried with them, as Lysias goes on to observe.[18] He continues to state that the city gave them the same *timai*, i.e. cult, that it awarded to citizens (*astoi*). In death, accordingly, these dead foreigners become *andres agathoi*, like the citizens, and both groups are honoured together for their *andragathia*. In this way, they conformed to the canon of proper behaviour for citizens and they also reinforced it. Meanwhile, the rewards for the non-Athenians show another way in which such men can become *andres agathoi*: they can actually die on behalf of Athens, a deed which has made them equal to citizens. At the moment of the funeral, the rituals will have

---

[17] Lys. 2.64; Loraux 1986: 35–6, 200. Encomium for the Athenians from Phyle: Lys. 2.61–6.
[18] Lys. 2.66. On the inscribed lists of war-dead, foreigners and barbarian archers are occasionally listed; see *IG* I³ 1172.35–7; 1180.5–7, 25–9; 1184.89–91; 1190.65–72, 136–41; 1192.152–7; cf. *IG* I³ 1144.34–8, 118–27; Loraux 1986: 32–3; Clairmont 1983: 50.

made explicit the status of these men, both citizens and foreigners, as war-dead. In these dynamics, the Thirty seem to have been forgotten, just as they go unmentioned in Lysias' funeral oration. We have no evidence for either the speech delivered over these dead or for the monument placed on their tomb, but, in view of our other evidence, it seems likely that the men's status as war-dead was emphasised and the Thirty were not. On the monument, this slide could be easily made by listing the places where the men were killed rather than the enemies whom they were fighting.[19] Subsequently, when the annual commemorations of the war-dead took place, these dead Athenians and foreigners were probably not singled out in the cult rituals; at this point, the assimilation will have been complete and the Thirty will have been completely forgotten. The rituals and their repetition will have created only this image of the dead democrats, so that once again all Athenians shared the same memories, just as they did with the announcement in the theatre.

The ways in which the sons of the dead democrats and the dead themselves were presented in these rituals would have been reinforced by the relationship between the topography of the city and the ceremonies (fig. 4). At the beginning of the Dionysia, the procession conveying the god to his sanctuary seems to have stopped in the Agora so that rituals could take place at the Eschara.[20] To reach this area, the participants would have walked by the Stoa Basileios, the probable location of Theozotides' great *stele* (fig. 2). In this way, the men who would be the audience in the theatre and possibly even the sons of the dead democrats themselves had in the course of the rituals to pass by the decree which would authorise the subsequent announcement about the sons in the theatre (fig. 4). These movements linked the ceremony with its emphasis that the fathers had died in war with the *stele* with its emphasis on the violence involved and its de-emphasis on the Thirty. The actual burial of the dead fathers ought to have created a similar set of connections between the spaces of the city and the rituals. If, as seems likely, the procession at the burial of the war-dead conveyed the bones from the Agora to the Demosion Sema, then the rituals for the dead democrats will have followed this pattern (fig. 4).[21] Those individuals involved, consequently, would have walked along the Panathenaic Way from the Agora to the Demosion Sema, a route

---

[19] For parallels on the lists of war-dead, see e.g. *IG* I³ 1144.32, 43, 130, 141; 1147.1–4, 127; 1162.1–3, 45–51; 1184.40, 44, 46, 48, 50, 52; Clairmont 1983: 48–50; Loraux 1986: 32.

[20] Above chapter 5 with note 10.

[21] Shear 2007a: 106. For the procession and the topography, see Gomme 1956: 102; Loraux 1986: 20; contra: Stupperich 1977: 32; Clairmont 1983: 3.

which required passing by the Stoa Basileios and the inscribed decree of Theozotides. In this way, the ritual connected the decree and the tomb in a setting which continually emphasised the dead men's status as killed in war and shifted all focus away from the Thirty. Together the ceremonies, the topography and the inscription worked to create a specific set of memories about the circumstances surrounding the dead democrats' deaths. Shared by all the Athenians, their remembering was reinforced each year by the repetition of the rituals in the theatre and the Demosion Sema.

Through these different rites on the Akropolis, in the theatre and in the Demosion Sema, the *demos* created a series of very specific memories and images (fig. 4). After the inaugural sacrifice to Athena, subsequent celebrations included all the Athenians so that they created memories of returning from Phyle for those individuals, like the men of the city, who had not in fact participated in the events. While the initial sacrifice served to separate out the actual participants from the other Athenians, all later repetitions included the whole *demos* and so they unified the men of the city and the men of the Peiraieus. This sacrifice singled out the return from Phyle as a critical moment in the history of the democratic city and it ensured that future generations had a memory of this important event. The rituals of the announcements in the theatre and of the burial of the dead democrats brought out the assimilation of the fathers and sons to the war-dead and the war-orphans respectively and de-emphasised the roles of the Thirty and the men of the Peiraieus. Again, these public ceremonies created a single memory for all Athenians and so served to unite them together into one body. Both rituals also allowed the *demos* to connect the present with the democratic past, as if the oligarchy had not taken place. Meanwhile, the addition of the sacrifice and the adaptation of existing rites also served to display the power and control of the *demos*. In the case of the City Dionysia, the audience will have included foreigners visiting Athens for the festival: upon their return home, they could spread the word that the Athenian *demos* was united again and firmly in control of the city. In this way, they were shown that the *stasis* had been a temporary aberration and they would not have the opportunity to interfere again in Athenian internal affairs.

REMEMBERING THE THIRTY?

The strategies of these rituals, accordingly, are to bring out the comparisons between the events of 404/3 and war and to de-emphasise the role of the Thirty, sometimes completely. In this way, they complement dynamics which we have already seen at work in the texts and monuments, but they also force us to ask whether the Thirty could actually be remembered by the Athenians. *Stasis*, too, was very much a part of the events of 404/3; could it also have a place in the Athenians' memories or was the topic too likely to instigate fracture and so to undo the unity created by the rituals? In the aftermath of the *demos*' return, how the Athenians addressed these issues would be critical not only for the future of the city, but also for the memories of these past events and the ways in which they would be celebrated. In fact, *stasis* proved to be so problematic that the Athenians could not actually remember it as such and the events of 404/3 had to be recast in the form of external war. While this strategy made room in the *demos* for the men of the city, it also largely removed the Thirty from the city's collective memory so that they could only be remembered in very circumscribed ways, if at all.

As civil strife, *stasis* is itself a problematic state of affairs because it pits citizens against other citizens. In the Greek *polis*, it brings out the divisions which, according to Nicole Loraux, are always latent in the city.[22] Consequently, it cannot be celebrated: 'there can be no "good victory" after a *stasis* in which blood was shed' writes Loraux.[23] Since it involves internal conflict, to rejoice in victory afterwards is to celebrate the defeat and death of one's fellow citizens, not external enemies, as in war.[24] If *stasis* is too problematic for celebration, then it cannot be commemorated; but, without monuments as nodes of memory, it also cannot be remembered. These dynamics suggest that the proper tactic for this problem is to forget *stasis* entirely, as if it had never taken place.[25] So the Athenians tried to do after the oligarchies of 411, but forgetting the events also allowed *stasis* to happen again, as the Athenians found to their cost in 404. After the reconciliation and the return of the *demos* in Boedromion of 403, these old models were no longer sufficient.

The Athenians did not, however, remember the events as *stasis*, as both the inscriptions and the rituals make clear. In his decree, Theozotides is quite specific about how the democratic citizens died and the circumstances under which they displayed their *andragathia*: they came to the aid of the democracy.[26] The term *stasis* has carefully been avoided in the initial clauses of the decree proper and there is no indication that it would have appeared elsewhere in the text. Indeed, it is hard to imagine how

---

[22] Loraux 2002: 93–104.   [23] Loraux 2002: 101.
[24] Compare Herodotos' contrast between ἔμφυλος στάσις, *stasis* among one's own people, and πόλεμος ὁμοφρονέων, war of common consent; Hdt. 8.3.1.
[25] Loraux 2002: 41–4, 64–7 and cf. 73–4.   [26] *SEG* xxviii 46.4–9.

it would have been relevant to the missing sections which contained the details of the award to the sons and the ways in which it was to be implemented. As it is now preserved, the honours for the Athenians returning from Phyle stress the fact of the return which they made possible, their actions in beginning to depose those ruling with 'unjust statutes' and the danger to which they exposed themselves.[27] Again, *stasis* and its cognates are absent from the preserved text. Since the decree itself is not preserved, we cannot be completely certain that these terms were avoided in it; their appearance, however, would certainly have clashed with the image provided in the rest of the monument and it seems unlikely. Similarly, there is no indication that these terms appeared in the lost text of the sales documents.[28] In the rewards for the foreigners who returned with the Athenians, the emphasis is on the ways in which the men helped the *demos,* not on the circumstances which made these actions necessary.[29] As far as we can ascertain, *stasis* and its related words are once again not used in this text. These terms are also avoided in the reinscribed proxeny decrees, which simply explain that the earlier decrees were taken down 'in the time of the Thirty'.[30] They do not make clear why the removal of these texts seemed logical or the circumstances in which the city found herself. Likewise, these terms also seem to have been avoided in the reconciliation agreement, a document in which we might well have expected to find *stasis* and its cognates. The inscribed texts, accordingly, very conspicuously avoided these terms, and, on the basis of this clear absence, it is hard to imagine that they appeared in the now lost sections of these documents.

The rituals which we have discussed also have other concerns which are incompatible with *stasis.* Both the oaths of reconciliation and the repetition of the sacrifices to Athena are concerned to create unity among the participants and to mark them all out as members of the *demos.* Even the dynamics of the initial sacrifice seem more concerned with identifying the men of the Peiraieus and excluding the men of the city than in celebrating *stasis.* When Xenophon and Lysias will come to describe the event, they will also not use this word and its cognates in this part of their narratives.[31] For Plutarch, subsequent celebrations are about freedom and, again, *stasis* does not figure in his description.[32] The announcements of the sons of the dead democrats and the burial of the dead fathers similarly have no emphasis on *stasis* and their focus is, instead, on the military connections.

---

[27] *SEG* xxviii 45.73–6; Aischin. 3.190.   [28] *SEG* xxxii 161.   [29] RO 4.4–8.
[30] *IG* i³ 229.1–4; *IG* ii² 6.11–14; *Agora* xvi 37.9–11; Walbank, *Proxenies* 26.4–6.
[31] Above notes 1 and 2.   [32] Above note 10.

In the public sphere of inscriptions and rituals, accordingly, the Athenians very clearly chose not to remember the events of 404/3 as *stasis*, as fighting between different citizens of the same city. Indeed, they resolutely forgot that it had existed. They did so conspicuously and frequently in both monuments and rituals celebrated on a regular cycle so that they also stressed, just as they had in the reconciliation agreement and its oaths, that they were forgetting.

Conspicuously forgetting *stasis* was an important part of the Athenians' strategy for remembering the events of 404/3 because it allowed them to be reconstructed as external war. This emphasis on war comes out very clearly in our documents and rituals and it was reinforced by the construction of three additional monuments, two trophies for their victory and a tomb for the Lakedaimonians on the road to the Academy (fig. 4). That war, not *stasis*, had taken place is brought out unambiguously in Theozotides' decree. Already at the beginning of the decree proper, the text stresses that fathers died a violent death.[33] In the lines that follow, the assimilation of the sons to the war-orphans emphasises that the events in question were external war, not *stasis*.[34] This connection is brought out again by the virtues attributed to the fathers: *euergesia* and *andragathia* are appropriate descriptions of the qualities of citizens killed fighting for the city.[35] The term *andragathia*, the quality of being an *aner agathos*, also picks up on the use of exactly this noun and this adjective in the announcement of the orphans at the Dionysia.[36] This relationship further reinforces the identification of the fighting as external war.

Similar strategies also appear in the rewards for the Athenians and the foreigners returning from Phyle. In the inscription for the Athenians, the epigram focuses on the honorands' attempts to depose those ruling the city unjustly and stresses that they hazarded their bodies in the process.[37] The awards which Aischines describes further bring out the nature of the conflict because the sacrifice and the dedications are exactly parallel to the normal procedures for thanking the gods for external military victory.[38] In the decree for the foreigners, the honorands are described as joining in the return from Phyle, a phrase which suggests a return from exile with force.[39] The military nature of the events is even more strongly brought out by the further description of foreigners who 'joined in fighting the battle of Mounichia'.[40] At this point in the decree, the text is extremely explicit about exactly what had taken place: it was certainly war, not *stasis*,

---

[33] *SEG* xxviii 46.4–6.   [34] *SEG* xxviii 46.6–11, 16–18.   [35] *SEG* xxviii 46.6–8.
[36] Above chapter 5.   [37] *SEG* xxviii 45.73–6; Aischin. 3.190.
[38] Aischin. 3.187; cf. Pritchett 1979: 186–92.   [39] RO 4.4–5.   [40] RO 4.7.

an image repeated in the other honorary inscriptions for the Athenians, dead and alive, who returned from Phyle.

The rituals also construct a similar image. We have already noticed that the sacrifice and dedications provided in the decree for the Athenians from Phyle follow the model of thanking the gods for military victory. Similarly, the announcement of the orphans at the Dionysia and the burial of the dead Athenians and foreigners in the Demosion Sema will have brought out the assimilation of these events to war and the dead to the city's regular war-dead. In these rituals, the dead Athenians and foreigners and the sons of the dead citizens are being treated no differently than if they had been killed fighting the Spartans in the Peloponnesian War. When the oldest of the orphans were announced, there will very probably also have been war-orphans involved, the sons of men killed in the final years of that great war. As far as we can see, both groups would have been treated exactly the same and no distinction would have been made between them. The connections with military success will also have been brought out by the democrats' sacrifice to Athena. On the initial occasion, when only the men from the Peiraieus participated, their actions will have evoked the image of rituals thanking the gods for military victory. That they marched in arms in the procession would have emphasised this particular image. In subsequent years, the participation of the whole *demos* should have reinforced this image. That this sacrifice was seen as a celebration of military victory is further brought out in Plutarch's description of it. He not only describes it as a thank-offering, a *charisterion,* but he included it in a series of rituals which are connected with other important victories, including Marathon, Naxos and Salamis.[41] Plataia and Mantineia are also invoked in this passage. Including the return from Phyle in this list of important victories brings out the status of the occasion as one celebrating military success and even on a par with the great battles against the Persians in the early fifth century. *Stasis,* in contrast, is strikingly absent from Plutarch's description. In the rituals, as in the inscriptions, consequently, the return from Phyle was repeatedly celebrated as a military victory. Each time one of these rituals was held, it constructed only this image of the event so that it became the only memory which the Athenians had about the overthrow of the Thirty.

The images presented by the texts and rituals were also reinforced by the three monuments connected with these events. Lysias reports that the *demos* set up a trophy over their enemies, but he does not indicate which battle was celebrated by this monument.[42] Since it seems to be an

---

[41] Above note 10.   [42] Lys. 2.63.

important structure which he links with the tomb of the Lakedaimonians, it seems most likely that it celebrated the *demos'* success at Mounichia.[43] If this inference is correct, then the monument will have been set up where Thrasyboulos and his forces routed the men of the city.[44] Xenophon also mentions an earlier trophy out in the countryside which Thrasyboulos and his forces set up near Phyle after they routed the forces sent against them by the Thirty.[45] These structures identified the conflicts very clearly as military engagements against external enemies and not as *stasis* against fellow citizens.[46] If Lysias' trophy is correctly associated with the Peiraieus, then it will have commemorated the events as war in a prominent place in the city. Another military monument was created by burying the Spartans killed in the fighting between Pausanias' forces and the men of the Peiraieus.[47] This tomb was located just outside of the Dipylon Gate on the road to the Academy and near to the Demosion Sema (fig. 4).[48] Now only fragmentarily preserved, the inscription will have set the monument apart from other neighbouring structures by its use of Laconian, rather than Attic, script to record not only the names of the individual men, but also, in larger letters, their ethnic, Lakedaimonians.[49] Through these strategies, the text marked the occupants as foreigners and *polemioi* of the Athenians; they were, consequently, killed in external war, not in *stasis*. In this setting, the tomb of the Lakedaimonians lay not far from the Demosion Sema and the grave of the democrats and their foreign supporters. This juxtaposition should have reinforced the military nature of the monuments and their emphasis that the engagements had been external war rather than civil strife.

Together, the inscriptions, the rituals and the monuments created a single image of the conflict which had occurred in Athens: it had been war fought against external enemies, the Lakedaimonians, and not *stasis* involving fellow citizens. By reproducing this message in texts, rituals and monuments, the Athenians repeatedly remembered the events as external war rather than civil strife. In this way, they stressed exactly how they were remembering these particular events. The inscriptions and monuments

---

[43] Trophy: see also Todd 2007: 262–3; battle: see Xen. *Hell.* 2.4.10–19.
[44] For battlefield trophies and their dynamics, see Pritchett 1974: 275 with further references.
[45] Xen. *Hell.* 2.4.6–7.
[46] Indeed, Pritchett's lists of battlefield trophies do not include any examples set up in *stasis* except for the trophy erected near Phyle; Pritchett 1974: 264–9.
[47] Xen. *Hell.* 2.4.33; Lys. 2.63.
[48] Willemsen 1977; Clairmont 1983: 203–4 no. 60a with further references; Stroszeck 2006. For a Spartan view of this tomb, see Low 2006: 98–9.
[49] *IG* II² 11678.

served to write this particular version of the events on to the topography so that they physically reminded viewers and readers that the events had been war, and not civil strife. These strategies further stressed that the *demos* was obeying the injunction of the reconciliation agreement not to remember past wrongs: victory over an external enemy is not a past wrong against fellow citizens, but *stasis* automatically is.

Focusing on the events from this perspective and turning the Spartans into the primary enemies of the *demos* also had consequences for the image of the Thirty. We have already seen that the reconciliation agreement made the Thirty and their closest associates into the men responsible for the events which had occurred and it absolved the men of the city from any part in the deeds of the Thirty.[50] In contrast, the strategies of the documents, rituals and monuments could only work if the enemies of the Athenians were either left unspecified or identified as the Spartans, as they are in the tomb of the Lakedaimonians by the Dipylon Gate. The Thirty, consequently, tend to disappear from view. In Theozotides' decree, we hear only of 'the oligarchy' and, in the rewards for the Athenians from Phyle, of 'those ruling the city with unjust statutes'.[51] In the preserved sections of the document for the foreign supporters, the opponents of the *demos* are not mentioned at all. In the other inscriptions, the Thirty appear in the sales documents along with the Eleven and oligarchs, while the proxeny decrees normally state that the earlier inscriptions were destroyed 'in the time of the Thirty'.[52] Turning *stasis* into external war, consequently, also required a significant erasure of the Thirty from the city's memorial and ritual landscape. In order to remove the focus from these particular men, the oligarchy is explicitly invoked in ways which find no parallel in the responses to the events of 411. Oligarchy is now juxtaposed with democracy in such a way that the rule of the *demos* is shown to be superior. This strategy is very clear in Theozotides' decree and it is also at work in the Bouleuterion complex where the honours for the Athenians from Phyle and the sales documents serve to juxtapose the behaviour of the good Athenian democrats and of the bad Athenian oligarchs, as we saw in chapter 8. Similarly, the new court facilities and the new Mint also suggest a comparison between democracy and oligarchy, as we saw in chapter 9. In these responses, tyranny plays much less of a role than it did in the aftermath of the events of 411. Democracy is no longer

---

[50] Above chapter 7.   [51] *SEG* xxviii 46.5; *SEG* xxviii 45.74–5; Aischin. 3.190.
[52] Sales: *SEG* xxxii 161 *stele* 1.4–5; *stele* 3.7; Proxeny decrees: above note 30; the exception is *IG* ii² 52 which says that the Thirty destroyed the earlier *stele*.

being defined simply as the opposite of tyranny, a category which covers too many possible options.[53] Now for the first time, democracy is also being defined as not being oligarchy.[54] If political systems cannot be so neatly characterised as they were before 404, now the possible options bear more relation to the Athenians' actual experiences. The location of at least some of these monuments in the Agora with its statues of Harmodios and Aristogeiton and Demophantos' decree also showed that the issue of tyranny was not simply being ignored and, at least in the construction of images of behaviour for the good citizen, it still had an important role to play.

CONSEQUENCES

In the city's monuments and rituals, the *demos* engaged in a serious effort to remake the events of 404/3 from *stasis* into external war. This strategy required forgetting that civil strife had actually taken place and it reconstructed the results as a 'good victory' for the Athenians. As an external war against the Spartans, the fighting occasioned by the return of the *demos* from Phyle became an event which both the men of the Peiraieus and the men of the city could celebrate together, as they seem to have done with the sacrifice to Athena in the years after 403. By turning these events into a 'good victory' over an external foe, the Athenians also kept their oaths not to remember past wrongs against their fellow citizens. Turning *stasis* into war, however, was not an uncontentious process. The disagreements over the process are now visible to us in the fates of two of the proposed honours for the men returning from Phyle. Theozotides faced a *graphe paranomon* because of his decree, while Thrasyboulos' initial proposal that all the foreigners should be given Athenian citizenship was also attacked with a *graphe paranomon*, despite having been passed by the *demos*.[55] In these two legal cases, only Theozotides succeeded in defending his decree, hence the inscribed *stele*. Not everyone was immediately willing to turn *stasis* into 'good victory' and the process was not complete when any of these individual measures was passed nor when specific monuments were erected.

---

[53] R. Osborne 2003: 267–9; contra: Ober 2003: 224–5.

[54] The strategies at work here do not support Ober's contention that, about 400, the principal opposition remained between democracy and tyranny or that the *stasis* was thought to have ended with tyrant slaying; Ober 2003: 224–5. On the use of the term 'Thirty Tyrants', see Krentz 1982: 16 note 2.

[55] Theozotides: Lys. fr. LXIV.128–50 (Carey); Todd 2000: 382–3; above chapter 7. Thrasyboulos: Arist. *Ath. Pol.* 40.2; above chapter 7.

Instead, creating victory was a continuing process which had to be repeated again and again through the city's rituals and topography. After 403, on an annual basis, the Athenians sacrificed to Athena to celebrate their victory and the return of the *demos* which it enabled. On every occasion, they were reminded that these events celebrated the end of war, not the end of *stasis*, and, irrespective of their actual actions in 404/3, they all shared the same memory of these events. In the same way, at the Dionysia, the presentation of the war-orphans made no distinction between the sons of men killed in war and the sons of the dead democrats, while the fathers were repeatedly memorialised as *andres agathoi* and good democrats who died to save the city from external enemies. Every year, the Athenians were reminded again that the overthrow of the Thirty was not *stasis*, but war, and the ritual created this specific memory of this event, which was shared by all the Athenians. The shared memories created by these two rituals also served to unify the *demos* and to erase the distinctions between the men of the Peiraieus and the men of the city. While the rituals caused the Athenians to remember the events of 404/3 as external war, they also required them to forget on a regular basis that it actually had been *stasis* and that the Thirty had been responsible. Simultaneously recalled and forgotten publicly in these ways, the (re)constructed events themselves became part of the Athenians' responses to oligarchy.

The memories created by the rituals were reinforced by the monuments erected in the cityscape. The tomb was located in the Demosion Sema with the graves of the other war-dead and the honours for the foreigners returning from Phyle were erected on the Akropolis (fig. 4). The Agora, meanwhile, was the location of Theozotides' decree (probably) at the Stoa Basileios, while the honours for the Athenians and the sales documents were located in the Bouleuterion complex (table 9; fig. 2).[56] In this setting, they were juxtaposed with the Stoa Poikile and its paintings and shields commemorating victory over external enemies, particularly the Persians and Spartans.[57] In this way, the new victory was made part of this series of successes against external enemies. These monuments also contrasted with the statues of Harmodios and Aristogeiton, the Tyrannicides, in the centre of the Agora (fig. 8). Success against internal enemies was contrasted with external military victory, but the visual juxtaposition also points to the real situation: overthrowing the Thirty has been *stasis* as well as a military success, a fact carefully ignored in the texts. For this reason, the 'good victory' had to be repeatedly constructed not only through the city's rituals, but

---

[56] Above chapter 8.   [57] Paus. 1.15.1–4; *IG* I³ 522.

also by individual viewers' movements from one monument to the next in the Agora and the Demosion Sema, settings which reinforced the texts' emphasis on military victory (fig. 4). Moving on to the Akropolis, the site of the honours for the foreigners and the sacrifice to Athena, brought yet another location into play, as did the presentation of the orphans in the theatre on the south slope of the Akropolis at the Dionysia. Using four different parts of the city required viewers and participants continually to (re)construct their memories of these events, a process aided by the monuments' use of the same set of images. The distances between the different areas, however, also created empty spaces, gaps into which competing memories of the same events and *stasis* itself could disappear and so be forgotten. The repetition on all the monuments and in all the rituals of the image of good victory won against external enemies ensured that only this particular memory prevailed against the gaps of forgetfulness. The monuments and the rituals together bring out repeatedly not only the *demos*' need to stress its remembrance of victory, but also its need to say that it was forgetting *stasis*.

This construction of 'good victory' out of the more complicated reality of civil strife had further consequences for the memory of the Thirty. As we have seen, in the inscriptions, they are remembered in very circumscribed ways, if at all, so that they largely fall into the gaps of oblivion. The strategies also affected the ways in which these events would subsequently be remembered. In Lysias' funeral oration, the democrats, both living and dead, have become heroic models worthy of citation and emulation.[58] They are the culmination of a series of earlier examples of the Athenians' great military deeds, which begin with the defeat of the Amazons, the Thebans and Eurystheus and include the Persian Wars and a selection of battles in the fifth century.[59] The only discordant note is the oblique reference to the disaster at Aigospotamoi and the cryptic allusions to further consequences, which are usually understood as references to the battle of Knidos.[60] This section serves to introduce the events of 404/3, the final engagement of the narrative. Lysias cannot deny that the exiled democrats were involved in *stasis*, but he also describes them as fleeing slavery, fighting (μαχόμενοι) on behalf of justice and engaging in *stasis* on behalf of democracy; the foreigners among them fought for the safety of the city.[61] In fact,

[58] Lys. 2.61–6.

[59] Amazons: Lys. 2.4–6; Thebans: Lys. 2.7–10; Eurystheus: Lys. 2.11–16; Persian Wars: Lys. 2.20–47; fifth century: Lys. 2.48–58.

[60] Lys. 2.58–60; Todd 2007: 258–9; Lamb 1930: 58–9 note b; Bizos 1967: 67; Medda 1995: 136 note 17.

[61] *Stasis*: Lys. 2.61, 63, 65; actions of the exiles: Lys. 2.61; foreigners: Lys. 2.66.

the democrats could not be defeated.[62] Their opponents are described as *polemioi* and the reference to the tomb of the Lakedaimonians provides further definition.[63] In this way, the events are turned into external war and the focus is shifted on to the Spartans, while the democrats' citizen opponents are only described in very general terms. By placing this section after his comments on Aigospotamoi, Lysias also implies that the successes of the democrats in 404/3 were actually the culmination of the war against the Peloponnesians. He further shows the influence of the public strategies when he describes the democrats as 'putting their own bodies in danger', a phrase very similar to the one used in the epigram for the Athenians returning from Phyle.[64] His characterisation of the foreigners 'who came to the aid of the *plethos* (or masses)' recalls the dead Athenians '[co]mi[ng] to the aid of the democracy' in Theozotides' decree, particularly because Lysias often uses the term *plethos* as a synonym for democracy.[65] Lysias, consequently, shows clearly the influence of the public responses and he has allowed the Thirty and oligarchy to slip into the gaps of forgetfulness.

The funeral speech which forms the greater part of Plato's *Menexenos* employs a comparable approach to the events of 404/3. Plato initially describes the situation as a 'domestic war' which was fought and he contrasts it with *stasis* which takes place in other cities.[66] That these events were war is reinforced by the later reference to 'those who died in this war' and the events at Eleusis are, likewise, described as war.[67] The enemy, however, is never named. Instead, the focus is on the moderation of the Athenians and the ways in which the men of the Peiraieus and the men of the city intermingled with each other; they also mixed together 'beyond hope with the other Greeks'.[68] This last phrase provides the only hint that the events were not purely an Athenian affair. In this version, the Thirty are conspicuously absent, as is the term oligarchs, and the focus is on reconciliation, not only of the living, but also of the dead.[69] In this way, the Spartans' role in the actual events is forgotten, while the context of the funeral oration reinforces the memory of war rather than internal strife. Since the *Menexenos* is generally identified as a parody or pastiche of speeches for the war-dead, the appearance of these strategies suggests

---

[62] Lys. 2.64.   [63] Lys. 2.61, 62, 63; cf. 65.
[64] Lys. 2.63: ἐν τοῖς σώμασι τοῖς ἑαυτῶν κινδυνεύσαντες; cf. *SEG* xxviii 45.76: κίνδυνον σώμασιν ἀράμενοι.
[65] Lys. 2.66: οἳ τῷ πλήθει βοηθήσαντες; cf. *SEG* xxviii 46.5–6: [β]ο̣[ηθ]όντ|ε̣ς τῆι δημοκρατίαι. Lysias' use of *plethos*: Todd 2007: 620.
[66] Pl. *Menex.* 243e1–4.   [67] Pl. *Menex.* 243e6–7; 244a3–4.   [68] Pl. *Menex.* 243e4–6.
[69] Reconciliation of the dead: Pl. *Menex.* 244a3–b3.

that they were not uncommon in such orations at this period.[70] While the overall dialogue brings out the emptiness of the patriotism celebrated in such speeches,[71] the section on the events of 404/3 also constitutes Plato's response to the Athenians' collective remembering (and forgetting) of them. By taking these strategies to the extreme, he brings out their absurdity and lack of connection with the actual events. That these words are spoken by Sokrates, a man whose condemnation was linked in part to his relationships with members of the Thirty, further exposes the hollowness of this rhetoric: if the reconciliation was really so mild, so easily achieved, so universally welcomed, why was the speaker later condemned to death? Bringing the Athenians back together again, Plato seems to suggest, was hard and painful despite the ways in which it was subsequently remembered.

The influence of these collective memories of the events is also apparent in 330 when Aischines comes to describe them in his attempt to deny Demosthenes a gold crown. Aischines compares Demosthenes' achievements unfavourably with the accomplishments and rewards of fifth-century Athenians such as Themistokles, Miltiades, the democrats from Phyle and Aristeides the just.[72] He next turns to the honours awarded in the fifth century and describes three monuments in order: the Eion Herms, the Marathon painting in the Stoa Poikile and the inscription with the rewards for the Athenians returning from Phyle at the Bouleuterion.[73] In this description, Aischines switches smoothly from one memorial to the next with no indication of the actual distances involved: 'pass on in thought to the Stoa Poikile' and 'furthermore, at the Metroon beside the Bouleuterion'.[74] By constructing his text in this way, he makes concrete the gaps in memory which allow the forgetting of competing memories. His sequence of monuments further presupposes that all three of these events were military victories over external enemies. When he comes to describe the attack on the democrats at Phyle, the Lakedaimonians come first and the Thirty are added on, almost as an afterthought, so that the focus remains on the external enemies.[75] The whole section shows how, in 330, the overthrow of the Thirty could be remembered easily and unproblematically as another 'good victory' won by the Athenians, while *stasis* had been forgotten. Similarly, Plutarch will place his description of the sacrifice to Athena in a list of religious rituals for external military victory,

---

[70] Parody or pastiche: Todd 2007: 153–4 with further references; Loraux 1986: 94, 324–5, 327. *Menexenos* as evidence: compare Loraux 1986: 94.
[71] Compare Loraux 1986: 94, 321; Loraux 2002: 219.   [72] Aischin. 3.181.
[73] Aischin. 3.183–91.   [74] Aischin. 3.186, 187 with chapter 8, note 81.   [75] Aischin. 3.187.

as we noted earlier, and he will forget completely that the events actually involved *stasis* and fighting between different groups of Athenians.

As these literary texts clearly show, the politics of remembering and forgetting the events of 404/3 were not limited to monuments and rituals because their imagery, in turn, affected the ways in which subsequent orators and writers would choose to recall the overthrow of the Thirty and the return of the *demos* from exile. Even while this episode was still within living memory, it could be presented as a 'good victory' won over external foes. In this way, Theozotides and the other Athenians who had returned from Phyle were successful in their (re)construction of the events of 404/3 and *stasis* could, indeed, be forgotten, as the Athenians took great care to remind everyone. Our evidence for the contentiousness of the process and for the contestation of the public memory of these events, however, should not make us forget that the whole process and every monument and inscription had to be approved by the *demos* and the *boule* before it could be undertaken. Many Athenians were evidently all too ready to remember only certain events and to forget the rest, a process repeatedly reinforced by the city's rituals and monuments.

THE POLITICS OF REALITY

The imagery of the Athenians' responses to the Thirty presented the city as united against external foes and once again properly democratic. Athens had been remade once more as the democratic city, while her political past was reclaimed and used to show that the rule of the *demos* was historically her proper type of constitution. Together, the Athenians repeatedly celebrated the events of 404/3 as external war and, together, they collectively consigned *stasis* and the Thirty to the gaps of forgetfulness through their rituals and monuments. The rise of the Thirty and the accompanying *stasis*, however, also showed that these public responses and the images which they created were not enough to prevent future problems: many of the same tactics had been used after 411, but they had not stopped oligarchs from once again seizing power. Practical measures were also needed. They fall into two categories: a series of important constitutional changes which interlock with the project of reinscribing the laws and the removal of the threat posed by the oligarchic enclave at Eleusis.

In discussing the project for (re)writing the laws, we saw that it included both the replacement of destroyed laws and the proposing of new laws. The effects of this process were not limited to the inscribed display in the Agora because it also inaugurated a period of important constitutional changes which effectively prevented further overthrow of the democracy. Of these measures, the most significant was the distinction now made between a law (*nomos*) and a decree (*psephisma*), documents which, in the fifth century, had not been considered to be different from one another.[76] At this time, the Athenians passed a law specifying that 'no decree of the *boule* or the *demos* is to override a law'.[77] From now on, laws would be permanent and of general application, while decrees were temporary measures applying to a specific situation or, in the case of honorary decrees, to a specific person or persons.[78] Furthermore, existing decrees in conflict with a new law were now repealed automatically.[79] These changes were probably introduced in 403/2 or just afterwards because the few documents which do not follow these requirements all seem to belong in this year.[80] This date is supported by Andokides who links the regulation giving laws priority over decrees both to the decree of Teisamenos and to another law mandating that the laws are to be used from the archonship of Eukleides in 403/2.[81]

This new distinction between laws and decrees also affected the ways in which legislation was now made. Decrees would be made by the *ekklesia* after they had been put forward by the *boule*.[82] In contrast, a new procedure was needed for laws, which would not be made by the assembly. Instead, a new body called *nomothetai*, who first appear in Teisamenos' decree, would make laws for the city. These *nomothetai* were to be drawn from the men who had taken the Heliastic oath and so were eligible to be jurors.[83] Laws could be proposed by any man who wished, as long as they had been displayed in writing in front of the Eponymoi in the Agora, but new laws were only made once a year in Hekatombaion, the first month, and they had to be read out in the *ekklesia*; the final product, however, was produced by the *nomothetai* who had been authorised by the assembly.[84] As this brief outline makes clear, this procedure was not an easy one to use and making decrees

---

[76] Fifth century: Hansen 1978: 316–17, 323; cf. Ostwald 1986: 523.

[77] Andok. 1.87; Dem. 23.87; 24.30; Hansen 1978: 324; Hansen 1979: 28–30, 52.

[78] Compare Dem. 23.218; Hansen 1979: 28–31. This distinction continued to be respected; see Hansen 1979: 31–53.

[79] Hansen 1978: 324–5.

[80] For the exceptions, see Hansen 1979: 32–43. Since Theozotides' decree concerns honours for the sons of the dead democrats, it is not an exception to the rule, as Hansen thinks; Hansen 1979: 32, 35, 37, 38.

[81] Andok. 1.87; cf. also Dem. 24.42 (law of Diokles), which should also belong in 403/2; above chapter 8.

[82] P. J. Rhodes 1979–80: 306; Hansen 1978: 317–24.

[83] Dem. 24.22; P. J. Rhodes 1979–80: 306; Ostwald 1986: 521; MacDowell 1975: 64, 68; Hansen 1985: 265.

[84] Dem. 24.20–3; cf. 20.89–96; P. J. Rhodes 1979–80: 306; Ostwald 1986: 520–2; MacDowell 1975: 64–5, 67–9; P. J. Rhodes 1985: 57, 60.

in the *ekklesia* remained a much simpler procedure.[85] Since laws and decrees were now distinguished, new procedures were needed to address an illegal decree and an illegal law. While the *graphe paranomon* continued to be used to attack the legalities of a decree, a new procedure, a suit against an illegally proposed law (γραφὴ νόμον μὴ ἐπιτήδειον θεῖναι), was created on the model of the *graphe paranomon*.[86] Consequently, adopting what appears to be a simple distinction between a law and a decree required considerably rethinking about the procedures for making the rules by which the Athenians would now live.

The strict new rules about making laws now prevented the *demos* from appointing *ad hoc* committees which would be empowered to change the city's laws and constitution, as the Thirty had been in 404. Similarly, these new procedures would also have prevented the repetition of the similar events in 411 when the constitutional issues were directly linked to the mandate of the Four Hundred. In combination with the inscribed version of the laws, the new procedures would also prevent the manipulation of the laws and the constitution for the needs of a particular regime or a particular group of Athenians. Consequently, instituting a regime other than the rule of the *demos* could only be done by overthrowing the whole legal system and replacing it with a new set of laws, a massive undertaking, as the work of the *anagrapheis* had shown. The city's existing laws, decrees and procedures could also not be used to legitimise any regime other than the democracy. In this way, the possibilities of political revolution by dissatisfied oligarchs or potential tyrants were greatly restricted by these measures.

This focus on the city's constitution was further reinforced by the textual and spatial politics which we have seen in the documents and buildings in the Agora. Since the inscribed laws were set up either between the columns of the two annexes of the Stoa Basileios or, in the case of the calendar, on the ledge in the back wall of the building, their appearance and physical location also distinguished them from decrees, which were inscribed on their own individual, free-standing *stelai* (figs. 7, 16); while they could be erected near the stoa, they could also be set up elsewhere in the Agora and even in the city. The documents' stress that democracy was the proper form of *politeia* for Athens reinforced the constitutional activity which strengthened this political system. These legal developments also helped to define further and in more detail the system under which the Athenians

---

[85] P. J. Rhodes 1979–80: 306; cf. MacDowell 1975: 73, 74; P. J. Rhodes 1985: 57. For future developments, see P. J. Rhodes 1979–80: 306; MacDowell 1975: 65–6, 69–72; and the subsequent discussion: Hansen 1979–80: 87–99; P. J. Rhodes 1985: 55–60; Hansen 1985: 345–60.

[86] Arist. *Ath. Pol.* 59.2; Dem. 24.33; Hansen 1978: 325–9; P. J. Rhodes 1981: 545.

had (tacitly) agreed to live when they swore the reconciliation agreement in Boedromion in 403. Constitutional change, consequently, was also part of the response to the Thirty.

While this new legislation focuses on the differences between laws and decrees, it also suggests that the *ekklesia* itself and its powers were under scrutiny at this time. If the documents about the *boule* showed in about 409 that the council was the servant of the *demos*, now the *demos* itself was shown not to have unlimited power.[87] The discussions about the composition of the *demos*, which we considered from the perspective of Athenian identity in chapter 8, also had a direct effect on who could and could not participate in the assembly. In the aftermath of all the contestation, the majority of the Athenians decided that citizenship would again depend on having two citizen parents. Only these men would be able to participate fully in the city's political life. Doing so took place primarily in two settings: in the *ekklesia* on the Pnyx and in the courts, now located in permanent facilities in the Agora (figs. 2, 4). Evidently, these decisions did not provide sufficient inducements to participate in the assembly because pay for doing so was also now introduced. Agyrrhios' initial payment of one obol was raised first by Herakleides to two obols and then again by Agyrrhios himself to three obols.[88] It had reached this third level already by the time of Aristophanes' *Ekklesiazousai*, performed sometime in the late 390s.[89] As this play makes clear, not every man received payment, which was restricted to the first comers, a figure perhaps determined by the number necessary for a quorum.[90] The decision to implement pay for at least some members of the *ekklesia* also brings out the continuing importance of doing one's civic duties.[91] Participation was still a hallmark of the democratic system and it was necessary if the city was to be properly run.

These developments focused on the long-term health of the democracy and on the ways of guarding it against future manipulations and they helped to lay out in legal form the new rules of engagement for the Athenians. Renewed *stasis* remained a very real threat, however, and a legal weapon was also needed to ensure that individual citizens continued to obey the reconciliation agreement and to abide by their oaths. To this end, Archinos

---

[87] Documents about the *boule*: *IG* I³ 105.   [88] Arist. *Ath. Pol.* 41.3.
[89] Ar. *Ekkl.* 289–93, 308–10, 380–95. On the date of the play, see Sommerstein 1998: 1–7 with further references.
[90] Ar. *Ekkl.* 289–93, 380–95; P. J. Rhodes 1981: 492; Gauthier 1993: 239–42, 247; Hansen 1996: 29–32.
[91] For increased participation by a broader range of Athenian citizens in the fourth century, see C. Taylor 2007.

introduced a new procedure, the *paragraphe*. It allowed a defendant who thought that the case against him violated the agreements to ask for a decision about the admissibility of the case.[92] The losing party was required to pay one sixth of the amount in question as a penalty.[93] According to the speaker of Isokrates 18, the first suit brought under this procedure, the purpose of the *paragraphe* was to ensure that men who broke the agreement suffered immediate punishment in addition to their eventual punishment from the gods for breaking their oaths.[94] As we saw in chapter 7, the existence of this procedure did not prevent speakers in legal cases from discussing previous deeds, both their own and their opponents', and the speaker of Isokrates 18 adopts precisely these tactics so that we hear in detail about how his problems with Kallimachos started when Athens was under the control of the Ten.[95] Since the agreement and the oaths are of central importance for the case, they, too, are repeatedly mentioned.[96] Strikingly for us, the speaker claims that many people are watching the outcome of the trial, not because they are interested in his personal affairs, but because 'they think it is a trial of the agreement'.[97] He also links the violation of the jurors' dikastic oaths and their oaths to uphold the agreement with a return to the situation which forced the reconciliation agreement to be made in the first place.[98] These statements emphasise the ways in which the courts and the law were instrumental in ensuring that the reconciliation agreement was upheld. In this formulation, the courts are the appropriate venue for negotiating differences created by the events under the Thirty, the same dynamic which we observed in the trials in chapter 7. Introducing the *paragraphe*, accordingly, allowed disputes arising from the *stasis* to be aired, but it prevented them from spiralling out of control and creating further division. In this way, it incorporated the agreement into the city's legal framework and it very much complemented the other contemporary legal reforms.

This emphasis on the rule of law and democracy as the city's proper *politeia* must have co-existed uneasily with the oligarchic enclave at Eleusis

---

[92] Isok. 18.1–3; P. J. Rhodes 1981: 473 with further references; Ostwald 1986: 510; Todd 1993: 136–7. The date of the introduction of the *paragraphe* is disputed. Although MacDowell's date of 401/0 has been frequently accepted, it has been called into question by Whitehead and Carawan, who prefer sometime in 402; MacDowell 1971b; Rhodes 1981: 473; Gagarin 2008: 186 note 24; Whitehead 2002: 71–90; Carawan 2006: 75–6. MacDowell's date would suggest a connection between the legislation and the re-incorporation of the oligarchs at Eleusis into the city, an occasion which may very well have raised further tensions.

[93] Isok. 18.3.   [94] Isok. 18.1–3.   [95] Isok. 18.5–12.

[96] E.g. Isok. 18.2, 4, 19–22, 25–7, 29, 30, 34, 35, 42, 44, 45, 47, 64, 67, 68.

[97] Isok. 18.42.   [98] Isok. 18.44.

in the months and years immediately after Boedromion of 403 (fig. 1). Despite the clauses of the reconciliation agreement, the oligarchs represented the potential for further *stasis*. How the *demos* would have handled this challenge in the long term we do not know because, in 401/0, the situation came to a head.[99] At this time, so Xenophon reports, the Athenians heard that the men at Eleusis were hiring mercenaries.[100] In response, the *demos* sent out the whole army and killed the generals from Eleusis when they came for a conference; the rest of the men at Eleusis then reconciled with the Athenians.[101] While Xenophon makes this action sound like an event which was over quickly, the speaker of Lysias 25 describes it as a siege.[102] In either case, the destruction of the leaders of the remaining oligarchs at Eleusis and the re-incorporation of the other men back into the city removed a potential source of future trouble for Athens. No longer would the oligarchs have a base from which they could potentially attack the city and those men discontented with the rule of the *demos* would either have to remain in Athens or go into exile, a step which would inevitably take them well away from the city so that they were unlikely to be able to cause trouble. Removing this possibility of further discord will have strengthened the rule of the *demos* and it will have left the courts and the law as the only way of resolving differences arising from the events under the Thirty. Since all the Athenians fought these oligarchs, the process will have also brought them together and provided them a concrete opportunity to act as a united *demos* against a common enemy. Image and reality were not so easily separated.

These political and constitutional developments interconnect with the other ways in which the Athenians responded to the Thirty. The links between the different parts of the response, however, should not blind us to their contentious nature. Both Thrasyboulos and Theozotides faced lawsuits when they tried to honour individuals involved with the return of the *demos*: remembering is not only a process, but it is also a contentious process. That Thrasyboulos' suit was brought by Archinos shows how men who had fought together against the Thirty did not necessarily agree on how the events should be memorialised. Since Archinos introduced the *paragraphe*, his particular concern with Thrasyboulos' proposal may well have

---

[99] Todd connects this date with the Spartans' inability to invade and the death of Agis; Todd 1985: 198–9; contra: Carawan 2006: 68–9, 75–6.
[100] Xen. *Hell.* 2.4.43. For the date, see Arist. *Ath. Pol.* 40.4. Xenophon merely describes it as 'at a later time'.
[101] Compare Arist. *Ath. Pol.* 40.4.   [102] Lys. 25.9.

been the constitutional issues.[103] Certainly, he was not completely against all rewards for individuals who fought the Thirty because he did propose the honours for the Athenians who returned from Phyle. The defeats both of Thrasyboulos' proposed rewards and of Phormisios' proposal restricting citizenship also emphasise that a leading role in overthrowing the Thirty did not necessarily translate into automatic support by the majority of the Athenians in the *ekklesia*. Similarly, as Euandros' *dokimasia* shows, activity on behalf of the Thirty did not necessarily preclude participation in the political life of the democratic city.

This contestation over honours and citizenship and the divisions brought out by the trials discussed in chapter 7 functioned at the level of the individual who, in every instance, repeatedly had to decide how he was going to respond to oligarchy on this particular occasion. These individual actions do not explain why our ancient sources are so insistent that the Athenians abided by the reconciliation agreement and did not remember past wrongs against their fellow citizens.[104] On the evidence of the legal speeches, such statements are simply not true. The decisions of individual men, however, did not prevent the Athenians from responding collectively to the Thirty: together, the documents, monuments and rituals showed how the Athenians were keeping to their agreement and this image was reinforced whenever any of the texts were read or the monuments were examined or the rites were celebrated. In the Agora, in the city's sanctuaries, in the theatre and in the Demosion Sema, the Athenians were shown to be united and lacking in recrimination as they remembered the events of 404/3 as external war rather than internal *stasis*. This collective memory of the democratic city's unity served to balance the individual actions of men working for their own ends. Responding to oligarchy and recreating the city for the *demos*, accordingly, were critical processes in allowing the Athenians to recover from *stasis* and to re-establish the democratic system on solid foundations. The politics of image were as necessary as the politics of reality.

---

[103] For Archinos' interest in constitutional issues, see R. Osborne 2003: 267; Strauss 1987: 96–7. As Strauss suggests, personal enmity may also have been involved.

[104] E.g. Xen. *Hell.* 2.4.43; Arist. *Ath. Pol.* 40.2; Wolpert 2002a: 48, 159 note 2 with further references.

The strategies of democracy

For Athenians looking back on the last decade or so of the fifth century, the overthrow of the democracy in 411 and 404 must have had an eerie similarity: on both occasions, the *demos* had been induced to appoint commissions to produce new laws for the city and then to vote itself out of existence. What guarantee was there, they must have wondered in the early fourth century, that such events would not take place again? Certainly, the threat of Spartan intervention and the new constitutional changes were important factors in preventing a repetition of these distressing events,[1] but equally significant were the Athenians' own public responses to oligarchy both after the oligarchies of 411 and after the events of 404/3. Ultimately, the rule of the *demos* could only be kept safe by the people themselves: their collective responses to oligarchy wrote democracy on to the city's landscape in a new way and they left no doubt that the *demos* cared to protect its rule and its control; the new legal developments further served to reinforce this imagery. Events, particularly in 411, had shown that democracy could not automatically be considered the proper *politeia* for the city. Now, perhaps for the first time, Athenians had to think consciously about what made democracy significant and how the rule of the *demos* was to be presented to the world. These responses to oligarchy, accordingly, also show us how the democracy wrote about itself and the ways in which it constructed its past.

The strategies of democracy after these two periods of oligarchy, however, were not identical. In the aftermath of the Thirty, the *demos* had to decide consciously that it would continue to use some, but not all, of the tactics developed after 411. Some of them had been shown to be ineffective and some of them did not match the different circumstances of the events in 404/3. In this sense, the response to the Thirty also reveals the *demos* responding to its own reactions to the oligarchies of 411 so that

---

[1] Compare R. Osborne 2003: 266–7; Todd 1985: 175–97, 200.

the period between 410 and 404 was now incorporated into the history of the democratic city. The *demos* positioned itself through its actions so that it was shown to be the proper ruler of the city and the legitimate successor to the earlier generations of democrats. The events after 404/3, accordingly, are both the *demos'* response to oligarchy and a reaction to its earlier actions after 411. Together, they demonstrated that Athens was now properly democratic, as she had historically been.

RESPONDING TO OLIGARCHY

In both 411 and 404/3, the oligarchies developed out of periods of intense discussion about the proper *politeia* for the city and, in both cases, commissions concerned with these issues were critical in gaining power for the oligarchs and dissolving the *demos*. Consequently, democracy had to be visibly established as the appropriate constitution for the city and it had to be shown to function. The oligarchies also appropriated the past for themselves in an effort to legitimise their rule and to show that it was *patrios*. The ways in which they used the city's physical spaces, and particularly the Agora and the Akropolis, also made the cityscape into places of contestation. Faced with these parallel circumstances in both 410 and 403, the *demos* used many of the same strategies to re-establish itself and its power.

In both periods, there was a concentrated effort to display democracy and its workings visibly in the city. In 410, for the first time, single copies of the city's inscriptions came to be set up in the Agora where, through their texts, they demonstrated the processes of democracy in action, as it were. Demophantos' decree together with the laws crucially showed that the rule of the *demos* was the only possible *politeia* for the city. The construction of the New Bouleuterion, the creation of the city's archives in the Old Bouleuterion and the display of the laws in the Stoa Basileios all served to reinforce these images. In 403 and the following years, the *demos* again used these same strategies to demonstrate once more that democracy was the only possible constitution for the city. Now dedicated court buildings were constructed in the Agora and additional inscriptions were erected both here and on the Akropolis. Their strategies once again served to put the workings of their rule on show and to demonstrate that the democracy was again functioning properly. In both periods, these actions also allowed the *demos* to reclaim the city's past for its own use. Through their actions, and particularly the republication and display of the laws, the iconic figures of Drakon, Solon and Kleisthenes were reclaimed from the oligarchs and shown to be the proper democratic ancestors of the current *demos* and its practices. These actions allowed the recovery more generally of the city's past and of traditions and offices which could not be linked to these three particular figures. The erection of decrees and other monuments both in the Agora and on the Akropolis also permitted the *demos* to reclaim these spaces in the city from the oligarchs. The Four Hundred's use of the Agora for their own purposes was particularly important in directing attention to this multi-purpose space which became the focus of attention both in 410 and again in 403 after the Thirty had also used the space as the centre of their own power. As a result of these oligarchic attentions, the *demos* over a period of about fifteen or so years turned the marketplace into the space of the democratic citizen.

The actions of the oligarchs in both 411 and 404/3 divided the Athenians and introduced *stasis* to the city. If the city was to have any chance of surviving, the citizens had to be reunited again and the fractures among them healed. In both cases, an important solution to these problems was an oath taken by all the Athenians. It was a brilliant choice because the very process itself reaffirms the unity of the community swearing the oath and assures its permanence. That the Athenians on both occasions were almost certainly arrayed by tribe and by deme served also to display the city in its democratic divisions to itself: the community being reaffirmed by this process was ruled by the *demos* and no one else. The rituals of the City Dionysia further provided another important occasion for creating unity within the *demos* and for displaying its control in an international setting.

Despite these similarities between the democrats' responses to the oligarchs of 411 and to the Thirty, there are also significant differences between the reactions to these two periods: responding to the Thirty was not merely a continuation of the *demos'* earlier actions after 411. That the Thirty were able to gain power at all demonstrated that not all problems had been fully resolved between 410 and 404. Most important, perhaps, was the issue of reconciliation. In 410/9, unity was created through the vehicle of Demophantos' decree and oath, but it presented a very uncompromising view: all the Athenians were shown to be democrats and prepared to kill tyrants. For supporters of the oligarchs, this image cannot have been very comforting and it made no accommodation for any other perspective. In 403, in contrast, reconciliation was the first step in responding to the Thirty. The resulting document and its accompanying oaths unified the divided city and they made clear the *demos'* rule of the city, but they also reconciled the two sides and re-incorporated the men of the city, the supporters of the oligarchs, into the community of the Athenian *demos*. Now, reconciliation and the creation of unity were separated from the display of the rule of the democracy. As far as we can tell, the stark and uncompromising tone of Demophantos' decree and oath were also absent from the reconciliation agreement.

If, in 403, reconciliation had to precede recreating the democratic city, then the events had further shown that the responses to the oligarchies of 411 were not sufficient. Demophantos' decree and oath had not prevented the Thirty from gaining power in 404. After 411, instead of considering the city's constitution, the democrats had become absorbed in a series of trials aimed at establishing blame for and complicity with the oligarchies. The *politeia*, meanwhile, was left unchanged. In 403, however, serious political reform was undertaken which made a repetition of the events of 411 and 404, if not impossible, then certainly far more difficult. Removing the ability to make laws from the *demos* and instituting a longer and more difficult process may have reassured some men of the city that the restored democracy was less radical than its predecessor. Instituting pay for the attendance of (at least some members of) the *demos* at the assembly, however, was hardly a move towards a restricted constitution. This decision also emphasised the important role which the *ekklesia* continued to play in the running of the city, even though it no longer had the power to make laws. The constitutional sphere shows some of the ways in which the democrats clearly learned the lessons of the inaction after 411: setting democracy on a solid footing again required serious thinking about how this system worked and not just the display of its power and its control of the city through monuments and inscriptions.

The patterns of commemoration after the two periods of oligarchy also differ. In the aftermath of 411, the focus was on the *demos* as a whole. All the Athenians had taken Demophantos' oath and their actions were memorialised by a single monument, the inscribed *stele* in the Agora. The only individuals honoured for their part in the overthrow of the oligarchs were the assassins of Phrynichos, none of whom were citizens at the time of their actions. This pattern of corporate commemoration is no different from the contemporary patterns of memorialising both victory in war and the war-dead in the Demosion Sema. In contrast, after 404/3, the actions of only a selected group of Athenians were celebrated: the men, both living and dead, who had brought the *demos* back from Phyle. This decision began to shift the focus from the corporate group to the individual, a transition which culminated with the statues for Konon and Euagoras in the Agora, the first bronze statues for living men.

Equally striking is the way in which commemoration after the return from Phyle failed to follow the pattern set by Demophantos' decree. This text is quite explicit about the honours for anyone killing the man who overthrows the democracy, who subsequently holds office, who sets himself up as tyrant, or who helps to set up a tyrant: if he lives, he is to receive half of the man's property and, if he dies, he and his sons are to receive the Tyrannicides' benefits.[2] The Thirty and their adherents had clearly overthrown the democracy, as well as fulfilling other criteria in Demophantos' list, but none of the returning Athenians were rewarded in the ways in which his decree prescribes. As Theozotides' decree shows, the dead democrats were treated as if they were war-dead and their sons as if they were war-orphans.[3] Consequently, the dead fathers were given a cult with the dead from other wars, rituals which clearly did not mark them out as the founders of democracy, and they certainly did not receive bronze statues in the Agora. Meanwhile, *sitesis* and *proedria* were definitely not awarded to the sons. These honours would have singled out specific individuals from the other Athenians returning from Phyle and they would have shown that all these men were not, in fact, equal. They would also have emphasised that their opponents had been Athenians and that what had taken place was *stasis*, rather than the war which the *demos* preferred to remember. Significant figures the dead democrats from Phyle certainly were, but they were not yet on a par with Harmodios and Aristogeiton. Such honours would be reserved for Konon and Euagoras, who defeated external enemies and killed no Athenians, tyrants or otherwise.

If the patterns of commemoration changed between the two responses to oligarchy, so, too, did the ways in which the Athenians remembered (and forgot) the deeds of the oligarchs. Demophantos' decree identifies both tyrants and oligarchs as *polemioi*, external enemies of the city, but, at the same time, the text makes clear that these men are Athenians.[4] The invocation of Harmodios and Aristogeiton and the juxtaposition of the decree and the statues also point towards the internal nature of the threat. In these relationships, there is a tension over whether the enemies of the city are really internal, the direction in which the statues point, or really external, the imagery of the text. In contrast, after 404/3, the Thirty were remembered only as external enemies who made war on the city and their status as Athenians was carefully glossed over. That the Lakedaimonians had intervened in the events and had fought against the men of the Peiraieus

---

[2] Andok. 1.97–8; above chapter 3, note 23.   [3] *SEG* xxviii 46.   [4] Shear 2007b: 150–1.

certainly aided these images, as they were linked together with the Thirty and their followers.

The oligarchs of 411, and particularly the Four Hundred, are not, however, mentioned in either Demophantos' decree or the honours for Thrasyboulos the assassin of Phrynichos. The very fact of these regimes is ignored and they are consigned to the gaps of memory. Subsequent events clearly showed the consequences of forgetting oligarchy: without any memory of oligarchy, it was impossible to prevent its recurrence. Consequently, the events of 404/3 could not simply be ignored, as the oligarchs of 411 had been. They could not, however, be remembered as *stasis*, as fighting between Athenian and Athenian. The Athenians' solution was to remember what had occurred as war and to create a 'good victory' out of the events. *Stasis*, meanwhile, was forgotten and the Thirty were only recalled selectively. These strategies further served to create unity among the Athenians and they allowed the men of the city to be re-incorporated into the community of the *demos* so that the Athenians were no longer divided.

These differing strategies of remembering and forgetting had further consequences for the ways in which Athenian identity was constructed. In the period after 411, the good Athenian was a democratic citizen who killed tyrants and modelled himself on the Tyrannicides Harmodios and Aristogeiton. With the events of 404/3 memorialised as external war, killing tyrants was no longer quite the right image of the good citizen. He continued to be a democratic citizen, but now he aided the democracy against oligarchy and fought on the city's behalf against her external enemies. Subsequently, the image of the tyrant slayer was invoked again for Konon and Euagoras, but now the emphasis was on the liberation which the tyrant slayers brought to the city, rather than the actual moment of killing the tyrant. In this way, the imagery could be used to celebrate victory in external war and it reinforced the identity of the good citizen as a democrat who fought the city's enemies. These changes in Athenian identity and in the strategies of remembering and forgetting also affected the ways in which democracy itself was defined. After 411, democracy continued to be juxtaposed with tyranny, just as it had been earlier in the century.[5] The events of 404/3, however, showed that this relationship was too simplistic. Instead, democracy was now juxtaposed both with tyranny and also with oligarchy, which events had shown was the real internal threat to the democratic city.[6]

Despite the similarities of the events in 411 and 404/3, the Athenians' responses to oligarchy were not identical and they did not simply continue

---

[5] Compare R. Osborne 2003: 268; Ober 2003: 224.   [6] Compare Lys. 28.11, 12–14; 18.25.

the same strategies. Democracy, unity, the city's past and her space were important aspects in both reactions to oligarchy. After the Thirty, the *demos* continued only those parts of the earlier project which had clearly worked; in the case of the *stelai* with the laws, reinscribing the text served to undo the actions of the oligarchs and to restore the display which had existed before they gained power. In the areas of reconciliation, the city's constitution and her memory practices, however, the *demos* made substantial changes to the existing ways of responding to oligarchy. These developments help to explain why the democracy was stronger after the Thirty than after the oligarchies of 411. This strengthened foundation allowed the *demos* to continue to rule the city and it prevented a further overthrow until external forces in the form of the Macedonians and military defeat once again exerted their twin influences on the city.

CREATING DEMOCRACY

These two responses had further consequences for both the city and the Athenians because now the *demos* had been forced to articulate exactly what it meant to be democratic. It required a male citizen to fight for the city against both internal and external foes who would destroy the rule of the *demos* and it was also intimately tied to performing one's civic duty in the *ekklesia*, the *boule* and the courts. Should the importance of these actions be forgotten, the citizen had only to visit the Agora, a space now focused directly on him, and to examine the monuments and buildings which together combined to show what being a good citizen entailed. These responses also allow us to see how the democracy chose to present not only itself, but also its own history, which, until this point, had not been distinguished from the history of the city as a whole.

The situation before the end of the fifth century is clearly brought out by the paintings in the Stoa Poikile (fig. 2). According to Pausanias, they showed the Athenians defeating the Spartans at Argive Oinoe, Theseus and the Athenians defeating the Amazons, the morning after the sack of Troy and the Battle of Marathon.[7] Pairing the two more recent battles against the Spartans and the Persians with the much earlier struggles against the Amazons and Troy suggested that there was no difference between them

---

[7] Paus. 1.15.1–3. The date of the battle of Oinoe, and so the painting, remains controversial; see with further references: J. G. Taylor 1998: 223–40; Sommerstein 2004: 138–45; Stansbury-O'Donnell 2005: 74–81; Castriota 2005: 90–2. Proponents of a date after the middle of the fifth century for the battle and painting need to explain why the four paintings together form an interlocking set of pendant pairs.

and that they all belonged to the history of the same city, irrespective of exactly what kind of city she was. Meanwhile, democracy itself was commemorated only by the statues of Harmodios and Aristogeiton which kept this foundational moment of the birth of the rule of the *demos* always present for the Athenians (fig. 8). No other points were remembered, however, so that the history of democracy stopped with its creation and it was given no lineage.

In contrast, the responses to the oligarchies focused on three more moments critical to the rule of the *demos*: swearing Demophantos' oath, reconciling the men of the Peiraieus and the men of the city and bringing back the *demos* from Phyle. Commemorated in monuments set up in the cityscape, these three events were marked out as significant for the *demos*. Like the statues of Harmodios and Aristogeiton, they were events internal to the city, rather than the defeat of external enemies, and they were closely connected with the continued existence of the democracy. Focusing on events subsequent to its foundation, they provided a history of the rule of the *demos* which was shown to have continued to exist beyond its initial institution. The monuments also made these three particular moments ever present for the Athenians so that they would not forget what it took to preserve democracy from oligarchy and tyranny. Selecting the reconciliation in particular also brought out an important aspect of this specific democracy: not only had the men of the Peiraieus and the men of the city reconciled, but they had also managed to keep *stasis* from re-occurring, unlike many contemporary Greek cities. Adding these events to the history of the rule of the *demos*, accordingly, brought out the success of this particular type of government.

If the responses to oligarchy showed that democracy had a history which extended beyond its foundation, then these actions also provided the rule of the *demos* with a lineage. Recovering Drakon and Solon for the *demos* identified good historical antecedents for democracy which was now shown not to have appeared out of nowhere at the end of the sixth century. Instead, it had a prehistory of significant figures whose actions led to the foundation of the rule of the *demos*. Reclaiming Kleisthenes added more definition to the moment of institution: if the Tyrannicides made democracy possible, then Kleisthenes provided the leadership and skill necessary to take advantage of this opportunity. In these ways, accordingly, the rule of the *demos* was shown not to be a form of *politeia* which had only existed for a short time. Instead, it had a good lineage stretching back to Drakon and Solon. In keeping with this emphasis on its longevity, its history after its foundation was now also made visible through monuments which reminded the Athenians of the importance of particular moments after the deed of the Tyrannicides.

Creating this democratic history for the *demos* also had further consequences. Once democracy was shown to have a history extending beyond Harmodios and Aristogeiton, then other events could be added to it. This process comes out very clearly with the bronze statues of Konon and Euagoras. Set up to honour these two men, they also added their victory to the history of the democratic city and, through their imagery, they configured the success as one won by the democratic Athenians. While the earlier significant moments focused on internal circumstances, now external events, and particularly military successes, were made part of the democracy's history. The particular emphasis on Solon as an ancestral figure looks ahead to the fourth century when he will be identified as the great democratic lawgiver of the city.[8] We can already see this process at work when Andokides without hesitation describes Demophantos' decree as a law of Solon, even though the text which he asks to be read out will make this misidentification obvious.[9] By the later fourth century, Solon and his role in establishing democracy would be made clear through the erection of a (posthumous) bronze statue of him in front of the Stoa Poikile, a decision which would, in turn, add another significant moment to the history of the democracy (fig. 2).[10]

The responses to the oligarchies of 411 and 404/3, consequently, allowed the democracy for the first time to write its own history and to display it in the city's spaces and monuments. In turn, the responses themselves would become part of that history and they would set the pattern for how the democratic city should respond to oligarchy and tyranny in the future. After the revolution from Demetrios Poliorketes in (almost certainly) 286, the democrats were faced with the (familiar) problem of commemorating and celebrating the events.[11] Despite the unrest which had occurred in the city, the events were configured as external war and the dead were buried in the Demosion Sema.[12] Meanwhile, the honorary decrees for three important Athenian participants looked back explicitly to the decree of Demophantos: these men did not act in opposition to the laws or the democracy 'of all the Athenians', held no office after the *demos* was overthrown and never

---

[8] On Solon the lawgiver in the fourth century, see Thomas 1994: 120–33 with further references; Mossé 2004: 243–59; Ober 1998: 360.
[9] Andok. 1.95.   [10] Dem. 26.23; Paus. 1.16.1; Ael. *VH* 8.16.
[11] For the problems of the date of the revolution, see Shear 2010 with further references.
[12] Paus. 1.29.13; Shear 2010: 149, 150.

acted against the democracy either 'by word or by deed'.[13] By the later 280s and the 270s, the ways in which democracy celebrated itself and its achievements had been set by the responses in the late fifth century to the Four Hundred, the Five Thousand and the Thirty and they were now continued and extended to commemorate the most recent revolution. What had begun as a project to recreate the democratic city and to negotiate the difficult events under the oligarchy had now become the model: even responding to oligarchy now had a history of its own.

[13] *SEG* xxviii 60.79–83; [Plut.] *X orat.* 851F; *IG* ii² 657.48–50; Shear 2010: 149–50.

References

Abbreviations of journal titles follow the scheme used in *L'Année philologique*.

Ajootian, A. (1998) 'A day at the races: the Tyrannicides in the fifth-century Agora', in *ΣΤΕΦΑΝΟΣ: Studies in Honor of Brunilde Sismondo Ridgway*, eds. K. J. Hartswick and M. C. Sturgeon. Philadelphia, PA: 1–13.

Alcock, S. E. (2002) *Archaeologies of the Greek Past: Landscape, Monuments and Memories*. Cambridge.

Anderson, B. (2006) *Imagined Communities: Reflections on the Origin and Spread of Nationalism*, 2nd edn rev. London.

Anderson, G. (2003) *The Athenian Experiment: Building an Imagined Political Community in Ancient Attica, 508–490 BC*. Ann Arbor.

Anderson, J. K. (1963) 'The statue of Chabrias', *AJA* 67: 411–13.

Andrewes, A. (1953) 'The generals in the Hellespont, 410–407 BC', *JHS* 73: 2–9.

    (1970) 'Lysias and the Theramenes papyrus', *ZPE* 6: 35–8.

    (1976) 'Androtion and the Four Hundred', *PCPS* 22: 14–25.

    (1992) 'The Spartan resurgence', in Lewis, Boardman, Davies and Ostwald (1992), 464–98.

Appadurai, A. (1981) 'The past as a scarce resource', *Man* 16: 201–19.

Assmann, J. (1995) 'Collective memory and cultural identity', *New German Critique* 65: 125–33.

    (2006) *Religion and Cultural Memory*. Stanford, CA.

Austin, C., and Olson, S. D. (eds.) (2004) *Aristophanes: Thesmophoriazusae, with Introduction and Commentary*. Oxford.

Avery, H. C. (1965) 'Heracles, Philoctetes, Neoptolemus', *Hermes* 93: 279–97.

    (1979) 'The Three Hundred at Thasos, 411 BC', *CP* 74: 234–42.

    (1999) 'The chronology of Peisander's mission to Athens', *CP* 94: 127–46.

Barringer, J. M., and Hurwit, J. M. (eds.) (2005) *Periklean Athens and its Legacy: Problems and Perspectives*. Austin, TX.

Berdahl, D. (1994) 'Voices at the Wall: discourses of self, history and national identity at the Vietnam Veterans Memorial', *History and Memory* 6.2: 88–124.

Bibauw, J. (1965) 'L'amendement de Clitophon (Aristote, *Ath. Pol.* 29, 3)', *AC* 34: 464–83.

Bizos, M. (ed.) (1967) *Lysias: Quatre discours: Sur le meurtre d'Ératosthène, Epitaphios, Contre Ératosthène, Pour l'invalide, introduction et commentaire*. Paris.

Blanshard, A. J. L. (1999) 'Rhetoric, identity and ideology in the Athenian lawcourt'. Ph.D. thesis, University of Cambridge.

(2007) 'The problems with honouring the Samians: an Athenian document relief and its interpretation', in *Art and Inscriptions in the Ancient World*, eds. Z. Newby and R. Leader-Newby. Cambridge: 19–37.

Blumenthal, H. (1973) 'Meletus the accuser of Andocides and Meletus the accuser of Socrates: one man or two?', *Philologus* 117: 169–78.

Boardman, J. (1985) *Greek Sculpture: The Classical Period, a Handbook*. London.

Boedeker, D., and Raaflaub, K. A. (eds.) (1998) *Democracy, Empire and the Arts in Fifth-Century Athens*. Cambridge, MA.

Boegehold, A. L. (1967) 'Philokleon's court', *Hesperia* 36: 111–20.

(1972) 'The establishment of a central archive at Athens', *AJA* 76: 23–30.

(1995) *Agora* XXVIII: *The Lawcourts at Athens: Sites, Buildings, Equipment, Procedure and Testimonia*. Princeton, NJ.

Bowersock, G. W. (1966) 'Pseudo-Xenophon', *HSCP* 71: 33–55.

Bowie, A. M. (1997) 'Tragic filters for history: Euripides' *Supplices* and Sophocles' *Philoctetes*', in *Greek Tragedy and the Historian*, ed. C. Pelling. Oxford: 39–62.

Boyd, T. D., and Rudolph, W. W. (1978) 'Excavations at Porto Cheli and vicinity: preliminary report IV: the lower town of Halieis, 1970–1977', *Hesperia* 47: 333–55.

Bruit Zaidman, L., and Schmitt Pantel, P. (1992) *Religion in the Ancient Greek City*. Cambridge.

Bruner, E. M. (1984a) 'Introduction: the opening up of Anthropology', in Bruner (1984b), 1–16.

(ed.) (1984b) *Text, Play and Story: The Construction and Reconstruction of Self and Society*. Prospect Heights, IL.

Bruner, E. M., and Gorfain, P. (1984) 'Dialogic narration and the paradoxes of Masada', in Bruner (1984b), 56–79.

Buckler, J. (1972) 'A second look at the monument of Chabrias', *Hesperia* 41: 466–74.

Burkert, W. (1983) *Homo Necans: The Anthropology of Ancient Greek Sacrificial Ritual and Myth*. Berkeley, CA.

(1985) *Greek Religion*. Cambridge, MA.

Burnett, A. P., and Edmondson, C. N. (1961) 'The Chabrias monument in the Athenian Agora', *Hesperia* 30: 74–91.

Bushaway, B. (1992) 'Name upon name: the Great War and remembrance', in Porter (1992), 136–67.

Calabi Limentani, I. (1986) 'Vittime dell' oligarchia: a proposito del decreto di Teozotide', in *Studi in onore di Cesare Sanfilippo* VI. Milan: 116–28.

Camp, J. McK. (1996) 'Excavations in the Athenian Agora: 1994 and 1995', *Hesperia* 65: 231–61.

(1999) 'Excavations in the Athenian Agora, 1996 and 1997', *Hesperia* 68: 255–83.

(2001) *The Archaeology of Athens*. New Haven, CT.

(2003) 'Excavations in the Athenian Agora: 1998–2001', *Hesperia* 72: 241–80.

(2007) 'Excavations in the Athenian Agora: 2002–2007', *Hesperia* 76: 627–63.

Camp, II, J. McK., and Kroll, J. H. (2001) 'The Agora Mint and Athenian bronze coinage', *Hesperia* 70: 127–62.

Carawan, E. (1991) 'Response to Julie Velissaropoulos', in Gagarin (1991), 107–14.

(1993) 'Tyranny and outlawry: *Athenaion Politeia* 16.10', in Rosen and Farrell (1993), 305–19.

(1998) *Rhetoric and the Law of Draco*. Oxford.

(2002) 'The Athenian amnesty and the "scrutiny of the laws"', *JHS* 122: 1–23.

(2006) 'Amnesty and accountings for the Thirty', *CQ* 56: 57–76.

Carey, C. (ed.) (2007) *Lysias: Orationes cum Fragmentis*. Oxford.

Cartledge, P. (1987) *Agesilaos and the Crisis of Sparta*. Baltimore, MD.

Castriota, D. (1992) *Myth, Ethos and Actuality: Official Art in Fifth-Century BC Athens*. Madison, WI.

(1998) 'Democracy and art in late-sixth- and fifth-century-BC Athens', in Morris and Raaflaub (1998), 197–216.

(2005) 'Feminizing the barbarian and barbarizing the feminine: Amazons, Trojans and Persians in the Stoa Poikile', in Barringer and Hurwit (2005), 89–102.

Cecchin, S. A. (1969) Πάτριος πολιτεία: *un tentativo propagandistico durante la guerra del Peloponneso*. Turin.

Chambers, M. (ed.) (1990) *Aristoteles: Der Staat der Athener*. Berlin.

(ed.) (1994) *Aristoteles: Athenaion Politeia*, corr. edn. Stuttgart.

Childs, W. A. P. (1994) 'The date of the Old Temple of Athena on the Athenian Akropolis', in Coulson, Palagia, Shear, Jr, Shapiro and Frost (1994), 1–6.

Clairmont, C. W. (1983) *Patrios Nomos: Public Burial in Athens during the Fifth and Fourth Centuries BC: The Archaeological, Epigraphic-Literary and Historical Evidence*. *BAR* International Series 161. Oxford.

Clinton, K. (1982) 'The nature of the late fifth-century revision of the Athenian law code', in *Studies in Attic Epigraphy, History and Topography Presented to Eugene Vanderpool. Hesperia* Supplement 19. Princeton, NJ: 27–37.

(1988) 'Sacrifice at the Eleusinian Mysteries', in *Early Greek Cult Practice: Proceedings of the Fifth International Symposium at the Swedish Institute at Athens*, eds. R. Hägg, N. Marinatos and G. C. Nordquist. Stockholm: 69–80.

(1994) 'The Epidauria and the arrival of Asclepius in Athens', in *Ancient Greek Cult Practice from the Epigraphical Evidence: Proceedings of the Second International Seminar on Ancient Greek Cult, organized by the Swedish School in Athens, 22–24 November 1991*, ed. R. Hägg. Stockholm: 17–34.

(2005) *Eleusis: The Inscriptions on Stone: Documents of the Sanctuary of the Two Goddesses and Public Documents of the Deme*. Athens.

Cloché, P. (1924) 'La boulè d'Athènes en 508/507 avant J-C', *REG* 37: 1–26.

Cohen, E. E. (2000) *The Athenian Nation*. Princeton, NJ.

Cole, S. G. (1996) 'Oath ritual and the male community at Athens', in *Demokratia: A Conversation on Democracies, Ancient and Modern*, eds. J. Ober and C. Hedrick. Princeton, NJ: 227–48.

Connerton, P. (1989) *How Societies Remember*. Cambridge.

Connor, W. R. (1988) '"Sacred" and "secular": ἱερὰ καὶ ὅσια and the classical Athenian concept of the state', *AncSoc* 19: 161–88.

(1991) 'The other 399: religion and the trial of Socrates', in *Georgica: Greek Studies in Honour of George Cawkwell*, eds. M. A. Flower and M. Toher. *BICS* Supplement 58. London: 49–56.

Coulson, W. D. E., Palagia, O., Shear, Jr, T. L., Shapiro, H. A., and Frost, F. J. (eds.) (1994) *The Archaeology of Athens and Attica under the Democracy: Proceedings of an International Conference Celebrating 2500 Years since the Birth of Democracy in Greece, held at the American School of Classical Studies at Athens, December 4–6, 1992*. Oxford.

Cressy, D. (1992) 'The fifth of November remembered', in Porter (1992), 68–90.

(1994) 'National memory in early modern England', in Gillis (1994), 61–73.

Csapo, E. (2007) 'The men who built the theatres: *theatropolai, theatronai* and *arkhitektones*', in *The Greek Theatre and Festivals: Documentary Studies*, ed. P. Wilson. Oxford: 87–121.

Cubitt, G. (2007) *History and Memory*. Manchester.

Culasso Gastaldi, E. (2003) 'Abbattere la stele: riscrittura epigrafica e revisione storica ad Atene', *CCG* 14: 241–62.

D'Angour, A. J. (1999) 'Archinus, Eucleides and reform of the Athenian alphabet', *BICS* 43: 109–30.

Detienne, M. (1989a) 'Culinary practices and the spirit of sacrifice', in Detienne and Vernant (1989), 1–20.

(1989b) 'The violence of wellborn ladies: women in the Thesmophoria', in Detienne and Vernant (1989), 129–47.

Detienne, M., and Vernant, J.-P. (eds.) (1989) *The Cuisine of Sacrifice among the Greeks*. Chicago, IL.

Develin, R. (1989) *Athenian Officials 684–321 BC*. Cambridge.

Dillon, S. (2006) *Ancient Greek Portrait Sculpture: Contexts, Subjects and Styles*. Cambridge.

Dover, K. J. (1968) *Lysias and the Corpus Lysiacum*. Berkeley, CA.

Dow, S. (1941) 'Greek inscriptions: the Athenian law code of 411–401 BC', *Hesperia* 10: 31–7.

(1953–7) 'The law codes of Athens', *Proceedings of the Massachusetts Historical Society* 71: 3–36.

(1960) 'The Athenian calendar of sacrifices: the chronology of Nikomakhos' second term', *Historia* 9: 270–93.

(1961) 'The walls inscribed with Nikomakhos' law code', *Hesperia* 30: 58–73.

Dunbar, N. (ed.) (1995) *Aristophanes: Birds, with Introduction and Commentary*. Oxford.

Durand, J.-L. (1989) 'Greek animals: toward a topology of edible bodies', in Detienne and Vernant (1989), 87–118.

Easterling, P. E. (1978) '*Philoctetes* and modern criticism', *ICS* 3: 27–39.

Edmondson, C. N. (1982) 'Onesippos' Herm', in *Studies in Attic Epigraphy, History and Topography Presented to Eugene Vanderpool*. *Hesperia* Supplement 19. Princeton, NJ: 48–50.

Edwards, M. (ed.) (1995) *Andocides. Greek Orators* IV. Warminster.

Elsner, J. (2003) 'Iconoclasm and the preservation of memory', in *Monuments and Memory, Made and Unmade*, eds. R. S. Nelson and M. Olin. Chicago, IL: 209–31.

Engels, J. (1993) 'Der Michigan-Papyrus über Theramenes und die Ausbildung des "Theramenes-Mythos"', *ZPE* 99: 125–55.

Farrar, C. (1998) *The Origins of Democratic Thinking: The Invention of Politics in Classical Athens*. Cambridge.

Fentress, J., and Wickham, C. (1992) *Social Memory*. Oxford.

Ferguson, W. S. (1932a) 'The condemnation of Antiphon', in *Mélanges Gustave Glotz* I. Paris: 349–66.

(1932b) *The Treasurers of Athena*. Cambridge, MA.

(1936) 'The Athenian law code and the old Attic trittyes', in *Classical Studies Presented to Edward Capps on his Seventieth Birthday*. Princeton, NJ: 144–58.

Figueira, T. J. (1993) 'The strange death of Draco on Aegina', in Rosen and Farrell (1993), 287–304.

Fingarette, A. (1971) 'A new look at the wall of Nikomakhos', *Hesperia* 40: 330–5.

Finley, M. I. (2000) *The Use and Abuse of History*. London.

(2004) 'Athenian demagogues', in P. J. Rhodes (2004), 163–84.

Forrest, W. G. (1970) 'The date of the pseudo-Xenophontic Athenaion Politeia', *Klio* 52: 107–16.

Forsdyke, S. (2005) *Exile, Ostracism and Democracy: The Politics of Expulsion in Ancient Greece*. Princeton, NJ.

Fuks, A. (1953) *The Ancestral Constitution: Four Studies in Athenian Party Politics at the end of the Fifth Century BC*. London.

Funke, P. (1983) 'Konons Rückkehr nach Athen im Spiegel epigraphischer Zeugnisse', *ZPE* 53: 149–89.

Gadbery, L. M. (1992) 'The sanctuary of the Twelve Gods in the Athenian Agora: a revised view', *Hesperia* 61: 447–89.

Gagarin, M. (1981) *Drakon and Early Greek Homicide Law*. New Haven, CT.

(ed.) (1991) *Symposion 1990: Vorträge zur griechischen und Hellenistischen Rechtsgeschichte (Pacific Grove, California, 24–25 September 1990)*. Cologne.

(ed.) (1997) *Antiphon: The Speeches*. Cambridge.

(2008) *Writing Greek Law*. Cambridge.

Gallia, A. B. (2004) 'The republication of Draco's law on homicide', *CQ* 54: 451–60.

Garvie, A. F. (1972) 'Deceit, violence and persuasion in the *Philoctetes*', in *Studi classici in onore di Quintino Cataudella* I. Catania: 213–26.

Gauthier, P. (1985) *Les cités grecques et leurs bienfaiteurs (IVᵉ–Iᵉʳ siècle avant J-C): contribution à l'histoire des institutions*. BCH Supplement 12. Athens.

(1993) 'Sur l'institution du *misthos* de l'assemblée d'Athènes (*Ath. Pol.* 41, 3)', in Piérart (1993), 231–50.

Gawlinski, L. (2007) 'The Athenian calendar of sacrifices: a new fragment from the Athenian Agora', *Hesperia* 76: 37–55.

Geary, P. J. (1994a) *Living with the Dead in the Middle Ages*. Ithaca, NY.

(1994b) *Phantoms of Remembrance: Memory and Oblivion at the End of the First Millennium*. Princeton, NJ.

Gernet, L. (1955) *Droit et société en Grèce ancienne*. Paris.

Gillis, J. R. (ed.) (1994) *Commemorations: The Politics of National Identity*. Princeton, NJ.

Goldhill, S. (1990) 'The Great Dionysia and civic ideology', in Winkler and Zeitlin (1990), 97–129.

(1994) 'Representing democracy: women at the Great Dionysia', in Osborne and Hornblower (1994), 347–69.

(2000) 'Civic ideology and the problem of difference: the politics of Aeschylean tragedy, once again', *JHS* 120: 34–56.

Gomme, A. W. (1956) *A Historical Commentary on Thucydides: The Ten Years' War* II: *Books II–III*. Oxford.

Gomme, A. W., Andrewes, A., and Dover, K. J. (1970) *A Historical Commentary on Thucydides* IV: *Books V 25–VII*. Oxford.

(1981) *A Historical Commentary on Thucydides* V: *Book VIII*. Oxford.

Graf, F. (1996) '*Pompai* in Greece: some considerations about space and ritual in the Greek *polis*', in *The Role of Religion in the Early Greek Polis: Proceedings of the Third International Seminar on Ancient Greek Cult, organised by the Swedish Institute at Athens, 16–18 October 1992*, ed. R. Hägg. Stockholm: 55–65.

Gribble, D. (1999) *Alcibiades and Athens: A Study in Literary Presentation*. Oxford.

(2006) 'Individuals in Thucydides', in Rengakos and Tsakmakis (2006), 439–68.

Griffin, J. (1998) 'The social function of Attic tragedy', *CQ* 48: 39–61.

Griffith, M. (1995) 'Brilliant dynasts: power and politics in the *Oresteia*', *ClAnt* 14: 62–129.

Habicht, C. (1997) *Athens from Alexander to Antony*. Cambridge, MA.

Halbwachs, M. (1992) *On Collective Memory*. Chicago, IL.

Hallett, C. H. (2005) *The Roman Nude: Heroic Portrait Statuary 200 BC–AD 300*. Oxford.

Hansen, M. H. (1975) *Eisangelia: The Sovereignty of the People's Court in Athens in the Fourth Century BC and the Impeachment of Generals and Politicians*. Odense University Classical Studies 6. Odense.

(1976) *Apagoge, Endeixis and Ephegesis against Kakourgoi, Atimoi and Pheugontes: A Study in the Athenian Administration of Justice in the Fourth Century BC*. Odense.

(1978) '*Nomos* and *psephisma* in fourth-century Athens', *GRBS* 19: 315–30.

(1979) 'Did the Athenian ecclesia legislate after 403/2 BC?', *GRBS* 20: 27–53.

(1979–80) 'Athenian *nomothesia* in the fourth century BC and Demosthenes' speech against Leptines', *C&M* 32: 87–104.

(1985) 'Athenian *nomothesia*', *GRBS* 26: 345–71.

(1986) 'The construction of Pnyx II and the introduction of assembly pay', *C&M* 37: 89–98.

(1990) 'Diokles' law (Dem. 24.42) and the revision of the Athenian corpus of laws in the archonship of Eukleides', *C&M* 41: 63–71.

(1991) *The Athenian Democracy in the Age of Demosthenes*. Oxford.

(1995) *The Trial of Sokrates: From the Athenian Point of View*. Copenhagen.

(1996) 'Reflections on the number of citizens accommodated in the assembly place on the Pnyx', in *The Pnyx in the History of Athens: Proceedings of an International Colloquium Organised by the Finnish Institute at Athens, 7–9 October, 1994*, eds. B. Forsén and G. Stanton. Helsinki: 23–33.

Hansen, M. H., and Fischer-Hansen, T. (1994) 'Monumental political architecture in archaic and classical Greek *poleis*: evidence and historical significance', in *From Political Architecture to Stephanus Byzantius: Sources for the Ancient Greek Polis*, ed. D. Whitehead. *Historia* Einzelschriften 87. Stuttgart: 23–90.

Hansen, M. H., and Heine Nielsen, T. (eds.) (2004) *An Inventory of Archaic and Classical Poleis: An Investigation Conducted by the Copenhagen Polis Centre for the Danish National Research Foundation*. Oxford.

Hansen, M. H., and Raaflaub, K. (eds.) (1995) *Studies in the Ancient Greek Polis*. *Historia* Einzelschriften 95. Stuttgart.

Harding, P. (1978) 'O Androtion, you fool!', *AJAH* 3: 179–83.

(1987) 'Metics, foreigners or slaves? The recipients of honours in *IG* ii² 10', *ZPE* 67: 176–82.

Harris, D. (1994) 'Freedom of information and accountability: the inventory lists of the Parthenon', in Osborne and Hornblower (1994), 213–25.

Harris, E. M. (1990) 'The constitution of the Five Thousand', *HSCP* 93: 243–80.

Harrison, A. R. W. (1955) 'Law-making at Athens at the end of the fifth century BC', *JHS* 75: 26–35.

Hedrick, Jr, C. W. (1994) 'Writing, reading and democracy', in Osborne and Hornblower (1994), 157–74.

(2000a) 'For anyone who wishes to see', *AncW* 31: 127–35.

(2000b) *History and Silence: Purge and Rehabilitation of Memory in Late Antiquity*. Austin, TX.

Heftner, H. (2001) *Der oligarchische Umsturz des Jahres 411 v Chr und die Herrschaft der Vierhundert in Athen: Quellenkritische und historische Untersuchungen*. Frankfurt.

Henderson, J. (ed.) (1987) *Aristophanes: Lysistrata, with Introduction and Commentary*. Oxford.

(1990) 'The *demos* and the comic competition', in Winkler and Zeitlin (1990), 271–313.

Henrichs, A. (1968) 'Zur Interpretation des Michigan-Papyrus über Theramenes', *ZPE* 3: 101–8.

Henry, A. S. (1977) *The Prescripts of Athenian Decrees*. Leiden.

(1982) '*Polis/acropolis*, paymasters and the Ten Talent Fund', *Chiron* 12: 91–118.

(1983) *Honours and Privileges in Athenian Decrees: The Principal Formulae of Athenian Honorary Decrees*. Hildesheim.

Hereward, D. (1952) 'New fragments of *IG* ii² 10', *ABSA* 47: 102–17.

Hesk, J. (2000) *Deception and Democracy in Classical Athens*. Cambridge.

Hignett, C. (1952) *A History of the Athenian Constitution to the End of the Fifth Century BC*. Oxford.

Hobden, F. (2007) 'The "men from Phyle" from Agora to *agōn*: the rhetorical life of Athens' democratic counterrevolutionaries', *Advances in the History of Rhetoric* 10: 151–74.

Hobsbawm, E. (1983) 'Introduction: inventing traditions', in Hobsbawm and Ranger (1983), 1–14.

Hobsbawm, E., and Ranger, T. (eds.) (1983) *The Invention of Tradition*. Cambridge.

Hölscher, T. (1998) 'Images and political identity: the case of Athens', in Boedeker and Raaflaub (1998), 153–83.

Hornblower, S. (1987) *Thucydides*. London.

(2000) 'The Old Oligarch (pseudo-Xenophon's *Athenaion Politeia*) and Thucydides: a fourth century date for the Old Oligarch?', in *Polis & Politics: Studies in Ancient Greek History Presented to Mogens Herman Hansen on his Sixtieth Birthday, August 20, 2000*, eds. P. Flensted-Jensen, T. H. Nielsen and L. Rubinstein. Copenhagen: 363–84.

(2002) *The Greek World 479–323 BC*, 3rd edn. London.

(2008) *A Commentary on Thucydides* III: *Books 5.25–8.109*. Oxford.

(2009) 'Thucydides and the *boule* (Council of Five Hundred)', in Mitchell and Rubinstein (2009), 251–64.

Humphreys, S. (1991) 'A historical approach to Drakon's law on homicide', in Gagarin (1991), 17–45.

Hung, W. (1991) 'Tiananmen Square: a political history of monuments', *Representations* 35: 84–117.

Hurwit, J. M. (1999) *The Athenian Acropolis: History, Mythology and Archaeology from the Neolithic Era to the Present*. Cambridge.

Jameson, M. H. (1971) 'Sophocles and the Four Hundred', *Historia* 20: 541–68.

(1998) 'Religion in Athenian democracy', in Morris and Raaflaub (1998), 171–95.

Jones, A. H. M. (1986) *Athenian Democracy*. Baltimore, MD.

Joyce, C. J. (2008) 'The Athenian amnesty and scrutiny of 403', *CQ* 58: 507–18.

Kagan, D. (1987) *The Fall of the Athenian Empire*. Ithaca, NY.

Kallet, L. (2001) *Money and the Corrosion of Power in Thucydides: The Sicilian Expedition and its Aftermath*. Berkeley, CA.

Karamoutsou-Teza, S. (1990) 'Αμοιβές στους ξένους που πολέμησαν για την αποκατάσταση της Δημοκρατίας στην Αθήνα το 403 πΧ (*IG* II² 10+ · Osborne, D6)', *Dodone* 19: 262–75.

Keaney, J. J. (1992) *The Composition of Aristotle's Athenaion Politeia: Observation and Explanation*. Oxford.

Kourouniotes, K., and Thompson, H. A. (1932) 'The Pnyx in Athens', *Hesperia* 1: 90–217.

Krentz, P. (1980) 'Foreigners against the Thirty: *IG* 2² 10 again', *Phoenix* 34: 298–306.

(1982) *The Thirty at Athens*. Ithaca, NY.

(1986) 'The rewards for Thrasyboulos' supporters', *ZPE* 62: 201–4.

(ed.) (1989) *Xenophon, Hellenika I–II.3.10, with an Introduction, Translation and Commentary*. Warminster.

(ed.) (1995) *Xenophon, Hellenika II.3.11–IV.2.8, with an Introduction, Translation and Commentary.* Warminster.

Kron, U. (1976) *Die zehn attischen Phylenheroen: Geschichte, Mythos, Kult und Darstellungen.* MDAI(A) Beiheft 5. Berlin.

Krumeich, R. (1997) *Bildnisse griechischer Herrscher und Staatsmänner im 5. Jahrhundert v Chr.* Munich.

(2007) 'Human achievement and divine favor: the religious context of early Hellenistic portraiture', in Schultz and von den Hoff (2007), 161–80.

Kuhn, G. (1985) 'Untersuchungen zur Funktion der Säulenhalle in archaischer und klassischer Zeit III: die Stoa Basileios in Athen', *JDAI* 100: 200–26.

Lahiri, N. (2003) 'Commemorating and remembering 1857: the revolt in Delhi and its afterlife', *World Archaeology* 35: 35–60.

Lalonde, G. V., Langdon, M. K., and Walbank, M. B. (1991) *Agora* XIX: *Inscriptions: Horoi, Poletai Records, Leases of Public Lands.* Princeton, NJ.

Lamb, W. R. M. (1930) *Lysias, with an English translation.* Cambridge, MA.

Lambert, S. D. (1996) 'Notes on two Attic *horoi* and some corrigenda to *The Phratries of Attica*', *ZPE* 110: 77–83.

(2002a) 'The sacrificial calendar of Athens', *ABSA* 97: 353–99.

(2002b) 'Parerga I: *IG* I³ 240K, a fragment of *IG* I³ 1185?', *ZPE* 139: 69–71.

(2004) 'Athenian state laws and decrees 352/1–322/1: I. Decrees honouring Athenians', *ZPE* 150: 85–120.

(2005) 'Athenian state laws and decrees 352/1–322/1: II. Religious regulations', *ZPE* 154: 125–59.

Laqueur, T. W. (1994) 'Memory and naming in the Great War', in Gillis (1994), 150–67.

Larsen, J. A. O. (1955) 'The Boeotian confederacy and fifth-century oligarchic theory', *TAPA* 86: 40–50.

Lawrence, A. W., and Tomlinson, R. A. (1996) *Greek Architecture*, 5th edn. New Haven, CT.

Lawton, C. (1992) 'Sculptural and epigraphical restorations to Attic documents', *Hesperia* 61: 239–51.

(1995) *Attic Document Reliefs: Art and Politics in Ancient Athens.* Oxford.

Leach, E. (1984) 'Conclusion: further thoughts on the realm of folly', in Bruner (1984b), 356–64.

Le Goff, J. (1992) *History and Memory.* New York, NY.

Lévy, E. (1976) *Athènes devant la défaite de 404: histoire d'une crise idéologique.* Paris.

Lewis, D. M. (1967) 'A note on *IG* i² 114', *JHS* 87: 132.

(1993) 'The epigraphical evidence for the end of the Thirty', in Piérart (1993), 223–9.

(1994) 'Sparta as victor', in Lewis, Boardman, Hornblower and Ostwald (1994), 24–44.

Lewis, D. M., Boardman, J., Davies, J. K., and Ostwald, M. (eds.) (1992) *The Cambridge Ancient History* V: *The Fifth Century BC*, 2nd edn. Cambridge.

Lewis, D. M., Boardman, J., Hornblower, S., and Ostwald, M. (eds.) (1994) *The Cambridge Ancient History* vi: *The Fourth Century BC*, 2nd edn. Cambridge.

Lewis, D. M., and Stroud, R. (1979) 'Athens honours king Euagoras of Salamis', *Hesperia* 48: 180–93.

Liddel, P. (2003) 'The places of publication of Athenian state decrees from the 5th century BC to the 3rd century AD', *ZPE* 143: 79–93.

Loening, T. C. (1987) *The Reconciliation Agreement of 403/402 BC in Athens*. Hermes Einzelschriften 53. Stuttgart.

Loraux, N. (1986) *The Invention of Athens: The Funeral Oration in the Classical City*. Cambridge, MA.

(1991) 'Reflections of the Greek city on unity and division', in *City-States in Classical Antiquity and Medieval Italy: Athens and Rome, Florence and Venice*, eds. A. Molho, K. Raaflaub and J. Emlen. Stuttgart: 33–57.

(1993) *The Children of Athena: Athenian Ideas about Citizenship and the Division between the Sexes*. Princeton, NJ.

(2002) *The Divided City: On Memory and Forgetting in Ancient Athens*. New York, NY.

Low, P. (2006) 'Commemorating the Spartan war-dead', in *Sparta & War*, eds. S. Hodkinson and A. Powell. Swansea: 85–109.

Ma, J. (2005) 'The many lives of Eugnotos of Akraiphia', *Studi ellenistici* 16: 141–91.

MacDowell, D. M. (ed.) (1962) *Andokides: On the Mysteries, with Introduction, Commentary and Appendixes*. Oxford.

(ed.) (1971a) *Aristophanes: Wasps, with Introduction and Commentary*. Oxford.

(1971b) 'The chronology of Athenian speeches and legal innovations in 401–398 BC', *RIDA* 18: 267–73.

(1975) 'Law-making at Athens in the fourth century BC', *JHS* 95: 62–74.

(2004) 'Epikerdes of Kyrene and the Athenian privilege of *ateleia*', *ZPE* 150: 127–33.

Marr, J. L., and Rhodes, P. J. (eds.) (2008) *The 'Old Oligarch': The Constitution of the Athenians attributed to Xenophon, with an Introduction, Translation and Commentary*. Oxford.

Mattingly, H. B. (1967) 'Two notes on Athenian financial documents', *ABSA* 62: 13–17.

(1997) 'The date and purpose of the pseudo-Xenophon constitution of Athens', *CQ* 47: 352–7.

McCoy, W. J. (1975) 'Aristotle's *Athenaion Politeia* and the establishment of the Thirty Tyrants', *YClS* 24: 131–45.

Medda, E. (ed.) (1995) *Lisia: Orazioni (I–XV), introduzione, traduzione e note*. 3rd edn. Milan.

Meiggs, R. (1972) *The Athenian Empire*. Oxford.

Meiggs, R., and Lewis, D. (1988) *A Selection of Greek Historical Inscriptions to the End of the Fifth Century BC*, rev. edn. Oxford.

Meritt, B. D. (1932) *Athenian Financial Documents of the Fifth Century*. Ann Arbor, MI.

(1936) 'Greek inscriptions', *Hesperia* 5: 355–430.

(1940) *Epigraphica Attica*. Cambridge, MA.

(1970) 'Ransom of the Athenians by Epikerdes', *Hesperia* 39: 111–14.

Meritt, B. D., Wade-Gery, H. T., and McGregor, M. F. (1950) *The Athenian Tribute Lists* III. Princeton, NJ.

Merkelbach, R., and Youtie, H. C. (1968) 'Ein Michigan-Papyrus über Theramenes', *ZPE* 2: 161–9.

Mikalson, J. D. (1975) *The Sacred and Civil Calendar of the Athenian Year*. Princeton, NJ.

Miller, S. G. (1995) 'Old Metroon and Old Bouleuterion in the classical Agora of Athens', in Hansen and Raaflaub (1995), 133–56.

Millett, P. (1998) 'Encounters in the Agora', in *Kosmos: Essays in Order, Conflict and Community in Classical Athens*, eds. P. Cartledge, P. Millett and S. von Reden. Cambridge: 203–28.

(2005) 'The trial of Socrates revisited', *European Review of History* 12: 23–62.

Mirhady, D. C. (2007) 'The dikast's oath and the question of fact', in Sommerstein and Fletcher (2007), 48–59.

Mitchell, L., and Rubinstein, L. (eds.) (2009) *Greek History and Epigraphy: Essays in Honour of P. J. Rhodes*. Swansea.

Mitchell-Boyask, R. (2007) 'The Athenian Asklepieion and the end of the *Philoctetes*', *TAPA* 137: 85–114.

(2008) *Plague and the Athenian Imagination: Drama, History and the Cult of Asclepius*. Cambridge.

Moore, M. B. (1995) 'The central group in the Gigantomachy of the Old Athena Temple on the Acropolis', *AJA* 99: 633–9.

Morgan, K. A. (ed.) (2003) *Popular Tyranny: Sovereignty and its Discontents in Ancient Greece*. Austin, TX.

Morison, W. S. (1998) 'Attic gymnasia and palaistrai inscriptions from the archaic period to 336/335 BC'. Ph.D. dissertation, University of California at Santa Barbara.

Morris, I., and Raaflaub, K. A. (eds.) (1998) *Democracy 2500? Questions and Challenges. AIA Colloquia and Conference Papers* 2. Dubuque, IA.

Mossé, C. (2004) 'How a political myth takes shape: Solon "founding father" of the Athenian democracy', in P. J. Rhodes (2004), 242–59.

Moysey, R. A. (1981) 'The Thirty and the Pnyx', *AJA* 85: 31–7.

Mügge, M. (2008) 'Politics, space and material: the "Memorial to the Murdered Jews of Europe" in Berlin as a sign of symbolic representation', *European Review of History* 15: 707–25.

Munn, M. H. (2000) *The School of History: Athens in the Age of Socrates*. Berkeley, CA.

Natalicchio, A. (1990) 'Sulla cosiddetta revisione legislativa in Atene alla fine del v secolo', *QS* 32: 61–90.

Nelson, M. (2006) 'The phantom stelai of Lysias, *Against Nicomachus* 17', *CQ* 56: 309–12.

Németh, G. (2006) *Kritias und die Dreißig Tyrannen: Untersuchungen zur Politik und Prosopographie der Führungselite in Athen 404/403 v Chr*. Stuttgart.

Nora, P. (1989) 'Between memory and history: *Les lieux de mémoire*', *Representations* 26: 7–25.

Ober, J. (1989) *Mass and Elite in Democratic Athens: Rhetoric, Ideology and the Power of the People*. Princeton, NJ.

(1998) *Political Dissent in Democratic Athens: Intellectual Critics of Popular Rule*. Princeton, NJ.

(2003) 'Tyrant killing as therapeutic *stasis*: a political debate in images and texts', in Morgan (2003), 215–50.

Ober, J., and Strauss, B. (1990) 'Drama, political rhetoric and the discourse of Athenian democracy', in Winkler and Zeitlin (1990), 237–70.

Ogden, D. (1996) *Greek Bastardy in the Classical and Hellenistic Periods*. Oxford.

Olick, J. K. (1999a) 'Genre memories and memory genres: a dialogical analysis of May 8, 1945 commemorations in the Federal Republic of Germany', *American Sociological Review* 64: 381–402.

(1999b) 'Collective memory: two cultures', *Sociological Theory* 17: 333–48.

Olick, J. K., and Robbins, J. (1998) 'Social memory studies: from "collective memory" to historical sociology of mnemonic practices', *Annual Review of Sociology* 24: 105–40.

Oliver, G. J. (2007) 'Space and the visualization of power in the Greek polis: the award of portrait statues in decrees from Athens', in Schultz and von den Hoff (2007), 181–204.

Oliver, J. H. (1935) 'Greek inscriptions: nos. 1–36', *Hesperia* 4: 1–70.

Osborne, M. J. (1981) 'Entertainment in the Prytaneion at Athens', *ZPE* 41: 153–70.

(1981–2) *Naturalization in Athens* I–II. Brussels.

(1999) 'Voyaging through strange seas of thought – the study of Athenian inscriptions', *PAA* 74.2: 67–80.

Osborne, R. (1998) 'Men without clothes: heroic nakedness and Greek art', in *Gender and the Body in the Ancient Mediterranean*, ed. M. Wyke. Oxford: 80–104.

(1999) 'Inscribing performance', in *Performance Culture and Athenian Democracy*, eds. S. Goldhill and R. Osborne. Cambridge: 341–58.

(2000) 'Women and sacrifice in classical Greece', in *Oxford Readings in Greek Religion*, ed. R. Buxton. Oxford: 294–313.

(2003) 'Changing the discourse', in Morgan (2003), 251–72.

(ed.) (2004) *The Old Oligarch: Pseudo-Xenophon's Constitution of the Athenians, Introduction, Translation and Commentary*, 2nd edn. LACTOR 2. London.

(ed.) (2007) *Debating the Athenian Cultural Revolution: Art, Literature, Philosophy and Politics 430–380 BC*. Cambridge.

Osborne, R., and Hornblower, S. (eds.) (1994) *Ritual, Finance, Politics: Athenian Democratic Accounts Presented to David Lewis*. Oxford.

Ostwald, M. (1955) 'The Athenian legislation against tyranny and subversion', *TAPA* 86: 103–28.

(1986) *From Popular Sovereignty to the Sovereignty of Law: Law, Society and Politics in Fifth-Century Athens*. Berkeley, CA.

Parker, R. (1996) *Athenian Religion: A History*. Oxford.

(1998) 'Pleasing thighs: reciprocity in Greek religion', in *Reciprocity in Ancient Greece*, eds. C. Gill, N. Postlethwaite and R. Seaford. Oxford: 105–25.

(2005) *Polytheism and Society at Athens*. Oxford.

Paton, J. M., and Stevens, G. P. (1927) *The Erechtheum*. Cambridge, MA.

Patterson, C. (1981) *Pericles' Citizenship Law of 451–50 BC*. Salem, NH.

Pébarthe, C. (2006) *Cité, démocratie et écriture: histoire de l'alphabétisation d'Athènes à l'époque classique*. Paris.

Pedley, J. (2005) *Sanctuaries and the Sacred in the Ancient Greek World*. Cambridge.

Phillips, D. D. (2008) *Avengers of Blood: Homicide in Athenian Law and Custom from Draco to Demosthenes*. Historia Einzelschriften 202. Stuttgart.

Pickard-Cambridge, A. (1988) *The Dramatic Festivals of Athens*, 2nd edn. rev. Oxford.

Piérart, M. (ed.) (1993) *Aristote et Athènes, Fribourg (Suisse) 23–25 Mai 1991*. Paris.

Plescia, J. (1970) *The Oath and Perjury in Ancient Greece*. Tallahassee, FL.

Pomeroy, S. B. (1982) 'Charities for Greek women', *Mnemosyne* 35: 115–35.

Porter, R. (ed.) (1992) *Myths of the English*. Cambridge.

Pritchett, W. K. (1970) *The Choiseul Marble. University of California Publications: Classical Studies* 5. Berkeley, CA.

(1974) *The Greek State at War* II. Berkeley, CA.

(1979) *The Greek State at War* III: *Religion*. Berkeley, CA.

(1996) *Greek Archives, Cults and Topography*. Amsterdam.

Quillin, J. M. (2002) 'Achieving amnesty: the role of events, institutions and ideas', *TAPA* 132: 71–107.

Raaflaub, K. A. (1990) 'Contemporary perceptions of democracy in fifth-century Athens', in *Aspects of Athenian Democracy*, ed. J. R. Fears. Copenhagen: 33–70.

(2003) 'Stick and glue: the function of tyranny in fifth-century Athenian democracy', in Morgan (2003), 59–93.

(2004) *The Discovery of Freedom in Ancient Greece*. Chicago, IL.

(2006) 'Thucydides on democracy and oligarchy', in Rengakos and Tsakmakis (2006), 189–222.

Rainbird, P. (2003) 'Representing nation, dividing community: the Broken Hill War Memorial, New South Wales, Australia', *World Archaeology* 35: 22–34.

Raubitschek, A. E. (1941a) 'The heroes of Phyle', *Hesperia* 10: 284–95.

(1941b) 'Two notes on Isocrates', *TAPA* 72: 356–64.

Rengakos, A., and Tsakmakis, A. (eds.) (2006) *Brill's Companion to Thucydides*. Leiden.

Rhodes, P. J. (1972a) *The Athenian Boule*. Oxford.

(1972b) 'The Five Thousand in the Athenian revolutions of 411 BC', *JHS* 92: 115–27.

(1979–80) 'Athenian democracy after 403 BC', *CJ* 75: 305–23.

(1981) *A Commentary on the Aristotelian Athenaion Politeia*. Oxford.

(1985) 'Nomothesia in fourth-century Athens', *CQ* 35: 55–60.

(1991) 'The Athenian code of laws, 410–399 BC', *JHS* 111: 87–100.

(2001a) 'Public documents in the Greek states: archives and inscriptions, part I', *G&R* 48: 33–44.

(2001b) 'Public documents in the Greek states: archives and inscriptions, part II', *G&R* 48: 135–53.

(2003) 'Nothing to do with democracy: Athenian drama and the *polis*', *JHS* 123: 104–19.

(ed.) (2004) *Athenian Democracy*. Edinburgh.

(2006) *A History of the Classical Greek World*. Malden, MA.

(2007) 'Oaths in political life', in Sommerstein and Fletcher (2007), 11–25.

(2008) 'After the three-bar *sigma* controversy: the history of Athenian imperialism reassessed', *CQ* 58: 500–6.

Rhodes, P. J., and Osborne, R. (eds.) (2003) *Greek Historical Inscriptions, 404–323 BC*. Oxford.

Rhodes, R. F. (1995) *Architecture and Meaning on the Athenian Acropolis*. Cambridge.

Robertson, N. (1990) 'The laws of Athens, 410–399 BC: the evidence for review and publication', *JHS* 110: 43–75.

Rolley, C. (1999) *La sculpture grecque* II: *La période classique*. Paris.

Rose, P. W. (1992) *Sons of the Gods, Children of Earth: Ideology and Literary Form in Ancient Greece*. Ithaca, NY.

Rosen, R. M., and Farrell, J. (eds.) (1993) *Nomodeiktes: Greek Studies in Honor of Martin Ostwald*. Ann Arbor, MI.

Rotroff, S. I., and Camp, J. McK. (1996) 'The date of the third period of the Pnyx', *Hesperia* 65: 263–94.

Roux, G. (1976) 'Aristophane, Xénophon, le pseudo-Démosthène et l'architecture du bouleutèrion d'Athènes', *BCH* 100: 475–83.

Rudhardt, J. (1958) *Notions fondamentales de la pensée religieuse et actes constitutifs du culte dans la Grèce classique: étude préliminaire pour aider à la compréhension de la piété athénienne au IVme siècle*. Geneva.

Ryan, F. X. (1994) 'The original date of the δῆμος πληθύων provisions of *IG* I³ 105', *JHS* 114: 120–34.

Ste Croix, G. E. M. de (1956) 'The constitution of the Five Thousand', *Historia* 5: 1–23.

(1972) *The Origins of the Peloponnesian War*. London.

Sakurai, M. (1995) 'A new reading in POxy. XIII 1606 (Lysias, against Hippotherses)', *ZPE* 109: 177–80.

Sartori, F. (1983) 'Aristofano e Agirrio nel 405 aC', in *Althistorische Studien Hermann Bengtson zum 70. Geburtstag dargebracht von Kollegen und Schülern*, ed. H. Heinen with K. Stroheker and G. Walser. *Historia* Einzelschriften 40. Stuttgart: 56–77.

Saunders, N. J. (2003) 'Crucifix, calvary and cross: materiality and spirituality in Great War landscapes', *World Archaeology* 35: 7–21.

Savage, K. (1994) 'The politics of memory: Black emancipation and the Civil War monument', in Gillis (1994), 127–49.

Schultz, P., and von den Hoff, R. (eds.) (2007) *Early Hellenistic Portraiture: Image, Style, Context*. Cambridge.

Seaford, R. (2000) 'The social function of Attic tragedy: a response to Jasper Griffin', *CQ* 50: 30–44.

Sealey, R. (1983) 'The Athenian courts for homicide', *CP* 78: 275–96.

(1987) *The Athenian Republic: Democracy or the Rule of Law?*. University Park, PA.

Seaman, K. (2002) 'Athletes and Agora-phobia? Commemorative athletic sculpture in classical Athens', *Nikephoros* 15: 99–115.

Shapiro, H. A. (1998), 'Autochthony and the visual arts in fifth-century Athens', in Boedeker and Raaflaub (1998), 127–51.

Shear, J. L. (2001) 'Polis and Panathenaia: the history and development of Athena's festival'. Ph.D. dissertation, University of Pennsylvania.

(2007a) 'Cultural change, space and the politics of commemoration in Athens', in R. Osborne (2007), 91–115.

(2007b) 'The oath of Demophantos and the politics of Athenian identity', in Sommerstein and Fletcher (2007), 148–60.

(2010) 'Demetrios Poliorketes, Kallias of Sphettos and the Panathenaia', in *Studies in Greek Epigraphy and History in Honor of Stephen V. Tracy*, eds. G. Reger, F. X. Ryan and T. F. Winters, Bordeaux: 135–52.

Shear, Jr, T. L. (1970) 'The monument of the Eponymous Heroes in the Athenian Agora', *Hesperia* 39: 145–222.

(1971) 'The Athenian Agora: excavations of 1970', *Hesperia* 40: 241–79.

(1973) 'The Athenian Agora: excavations of 1971', *Hesperia* 42: 121–79.

(1975) 'The Athenian Agora: excavations of 1973–1974', *Hesperia* 44: 331–74.

(1984) 'The Athenian Agora: excavations of 1980–1982', *Hesperia* 53: 1–57.

(1993) 'The Persian destruction of Athens: evidence from the Agora', *Hesperia* 62: 383–482.

(1994) ''Ισονόμους τ' Ἀθήνας ἐποιησάτην: the Agora and democracy', in Coulson, Palagia, Shear, Jr, Shapiro and Frost (1994), 225–48.

(1995) 'Bouleuterion, Metroon and the archives at Athens', in Hansen and Raaflaub (1995), 157–90.

Sherman, D. J. (1994) 'Art, commerce and the production of memory in France after World War I', in Gillis (1994), 186–211.

(2001) *The Construction of Memory in Interwar France*. Chicago, IL.

Sickinger, J. (1999a) 'Literacy, documents and archives in the ancient Athenian democracy', *American Archivist* 62: 229–46.

(1999b) *Public Records and Archives in Classical Athens*. Chapel Hill, NC.

Siewert, P. (1979) 'Poseidon Hippios am Kolonos und die athenischen Hippeis', in *Arktouros: Hellenic Studies Presented to Bernard M. W. Knox on the Occasion of his 65th Birthday*, eds. G. W. Bowersock, W. Burkert and M. C. J. Putnam. Berlin: 280–9.

(1982) *Die Trittyen Attikas und die Heeresreform des Kleisthenes. Vestigia* 33. Munich.

Sivan, E. (1999) 'Private pain and public remembrance in Israel', in *War and Remembrance in the Twentieth Century*, eds. J. Winter and E. Sivan. Cambridge: 177–201.

Sommerstein, A. H. (1977) 'Aristophanes and the events of 411', *JHS* 97: 112–26.

(ed.) (1987) *Birds, with Translation and Notes. The Comedies of Aristophanes* VI. Warminster.

(ed.) (1990) *Lysistrata, with Translation and Notes. The Comedies of Aristophanes* VII. Warminster.

(ed.) (1994) *Thesmophoriazusae, with Translation and Notes. The Comedies of Aristophanes* VIII. Warminster.

(ed.) (1998) *Ecclesiazusae, with Translation and Commentary. The Comedies of Aristophanes* X. Warminster.

(2004) 'Argive Oinoe, Athenian *epikouroi* and the Stoa Poikile', in *Greek Art in View: Essays in Honour of Brian Sparkes*, eds. S. Keay and S. Moser. Oxford: 138–47.

Sommerstein, A. H., and Fletcher, J. (eds.) (2007) *Horkos: The Oath in Greek Society*. Exeter.

Sourvinou-Inwood, C. (1994) 'Something to do with Athens: tragedy and ritual', in Osborne and Hornblower (1994), 269–90.

(1995) *'Reading' Greek Death to the End of the Classical Period*. Oxford.

(2003) *Tragedy and Athenian Religion*. Lanham, MD.

Sparkes, B. A., and Talcott, L. (1970) *Agora* XII: *Black and Plain Pottery of the 6th, 5th and 4th Centuries BC*. Princeton, NJ.

Spence, I. G. (1993) *The Cavalry of Classical Greece: A Social and Military History with Particular Reference to Athens*. Oxford.

Stähler, K. (1972) 'Zur Rekonstruktion und Datierung des Gigantomachiegiebels von der Akropolis', in *Antike und Universalgeschichte: Festschrift Hans Erich Stier zum 70. Geburtstag am 25. Mai 1972*. Münster. 88–112.

Stansbury-O'Donnell, M. D. (2005) 'The painting program in the Stoa Poikile', in Barringer and Hurwit (2005), 73–87.

Stanton, G. R., and Bicknell, P. J. (1987) 'Voting in tribal groups in the Athenian assembly', *GRBS* 26: 51–92.

Starkie, W. J. M. (1897) *The Wasps of Aristophanes, with Introduction, Metrical Analysis, Critical Notes and Commentary*. New York, NY.

Steiner, D. T. (1994) *The Tyrant's Writ: Myths and Images of Writing in Ancient Greece*. Princeton, NJ.

(2001) *Images in Mind: Statues in Archaic and Classical Greek Literature and Thought*. Princeton, NJ.

Stewart, A. (1990) *Greek Sculpture: An Exploration*. New Haven, CT.

(1996) *Art, Desire and the Body in Ancient Greece*. Cambridge.

Strauss, B. S. (1985) 'Ritual, social drama and politics in classical Athens', *AJAH* 10: 67–83.

(1987) *Athens after the Peloponnesian War: Class, Faction and Policy 403–386 BC*. Ithaca, NY.

Stroszeck, J. (2006) 'Lakonisch-rotfigurige Keramik aus den Lakedaimoni-ergräbern am Kerameikos von Athen (403 v Chr)' *AA* 2006.2: 101–20.

Stroud, R. S. (1968) *Drakon's Law on Homicide*. University of California Publications: Classical Studies 3. Berkeley, CA.

(1971) 'Greek inscriptions: Theozotides and the orphans', *Hesperia* 40: 280–301.

(1979) *The Axones and Kyrbeis of Drakon and Solon*. University of California Publications: Classical Studies 19. Berkeley, CA.

(1998) *The Athenian Grain-Tax Law of 374/3 BC*. Hesperia Supplement 29. Princeton, NJ.

(2006) *The Athenian Empire on Stone*. Athens.

Stupperich, R. (1977) 'Staatsbegräbnis und Privatgrabmal im klassischen Athen'. Ph.D. dissertation, Westfälischen Wilhelms Universität. Munster.

Sturken, M. (1991) 'The wall, the screen and the image: the Vietnam Veterans Memorial', *Representations* 35: 118–42.

Tanner, J. (2006) *The Invention of Art History in Ancient Greece: Religion, Society and Artistic Rationalisation*. Cambridge.

Taylor, C. (2007) 'A new political world', in R. Osborne (2007), 72–90.

Taylor, J. G. (1998) 'Oinoe and the Painted Stoa: ancient and modern misunder-standings?', *AJP* 119: 223–43.

Taylor, M. C. (2002a) 'One hundred heroes from Phyle?', *Hesperia* 71: 377–97.

(2002b) 'Implicating the *demos*: a reading of Thucydides on the rise of the Four Hundred', *JHS* 122: 91–108.

Taylor, M. W. (1991) *The Tyrant Slayers: The Heroic Image in Fifth Century BC Athenian Art and Politics*, 2nd edn. Salem, NH.

Thomas, R. (1989) *Oral Tradition and Written Record in Classical Athens*. Cambridge Studies in Oral and Literate Culture 18. Cambridge.

(1992) *Literacy and Orality in Ancient Greece*. Cambridge.

(1994) 'Law and the lawgiver in the Athenian democracy', in Osborne and Hornblower (1994), 119–33.

(2009) 'Writing, reading, public and private "literacies": functional literacy and democratic literacy in Greece', in *Ancient Literacies: The Culture of Reading in Greece and Rome*, eds. W. A. Johnson and H. N. Parker. Oxford: 13–45.

Thompson, H. A. (1937) 'Buildings on the west side of the Agora', *Hesperia* 6: 1–226.

(1968) 'Activity in the Athenian Agora: 1966–1967', *Hesperia* 37: 36–72.

(1982) 'The Pnyx in models', in *Studies in Attic Epigraphy, History and Topography Presented to Eugene Vanderpool*. Hesperia Supplement 19. Princeton, NJ: 133–47.

Thompson, H. A., and Wycherley, R. E. (1972) *Agora* xiv: *The Agora of Athens: The History, Shape and Uses of an Ancient City*. Princeton, NJ.

Thompson, W. E. (1966) '*Conspectus traditionum*', *CQ* 16: 286–90.

(1970) 'Notes on the treasurers of Athena', *Hesperia* 39: 54–63.

Todd, S. C. (1985) 'Athenian internal politics, 403–395 BC, with particular reference to the speeches of Lysias'. Ph.D. thesis, University of Cambridge.

(1993) *The Shape of Athenian Law*. Oxford.

(1996) 'Lysias against Nikomakhos: the fate of the expert in Athenian law', in *Greek Law in its Political Setting: Justification and Justice*, eds. L. Foxhall and A. D. E. Lewis, Oxford: 101–31.

(2000) *Lysias. The Oratory of Classical Greece* II, series ed. M. Gagarin. Austin, TX.

(2007) *A Commentary on Lysias, Speeches 1–11*. Oxford.

Townsend, R. F. (1995) *Agora* XXVII: *The East Side of the Agora: The Remains Beneath the Stoa of Attalos*. Princeton, NJ.

Traill, J. S. (1986) *Demos and Trittys: Epigraphical and Topographical Studies in the Organization of Attica*. Toronto.

Travlos, J. (1971) *Pictorial Dictionary of Ancient Athens*. London.

Tsakirgis, B. (2005) 'Living and working around the Athenian Agora: a preliminary case study of three houses', in *Ancient Greek Houses and Households: Chronological, Regional and Social Diversity*, eds. B. A. Ault and L. C. Nevett. Philadelphia, PA: 67–82.

Vanderpool, E. (1974) 'The "Agora" of Pausanias, I, 17, 1–2', *Hesperia* 43: 308–10.

Velissaropoulos-Karakostas, J. (1991) 'Νηποινεὶ τεθνάναι', in Gagarin (1991), 93–105.

Vidal-Naquet, P. (1986) 'Le *Philoctète* de Sophocle et l'éphébie', in *Mythe et tragédie en Grèce ancienne* I, eds. J.-P. Vernant and P. Vidal-Naquet. Paris: 159–84.

Vlassopoulos, K. (2007) 'Free spaces: identity, experience and democracy in classical Athens', *CQ* 57: 33–52.

Volonaki, E. (2001) 'The re-publication of the Athenian laws in the last decade of the fifth century BC', *Dike* 4: 137–67.

Wade-Gery, H. T. (1932–3) 'Studies in Attic inscriptions of the fifth century BC', *ABSA* 33: 101–36.

(1958) *Essays in Greek History*. Oxford.

Wagner-Pacifici, R., and Schwartz, B. (1991) 'The Vietnam Veterans Memorial: commemorating a difficult past', *American Journal of Sociology* 97: 376–420.

Walbank, M. B. (1978) *Athenian Proxenies of the Fifth Century BC*. Toronto.

(1982) 'The confiscation and sale by the poletai in 402/1 BC of the property of the Thirty Tyrants', *Hesperia* 51: 74–98.

(1994) 'Greek inscriptions from the Athenian Agora: lists of names', *Hesperia* 63: 169–209.

Wallace, R. W. (1985) *The Areopagos Council, to 307 BC*. Baltimore, MD.

Walters, K. R. (1976) 'The "ancestral constitution" and fourth-century historiography in Athens', *AJAH* 1: 129–44.

Westlake, H. D. (1968) *Individuals in Thucydides*. Cambridge.

Whitehead, D. (1982–3) 'Sparta and the Thirty Tyrants', *AncSoc* 13/14: 105–30.

(1983) 'Competitive outlay and community profit: φιλοτιμία in democratic Athens', *C&M* 34: 55–74.

(1984) 'A thousand new Athenians (*IG* II².10+)', *LCM* 9: 8–10.

(1993) 'Cardinal virtues: the language of public approbation in democratic Athens', *C&M* 44: 37–75.

(2002) 'Athenian laws and lawsuits in the late fifth century BC', *MH* 59: 71–96.

(2009) '*Andragathia* and *arete*', in Mitchell and Rubinstein (2009), 47–58.

Wilhelm, A. (1922–4) 'Fünf Beschlüsse der Athener', *JÖAI* 21–22: 123–71.

Willemsen, F. (1977) 'Zu den Lakedämoniergräbern im Kerameikos', *MDAI(A)* 92: 117–57.

Wilson, P. (2009) 'Tragic honours and democracy: neglected evidence for the politics of the Athenian Dionysia', *CQ* 59: 8–29.

Wilson, P., and Hartwig, A. (2009) '*IG* I³ 102 and the tradition of proclaiming honours at the tragic *agon* of the Athenian City Dionysia', *ZPE* 169: 17–27.

Winkler, J. J., and Zeitlin, F. I. (eds.) (1990) *Nothing to Do with Dionysos? Athenian Drama in Its Social Context*. Princeton, NJ.

Winter, J. (1995) *Sites of Memory, Sites of Mourning: The Great War in European Cultural History*. Cambridge.

Wolpert, A. (2002a) *Remembering Defeat: Civil War and Civic Memory in Ancient Athens*. Baltimore, MD.

(2002b) 'Lysias 18 and Athenian memory of the Civil War', *TAPA* 132: 109–26.

(2006) 'The violence of the Thirty Tyrants', in *Ancient Tyranny*, ed. S. Lewis. Edinburgh: 213–23.

Wood, N. (1994) 'Memory's remains: *Les lieux de mémoire*', *History and Memory* 6.1: 123–49.

Woodhead, A. G. (1954) 'Peisander', *AJP* 75: 131–46.

(1997) *Agora* xvi: *Inscriptions: The Decrees*. Princeton, NJ.

Wycherley, R. E. (1957) *Agora* iii: *Literary and Epigraphical Testimonia*. Princeton, NJ.

(1978) *The Stones of Athens*. Princeton, NJ.

Young, J. E. (1993) *The Texture of Memory: Holocaust Memorials and Meaning*. New Haven, CT.

(1994) 'The art of memory: Holocaust memorials in history', in *The Art of Memory: Holocaust Memorials in History*, ed. J. E. Young. Munich: 19–38.

(2000) *At Memory's Edge: After-Images of the Holocaust in Contemporary Art and Architecture*. New Haven, CT.

Yunis, H. (1996) *Taming Democracy: Modes of Political Rhetoric in Classical Athens*. Ithaca, NY.

(1997) 'Thrasymachus B1: discord, not diplomacy', *CP* 92: 58–66.

Index locorum

LITERARY TEXTS

AELIAN

Varia Historia
8.16, 321

AISCHINES

1.173, 219
2.32, 118
2.58, 118
2.89, 118
2.92, 118
2.135, 118
3, 142
3.24, 118
3.75, 118
3.154, 149, 291
3.181, 305
3.183–5, 255
3.183–91, 255, 305
3.186, 305
3.187, 230, 234, 237, 245, 250, 252, 253, 256, 258, 260, 274, 281, 290, 297, 298, 300, 302, 305
3.187–8, 254
3.190, 234, 248, 296, 297, 300
3.190–1, 230, 237, 245, 250, 252, 253, 256, 258, 260, 274, 281, 300, 302
3.195, 224, 261
3.234, 282

ANDOKIDES

1, 220
1.11–70, 220
1.45, 137
1.71, 220

1.71–91, 221
1.75, 62
1.78, 62, 266
1.79, 118
1.81, 197, 199
1.81–2, 229
1.82, 91, 239, 240
1.83, 168
1.83–4, 91, 95, 100, 229, 239, 240, 251, 252, 307
1.84, 46, 91
1.85, 91
1.87, 307
1.90, 196, 197, 203
1.91, 216, 273
1.94, 219
1.94–5, 221
1.95, 89, 171, 241, 321
1.95–6, 85
1.96, 52
1.96–8, 1, 5, 20, 73, 75, 89, 96–7, 98, 99, 101, 102, 104, 107, 110, 111, 136, 137, 138, 147, 150, 153, 160, 161, 162, 163, 190, 196, 208, 215, 225, 241, 253, 254, 255, 258, 260, 261, 273, 274, 278, 280, 284, 301, 314, 315, 316, 317, 318, 321
1.105, 221
1.121, 221
1.133–5, 221
1.140, 226
1.150, 221
2.23, 118
3.11–12, 169
3.12, 169

ANDROTION (*FGRHIST* 324)

F43, 41

ANECDOTA GRAECA (BEKKER)

s.v. καταλογεύς, 41
s.v. συγγραφεῖς, 41

ANTIPHON

5.10–11, 268
fr. 1c col. 6 lines 17–18, 64
frs. 1–6, 60

ARISTOPHANES

Birds
  1072–84, 151
  1074–5, 151
Ekklesiazousai
  289–93, 309
  308–10, 309
  380–95, 309
Frogs
  687–702, 60
  689–91, 64
Knights, 19
  225–7, 38
  280–1, 141
  551–64, 38
  573–6, 141
  580, 38
  702–9, 141
  766, 141
  1404–5, 141
Lysistrata, 26
  273–80, 43
  616–35, 43
  626–35, 140, 278
  630–5, 102
  664–70, 43
  1150–6, 43
Thesmophoriazousai, 26
  335–51, 43
  352–71, 44
Wasps
  389–94, 266
  818–21, 266
  1108–9, 266, 268

ARISTOTLE

Athenaion Politeia
  3.1–4, 35, 47
  3.6, 46

4.2, 45, 47
4.2–4, 45
4.3, 46, 47
4.4, 46
7.1, 105
8.1, 48
8.1–2, 35, 47
8.4, 46, 47
21.3, 47
22.2, 107
25.2, 46
27.3, 35
29.1, 31
29.1–3, 36, 50
29.2, 31, 41
29.3, 31, 42
29.5, 33, 34
30.1–32.1, 20
30.2, 47, 48
30.2–31.3, 33
30.3, 48
30.6, 47, 48
31.1, 48
31.3, 48
32.1, 36, 52
32.1–2, 36
32.2, 36
32.3, 36, 112
33.1, 50, 51, 52
34.3, 168, 169, 170
34.3–35.1, 170
35.1, 171, 172
35.1–2, 169, 182
35.2, 85, 173, 174
35.3, 174
35.3–4, 182
35.4, 272
36.1–2, 179, 182
37.1, 173, 182, 184
37.1–2, 179
37.2, 177, 182, 288
38.1, 184, 185
38.3, 185
38.3–4, 190
38.4, 185, 195
38.4–40.1, 208
39.1, 191, 201, 206
39.1–3, 191
39.1–6, 191
39.2, 168, 191, 201, 202, 203, 204
39.4, 207, 209, 214
39.4–5, 191
39.5, 201
39.5–6, 191
39.6, 191, 196, 197, 203, 206, 238

ARISTOTLE (*cont.*)

40.1, 209
40.2, 15, 224, 226, 261, 301, 312
40.4, 191, 311
41.3, 271, 309
43.3, 126
44, 56
47.1, 48
47.2–3, 246
55.5, 105
57.1–2, 105
57.2–4, 104
59.2, 308
Rhetoric
1.14.3, 61
2.23.25, 222
3.15.3, 61
3.18.6, 61

ARRIAN

Anabasis
3.16.8, 102

ATHENAEUS

13.577b, 261
15.695a–b, nos. 10–13, 140

DEMOSTHENES

18, 142
18.55, 118
18.142, 118
18.312, 176
19.129, 118
19.280–1, 278
20.18, 75
20.42, 130, 143
20.69, 255
20.69–70, 230, 231, 237, 246, 252, 255, 259, 277, 278, 279, 280, 281
20.70, 102, 264, 275, 276, 278
20.72–4, 280
20.75–86, 282
20.89–96, 307
20.127–30, 75
20.159, 85
23.33, 176
23.65–78, 266
23.87, 307

23.196–8, 282
23.218, 307
24.20–3, 307
24.30, 307
24.33, 308
24.42, 239, 307
24.144, 78
24.180, 282
26.23, 321
45.17, 268
57.30, 261

[DEMOSTHENES]

13.21–2, 282
25.23, 117
58.67, 163

DEUTERONOMY

25: 17–19, 7

DIODOROS

13.107.4, 169
14.3.1, 172
14.3.2, 169
14.3.3, 168
14.3.5–7, 170
14.4.1, 171
14.4.1–6.3, 181
14.5.5–7, 182
14.5.6, 182
14.32.1, 184
14.32.1–33.1, 181
14.32.4–33.1, 182
14.33.1–2, 184
14.33.2–3, 184
14.33.5, 184, 185
14.33.6, 185
15.32.5, 282
15.33.4, 282

DIOGENES LAERTIUS

2.40, 219
2.44, 219

DIONYSIOS OF HALIKARNASSOS

Lysias
32, 199, 201, 260

DOURIS (*FGRHIST* 76)

F66, 78

ETYMOLOGICUM MAGNUM

s.v. συγγραφεῖς, 41

EUMELOS (*FGRHIST* 77)

F2, 261

EURIPIDES

Suppliants
399–466, 19

EXODUS

17: 8–15, 7

HARMODIOS *SKOLIA*

PMG nos. 893–6, 140

HARPOKRATION

s.v. λίθος, 105
s.v. συγγραφεῖς, 41

HELLENIKA OXYRHYNCHIA

16.2, 48
16.4, 48

HERODOTOS

3.80.1–84.1, 19
5.33.3, 176
6.109.3, 102
6.109.3–6, 278
6.123.2, 278
8.3.1, 295
8.28, 176

HOMER

Iliad, 4
Odyssey, 4

HYPEREIDES

Epitaphios
34–9, 278

ISAIOS

5.47, 75
8.43, 261

ISOKRATES

8.82, 149
8.82–3, 148
9.54, 256, 277
9.54–6, 281
9.56–7, 246
9.57, 102, 276
18.1–3, 310
18.2, 310
18.3, 310
18.4, 310
18.5, 172, 275
18.5–12, 310
18.19–20, 190, 197
18.19–21, 190
18.19–22, 310
18.20, 191, 196, 202
18.23, 219
18.25–7, 310
18.29, 310
18.30, 310
18.34, 310
18.35, 310
18.42, 310
18.44, 310
18.45, 310
18.45–6, 226
18.47, 310
18.52, 266
18.64, 310
18.67, 190, 310
18.68, 310

KARYSTOS (*FHG* 4.358)

fr. II, 261

KRATEROS (*FGRHIST* 342)

F5b, 22, 57, 60

LYKOURGOS

Leokrates
46–51, 278
51, 264, 283
112, 66
112–15, 163
115, 62
117–19, 58
124, 85, 89
124–5, 163
126, 85, 89, 102
126–7, 161

LYSIAS

2.4–6, 303
2.7–10, 303
2.11–16, 303
2.20–47, 303
2.48–58, 303
2.58–60, 303
2.61, 230, 303, 304
2.61–6, 292, 303
2.62, 304
2.63, 185, 230, 298, 299, 303, 304
2.64, 255, 292, 304
2.65, 230, 303, 304
2.66, 235, 255, 292, 303
7.4, 67, 142
12.6–23, 272
12.42, 64
12.54–7, 185
12.62–3, 64
12.62–79, 183
12.64–5, 63
12.72–3, 170
12.72–7, 169
12.73, 170
12.78, 63
12.94, 177, 288
13.2, 218
13.12–42, 218
13.17–18, 218
13.36–8, 171
13.41–3, 218
13.46, 177, 288
13.65, 218
13.70–3, 66, 142
13.71–2, 142
13.72, 67
13.77–9, 218
13.77–82, 218
13.78–9, 219

13.80–1, 208, 287
13.85–7, 218
13.88, 190
13.88–9, 218
16.4–8, 222
16.10, 222
16.13–18, 222
16.15–17, 222
16.17, 222
16.20, 222
18.10–12, 185
18.24, 235
18.25, 318
21.4, 209
25.1, 223
25.1–2, 223
25.2, 223
25.5, 223
25.9, 64, 222, 311
25.14, 64, 223
25.15–16, 223
25.16, 223
25.18, 223
25.18–19, 223
25.19, 223
25.22, 179
25.23, 190
25.25–6, 61
25.27, 223
25.28, 190, 213, 226
25.29–31, 223
25.34, 190
26.10, 222
26.13–15, 222
26.16–20, 222
26.21, 222
26.21–4, 222
28.11, 318
28.12–14, 318
30, 220
30.2, 73, 83
30.3, 74, 83
30.4, 74, 229, 240
30.5–6, 100
30.7–8, 64
30.7–9, 220
30.9–14, 100
30.10–13, 83
30.10–14, 74
30.15–16, 74, 220
30.17, 100, 229
30.17–25, 238
30.20, 238
30.25, 83, 232
30.26, 176

30.28, 239
30.30, 100
30.35, 100
31.8, 235
34, 260
34.2, 260
34.6, 260
fr. LXIV
    128–50, 15, 224, 301
    129 lines 26–47, 291
    129 lines 30–8, 149
    130 lines 72–81, 235
fr. LXX
    165 lines 34–48, 191, 195, 202
    170 lines 182–92, 64

[LYSIAS]

6, 220
6.9, 220
6.24, 220
6.38, 190
6.39, 190
6.40, 190
6.45, 190
20, 165
20.1, 50, 61, 63
20.5, 63
20.6, 63
20.7, 63
20.8, 63
20.8–9, 63, 65
20.9, 63
20.10, 63
20.13, 63
20.13–14, 50, 61
20.14, 50, 63
20.14–45, 61
20.16, 50, 61, 63
20.17, 61
20.18, 61
20.19, 63, 141
20.22, 61, 63

NEPOS

Chabrias
    1.2–3, 282
Thrasybulus
    3.2, 199
Timotheus
    2.3, 282

P. MICHIGAN

5982, 183

PAUSANIAS

1.3.2–3, 246, 276, 282
1.8.4–6, 102
1.15.1–3, 319
1.15.1–4, 255, 302
1.16.1, 321
1.29.13, 321
1.30.4, 38

PHILOCHOROS (FGRHIST 328)

F30, 137
F136, 41

PHOTIOS

Lexikon
    s.v. καταλογεύς, 41
    s.v. λίθος, 105

PLATO

Apology
    32c3–d7, 220
Crito
    50a6–54d1, 254
Menexenos
    234a1–b7, 117
    243e1–4, 304
    243e4–6, 304
    243e6–7, 304
    244a3–4, 304
    244a3–b3, 304

PLINY

Naturalis historia
    34.17, 275

PLUTARCH

De gloria Atheniensium
    349F, 197, 208, 289, 298, 305
Praecepta gerendae reipublicae
    814B, 199

PLUTARCH (*cont.*)

Alkibiades
25.14, 66
Aristeides
7.5–6, 137
7.6, 201
Kimon
7.4–8.1, 255
8.7–9, 148
Lysandros
14.8, 169
15.6, 177
21.3–4, 185
21.4–5, 185
21.6, 185
Lysias
15.6, 288
Solon
19.1–2, 47
25.3, 105
Themistokles
19.6, 177

[PLUTARCH]

Vitae decem oratorem
833A, 57
833D, 57
833D–E, 57
833E–F, 22, 57, 60
834A–B, 60
834B, 57
835F, 172
835F–836A, 261
851F, 322

POLLUX

Onomastikon
8.19–20, 137
8.86, 105
8.112, 230

POLYAINOS

2.1.2, 282

SCHOLIA ON AISCHINES

1.39, 169, 173, 199, 230, 238, 261
3.195, 261

SCHOLIA ON ARISTOPHANES

Knights
855b, 137
Lysistrata
421a, 41

SCHOLIA VETERA ON ARISTOPHANES

Wealth
1146a, 199

SCHOLIA OF TZETZES ON ARISTOPHANES

Wealth
1146, 199

SCHOLIA RECENTIORA ON ARISTOPHANES

Wealth
1146b, 199

SOPHOKLES

Oedipus Coloneus
54–61, 38
855, 176
887–9, 38
1156–9, 38
1491–5, 38
Philoktetes, 16
4, 155
54, 157
55–131, 157
57, 155
58–64, 155
72–4, 156
79, 156
96, 156
119, 156
121–2, 157
130, 156
133–4, 155
141, 156
201, 156
210, 156
229, 158
236, 156
240–1, 155

242, 156
249, 156
253–316, 158
260, 155, 156
262, 156
268–84, 157
276, 156
284, 156
300, 156
307, 156
314–15, 157
315, 156
327, 156
337, 156
343–53, 157
343–84, 157
354–81, 156
359–73, 155
372, 156
403–55, 156
421, 158
456, 156
466, 156
468, 156
478, 156
484, 156
531, 156
533, 156
542, 155
561–2, 159
578, 156
582, 155
586, 158
589, 156
598–600, 157
620, 156
622–3, 156
628, 156
628–34, 158
635, 156
658, 156
662, 156
665, 158
671, 158
733, 156
742, 156
745, 156
747, 156
750, 156
753, 156
776, 156
782, 156
799, 156
802, 156
804, 156

805, 156
807, 156
807–13, 156
811, 156
833, 156
843, 156
845, 156
855, 156
864, 156
869, 156
875, 156
878, 156
879, 156
889, 156
896, 156
898, 156
910, 156
910–11, 157
914, 156
923–4, 157
925–6, 157
927–62, 157
932, 156
940, 155
941, 156
947–9, 157
967, 156
981, 156
986–94, 157
999–1000, 158
1001–39, 157
1008, 156
1026–8, 157
1050, 156
1066, 155
1072, 156
1197–9, 157
1200–2, 158
1222–58, 157
1237, 155
1268–9, 157
1275–6, 158
1280–6, 157
1288, 157
1291–4, 157
1292, 156
1293–8, 158
1295, 156
1298, 155
1301, 156
1310, 156
1324, 156
1348–72, 158
1367, 156
1367–8, 156

SOPHOKLES (*cont.*)

1375, 158
1385, 158
1390, 157
1392, 158
1399, 156
1423, 156
1433, 155
1467, 159

SUDA

s.v. ἀσκοφορεῖν, 153
s.v. λίθος, 105
s.v. πρόβουλοι, 41

THEOPOMPOS (*FGRHIST* 115)

F154, 78
F155, 78

THRASYMACHOS

85 B1, 42

THUCYDIDES

1.126.8, 35, 47
2.65.7, 66
2.65.11–13, 66
3.69–85, 19
3.70.6, 65
3.72.3–74.2, 65
3.81.2–5, 65
5.26.5, 65
5.38.2–4, 48
6.27.1–29.3, 220
6.53.1–2, 220
6.54.1–59.1, 29
6.55.1–2, 58
6.60.1–61.7, 220
7.28.3–4, 148
8.27.1–6, 27
8.47.2, 22
8.48.1, 22, 29
8.48.2, 42
8.48.4, 44
8.48.4–7, 26
8.49, 26, 29
8.50.1–51.3, 27

8.51.3, 27
8.53.1, 26, 29, 42
8.53.1–54.1, 30
8.53.3, 26
8.54.2, 29
8.54.3, 26
8.54.4, 26
8.54.5, 29
8.63.3, 29
8.64.1–2, 29
8.64.2, 29
8.65.1, 29
8.65.2, 29, 31
8.65.2–3, 29
8.65.2–66.5, 26
8.65.3, 45
8.66.1, 29, 39, 52
8.66.1–3, 30
8.66.2, 31, 65
8.66.3–5, 30
8.67.1, 29
8.67.1–3, 26
8.67.2, 38
8.68, 29
8.68.1, 26
8.68.2, 61, 65
8.68.3, 27
8.69, 31
8.69.1, 26
8.69.1–70.1, 39, 112
8.69.2, 29
8.69.4, 39, 52
8.70.1–2, 31
8.71.1, 29
8.71.3, 40
8.72.1, 29
8.73.3, 29
8.73.4, 29
8.74.3–75.1, 31
8.76.1, 37
8.76.2–77, 44
8.76.6, 44
8.77, 29
8.86.1, 29
8.86.9, 29, 40
8.89.1, 29
8.89.1–2, 40
8.89.2, 29
8.90.1, 29, 51
8.90.1–5, 39
8.90.2, 26, 28
8.92.2, 29, 39, 40
8.92.4–9, 39
8.92.4–11, 30
8.92.5, 29

8.92.6, 39
8.92.10–11, 40
8.93.1, 39, 40
8.95.2, 29
8.97.1, 38, 179
8.97.1–2, 51
8.97.2, 51
8.98, 29
8.98.1, 26, 61
8.98.1–4, 62

VALERIUS MAXIMUS

2.10.ext. 1, 102
4.1.ext. 4, 199

VELLEIUS PATERCULUS

2.58.4, 199

XENOPHON

Hellenika
  1.3.8–9, 148
  1.7.28, 62
  2.2.20, 169
  2.3.1, 172
  2.3.2, 169, 170, 171
  2.3.11, 170, 171
  2.3.12, 174
  2.3.12–13, 181
  2.3.14–16, 181
  2.3.17–20, 181
  2.3.18–19, 179
  2.3.21, 181
  2.3.21–2, 272
  2.3.22–56, 181
  2.3.23, 171
  2.3.23–55, 171
  2.3.24, 171
  2.3.40, 272
  2.3.42, 219
  2.3.44, 219
  2.3.46, 29
  2.3.50, 117, 171
  2.3.51, 171, 173, 179
  2.3.55, 117, 171
  2.4.1, 181
  2.4.1–2, 184
  2.4.2, 179, 181
  2.4.6–7, 299
  2.4.8, 172

2.4.8–9, 181
2.4.10, 184
2.4.10–19, 299
2.4.10–22, 184
2.4.19, 219
2.4.20–2, 204
2.4.23–4, 184, 185
2.4.24, 172
2.4.25, 234
2.4.26, 172
2.4.28, 185
2.4.28–9, 185, 188
2.4.29–30, 185
2.4.30–5, 185
2.4.31, 185
2.4.33, 185, 299
2.4.35, 185
2.4.35–8, 190
2.4.36–7, 185
2.4.38, 185, 195, 197, 200, 205
2.4.38–9, 197
2.4.38–43, 208
2.4.39, 287
2.4.39–42, 289
2.4.43, 172, 196, 197, 207, 226, 311, 312
3.1.1, 230
Memorabilia
  1.1.1, 219
  1.2.31, 173, 180
  4.4.3, 220

[XENOPHON]

Athenaion Politeia, 19
  1.3, 35

INSCRIPTIONS

Agora XVI
  37, 176, 231, 235, 236, 258
  37.9–11, 296
  39, 176, 235
  114.19–24, 10
  187.26–30, 144
  214, 280
  270, 38
Agora XIX
  P2 + LA2, 191, 230, 238
I.Eleusis
  24, 59
IG I³
  1, 59
  2, 59

IG I³ (*cont.*)
5, 59
11, 197
17.7–9, 145
28.14, 235
30.4–5, 145
31.2, 198
37, 196
43.4–5, 145
57.9–10, 235
62, 196
65.10–11, 145
73.24–5, 145
75, 196, 197, 198
75.1–6, 198
75.5, 198
75.29, 198
76, 196, 197, 198
76.21–2, 198
76.26–7, 198
83, 197, 198
84.28, 48
86, 196
89.26, 198
89.34, 198
91.15–16, 235
92.7–9, 145
96.16, 145
97, 145
98, 22, 56
98.1–7, 56
98.3, 56
98.4, 56
98.5–7, 56
98.8–28, 56
98.14, 56
98.26, 56
98.28, 56
100, 148
101, 128
101.9–10, 145
101.47, 148
102, 5, 66, 67, 128, 161, 162,
    318
102.1–14, 142
102.5–14, 143
102.6–7, 144, 145, 149
102.6–8, 130, 150
102.8–10, 150
102.14–38, 142
102.14–47, 161
102.25–38, 67
102.38–47, 67, 142
103, 128

104, 5, 72, 75, 84, 85, 91, 95, 96, 98, 99, 101,
    104–5, 106, 110, 111, 162, 198, 199, 240,
    251, 254
104.1–2, 100
104.1–9, 73, 76, 109, 162
104.4–6, 73
104.5–7, 104
104.5–8, 91
104.5–9, 99
104.7, 73, 99
104.7–8, 101
104.10, 100
104.10–11, 76
104.56, 100
104.56–7, 76
104.57, 76
105, 5, 72, 76, 84, 86, 95–6, 97–8, 99, 100, 101,
    102, 105, 108, 110, 111, 162, 309
105.9, 78
105.17, 78
105.18, 78
105.23–34, 77, 100, 107
105.25, 78
105.27, 78
105.30, 78, 107
105.33, 78
105.34, 78, 98, 108
105.34–5, 78, 98
105.34–43, 77, 100
105.35, 78
105.36, 78, 98
105.37, 78
105.40, 78
105.40–1, 78, 98
105.42, 78
105.43, 78, 84
105.44–5, 107
105.44–51, 77
105.45, 78, 107
105.45–6, 78
105.47, 78
105.49, 78
105.52, 78
105.53, 78
105.54, 78
105.56–7, 78
105.59, 78
106, 128
108, 128
109, 128
110, 128
113, 128, 256, 277
114, 128
115, 128

116, 128
117, 128
123, 128
124, 128
125, 128, 143, 145
125.6–8, 145, 149
125.6–17, 130
125.17, 143
125.23–9, 143, 144, 151
125.25–9, 130
125.28–9, 145
126, 128
127, 14, 128, 176, 231, 236, 252, 258, 259
127.1–2, 249
127.1–4, 236
127.3–4, 249
127.7–9, 237
127.25–32, 118
127.34, 249
127.36–7, 237
127.38–9, 247
131, 141
131.1–9, 75
161.5–6, 235
162.9–10, 235
164.24–5, 235
179.6–7, 235
227.13–14, 145
227.22–3, 235
228.11–12, 235
229, 176, 231, 235, 251, 252, 258
229.1–4, 296
229.4–6, 247
229.5–6, 231
236, 72, 78, 83, 86, 93, 95
236.5–6, 99
236.9, 99
236.38, 99
236.41, 99
237, 72, 79, 86, 95
237.13, 99
237*bis*, 79
240K, 79
248, 59
249, 59
253, 59
259–72, 129
292, 59
311.35–51, 22, 53
312.52–68, 22, 54
313.72–86, 54
314, 129
315, 129
316, 129

317, 59
333.4, 54
334.18, 54
335.30–2, 22, 53
335.32, 54
336.44, 54
336.44–57, 22, 54
337.60–2, 54
338, 128, 129
339, 129
340, 129
341, 129
342, 129
343, 59
357.54–82, 22, 53
358, 54
359, 128, 129
363, 59
365, 55
366, 55
371, 55
372, 55
373, 22, 55
373.1–2, 50
374, 22, 55
375, 48, 55, 129
375.1–3, 20, 73
375.14, 148
375.16–18, 148
375.27, 67, 142
375.30–1, 148
375.35–6, 148
376, 129
377, 129
378, 129
379, 129
380, 172
380.1–4, 172
380.6–7, 172
380.11–12, 172
380.27, 171
384, 59
402, 59
405, 38
433, 59
435, 59
436, 59
453, 59
461, 59
462, 59
474 + *SEG* xxxiii 22, 123
474 + *SEG* xxxiii 22.1–7, 126
474 + *SEG* xxxiii 22.8–43, 123
474 + *SEG* xxxiii 22.44–76, 124

IG I³ (*cont.*)
474 + *SEG* XXXIII 22.83–92, 124
474 + *SEG* XXXIII 22.93–237, 124
476, 129
477, 129
478, 129
479, 129
522, 255, 302
951, 102, 275
1144.32, 293
1144.34–8, 292
1144.43, 293
1144.118–27, 292
1144.130, 293
1144.141, 293
1147.1–4, 293
1147.127, 293
1154, 93
1162.1–3, 293
1162.45–51, 293
1172.35–7, 292
1180.5–7, 292
1180.25–9, 292
1184.40, 293
1184.44, 293
1184.46, 293
1184.48, 293
1184.50, 293
1184.52, 293
1184.89–91, 292
1185, 79
1190.65–72, 292
1190.136–41, 292
1192.152–7, 292
IG II²
1, 14, 176, 231, 236
1.1–4, 236
6, 176, 231, 235, 247, 250, 252,
     258
6.11–14, 296
10, 246
13 + addenda p. 655 + *SEG* XL 54, 176, 231,
     235, 236, 250, 252, 258
13 + addenda p. 655 + *SEG* XL 54.8–11, 247
44, 198
52, 176, 231, 235, 236, 250, 258, 300
52.4–5, 261
52.5–7, 247
222.11–16, 145
223.13–14, 145
300.2–5, 145
448.16–19, 145
487.10–12, 145
505.41–3, 145

555.9–11, 145
657.43–5, 10
657.48–50, 322
657.50–2, 145
657.58–62, 144
680, 10
1374, 14
1496.80–1, 152
1496.III–12, 152
1496.126–33, 289
1496.138–42, 289
1498.20–2, 172
1641.25–33, 268
1656, 18
2720, 95
4992, 289
5224, 93
11678, 185, 299
IG XII.5
444, A54, lines 70–1 (= *FGrHist* 239, A54,
     lines 70–1), 275
RO
2, 14, 176, 231, 236, 252, 258, 259
2.43, 237
2.43–4, 258
2.52–4, 258
2.57, 231
2.58, 237
2.64–5, 237
2.66, 258
2.66–8, 247
2.71, 237
2.71–2, 237
4, 5, 218, 231, 233, 234, 250, 252, 261, 300, 302,
     303
4.1–2, 249
4.4–5, 297
4.4–8, 296
4.6, 249
4.7, 297
4.8, 249
4 col. 5.45, 249
4 col. 6.56–7, 234, 249
4 col. 6.58, 249
4 col. 7.10, 249
6, 198
11, 230, 231, 237, 252, 255, 259, 277, 279,
     281
11.5–6, 237
11.12–13, 237
11.14–17, 253
11.17, 237
11.20–1, 246
41, 198

95.65–6, 145
95.76–8, 145
SEG
  XIX 204, 242, 282
  XXIII 81.1–8, 172
  XXVIII 45, 5, 230, 232, 237, 245, 250, 252,
     253, 256, 258, 260, 274, 281, 300,
     302, 305
  XXVIII 45.73–6, 248, 296, 297
  XXVIII 45.74–5, 251, 272, 300
  XXVIII 46, 1, 5, 224, 230, 235, 237, 246, 248,
     249, 250, 252, 254, 255, 256, 258, 259, 261,
     274, 279, 281, 291, 293, 294, 300, 301,
     302, 307, 317
  XXVIII 46.4–6, 235, 248, 297
  XXVIII 46.4–9, 295
  XXVIII 46.5, 300
  XXVIII 46.5–6, 304
  XXVIII 46.6–8, 297
  XXVIII 46.6–11, 297
  XXVIII 46.16–18, 297
  XXVIII 60.79–83, 322
  XXVIII 60.83–6, 145
  XXXII 161, 191, 230, 238, 246, 252, 253, 254, 258,
     260, 261, 296, 300, 302
  XXXII 161 *stele* 1.1–5, 238, 250
  XXXII 161 *stele* 1.4–5, 300
  XXXII 161 *stele* 3.7, 238, 300
  XXXII 239, 275

XL 54, *see IG* II^2 13
XLIV 34, 234
LII 45, 230
LII 48, 72, 79, 86–9, 95, 100, 104, 105, 109, 110,
  111, 141, 162, 228, 232, 241–3, 244, 251,
  254, 257
  fr. 1A.6–22, 254
  fr. 1B.14, 88, 100
  fr. 2, 240, 243
  fr. 2A, 175, 179
  fr. 2A.1, 232
  fr. 2A.8, 257
  fr. 2B, 93, 95
  fr. 3, 240, 243
  fr. 3A, 78, 175, 179
  fr. 3A.30, 232
  fr. 3A.31–58, 254
  fr. 3A.77, 257
  fr. 3B, 72, 78, 83, 86, 93, 95
  fr. 4, 89
  fr. 7A.1–4, 254
  fr. 9B col. 2.7, 100
  fr. 9B col. 2.8, 100
  fr. 10, 89, 242, 243
  fr. 11, 89
  fr. 13B, 79
Walbank, *Proxenies*
  26, 176, 231, 235
  26.4–6, 296

General index

Academy, 297, 299
Acharnai
 defeat of oligarchs, 182
Achilles, 155
 arms of, 156
agalma, definition of, 246
Agis, 29
Agora
 Aiakeion, 266
 Altar of Twelve Gods, 138, 275
 and commercial buildings, 284
 and Dionysia, 137
 and Four Hundred, 22, 112, 119, 314, 315
 and honorary statues, 281, 284
 and inscriptions, 71, 96, 101–5, 106, 108, 109,
  110, 111, 113, 128, 129, 132, 135, 160, 176,
  215, 243, 245, 246, 253–6, 261, 264, 276,
  286, 314
 and military activity, 137
 and military victory, 283, 303, 312
 and ostracism, 137
 and politics of space, 131, 132, 133, 164, 243,
  257, 263, 276, 280
 and Thirty, 172, 179, 186, 188, 256, 263, 314,
  315
 and trials, 268
 and war-dead, 293
 as democratic space, 17, 71, 104, 106, 121, 122,
  132, 135, 164, 247, 256, 264, 270, 273, 275,
  277, 280, 284, 286, 315, 319
 as memorial space, 162, 164, 259, 275, 283,
  286
 as multi-use space, 17, 71, 106, 122, 284, 315
Bouleuterion
 activities of, 106
 and *boule*, 99, 107, 108, 110, 111
 and Demophantos' decree, 89
 and Four Hundred, 22, 31, 39, 61, 112, 113,
  120
 and inscriptions, 101, 102, 103
 and Theramenes' trial, 117, 120

construction of, 36, 108
 in 411, 28, 36, 39, 52, 56
Bouleuterion complex, 264
 and inscriptions, 253, 300, 302
 and sales documents, 246, 254
Building A, 268, 272, 284
 and democracy, 271
 and dikastic equipment, 266
 as court, 268
 construction of, 264–5, 266
Building B, 268, 272, 284
 and democracy, 271
 and dikastic equipment, 266
 as court, 268
 construction of, 265–6
Building C, 266
Building D, 266
Building E, 266
 construction in, 16, 17, 113, 119
courts, 266, 272; *see also* Buildings A and B
 and citizen, 283, 309
 and democracy, 271, 272, 273, 300
 and Demophantos' decree, 273
 and Tyrannicides, 273
 construction of, 5, 263, 270, 314
 location, 283
Eschara, 137, 293
Great Drain, 246
herm of Onesippos, 275
 in *c*. 500, 121
 in 411, 38, 40, 68, 70
Kolonos Agoraios, 116, 118
Metroon, 245, 305
Mint, 272, 283
 and democracy, 271, 272, 273, 300
 construction of, 264, 268–70
New Bouleuterion, 113, 118
 and *boule*, 119, 120, 122, 132, 133, 166
 and Theramenes' trial, 117, 272
 and Thirty, 171, 179, 186, 218, 254
 construction of, 116–17, 121, 314

356

design, 122
grilles, 117
reconstruction of, 5
Old Bouleuterion, 116, 122; *see also*
Bouleuterion
after 479, 121
and archives, 118, 119, 122, 132, 166, 273,
314
and *boule*, 121
and Demophantos' decree, 89, 137, 138, 147,
161, 215, 241, 273, 278
and Four Hundred, 121, 133, 164
and inscriptions, 113, 133
and Phyle honours, 245, 253, 305
and Theramenes' trial, 117
c. 500, 121, 131
design, 116, 117, 122
Panathenaic Way, 264, 293
South Stoa I, 92, 268
Southeast Fountain House, 264
Square Peristyle, 266
statues
Chabrias, 242, 281, 282–3
Eponymous Heroes, 91, 92, 276, 307
Euagoras, 237, 246, 259, 264, 275, 276, 277,
278, 279, 280, 281, 282, 283, 316, 321
appearance, 279
location, 276
generals, 264, 283
Iphikrates, 282
Konon, 237, 246, 259, 264, 275, 276, 277,
278, 279, 280, 281, 282, 283, 316,
321
appearance, 279
location, 276
Leagros, 102, 275
Solon, 321
Timotheos, 282
Tyrannicides, 29, 39, 102, 103, 104, 110, 111,
132, 137, 140, 225, 237, 264, 273, 274, 275,
278, 279, 283, 284, 301, 302, 317, 320
Zeus Soter, 246, 255, 259, 275, 276, 277
Stoa Basileios, 72, 92, 264
after 479, 121
and *basileus*, 110, 111, 119, 120
and Drakon's law, 91, 92, 101, 254
and inscriptions, 92–5, 101, 104, 113, 114,
166, 175, 253
and laws, 76, 105, 108, 114, 115, 119, 120, 121,
132, 239, 240, 244, 245, 251, 254, 270,
273, 308, 314
and sacrificial calendar, 228, 244, 245, 254,
258, 308
and Theozotides' decree, 246, 254, 255, 293,
294, 302

and Thirty, 175, 179, 186
annexes, 72, 92–5, 113, 114, 115, 116, 117, 120,
121, 175, 239, 240, 275
c. 500, 119, 121, 131, 258
laws, 272
lithos, 105, 137, 138
north wall, 244
Stoa of Zeus, 92, 114, 268, 283
and freedom, 277
and inscriptions, 246, 253, 255, 259
and statues, 276, 277, 279
Stoa Poikile, 92, 284
and military victory, 255, 274, 275, 279, 283,
302
and Theozotides' decree, 254, 255, 258
and trials, 268
Marathon Painting, 305
paintings, 319
Solon's statue, 321
Strategeion, 284
Tholos, 266, 284
Agoratos
and procession to Akropolis, 288
at Phyle, 218
killed Dionysodoros, 218
trial of, 218, 219
Agrai
sanctuary of Meter, 204, 226, 289
and reconciliation agreement, 212, 214,
215
Agyrrhios, 221, 309
Aigospotamoi, battle of, 74, 280, 303, 304
Aischines
and award of crowns, 142
memory strategies, 305
on Demosthenes, 305
Aisimos, 288
Akropolis
after Thirty, 263
and Five Thousand, 123
and Four Hundred, 123, 314
and honours for Samians, 246
and inscriptions, 14, 56, 58, 59, 69, 71, 112, 123,
128–9, 130, 131, 132, 133, 164, 177, 215,
243, 246, 247, 256, 286, 314
and men of Peiraieus, 208, 287, 288, 294
and oligarchs of 411, 128
and Phyle honours, 246, 302, 303
and politics of space, 130, 131, 133, 164, 243,
257, 263, 284
and statues, 283, 284
and Thirty, 177, 179, 186, 188, 256, 314
archaic temple of Athena, 127, 130
as memorial space, 162, 259, 283, 284, 286
construction on, 16, 113

Akropolis (*cont.*)
  Erechtheion, 113
    and democrats, 126, 127
    and oligarchs, 126
    and past, 127–8
    completion, 130, 141
    construction, 123–6
    unfinished, 123
  Hekatompedon, treasures of, 53, 54, 128
  in 411, 70
  Parthenon
    and Erechtheion, 123
    treasures of, 53, 54, 128
  Periklean plan, 123
  Pronaos, treasures of, 53, 54, 128
  Propylaia, 123
Alexander III, king of Macedon, 2
Alexikles, 29, 30, 39, 62
Alkibiades, 29, 36
  and overthrow of democracy, 22
  and Phrynichos, 26, 27
  negotiations with, 26, 42
  recall of, 30, 42
Amazons, 259, 303, 319
Amorges, 26
anagrapheis
  after 411, 73, 74, 76, 78, 79–85, 91, 95, 100,
    104, 115, 118, 120, 239, 240
  after 404, 78, 173, 232, 238, 251
  definition of, 73
anathyrosis, definition of, 87
ancestral constitution, *see patrios politeia*
Andokides
  and decree of Demophantos, 73
  and events of 415, 220
  and exile, 220
  and Kallias, 221
  trial of, 220, 221, 224
andragathia, 145, 146
  of benefactor, 237
  of dead democrats in 403, 235, 295, 297
  of dead in 403, 292
  of war-dead, 149, 292
Andrewes, Antony, 44, 54
Androkles, 31
Andron, 60, 62
aner agathos
  and *andragathia*, 297
  and democracy, 146, 153
  and *Philoktetes*, 156
  of benefactor, 144, 145, 146, 153, 162, 163, 164,
    237, 279
  of dead foreigners, 292
  of democrats killed in 404/3, 291, 302
  of *proxenoi*, 235

  of Samians, 237
  of war-dead, 149, 150
Antiphon
  and past, 51
  as ambassador, 27
  as oligarch, 29, 36
  as tyrant, 58
  decree concerning, 58, 69
  defence speech, 44, 67
  defence strategy, 64, 65
  trial of, 44, 57, 60, 61, 62
Anytos, 168, 219, 221
Apolexis, 62
Apollodoros of Megara
  assassin of Phrynichos, 66, 67, 146, 150,
    151
  honours for, 67, 141, 142, 146, 151, 154, 161
  rewarded, 61
Archeptolemos, 57, 58, 60, 61, 62, 69
Archestratos, 172, 173, 176, 179, 232
Archinos
  and *paragraphe*, 309, 311
  and *patrios politeia*, 168
  and registration, 209
  as prosecutor, 224, 261, 311
  honours proposed by, 233, 312
archives, 118, 120, 133, 197, 240; *see also* Old
    Bouleuterion
archon (eponymous), 35, 47
  dokimasia in 383/2, 221
  of 403/2, 78, 191, 230, 239, 261, 307
  of 382/1, 222
  under Five Thousand, 52
  under Four Hundred, 50, 52
  under Thirty, 172
archons, nine, 34, 35, 47; *see also* oath
  and laws, 105
Areiopagos
  and homicide court, 266
  and laws, 46
  and Thirty, 172, 173, 176, 177, 179, 186, 188
  boule of, 91, 239
Arginousai, battle of, 62
Argos, 198
Aristarchos, 29, 62
Aristeides, 305
Aristokrates, 29
Aristophanes, 43, 44, 64, 151, 268, 309
Aristotle
  and *patrios politeia*, 49
  on events of 411, 20, 22, 31–40, 67
  politics of space, 36–7, 112
astu, definition of, 185
Astyochos, 27
ateleia, definition of, 237

Athena, 14, 131, 132
12 Boedromion
after 403/2, 289–90, 301, 302
and division, 288, 289
and memory, 290
and men of city, 288
and men of Peiraieus, 288
procession, 208, 287, 288
sacrifice, 208, 209, 287, 288, 289, 294, 296,
298, 303, 305
and democrats, 126, 127
and oligarchs, 127
Polias, 73, 129, 155, 172
Atreus, sons of, 157
Autolykos, 182

basileus, 35, 47, 104, 108, 111, 120
actions of, 120
and Drakon's law, 76, 91, 99, 104
and *kurbeis*, 104
and Stoa Basileios, 104, 119
in 404/3, 172
role of, 104, 105, 106, 109, 119, 254
Berlin
Gestapo-Gelände, 12
Memorial for the Murdered Jews of Europe,
12
Birkenau, concentration camp at, 13
Boethos, 73
Boiotia, 48, 282
Bottiaians, 198

Chabrias
as general, 281, 282, 283
honours for, 282
statue of, *see* Agora
Chaireas, 31
charisteria, definition of, 289
Charmides, 184, 219
City Eleusinion, 204, 221
city walls of Athens
destroyed, 18
rebuilt, 18
'constitution for the future', *see* Aristotle,
Athenaion Politeia 30.2–6
'constitution for the present', *see* Aristotle,
Athenaion Politeia 31.1–3
'constitution of Drakon', *see* Aristotle, *Athenaion
Politeia* 4.2–4
contestation, 11, 12
after 411, 75
after Thirty, 224, 301, 306, 309, 311, 312
between Athenians, 15; *see also* trials
museum display, 11
rituals, 12

Corinth, 282
Cyprus, 280

decrees
appearance, 308
distinct from laws, 307
location, 308
procedures for, 307, 308; *see also graphe
paranomon*
Dekeleia, 26, 61, 64
Delphinion, 266
Demetrios Poliorketes
response to, 321
revolution from, 321
Demophanes, 61
Demophantos
decree of, *see* Andokides 1.96–8
oath of, *see* Andokides 1.96–8
demosion, 118
Demosion Sema, 312
and commemoration, 316
and monuments, 303
and Spartan tomb, 299
burial after 286, 321
burial procession, 293
rituals, 287, 292–3, 294, 296, 298
tombs, 302
Demosthenes, 78
and award of crowns, 142
and crown, 305
and honours for Konon, 231
diaitetai, definition of, 105
dikastai; see also oath
and Agora, 271, 272, 273
and memory, 273
definition of, 271
Diognetos, 73, 100
Diokles, 73, 100, 239, 240
Dionysia
after 404/3, 291–2, 294
allies, 153
and Demophantos' oath, 75, 135, 136, 138, 140,
147, 152, 154
and memory, 17, 135, 147, 150, 153–4, 160, 163
and response to oligarchy, 16, 152, 154, 155, 158,
164, 287
announcement of crowns, 130, 135, 141–4, 146,
150–1, 152, 153, 154, 163, 237, 252
colonists, 153
generals' libation, 147, 148, 152, 153
of 411, 43
of 409, 1, 16, 130, 140, 141, 143, 146–59, 160,
163, 164, 208, 273
of 404, 143
Proagon, 136

Dionysia (*cont.*)
  procession, 137, 293
  proclamation against tyrants, 147, 151, 152,
    154
  tribute, 147, 148–9, 152, 153
  war-orphans, 147, 149–50, 152, 153, 154, 163,
    286, 291–2, 294, 296, 297, 298, 302,
    303
Dionysodoros, 218
  killed by Agoratos, 218
  murdered by Thirty, 218
Dipylon Gate, 185, 299, 300
dokimasia
  after Thirty, 221, 222, 223
  definition of, 217
Dow, Sterling, 72, 86, 87
Drakon
  and democracy, 320
  and democrats, 106, 107, 109, 110, 112, 164,
    166, 257, 259, 314, 320
  and oligarchs, 54, 58, 59, 68, 109, 110
  as lawgiver, 133
  law on homicide, *see IG* I³ 104
  laws of, 35, 47, 91, 173, 175, 229, 232, 239, 251,
    257
Drakontides, 170

Eetioneia, *see* Peiraieus
Eion Herms, 305
Eleusinian Mysteries, *see* Mysteries
Eleusis
  and Thirty, 181, 182, 184, 188, 212
  oligarchic enclave, 191, 195, 200, 201, 202, 203,
    310
  destruction of, 197, 304, 306, 311
  sanctuary of Demeter, 191, 203, 204, 205, 212
  and reconciliation agreement, 215
Eleven
  and reconciliation agreement, 213
  and trial of Agoratos, 218
  in reconciliation agreement, 191, 196, 200,
    203, 205, 216
  property of, 238, 261, 300
Elis, 198
enktesis, definition of, 141
Ephialtes
  laws of, 172, 173, 176, 179, 232
  reforms of, 47, 59, 104
Epichares, 221
Epigenes, 61, 126, 127
Epikerdes
  benefactions, 130, 143, 145
  honours for, 130; *see also IG* I³ 125
epistates of *boule*, definition of, 56
Erasinides, 144

Eratosthenes
  and Lysias, 63, 183
  Theramenes, 64
Euagoras
  and Greeks, 237, 281
  and honours, 317
  as Athenian, 256, 277
  as democrat, 280
  as liberator, 278, 281, 283
  as tyrant slayer, 278, 281, 283, 318
  honours for, *see* RO 11
  statue, *see* Agora
Euandros, 222, 312
euergesia
  definition of, 235
  of dead democrats in 403, 297
Eukleides, 78, 191, 230, 239, 261, 307
Euktemon, 61
Eumolpidai, 203, 204
eunoia, definition of, 145
Euripides, 43
Eurystheus, 303
euthunai, definition of, 54

Farrar, Cynthia, 40, 69
fascia, definition of, 86
Finley, Moses, 44
Five Thousand
  and Four Hundred, 52
  and Kleisthenes, 52
  and past, 50, 51, 52, 53, 54, 55, 57, 68, 70, 106,
    109
  and *patrios politeia*, 22, 68
  and Pnyx, 51
  establishment of, 54
  fall of, 189
  oligarchy of, 3, 44
  response to, 2, 257, 259; *see also* oligarchies of
    411
  strategies of, 16, 50, 52, 53, 54, 58, 59, 60
  trials under, 57
  under Four Hundred, 30, 39
forgetting, 7, 9, 11, 17; *see also* oligarchies of 411,
    Thirty
  and reconciliation agreement, 203, 205–6, 214,
    216, 217
  and *stasis*, 214, 297, 301, 302, 303, 305, 306, 318
  and unity, 200, 203
Four Hundred
  and *boule*, 31, 38, 99, 102, 107, 108, 112, 121, 171
  and Bouleuterion, 50; *see also* Agora,
    Bouleuterion
  and Eetioneia, *see* Peiraieus
  and past, 20, 35, 36, 50–1, 53, 68, 70, 106, 109
  and *patrios politeia*, 22, 51

and Samos, 29
and sources, 22–41
and Sparta, 29
establishment of, 21, 26, 29, 31, 39, 44, 45, 56,
  170
fall of, 20, 26, 29, 38, 39, 40, 51, 54, 184,
  189
forgetting, 163
oligarchy of, 3, 5, 21, 40, 98
response to, 2, 20, 136, 256, 257, 259; *see also*
  oligarchies of 411
  forgetting, 122, 162
rule of, 31, 102, 122
strategies of, 16, 50, 53, 58, 59; *see also* and
  past
Fuks, Alexander, 44

Geary, Patrick, 8, 11
Geleontes, 254, 257
generals, 47
  and assembly, 289
  denounced by Agoratos, 218
  in 410/9, 147, 159
  in 404/3, 172
  of oligarchs at Eleusis, 311
  trial under Thirty, 171
  under Five Thousand, 57, 58
Genesia, 254
Germany, 6
  8 May 1945, 12
Glaukippos, 73
Glaukos, 184
grammateus, definition of, 73
graphe paranomon, 301, 308
Guy Fawkes Day, England, 12

Hagnon, 21
Halieis, 198
Halikarnassos, 128
Hansen, Mogens, 219
Harmodios and Aristogeiton
  as founders of democracy, 320, 321
  as liberators, 278
  as models, 1, 101, 102, 147, 260, 274, 317,
    318
  cult, 39, 274, 278
  honours for, 237, 264, 275, 317
  kill Hipparchos, 28, 321
  statues of, *see* Agora
hellenotamiai
  definition of, 48
  in 404/3, 172
  of 410/9, 48, 143
  of 409/8, 99
  under Four Hundred, 55, 58

Hellespont, 136, 159, 282
Hera, 14
Herakleides, 309
Herakles, 155, 156, 159
Hermon, 29
Herms, mutilation of, 220
hetaireiai, definition of, 26
hipparchoi
  definition of, 47
  in 404/3, 172
Hipparchos, 28, 29, 103, 104
Hipparchos, son of Charmos, 57, 58
Hippias, 28
Hippomachos, 184
Hippotherses, 64, 195
hupogrammateus, definition of, 73

Iasos, 26
Ilissos River, 212
inscription
  as monuments, 105, 113, 251, 252
  authorising decree, 73, 84, 91, 96, 98, 99, 100,
    106, 162, 199, 225, 251
  display, *see* stele
  memory politics, 161, 162
  politics of display, 249
  prescript, 54, 73, 75, 97, 98, 99, 100, 162, 198,
    249, 251, 258
  publication clause, 253
  reading, *see* reading
Iphikrates
  as general, 282
  statue of, *see* Agora
isonomia, definition of, 164
isoteleia, definition of, 234
Isotimides, 220, 221

Japan, 6

Kallias, 221
Kallibios, 182
Kallimachos, 190, 196
Kephisios, 221
Kerkyra, 19, 65, 282
Kerykes, 203, 204
Kinyras, daughter of, 277
Kleigenes, 73
Kleisthenes, 122
  and *boule*, 36, 56, 58, 107, 108, 171
  and buildings, 119
  and constitution, 31, 47, 67, 97, 107, 128,
    139
  and decrees, 59
  and demes, 107
  and democracy, 320

Kleisthenes (*cont.*)
and democrats, 106, 107, 109, 110, 112, 121,
130, 133, 164, 166, 257, 258, 259, 314, 320
and laws, 33
and oligarchs, 33, 36, 48, 50, 56, 58, 59, 68,
109, 110
and Thirty, 172
and tribes, 48, 107
equal to Drakon and Solon, 133
Kleisthenes (fifth-century Athenian), 61
Kleitophon
amendment of, 31, 33, 36, 42, 50, 67
and Kleisthenes, 50
in 411, 22, 36, 40, 49, 51
in 404, 168
Kleokritos, 203
Kleon, 38
Kleophon, 83, 84
Knidos, battle of, 18, 231, 237, 276, 277, 280, 281,
303
Kolonos
and Four Hundred, 22
and oligarchs, 38
assembly at, 21, 26, 33, 36, 38, 41, 42, 53,
157
hippeis, 38
sanctuary of Poseidon, 38
Konon, 256
and honours, 317
and Persians, 277
and Thirty, 280
as democrat, 280
as liberator, 277, 278, 281, 283
as tyrant slayer, 278, 281, 283, 318
honours for, *see* Demosthenes 20.69–70
statue of, *see* Agora
Kritias
and Eleusinians, 181
and laws, 173, 180
and response to democracy, 180
and Sokrates, 219
and violence, 181
death of, 184
kurbeis, 104, 257
definition of, 104
Kynosarges, 212

Lakedaimonians, tomb of, *see* Sparta, tomb at
Athens
Lambert, Stephen, 86
Lapis Primus (first inscription of tribute), 129
laws, *see also* Thirty
and stoa, 91, 92, 239
concerning *boule*; *see also IG* I³ 105
location, 95–6

distinct from decrees, 307
on taxes, *see IG* I³ 237
procedures for, 307, 308, 316
reorganisation of, 5, 72, 73, 79, 85, 106,
115, 118, 173, 175, 229, 238, 251, 257,
270, 306
trierarchic, *see IG* I³ 236, *SEG* LII 48 fr. 3B
Lemnos, 155
Lenaia, 43
Leodamas, 222
Leokoreion, 29
Leon, 221
Lesbos, 282
Leukotainioi, 254, 257
Lewis, David, 56, 79
literacy, 13
and memory, 8
lithos, *see* Stoa Basileios
Loening, Thomas, 4
Loraux, Nicole, 3, 4, 295
Lykeion, 108
Lykon, 219
Lykourgos
and Demophantos' decree, 160
and forgetting, 163
Lysandros
and Athens, 185
and Thirty, 170
Lysias
and *stasis*, 296
forgetting Thirty, 293
memory strategies, 303–4
speeches by, 4

Macedon, 2, 319
Mantineia, 198
battle of, 298
Mantitheos, 222
Marathon, battle of, 258, 298, 319
me mnesikakein, *see* reconciliation agreement
Meiggs, Russell, 56
Meletos, 219, 221
memory
and civil strife, *see stasis*
and communication, 10
and identity, 10
and inscriptions, 8, 9, 13, 14, 106, 217
and literacy, 8
and public monuments, 8, 9, 106, 136, 154,
160–3, 214, 286, 302–3, 320
and reading, 12, 13, 14, 160–1, 162, 216, 217,
286
and ritual, 10, 135, 153–4, 160, 163, 226, 286,
287, 302; *see also* Dionysia; Athena, 12
Boedromion

and writing, 8, 13
collective, 6, 7, 8, 9, 10, 225, 286, 287, 295, 305, 312
cultural, 7
individual, 6, 7, 8, 9, 15, 219, 225, 286, 303–5, 306
malleability of, 7
national, 10, 11
of Athenians, 161, 162, 216, 287, 292, 294, 302
of Athenian fleet in 409, 161
social, *see* collective
Metropolitan Church, of Athens, 91
Miletos, 27
Miltiades, 305
Mnasilochos, 50, 52, 55
Mounichia, battle at, *see* Peiraieus
Mysteries, 164, 201, 204, 220
  Great
    and initiation, 204
    of 403, 209, 211
    of 400, 220
    procession, 204, 209
    Prorrhesis, 209
  Little, 212, 214
    and initiation, 204
  not carried out, 204
  profanation of, 220
Mytilene, 282

Nakone, 4
Naxos, battle of, 282, 298
Neapolis, 128
Neoptolemos, 155
  and deception, 157, 158
  and friendship, 158
  and oaths, 156, 159
  and Philoktetes, 159
  as war-orphan, 155–6, 158
  educating, 156
Nike, 73, 129, 155, 172
Nikeratos, 182
Nikias, 182
Nikomachos
  anagrapheus
    first term, 73–4, 79, 83, 84
    second term, 74, 78, 229, 232, 238, 239, 240
  and laws of Solon, 176
  trial of, 64, 220
nomos, definition of, 307
nomothetai
  and laws, 307
  definition of, 91
  in 403, 91, 229, 239, 240

oath
  and gods, 140, 214
  and unity, *see* unity
  bouleutic, 100, 107, 108
  dikastic, 216, 224, 273, 310
  Heliastic, 307
  in *Philoktetes*, 155, 156–7
  of alliance, 198
  of archons, 105, 137
  of reconciliation agreement, *see* reconciliation agreement
  reperformance, 101, 216, 253
  swearing, 137, 138–41, 207–14, 225
Odeion of Perikles, 266
Odysseus, 155
  and deception, 157, 158
  and events of 411, 158
  and Neoptolemos, 155, 157
  and oaths, 156, 157
  and Philoktetes, 157
Oedipus, 176
Oinoe, 62
Oinoe, Argive, battle at, 319
oligarchies of 411, 3
  and past, 56, 58, 109, 174
  and response to Thirty, 284
  response to, 2, 3, 6, 14, 74, 130, 159, 160, 166, 189, 306
  and commemoration, 316, 320
  and response after 286, 322
  and response to Thirty, 17, 247, 258, 300, 314–15, 319
  dates of, 72, 74, 109
  democracy, 16, 96–101, 109, 110, 113, 119–21, 122, 164, 165
  display, 16, 98–101, 109, 113, 119–21, 122, 133
  forgetting, 17, 71, 111, 122, 128, 129, 130, 131, 133, 134, 162–3, 164, 165, 259, 318
  identity, 110, 132, 140, 142, 164, 315, 318
  importance of, 313
  past, 16, 106–9, 110, 111, 113, 119, 121–2, 123, 127–8, 132, 133, 164, 168
  political reform, 167, 316
  sources for, 20, 21
Onomakles, 57, 60, 61, 62, 69
Osborne, Michael, 234
Osborne, Robin, 167
ostracism, 16, 58, 137
Ostwald, Martin, 21

Palladion, 266
Panathenaia, 164
  Little, 288
  of 410, 154

paragraphe, 310, 311
patrioi nomoi
  definition of, 20
  in 404, 169
  in 411, 20, 44, 45
  of Kleisthenes, 31, 33, 42
patrios politeia
  after 411, 106, 108, 109, 110, 112, 121,
    164
  and 'constitution for the future', 48
  and Five Thousand, *see* Five Thousand
  and Four Hundred, *see* Four Hundred
  and moderates, 42, 44, 180
  and peace of 404, *see* peace
  and Thirty, *see* Thirty
  and Thucydides, 42
  debates in 411, 16, 20, 22, 41, 42, 43, 44, 47,
    48, 49, 68
  definition of, 16
  in 404, 168, 169, 170, 173
  scholarship on, 21
Patrokleides, 61, 118
Patrokles, 172
Pausanias, king of Sparta, 4
  and reconciliation, 185, 188, 190
  disbands army, 208, 287
  fights democrats, 185
  intervention of, 167, 185
  leads army, 185, 188
  trial of, 260
peace
  of 404 with Sparta, 2, 168
    terms, 168–9
  of 403 between Athenians, 191
Peiraieus, 132
  democrats capture, 184
  Eetioneia, 22, 30, 39, 40
  in 411, 38, 39, 40, 68
  in 403, 40, 184, 185, 234, 249, 260,
    261
  Mounichia
    battle at, 184, 186, 204, 234, 261, 297,
      299
    possible trophy, 299
Peisandros, 64
  and Antiphon, 64
  and Four Hundred, 26
  and Odysseus, 157
  and past, 51
  and Spartans, 26
  as oligarch, 26, 29, 36
  first visit to Athens, 26, 27, 41, 42, 43
  on Samos, 26
  second visit to Athens, 26, 30, 31
  trial of, 61

Peisistratidai, 151
Peisistratos, 57
Peloponnese, 282
Peloponnesian War, 2, 143
  after 411, 2, 20
  Athenian dead from, 298
  Athenian defeat in 404, 2, 17, 166,
    213
  end of, 3, 5, 18, 304
  in 411, 48
Perikles, 35, 69
  law on citizenship, 261
peripoloi, definition of, 28
Persia
  alliance with Sparta, 31
  and honours for Knidos, 281
  and relations with Athens, 281
  defeated by Athens, 254, 302, 319
  destruction of Athens, 121, 127, 128
  fleet at Knidos, 237, 277, 281
  king of, 42
Persian Wars, 275, 298, 303
Pharnabazos, 281
Philoktetes, 155
  and anger, 157, 158, 159
  and deception, 157, 158
  and events of 411, 158
  and friendship, 158
  and home, 157
  and Neoptolemos, 155
  and oaths, 156, 157, 159
  arms of, 155, 156
Phormisios, 168, 260, 312
Phreatto, 266
Phrynichos, 64
  accused by Peisandros, 26, 27
  and Antiphon, 64
  and betrayal, 27
  and fighting, 27
  and Four Hundred, 22
  as oligarch, 27, 28, 29, 36, 150
  as traitor, 163
  as tyrant, 39, 58, 66, 67, 150
  assassination of, 28, 29, 30, 39, 40, 60, 66, 67,
    163
  decree concerning, 57, 58, 69
  on Samos, 26
  trial of, 60, 62, 64, 66, 67
phulobasileis, 257
  definition of, 254
Phyle
  attack of oligarchs, 234, 305
  defeat of oligarchs, 181, 182
  democrats at, 219
  occupied by democrats, 181, 182, 184

return from, 224, 233, 234, 250, 289, 290, 292, 294, 297, 298, 301, 305, 306
  honours for Athenians, *see SEG* XXVIII 45, Aischines 3.187, 190–1
  sacrifice, 233, 290
  honours for non-Athenians, *see* RO 4
  sacrifice to Athena, *see* Athena
  trophy near, 299
Plataia, battle of, 298
Plato
  memory strategies, 304–5
Plutarch
  and *stasis*, 296, 298
  memory strategies, 305
Pnyx
  activities of, 106
  and *demos*, 38
  and *ekklesia*, 38, 99, 263, 309
  and Thirty, 177, 178, 179, 186, 188, 263
  in 411, 36, 38, 51, 179
  original form, 51, 177
  phase 2, 177, 178, 263
  phase 3, 177
polemarchos, 35, 47
polemios
  and Athenian identity, 110, 140, 253
  definition of, 75
  in Demophantos' decree, 75, 139, 148, 150, 317
  killing, 279, 280
  oligarchs as, 163, 255, 304
  Spartans as, 299
poletai
  and Drakon's law, 99
  and property of Thirty, 249
  definition of, 246
politeia, definition of, 2
Polystratos, 50, 62
  and *demos*, 63
  and Four Hundred, 63
  as oligarch, 50
  first trial, 61
  second trial, 61, 63
proedria, 149, 317
  definition of, 141
proedroi, of Four Hundred, 56
proxenoi
  decrees for, 176, 231, 235, 247, 249, 250, 252, 258, 261, 272, 296, 300
  definition of, 176
  rewards for, 141
prutaneis, 47
  and laws concerning *boule*, 78
  and *sungrapheis*, 34
  and Tholos, 266

definition of, 34
  of Four Hundred, 56
Prytaneion, 141, 235, 266
psephisma, definition of, 307
Pythodoros, 31, 50, 172
Pythophanes, 56, 57

Quillin, James, 4

Rapoport, Nathan, 13
reading
  and Athenians, 13
  and individual, 135
  and inscriptions, 12, 13, 14, 100, 101, 105, 129, 130, 146, 160, 161, 215, 216, 217, 223, 226, 247, 252, 259
  and *kurbeis*, 104
  and memory, *see* memory
  and reconciliation, 217
  and reperformance, 253; *see also* oath Demophantos' decree, 160–1
reconciliation agreement, 2, 4, 189, 224, 229; *see also* forgetting
  and courts, 310
  and memory, 154, 214
  and *paragraphe*, 310
  and unity, 189, 200–7, 217, 227, 315, 316
  form of document, 197–9
  location of, 215
  me mnesikakein, 3, 4, 190, 191, 196, 213, 216, 217, 300
  oath, 17, 189, 191, 196, 197, 199, 207, 224, 289, 296, 309, 310
  strategies of, 200–7, 213, 228, 262, 296, 300
  success of, 312
  terms, 190–8, 199, 229, 238, 316
Rhodes, Peter, 47, 196

sacrifice
  and unity, *see* unity
  at *ekklesia*, 289
  dynamics of, 152, 205, 288
  to Athena, 12 Boedromion, *see* Athena
sacrificial calendar; *see also SEG* LII 48
  and past, 109
  appearance
    after 411, 86–9
    after 404, 86, 88, 241–3, 245
  location
    after 411, 93, 95, 244
    after 404, 243, 244, 245, 254
Salamis on Cyprus, 230, 237, 256, 264, 277
Salamis, battle of, 298
sale of property of Thirty, accounts of, *see SEG* XXXII 161

Samians
    honours for, *see IG* I³ 127, RO 2
Samos, 22, 29, 42
    army on, 26, 31, 36, 44, 159
    democracy and, 37
    generals on, 159
sanctuary of Dionysos, 137
sanctuary of Lykos, 266
sanctuary of Meter at Agrai, *see* Agrai
sanides, definition of, 91
Second Athenian League, 2, 18
Shear, Jr, T. Leslie, 104
Sicilian disaster, 16, 19, 31, 66, 113
Sicilian expedition, 16, 220
Sicily, 16
Sickinger, James, 84
sitesis, 141, 317
Sokrates
    and Thirty, 173, 219, 305
    in *Menexenos*, 305
    trial of, 219, 220, 224, 254, 305
Solon
    and *boule*, 46, 47, 48, 50, 58, 107, 171
    and constitution, 31
    and democracy, 320, 321
    and democrats, 106, 107, 109, 110, 112, 164,
        166, 257, 259, 314, 320, 321
    and oligarchs, 50, 54, 58, 59, 68, 109, 110
    and past, 258
    and tribes, 254
    as lawgiver, 133, 321
    laws of, 35, 47, 79, 83, 84, 91, 107, 173, 174,
        175, 229, 232, 239, 251, 257
Sommerstein, Alan, 44
Sophokles
    prosecutes Peisandros, 61
    response to oligarchy, 17, 155, 159, 164, 165
South Africa, 6
Sparta
    alliance with Persia, 31
    and Athenian reconciliation, 185, 190
    and Corinthian War, 18
    and Four Hundred, 28
    and Phyle, 305
    and Thirty, 183
    defeat at Argive Oinoe, 319
    defeat at Knidos, 276, 281
    defeated by Athens, 255, 302, 319
    garrison at Athens, 181, 182, 288
    intervention at Athens, 184, 185, 187, 304, 317
    threat of intervention, 2, 4, 313
    tomb at Athens, 185, 297, 299, 300, 304
Sphakteria campaign, 259
stasis
    and memory, 295

    and ritual, 296–7
    as war, 216, 224, 291, 297–300, 301, 302, 303,
        304, 305, 312, 317, 318
    after 286, 321
    at Athens
        after 411, 139, 295
        after 404/3, 309, 311, 320
        in 411, 19, 29, 65, 68
        in 404/3, 167, 184, 185, 188, 213, 286, 295,
            302, 303, 306
        in 280s, 321
    at Kerkyra, 19, 65
    contrasted with war, 150, 287
    definition of, 2, 295
    in fifth century, 19
    prevention of, 310
    term avoided, 235, 295–6
stele; see also inscription
    and display, 99, 100
    appearance of, 85, 245
    definition of, 1
    free-standing, 85, 86, 89, 308
    inscribing, 59
    location of, 215; *see also* Akropolis, Agora
    opisthographic, definition of, 78
    stoichedon, *see* stoichedon
stoichedon, definition of, 88
sungrapheis, 33, 41
    at Kolonos, 33, 35
    definition of, 31
    politeia of, 33
Synoikia, 254, 257

taxiarchoi
    definition of, 171
    denounced by Agoratos, 218
    trial under Thirty, 171
Teisamenos
    colleague of Nikomachos, 239
    decree of, *see* Andokides 1.83–4
Ten
    and *basileus*, 172
    and reconciliation agreement, 213
    control of Athens, 310
    election of, 184
    in reconciliation agreement, 191, 196, 203, 205,
        216
    property of, 238
Ten in Peiraieus, 184
    and reconciliation agreement, 213
    in reconciliation agreement, 191, 195, 196, 197,
        200, 203, 205, 216
    property of, 238
Teukros, 277
Theatre of Dionysos, 19, 137, 294, 303, 312

Thebes, 184, 303
Themistokles, 305
Theopompos, 52
Theozotides
    and events of 404/3, 306
    decree of, *see SEG* XXVIII 46
    honours proposed by, 15
    trial of, 224, 301, 311
Theramenes, 40, 52
    accused by Lysias, 63
    after 411, 29
    and Eetioneia, 39
    and *patrios politeia*, 21, 51, 168
    and response to democracy, 183
    as moderate, 49, 51, 167, 169
    as oligarch, 29, 36
    death of, 181
    in 404/3, 181, 182, 183
    memory of, 169, 183
    prosecutes Antiphon, 62
    trial of, 5, 117, 120, 171, 173, 181, 182, 183, 186,
        272
Theseus, 259, 319
    sons of, 158
thesmothetai, 35, 47
    under Five Thousand, 57, 58
Thirty
    and *boule*, 171
    and constitutional reform, 166, 167, 169, 170,
        171, 172, 173, 174, 175, 179, 182, 183, 186,
        196, 227, 270, 272
    and democratic city, 166
    and Eleusis, *see* Eleusis
    and inscriptions, 176, 177
    and laws, 17, 172–3, 174, 175, 176, 180, 227,
        232, 239, 240, 250, 257
    and Leodamas, 222
    and New Bouleuterion, *see* Agora
    and past, 171–2, 174, 180, 186, 227
    and *patrios politeia*, 169, 174, 180, 186
    and reconciliation agreement, 213
    and Sparta, 185, 186, 318
    and trials, 5, 171
    and violence, 167, 180–4, 185, 186
    as exiles, 260
    as tyrants, 181
    attack Phyle, 184, 305
    conflated with Four Hundred, 163
    defeated at Mounichia, 184
    erasure of, 3
    establishment of, 17, 117, 169, 170, 315, 316
    fall of, 15, 172, 184, 187, 189, 261, 298, 302, 305,
        306
    in reconciliation agreement, 191, 196, 200,
        203, 205, 216, 300
    memory of, 17, 286, 295, 300–1, 303
    oligarchy of, 3, 5
    property of, 238, 261, 300
    punishment by *demos*, 253
    response to, 2, 3, 4, 6, 14, 74, 106, 167, 184,
        185, 188, 189, 227, 263, 311, 312
    and commemoration, 316–17, 320
    and constitution, 18, 228, 286, 306–10, 316
    and response after 286, 322
    and response to 411, 2, 314–15, 319
    anger, 223, 224
    dates of, 229, 231, 287
    democracy, 101, 227, 247, 248, 256, 259,
        270, 284, 286, 287, 292, 294, 300, 306
    display, 227, 247, 251–2, 253, 256, 257, 259,
        270, 284, 286, 287, 292, 294
    external war, 18, 224, 294, 295, 301, 303,
        306, 312, 317; *see also stasis*
    forgetting, 18, 189, 190, 225, 228, 258, 259,
        287, 292, 293, 294, 302, 303, 304, 306,
        318
    identity, 228, 253, 259, 260, 261, 264, 270,
        274, 284, 318
    importance of, 313
    past, 187, 247, 257–9, 284, 294, 306, 314
    reconciliation agreement, *see* reconciliation
        agreement
    speeches, 4, 17, 190, 218–23
    response to democracy, 17, 170, 175, 177, 180,
        183, 186, 188, 189, 227, 263, 286
    forgetting, 175, 179
    trial of Theramenes, *see* Theramenes
Thrasyboulos, 288, 290
    attacks Peiraieus, 184
    honours proposed by, 15, 224, 260, 301, 311,
        312
    in 404/3, 182
    leaves Thebes, 184
    seizes Phyle, 181, 182, 184
    trial of, 224, 261, 311
Thrasyboulos of Kalydon, 128
    assassin of Phrynichos, 66, 67, 146, 150, 151,
        318
    honours for, 66, 129, 131, 141, 146, 150, 154,
        162; *see also IG* I³ 102
Thrasyboulos of Kollytos, 222
Thrasyllos, 148
Thrasymachos, 42
Three Thousand, 173, 179, 181, 182, 184
    depose Thirty, 184
    selection of, 181, 182
Thucydides
    and *patrios politeia*, 44, 45, 49, 68
    as democrat, 40, 65, 69
    critique of oligarchy, 65

Thucydides (*cont.*)
    narrative strategies, 66
    on events of 411, 20, 22–31, 36, 40, 42, 60, 65,
        67, 68, 69, 157
    on Peisistratidai, 29
    politics of space, 37–40, 96, 106, 112, 119, 131
Thymochares, 62
timai, definition of, 292
Timokrates, 78
Timotheos
    as general, 282
    statue of, *see* Agora
Todd, Stephen, 4, 83
Townsend, Rhys, 5
tradition, invention of, 11
treasurers of Athena, 53
    amalgamation of, 48
    and Solon, 47
    of 412/1, 53
    of 410/9, 55, 128, 129
    under Five Thousand, 54, 55, 58
    under Four Hundred, 53, 54, 55, 58
treasurers of Athena and the Other Gods
    of 404/3, 172
    of 403/2, 172
    of 399/8, 14
treasurers of the Other Gods, 48
trials, *see also* named individuals
    after 411, 29, 60, 61, 67, 165, 316
    after Four Hundred, 21
    after Thirty, 189, 190, 217, 218, 221, 223, 224,
        225, 260, 273, 310, 312
    of Arginousai generals, 62
trierarchoi, definition of, 22
Trojan War, 155
trophy over Thirty, *see* Phyle, Peiraieus
Troy, 155, 156, 157, 158, 159, 259, 319
Truth and Reconciliation Commission, of South
        Africa, 6
Twelve Gods, 102
Tyndareos, 157
Tyrannicides, *see* Harmodios and Aristogeiton
Tyrannicides' benefits, 75, 253, 255, 317

unity
    and Dionysia, 147, 149, 151, 152, 153, 163, 315
    and disagreement, 15, 206, 224

and exclusion, 16, 200, 203, 207, 213
and memory, 161, 162
and Mysteries, 204, 205, 207, 212, 214
and oaths, 139, 149, 152, 159, 200, 207, 213,
    315
and Panathenaia, 154, 288
and sacrifice, 152, 205, 288
and tacit agreement, 15, 152, 200, 203, 206,
    207, 213
creation of, 15
    after 411, 16, 111, 120, 127, 135, 138, 139, 141,
        159, 315
    after 404/3, 189, 289, 290, 292, 294, 296,
        302, 306, 311, 315, 318; *see also*
        reconciliation agreement
oaths, 214

Vietnam Veterans Memorial, *see* Washington,
    D.C.

war-dead, 149
    as models, 150, 153
    assimilation to, 163, 255, 291, 292, 293, 294,
        317
    burial procession, 293
    rituals for, 287
war-orphans, *see also* Dionysia, Neoptolemos
    assimilation to, 235, 255, 291, 292, 294, 297,
        317
Warsaw, Ghetto Memorial, 13
Washington, D.C,
    National Air and Space Museum, 11
    Vietnam Veterans Memorial, 9, 12, 14
Wolpert, Andrew, 4
World War I, 9, 11
World War II, 6, 12

Xenainetos, 231
xenia, definition of, 235
Xenophon
    and *stasis*, 296

Yad Vashem, Pillar of Heroism, 14
Yugoslavia, former, 6

Zeus Horkios, 156